*Writing, Directing,
and Producing
Documentary Films
and Videos*

Other books by Alan Rosenthal

Jerusalem, Take One! Memoirs of a Jewish Filmmaker
Why Docudrama? Fact-fiction on Film and TV

Writing, Directing, and Producing Documentary Films and Videos

FOURTH EDITION

Alan Rosenthal

SOUTHERN ILLINOIS UNIVERSITY PRESS / CARBONDALE

10 09 08 07   4 3 2 1

Library of Congress Cataloging-in-Publication Data
Rosenthal, Alan, [date].
Writing, directing, and producing documentary films
and videos / Alan Rosenthal.—4th ed.
    p. cm.
Includes bibliographical references and index.
ISBN-13: 978-0-8093-2742-3 (pbk. : alk. paper)
ISBN-10: 0-8093-2742-2 (pbk. : alk. paper)
1. Documentary films—Production and direction.
2. Documentary films—Authorship. I. Title.
PN1995.9.D6R65 2007
808′.06607—dc22   2006035786

Printed on recycled paper. ♻

The paper used in this publication meets the minimum
requirements of American National Standard for Information Sciences—Permanence of Paper for Printed Library
Materials, ANSI z39.48-1992. ⊗

For Tirtza

CONTENTS

ILLUSTRATIONS

PREFACE TO THE FOURTH EDITION

Some elderly sage is once reputed to have said, "The only constant is change." Those were indeed words spoken in wisdom.

About five years ago I pushed away my pen (actually, my word processor) after completing the third edition of this book. I was happy. I could take a holiday. Now I could lie low for at least ten years before it would be necessary to update the text. Well, I was wrong once again.

New equipment, new broadcast systems, new approaches, new filming methods, the use of computer-generated imagery, the growth of hybrid forms, the intersection of documentary and docudrama, not to speak of the Web and digital video, have all forced me to reconsider how one approaches documentary filmmaking in the twenty-first century. The fruits of that thinking underpin this new edition.

Again, the emphasis in the book is on what to say and what to show and how to do both of these things in the best possible way. So this is a book about storytelling—how to tell great and moving stories about fascinating people, whether they be villains or heroes.

My goal in this new edition has been first of all to enlarge and amplify certain key elements that were discussed in the earlier texts. Thus, the chapter on editing has been revised to take into account the massive strides in the use of nonlinear editing. Because cable television stations like Discovery and A&E demand such precise and exacting proposals, I have provided even more examples of how one accomplishes these tasks. In fact, demonstration through examples from key filmmakers' work is one of the key teaching techniques I have used throughout the book. Budgeting has also been rethought, with examination of a fairly complex budget example to show how it is all done. The chapter called "Family Films" has also been vastly expanded. This seems to me a genre that has been growing by leaps and bounds the past few years, so that a few words on its possibilities and its pitfalls seemed to me very necessary for both new and mature video- and filmmakers.

In the years that have passed since the last edition, we have seen the growth of the documentary hybrid, a greater willingness to experiment in form, and a growing interest in both docudrama and the history documentary. Again, the discussion of these forms has been vastly expanded, with many suggestions given as to how to master these changes and challenges.

I have also added a new chapter titled "Making Your First Film." This is intended for first-year film students and novice documentary makers who want some solid, simple advice on how to get started. They know the water is attractive, but they are not sure whether to jump in, dive in, or just put in two toes at a time. I hope that this chapter will make them see that there are few sharks, the water is warm, swimming is dead easy, and the whole enterprise is rather easy and pleasant.

Finally, I have enormously expanded the chapter "Staying Alive." This chapter is meant for those who want to be their own producers, and it deals in detail with financing, festivals, distribution, marketing, and the likenesses and differences between the U.S. and European television scene. In short, it deals with those subjects that dominate so much of our lives as independent filmmakers but are rarely touched upon at film school.

Once more, many friends helped in providing stimulating ideas, provocations, and assistance, namely Ben Levin, Jost Hunnigher, John Marshall, Len McClure, Derek Paget, Steve Lipkin, and Dennis O'Rourke. To all of them, my thanks. Extra special thanks must go to Simon Armitage, Sue Collins, Nicole Lorraine Draper, John Else, Alex Grigor, Brian Hill, Julie Innes, Faramarz K-Rahber, Jan Krawitz, Michèle Ohayon, Patricia Phillips, Agnieszka Piotrowska, the National Film Board of Canada, and Sami Saif, all of whom took time off to discuss their films with me at length, and in many cases allowed me to use photos, excerpts, and graphics from their work. Again, along with thanks, I would also like to acknowledge that all the script, graphics, or document extracts used herein retain the copyright of the original owners.

This is my third book for Southern Illinois University Press, and no one could have a better patron. Here my thanks go in particular to my editor Karl Kageff, to Bridget Brown, who took care of the small details, and to Jim Simmons, who helped me for so many years. Finally, I would like to express my gratitude to my copy editor, Katherine Faydash, and to Tirtza Elnathan, who was always there for me.

PREFACE TO THE FIRST EDITION

I have always distrusted how-to books, whether they are about sex or about making a million. The authors of such texts seem to me a bit presumptuous in trying to teach you things best learned by experience.

And as in love and business, so in film. Documentary is learned by doing, by trial and error. This is not a how-to book. It is meant to be a companion to you along the way, helping you see some of the pitfalls and problems and helping you find solutions to the difficult but fascinating task of filmmaking.

Except briefly in the first and last chapters, I have said little about the aims and purposes of documentary. Yet this is probably the most important question, and at some point, we all have to answer it. For me, working in documentary implies a commitment that one wants to change the world for the better. That says it all.

First, my thanks to all those people and organizations that let me look at their films and burrow through their scripts. In particular, I would like to thank Will Wyatt, of the BBC, and Leslie Woodhead, of Granada; both gave me immense help and made this book possible. I would also like to thank Jeremy Isaacs, David Elstein, and Jerry Kuehl, who helped me tie up some loose ends.

Thanks are also due to the University of California Press, which allowed me to publish notes and interviews from some of my previous books—in particular, discussions with Arthur Barron, Ellen Hovde, Sue McConnachy, Jeremy Sandford, George Stoney, Peter Watkins, and Charlotte Zwerin.

P. J. O'Connell's manuscript "Robert Drew and the Development of Cinema Verité in America" was essential to me in understanding the real workings of cinema verité, and I am grateful to P. J. for letting me reprint discussions with Ricky Leacock and Don Pennebaker.

I am, of course, tremendously grateful to the following stations and authors who allowed me to reproduce script extracts: the BBC, Granada Television Limited, the National Film Board of Canada, Thames Television, WNET, James Burke, Kate Davis, Jon Else, Jill Godmilow, David Hodgson, Stuart Hood, Antony Jay, Robert Kee, and Morton Silverstein.

Many of my friends assisted with this book, but six people above all helped guide my steps. The first was John Katz, who drank a lot of coffee with me and pointed me in the right direction. Later, Ken Dancyger and Brian Winston went over different sections of the book and gave me very constructive and detailed criticism. My debt to them is enormous, and I also have to thank Brian for letting me reproduce extracts from one of his scripts.

Another tremendous influence on me was Antony Jay. I met Tony many years ago while writing another book. After talking to me about one of his films, he showed me the teaching notes he used at the BBC and gave me an informal half hour when we discussed script-writing techniques. Tony was then acknowledged as possibly the finest script-writer at the BBC and is now world famous for his joint scripting of the series *Yes, Prime Minister.* That half-hour discussion was worth its weight in gold, and I have been grateful to Tony ever since.

Unbounded thanks also to Dan Gunter, who did a superb job of copyediting and helped translate my native English idioms into understandable American speech.

My last guiding light was James Simmons, my editor at Southern Illinois University Press, who waited patiently through all my delays and provided excellent advice and tremendous enthusiasm along every inch of the way. To all six, my thanks and gratitude.

*Writing, Directing,
and Producing
Documentary Films
and Videos*

1

INTRODUCTION

In the last twenty years, tremendous changes have taken place in documentary and nonfiction filmmaking. These changes include subject matter, form, rise in the number of university film and video courses, but very few books explain how to consider, create, write, produce, and direct the "new" film. One object of this book is to fill that gap: to provide you with a thorough, down-to-earth grasp of documentary filmmaking, from idea to finished work, and from raising money to enjoying the fruits of your efforts. But above all, this is a book about ideas and concepts. Its goal is to help you to think about the film as a totality before the camera is switched on. This approach may seem obvious, but it is not always so obvious in practice. Many people jump into a film, shoot hours of material, and then wonder what it's all about. To me, that is putting the horse before the cart with a vengeance.

In essence, this book is about the daily problems that the filmmaker faces: from concept to finished film, from financing to distribution, from censorship and political problems to breaking into the networks, from the complexities of location shooting to problems of ethics and morality, from difficulties with the crew to the problems of dealing with real people and the complexities of their lives. Finally, the book deals with research, problems of style, varieties of approach, and the challenge of new technologies.

This book does not deal with equipment. This omission is deliberate because this subject is thoroughly covered in other books and is well taught in most film schools and universities. And therein lies one of the problems. Most film schools provide a level of technical training that would have been unthinkable only a few years ago. Students graduate having handled more editing equipment than Eisenstein ever did; they know how to take apart and rebuild a Nagra in ten minutes and how to light a set using the best techniques of Néstor Almendros and Vilmos Zsigmond. So the last thing they need is additional advice on bounce or direct lighting. But students do tend to be deficient in what to say and how to say it. Documentary writing, for example, is often the weakest subject in the curriculum. One of the aims of this book is to redress the imbalance.

A second topic deliberately left out of this book is that of documentary history. The subject is tremendously important, but I assume that most readers of this book are familiar with the history of documentary filmmaking. If not, then Erik Barnouw's *Documentary: A History of the Non-fiction Film* is the best introduction around. If you know some history, you can proceed without reinventing the wheel. If you are familiar with the films of Flaherty, Riefenstahl, Jennings, the Maysleses, Drew, Leacock, and Pennebaker, you already have a good sense of evolving styles and objectives. So, for the rest of this book, I will assume that you learned about cinema verité at your mother's knee, and that you know that *Nanook of the North* is a film rather than a Canadian hockey star.

ORIGINS

This book arose out of a series of discussions and seminars I had with students, first at the Australian National Film School and later at Stanford University. These students knew everything about technology but undervalued ideas. Most of them had grown up in the tradition of cinema verité, which one student interpreted to me as "shoot before you think."

Cinema verité has an absolutely vital spot in any film curriculum, but if mishandled it can act detrimentally on other film disciplines, especially writing. This is exactly what I found: raised on a diet of cinema verité, the students knew nothing about planning a standard documentary or industrial film and were completely lost when it came to writing commentary. Further exploration showed that they had a highly romantic vision of what happens on location and a completely unrealistic view of how a documentary film director works. When I gently suggested that a documentary director's main task was listening to people, they thought I was joking.

One thing was clear. Though the students knew everything concerning the realities of feature filmmaking, they had only the faintest idea of what documentary was all about. So we talked, and gradually the idea of this book was born.

At first I thought the essay would discuss only writing, as that seemed to be the biggest problem. However, that soon seemed too limiting, because where did writing end? Writing was not just idea and commentary; it was the overall concept of the film. And if you look at the problem more broadly, don't documentary directors write the film as they go along? They have to face the unexpected. They have to make choices on the spot. They can shape the film any one of a dozen ways while supervising the editing. So how could you have a book on writing that failed to deal with directing?

Writing and directing are inextricably linked in the making of documentary and industrial films. I know that many people just write and others just direct. But the usual situation is to find both tasks combined in one person, and necessarily so, because it is hard to say where one ends and the other begins. So once I was committed to exploring writing problems, it was inevitable that directing had to be covered as well.

OBSERVATIONS

This book follows what I see as the natural progression of the documentary film. It starts with a discussion of ideas, research, proposal, and script structure; proceeds through preproduction and production; and then deals in depth with editing and commentary writing. By the time you have finished part 4, you should be familiar with the preparation and production of the standard documentary or industrial film. Part 5 covers a few distinct types of film and some special techniques. Thus, there is one chapter on the historical film and another on cinema verité. The final chapters, the "wrap," offer advice on fund-raising, distribution, and marketing, and a perspective on the entire process.

Within this framework I have made one or two policy decisions. The first concerns the subject of video and film. This book is intended to help both film and video makers. Whether you are making a documentary on film or video, for at least half the time, your path and approach will be exactly the same. Only during editing will the paths separate. Reasons for choosing video over film, or vice versa, will be discussed in chapter 3. But in terms of approach, script writing, and directing, what applies to one applies to the other.

The book also addresses both documentary filmmakers and makers of other forms of nonfiction film, for instance, industrial, travel, and educational films. Obviously, the objectives of these different kinds of film vary enormously. The documentary often has a strong reform or social purpose, while an industrial may serve to improve a company's corporate image or to act as a fund-raiser. However, though their purposes differ, both genres share a great number of methods and techniques. For example, if you are dealing with research or script writing, your methods will be as valid for the industrial film as for the documentary. Finally, on a practical level, most makers of nonfiction films exist in both the sponsored world and the documentary world. Today they will make an investigatory documentary; tomorrow they will make an industrial film. The more knowledge you have of the techniques of both, the better off you are.

My last observation concerns money. Only purists, angels, and millionaires make films without thinking about money. Films cost money, usually a hell of a lot, and the sooner you start thinking about that fact, the better. Neither writing nor directing is done in a vacuum; scriptwriter and director alike must be aware of budget limitations. Once you start talking about money, you might as well discuss fund-raising and the role of the producer. Both subjects are in fact discussed in this book at length, and I make no apologies. Someone once expressed it this way: "The successful filmmaker has his head full of dreams, his eyes on the mountains, but his feet on the ground." That puts it bluntly, but it makes sense.

METHOD

Though I didn't climb any mountains to consult the sages, I did try to talk to the best professionals around before writing this book. The questions were always, "How do you work?" and "Why do you do things this way?" Occasionally I would also ask, "What is the most important thing that you have learned over the years?" This book is a distillation of their answers and advice and represents how experienced professionals tackle film and video problems. But the book also comes out of my own experiences as a filmmaker and is affected by my quirks, background, and experience. I have been making films for about twenty-five years and have developed various techniques and approaches that make sense to me. They represent an attempt to put logic as well as emotion into that very peculiar process we call filmmaking.

However, a warning is in order. First, all filmmakers are different. My method of filmmaking may not work for you. Our temperaments and our approaches to film may be light-years apart. And that's fine.

Second, this book is not sacrosanct. There are no rules in filmmaking. What is accepted as gospel today is rejected tomorrow. I hope that you will read the book, accept what is useful, and then go out, break all the rules, and make the greatest film ever.

PART ONE

From Idea to First Draft

2

CLEARING THE DECKS

From time to time I meet with my partner, Larry, and we toss documentary ideas at each other. Larry sits, taking notes furiously, and I wander around with a cup of coffee. "How about," I'll say, "a series on cities. How we lived yesterday, today, and tomorrow, and how the environment has changed, and what the changes do to the quality of our lives. The disaster in New Orleans would provide a good first film. Or we could do the divided cities—Beirut and Berlin, Jerusalem and Belfast. Or we could look at abandoned cities like Angkor Wat or Fatehpur Sikri. Then there are the rebuilt cities like Tokyo or Coventry. And we could use material from the film *Metropolis* as a motif. Well, what do you think?"

Then it's Larry's turn. "I'd like to do *Union Jack over Eden*, about the British writers and actors in Hollywood in the 1930s. There were hundreds of them, from Cary Grant to Boris Karloff. They even had a cricket team with David Niven and Erroll Flynn. And here's another idea. We take famous generals to the scenes of their battles and relive their experiences with them."

Of course, these are not just ideas of the moment. Our general reading and observation of people, politics, and current events, our sense of where the documentary market is going, and changes in different genres, all taken together, establish a whole body of potential material in our minds. This material matures over time, so we bring to our programming sessions a series of ideas that have been developing and that we now want to try out on each other. Some of the ideas are old, some new. Often the old ideas suddenly became feasible because an external event makes them newsworthy. Thus, the earthquake in Pakistan and the tsunami disaster rekindled my interest in the environment and cities, and the Sudan and Darfur atrocities reawoke my interest in the subject of genocide.

YOUR CHOICE OF TOPIC

The above may sound a bit arbitrary, but it hides a deeper process. With all the banter and the joking, Larry and I are moving toward a commitment to spend anything from a few months to a few years on making a film. And we have to answer one vital question before we do anything: why do we really want to make this film? This, above anything else, is what you really have to ask yourself before you start.

Often the answer is that you have no choice. The subject obsesses you. It has been haunting you for years. It appeals to you. It appeals to your imagination, to your emotions, to your political views. Your topic covers a range of human experience that you feel you have to talk about, an experience that you feel you can best deal with on film.

I feel, very strongly, that this is the way the best films arise. They are generated from the burning passion to say something interesting, vital, and moving about the human condition, as exemplified by Jan Krawitz's *Big Enough*, Rob Epstein's *The Times of Harvey Milk*, or Jonathan Stack's *The Farm*. Sometimes they want to raise and discuss an issue, as Marlon Riggs does very seriously in *Color Adjustment* or as Michael Moore does with a lighter hand in *Fahrenheit 9/11*.

Occasionally films will want to celebrate a lifetime's musical achievement, as in *The Buena Vista Social Club*, or to reflect on an amazing career, as in *My Architect*, about Louis Kahn, or *Tell Them Who You Are*, about cinematographer Haskell Wexler. Often they are an appeal for social and political change, like Barbara Kopple's *Harlan County* or Nettie Wild's *A Place Called Chiapas*. Sometimes they are a warning from the past that offers us a guide to the future, like Claude Lanzmann's *Shoah*, Peter Cohen's *Homo Sapiens 1900* about Nazi eugenics, and the moving and heartrending *Las Madres: The Mothers of Plaza de Mayo*.

Although a topic may obsess you for years, that obsession is not enough. You also have to ask yourself the question, Is there a good *story* there? I really consider this to be vital. If you merely have material for a discussion, then you should be making current-affairs talk shows. To make good documentaries, you need a strong narrative thrust and a tale that can be recounted in the most compelling, dramatic way possible. And when you have a story as compelling as that told by Spike Lee in *Four Little Girls*, about the racist bombings in the South in 1963 and the death of four black children, then you begin to believe there is nothing quite as powerful in film as a well-told documentary.

Now, obviously, I am aware that wonderful nonnarrative impressionist documentaries have been made. Bert Haanstra's *Glass* is a marvel by any standard. *Satya* by Ellen Bruno and *Empire of the Moon* by Kris Samuelson are superb recent examples of what can be done in the impressionist style. However, I would suggest that, in general, the strong story is a vital element of the successful documentary.

When you have a story that captures the imagination, the film often passes from the interesting to the unforgettable. Ric Burns's documentary *The Donner Party* told the tragic story of the life and death of a few American pioneers in an absolutely riveting way. *Hearts of Darkness* told of the challenges and problems involved in the making of *Apocalypse Now*, while *Hoop Dreams*, about the hopes of two young boys to rise to basketball stardom, captured the aspirations of thousands of black youngsters everywhere.

Powerful narratives can also range far beyond one individual's story. John Pett's *Morning* gives us the story of the Allied invasion of Normandy. *Born into Brothels* shows us glimpses of life as observed by young Indian children. Antony Thomas's *Thy Kingdom Come . . . Thy Will Be Done* tells us compellingly about the ways of fundamentalist religion in Texas, while Ken Burns's *Civil War* series made documentary history.

And then there is documentary's capacity to embrace the weird, the wonderful, and the wacky. Who can forget Mark Lewis's *Cane Toads*, about the strange invasion of a small Australian town by thousands of plump, squat, gray toads, or the mating rituals of young females in the American South as wryly recounted in *Sherman's March*. Dennis O'Rourke's *Cannibal Tours* helped turn Western exotic tourism upside down, while more recently Roko and Adrian Belic's *Genghis Blues* told the story of Paul Pena, an American blues legend who traveled to Siberia and Mongolia to compete in a *khoomei*, or throat singing, competition.

So the starting point for me is to tell a story that fascinates me and that I also think is dramatic. But what then? Once we get an idea that seems worth spending a few months of our lives on, Larry and I begin to ask questions.

Is it practical? Is it feasible? Does it have strong and interesting characters who can carry the story? Would it be high or low budget? Does it have broad or narrow audience appeal? What approach could we take to the subject? We are clearing the decks, seeing whether the first idea looks promising enough to develop. You could say that if the idea is fine, we should just go ahead, but we first ask one important question: can we sell this brilliant idea, and if so, how? In other words, will there be a serious chance of financing our film and getting it out later into television or cinemas, or will it just remain a self-financed applauded festival film that never recoups its costs?

It's all very well to be a writer, but usually the serious writer-director must also get involved in fund-raising from the beginning, particularly when the writer is also the producer. So the writer's job often becomes threefold.

First, he or she must write a proposal: a document that presents the basic idea in an attempt to persuade some funding agency (sponsor, commissioning editor, foundation, or television station) to back the film. Second, the writer must write the script. Finally, the writer often directs the film.

A good part of this book is devoted to the problems and questions surrounding the writing of the proposal. If you have the film given to you on a golden plate and don't have to worry about raising money or having to define your ideas to anyone, then you may want to skip those pages. But you may also want to drop me a note and tell me how you did it so easily, because I am green with envy.

WHY DO WE DO IT?

Why bother to make documentaries? The question has haunted me for years. Most of the time, I don't think about it. I just go ahead and make films, but occasionally, in a quiet reflective mood I return to that basic question. Why invest so much energy in a pursuit that is not particularly well paid, that can make you old before your time, that can split you from your family, and that more often than not may hang on the screen for a mere fifty minutes before vanishing unmourned into eternity?

Part of the answer, of course, is that documentary filmmakers are mad. If they weren't, they would use their talents making a bundle in feature films and luxuriate in fame and fortune. And part of the answer is in that old cowboy cliché, "A man's gotta do what a man's gotta do," In other words, we are compulsive and driven, somehow believe in this crazy medium, and wouldn't swap it for any other kind of work or play.

However, as beginning filmmakers or even experienced veterans it really is worthwhile to think seriously about why you make films. In 1998 various filmmakers tried to answer that question in a book called *Imagining Reality*, edited by Kevin Macdonald and Mark Cousins. Most of the filmmakers admitted that a demon possessed them but then went on to quantify what personally drove them. Most admitted to curiosity and a need to communicate. Ricky Leacock talked about a passion for experiences, both good and bad. Albert Maysles spoke about recording events so that they could be shared. Mike Grigsby talked about giving a voice to the voiceless. Others talked about providing a space where people could be themselves and express their deepest emotions. Most defined a concern for the world around them, though the expression was very gently put. All talked of vision, passion, commitment. For myself, I live in Israel, where everything is in flux, in transition, and my own driving force is both to mirror that change and to try to help make Israel a better place in which to live, both now and in the future. So, some of the answers are shared. Some are uniquely individual. The main thing to understand is that there is a basic question that sooner or later you are going to have to answer.

In *Imagining Reality* many of the filmmakers interviewed were also asked about their favorite techniques. Many swore by cinema verité. Others talked of assimilating traditions from the past, from Humphrey Jennings and from Chris Marker, or of noting the experimental traditions of South America. Often there was a scorn for heavily narrated films. Reflecting on form and style, Michael Jackson, a British producer, wrote, "The world is becoming more open, complex, more confusing, and more fragmented and to reflect the many new realities new documentary forms may be necessary."

My own view of technique is relatively simple and was expressed very well by Nicholas Fraser, a BBC producer, who put things this way: "Documentaries must surely be regarded like non-fiction books or journalism—anything should go in the matter of technique, and the only real criterion for a good film is whether it tells the truth or not." Here I would maybe add a second criterion: that the film works upon the audience.

In the end, what I think one has to do is avoid dogmas and straitjackets and stop oneself from thinking there is only one way to make documentaries. You are a filmmaker, you have a goal to reach, and you have a *variety of techniques* that will help you—cinema verité, narration, experimentation, graphics, music, verse, and so on. Your techniques are like the colors on an artist's palette. They are the tools for the job. You simply choose the techniques most appropriate for the job in hand and go ahead. And that's all there is to it.

IS A SCRIPT NECESSARY?

If somebody asked you to name ten or twelve outstanding documentaries or documentary series, it is highly possible that your list might include *Nanook of the North, The Corporation, Hoop Dreams, Best Boy, The Good Woman of Bangkok, Harlan County, 7 Up/49 Up, One Day in September, The Nazis: A Lesson from History, Soldiers in the Army of God, Fahrenheit 9/11, The War Game, Letters from Vietnam, Diary for Timothy, A Walk through the Twentieth Century,* and *Tongues Untied.* What strikes us about the list? First is the sheer variety of the films. They range from Flaherty's classic description of Inuit life to an institutional portrait, to Jennings's gentle observation of life in England at the end of World War II. *Best Boy* tells us about the life of a mentally retarded man, *Harlan County* deals with striking miners, *The War Game* is a horrifying documentary drama of the effects of an atomic bomb on a small British town, and *Fahrenheit 9/11* excoriates President Bush. All are, in their own ways, outstanding examples of really excellent documentary films.

But what was the writer's part in these projects and in the success of the films? Apart from *The Nazis: A Lesson from History,* only five or six of the works—including *The War Game, The Corporation, Twentieth Century, Tongues Untied,* and perhaps *Diary for Timothy*—had anything resembling a full preproduction script or final narration. All the other films were largely unscripted. Notes were probably jotted down and long discussions held as to what sequences to shoot, but no long preproduction scripts with suggested visuals and tentative commentary were prepared. Instead, most of these films were built on the editing table. Clearly, then, you can have a successful film without a script, or at least without a conventional script that defines action and progression and carefully lays in all the narration or guidelines for the narration. All this, of course, is illustrated by the success of cinema verité in the 1960s and by the esteem granted to Drew, Pennebaker, Wiseman, the Maysleses, Leacock, and other pioneers of the genre.

Granted, then, you can have a film without a prewritten script, or even a clear outline of ideas, but if you are going to do a commissioned film for television, then usually both become necessary. And here it's worthwhile to think about how the world of television really works and what it really wants. While researching this book I looked at television program schedules in the United States, England, Canada, and France. What became clear is that 80 percent of the scheduled documentaries *were fully scripted*, which is quite a sobering fact. So, the sooner you learn how to deal with the written script, the better.

THE PURPOSE OF THE SCRIPT

If verité filmmakers can dispense with a script, perhaps filmmakers in other genres can also abandon it. Think of the savings in hours, coffee, cigarettes, and frayed nerves if we could just make do with a few rough notes. What a beautiful dream!

So, why a script? Because using a script is usually the most logical and helpful way to make a film. I think of the script as something akin to the architect's plan. Buildings can be erected without master designs and working drawings, and in the same way, all sorts of films can be made without scripts. But there are myriad reasons in both cases for writing down and formalizing the creative ideas. To put it very simply, a decent script makes the task of filmmaking a hundred times easier. Why is that? How does the script help us and what are its prime functions?

1. The script is one of the chief means by which a television company assesses your worth. It's also an organizing and structural tool, a reference, and a guide that helps everyone involved in the production.

2. The script communicates the idea of the film to everyone concerned with the production, and it tries to do this clearly, simply, and imaginatively. The script helps everyone understand what the film is about and where it is going. The script is particularly vital to the sponsor, or television commissioning editor, telling him or her in detail what the film is about and whether what has been loosely discussed in conference has been translated into acceptable film ideas.

3. The script is also essential to both the cameraperson and the director. It should convey to the cameraperson a great deal about the mood, action, and problems of the camera work. It should also help the director define the approach and the progress of the film, its inherent logic, and its continuity.

4. The script is also an essential item for the rest of the production team because, apart from conveying the story, it helps the crew answer a series of questions:

- What is the appropriate budget for the film?
- How many locations are needed and how many days of shooting?
- What lighting will be required?
- Will there be any special effects?
- Will archival material be needed?
- Are special cameras or lenses called for because of a particular scene?

Last, the script will also guide the editor, showing the proposed structure of the film and the way the sequences will fit together. In practice, the editor may read the original script but will eventually work from a slightly different document, the *editing script*. (For reasons discussed later, the editing script may differ radically from the original script.)

Implicit in the above comments is the idea that the script is a *working document* and not a *literary document*. It is the basis from which plans can be made and action carried out. It might incidentally be a superb piece of prose (unusual!), but that is not the prime requisite. The first object of the script is to show what the film is about and suggest how its main idea can be carried out in the best possible way.

I have suggested the analogy of an architect's plan, but the comparison works only to a certain point. A script is a guide or first battle plan, the best device for getting the film under way on the basis of the information known at the time of writing. However, in reality it is only a best-guess guide to uncharted territory. It states where you want to go and suggests what seems, initially, to be the best route.

But the actual experience of the filming may cause you to change many ideas. For example, planned sequences may just not work out. The marvelous person who seemed so alive and forthcoming during the research interview turns out to be flat and useless on camera. The vaunted pageant, which sounded so good when described to you and that you thought would provide the climax to the film, turns out to be abysmally dull. Or new possibilities may be discovered while shooting. Strange characters may turn up and marvelous, unexpected events happen even in the best-planned film. In each case you may need to drastically revise your thinking about both the film and the script. You may find yourself reevaluating sequences, throwing some away, adding others, and even reordering some of the main acts.

Another frequent problem is that theory does not always match reality. The script that looked so appealing on paper refuses to work when the material is assembled. You find, for example, that the whole rhythm of the film is wrong or that it is overloaded with information. At that point the script will have to be adjusted, and again, sequences may have to be dropped, cut, or reordered. In most cases this can be done relatively easily, and the script can be altered to accommodate the changes without damaging the essential structure and message of the film.

THE OVERALL FILM STAGES

In order to understand the problems involved in the script, it helps to visualize the entire production process, which is outlined below. In a prescripted documentary the film will probably go through the following stages:

1. Writing the proposal
2. Seeking backing or a coproduction deal
3. Script development
   - the idea and its development
   - discussion of proposal with commissioning editors, sponsors, or funding agencies
   - preliminary research
   - possibly modifying the proposal
   - agreement on budget
   - research
   - writing the shooting script
   - acceptance and modification of script
   - (At this point the writer can relax slightly, but only slightly, as he or she will probably be highly involved throughout production stages as well.)
4. Preproduction (based on script)
5. Filming
6. Editing
   - the visual edit based on a revised editing script
   - editing sound and laying in narration from an approved narration script
7. Final lab work for films or on-lining for videos
   - (The final order of work varies slightly when you are working in video, and that will be discussed later.)

What can sometimes be confusing is that the word *script* is used in half a dozen different ways and may mean something entirely different depending on where you are in the production. You will also hear the words *treatment* and *outline* bandied about, which adds to the confusion. In reality, it is all quite simple, and the script stages proceed as follows.

1. *The idea.* We know what that is. It is the sharp concept, the raison d'être, that underlines the whole film structure.

2. *The treatment or outline.* The treatment or outline is usually just a few pages sketching in what the film is about. It will suggest an approach and tell the overall story of the film. Its usual aim is to clarify the purpose and progression of the film with the funding agency.

3. *The shooting script.* The shooting script is the approved master plan. It usually has a fairly full description of all the visual sequences and an accompanying outline of the ideas to be discussed in the sequence or some tentative narration. As its name indicates, this script also suggests to the director what to shoot and will be used to make a daily shooting plan and a proper budget. As mentioned earlier, it also helps the cameraperson see what special camera and lighting provisions have to be made.

4. *The editing script.* The editing script (visuals) may be the same as the shooting script or something radically different. Normally the director sits down with the editor after filming to review the material already shot (called *rushes* or *dailies*). If the director decides to drop, add, or modify a sequence, he or she will probably draw up a new script or set of notes to guide the editor. This is what we call the editing script. What must be emphasized is that during editing, the rushes, not theory, must guide the film, and this material may necessitate many departures from the original script—thus, the occasional necessity to formulate a special editing script.

5. *The narration script.* This is not really a script but rather the final narration text that has to be read over the visuals. In most current event or biographical documentaries, the shooting script contains only a rough guide to the main ideas of the film. The writing of the exact narration is usually left until almost the end of the process, when all the visual material has been locked into place. However, even in films for which a full narration has been written at an early stage, it is not unusual to see major changes being made in editing, necessitating a new narration script when the editing is almost complete. (Recording and laying in the narration track is one of the last stages in the editing process.)

3

GETTING TO WORK

The writer-producer's first work on a project can be broken down into two stages: (1) from birth of the idea to completion and acceptance of the proposal and (2) from the research stage to acceptance of the shooting script. A great deal of writing will be done at both stages, but to different ends. The final objective of the first stage is to sell potential backers, like a television commissioning editor, on the idea of a film. The objective of the second stage is to prepare a working document that will guide the film from shooting through completion.

So, is the writer a huckster, a common salesperson? In many cases, yes! Occasionally, a writer is invited into a project that has already been set in motion and for which the sole task is merely to write the script. More often than not, though, the writer will also be the producer or will work closely with the producer; in that case, his or her first job is to generate a piece of paper that will sell the idea of the film.

Of course, there are other objectives during the first stage, such as clearing the head of the writer, formulating the ideas in a lucid way, and agreeing on objectives with the sponsor. Nevertheless, in most cases the real aim of the first stage is to get somebody to accept the proposal and fund a film that might cost anything from $5,000 to $250,000. There are five milestones along the way:

1. Conceptualizing the idea
2. Delivering the basic suggestion
3. Writing and delivering the proposal
4. Discussing the suggestion or idea with the sponsor, television station, or support organization
5. Discussing the proposal and signing the contract

All five stages are usually necessary when the idea originates from you personally, but sometimes stages 2–4 overlap. If the idea or request for a film comes from a television station or a sponsoring organization, then you will most likely go straight to the proposal. In this chapter I want to deal with stages 1 and 2.

THE BASIC IDEA OR SUGGESTION

The basic suggestion is the written definition of the idea that gets the film moving. It is the power and driving force that impels your whole production. Ideas come from everywhere. Ideas can be impelled upon you by childhood experience, by something you saw on television, by your newspaper reading, or by something a friend told you. Wherever the idea comes from something has stirred within you. Your intellectual or emotional curiosity has been aroused, and you feel ready to commit time and an immense amount of energy to transform that vague idea into a film.

Where do you go from there? You try to commit the idea to one simple statement, and the simpler the better. If you can't do this and your definition of the idea turns into an essay, then you know something is wrong. So you jot down something like this.

Debbie and David: This is the story of a mother who is determined that through her inventions her invalid child will learn to walk.
Because It's There: This film investigates the race to conquer Mount Everest.
Shaheed: This film looks at the life of Ahmed Salim, one of the first of the Islamic suicide bombers.
Two Wheels to Love: This film deals with love among the handicapped.
Mysteries of Rome: This film looks at the secret treasures that are rumored to be held by the Vatican.

Once you've defined your idea, you have to get your act on the road. You can do this via a note, a letter, or a memo that raises someone's interest so that he or she will back the film. The key here is to raise interest. The note can be formal or informal, jocular or serious, but whatever format it takes, its purpose is to intrigue the reader, to stimulate his or her interest and imagination. The response you are looking for is, "What a great idea! Let's think more about this." This approach works fairly well with corporate sponsors, but a television company will usually request a full proposal before proceeding further.

More often than not, the note or letter is short and to the point. If the idea is good, then its attractiveness will be seen immediately. The task of the suggestive note is to say briefly what the film is about, why the idea is attractive to you, and why it might be of interest to the sponsor. Here are a few examples, mainly addressed to corporate or charity sponsors.

Help Me

If hospitals scare adults, then what are the effects of the institution on children? We believe that the problems facing children going into the hospital have been neglected for too long.

We therefore propose to make a ten-minute film for children between the ages of four and ten, which will help dispel their fears. There is a dire need to make such a film, and we believe that the Wellington Hospital, with its worldwide reputation for the care and welfare of children as well as its reputation for healing, is the ideal institution to make and back such a pioneering film.

We estimate the production cost to be in the region of $12,000.

The suggestion is brief but easily grasped. Such an idea would probably be accompanied by a letter suggesting a meeting to discuss the idea in more detail if there is any initial interest. The letter would also amplify why it would benefit the hospital to make such a film.

Another idea might be put this way:

Dear Dr. Courts:
Is it just coincidence or is it the fashion of the times? In the last month I have read at least three articles in magazines ranging from *Newsweek* to the *New Yorker* discussing the prevalence of student stress and teenage suicide.

This started me thinking about your department, which has received so much well-deserved publicity in regard to its research on student stress and your innovative methods for dealing with the same.

I would like to suggest doing a film with you on the whole subject of stress, which would serve to publicize your methods and approach around the world. We could do this either as a

straightforward instructional film, or we could play around a
little more imaginatively using two or three student types. We
could take a first-year student and a graduate student as typical
cases and examine their problems and treatment.

I think—and I don't believe I'm wrong—that there is a
tremendous demand for such a film (or videotape). I also think
it would be fairly easy to get the university and the Science
Research Council to fund us up to the tune of $20,000, which
should be sufficient. What do you say? Can we get together to
discuss the matter further?

In the above two examples, the writer-producer is the originator of
the suggestions. However, it sometimes happens that a sponsor or a
television documentary series solicits proposals on a general topic. It
is then up to the writer to develop a specific approach. A recent memo
from the British Home Office read as follows:

Request for Suggestions

We wish to make various short films showing the problems confronting new immigrants to England, and the successful integration of the
immigrants. We welcome suggestions from producers, which should
be less than three pages in length and turned in, in triplicate. The films
should be under twenty minutes in length and should be capable of
being executed on a budget of $15,000. Proposals must be submitted
to this office by July 31.

An interested writer-producer might have responded as follows:

The Orchestra

This is a film about a unique orchestra in Manchester composed of
thirty Indians from New Delhi and Madras who have been in England
five years. Some are fluent in English, but not all. Many were professional musicians in India, but they now have to support themselves
in Manchester by learning new trades and professions.

Three years ago, under the leadership and inspiration of Asoke
Badra, they decided to form a specialized Indian folk orchestra.

The orchestra rehearses three times a week, and in the last year has
given major concerts in Manchester and in London's Festival Hall.
Next year the orchestra has been invited to appear at New York's
Lincoln Center.

We believe that a look at the orchestra and its members will provide a different and fascinating way of approaching the problems of
immigrant absorption.

Implicit in this suggestion is the idea that the writer-producer will explore individual immigrant backgrounds, problems, and attitudes to the new country, and will emerge with a story of hope. Quite clearly, the orchestra motif is a neat frame for this exploration.

Though I thought about the orchestra idea, I never submitted it. I was therefore very interested when, a few years later, I saw that Jim Brown, a New York filmmaker and university professor, had just finished a documentary on the experiences of a Russian émigré orchestra in the United States.

When you write to a television station it is vital to know if it has particular documentary strands, the arts or history or current events, into which your film will fit. For example, the BBC ran a series called *Secret History*. If you were writing to its commissioning editor you might just drop a note as follows:

> Dear Mr. Lawson:
> I am a documentary producer who specializes in films on history and politics. Recently I followed with great fascination your series *States of Terror*. Your analysis of the situation in Iran backed up everything I have seen there with my own eyes on my three visits last year.
>
> They were not casual visits, but were made in the course of my research on a new series my company is planning called *The Masters of Murder*. In this six-part series, we plan to profile major world terrorists such as bin Laden, the Jackal, the Baider Meinhoff Group, and Ohlendorff, one of the leaders of the Waffen SS. Danny Setton, whose work you know from his films on Mengele and Bormann will be the writer, I will direct, and Prof. Frankel, whose books on terror you know, will be our consultant.
>
> I think the subject speaks for itself, as well as the quality of the production personnel. I think the idea is a dynamic one, well suited to *Secret History*, and I would very much appreciate your sparing some time for us to meet to see whether we can develop this idea in tandem.

Given a letter like this, a commissioning editor might invite you to a meeting, but he or she is most likely to reply "Could be, but let's see a proper proposal." Or, to be very cynical, they might not reply at all and just pinch your idea.

If you know that local television or the BBC is doing a series on writers called *Bookends*, your introductory letter might go:

Dear Mr. Monson

I am a writer-producer of arts documentaries and would be obliged if you would consider the following idea for inclusion in *Bookends*.

As you know, Frank McCourt's book *Angela's Ashes* skyrocketed from nowhere to 120 weeks on the best-seller charts. As you also know, various films have already been made on Frank, but all concentrating on his childhood in Ireland. His contemporary life however is a closed book to us.

Frank is a very good friend of mine and has agreed to allow me an entry into his private life denied to most other filmmakers. What I would like to propose to you is an hour film, *The Price of Fame*, looking at how Frank's life has changed since fame and riches came his way. I think the film would secure a very wide audience and can be made on a very limited budget.

If the idea intrigues you I would appreciate hearing from you and you can reach me at the above address or phone.

THE DISCUSSION AND THE AGENDA

The response to your initial suggestion has been favorable. The doctor, the sponsor, the station, or the agency is intrigued. They are willing to explore further, though they have told you they are far from committed. They want to meet and, depending on the discussion, will decide whether they want to pursue the matter. The following topics are likely to be on the meeting's agenda: the subject matter and purpose of the film; its intended audience; its approach; and its limitations, such as budget and timing. Knowing that these topics will come up, you have to prepare so that you will have the answers at hand when a problem is raised. You will also know what issues to raise with the sponsor so that there will be no misunderstandings once you start to work seriously on the film.

Subject Matter and Purpose

No matter what the film, and no matter who is supporting it, it is essential that the boundaries of the topic and the purpose of the film be clarified from the start. As I've mentioned, you must aim for a target definition or basic assertion that states clearly what the film is about, what it is trying to say and to whom, and what it hopes to achieve. You must have those things straight before participating in any meetings.

This target definition isn't just for the sponsor; it will also keep your thinking on track as the film progresses.

You also have to be clear from the start what you want the film to do. It may have a multiplicity of purposes, but you should know what they are. Is it meant as a television current-affairs film? Is it meant to comment on and inform on a political crisis? Will it merely entertain? Will it help in fundraising? Will it alarm the population to a hidden danger and shake them from their complacency, like *The War Game* does? Is it meant to change political or social attitudes, as Michael Moore attempted to do in *Fahrenheit 9/11* and in *Bowling for Columbine?* Will it instruct? Is it meant to change certain habits and behaviors? Is it meant to illuminate and track strange human behavior? You may want the film to do all these things or none of them, but you must be sure of your central purpose from the beginning.

In these early discussions, if the film is not your own personal project, you also need to probe the sponsors' attitude to the subject. Why are they interested? What do they want? Ideally, their interests and attitudes will coincide with your own, but not always. Therefore, it is best to flush out any sponsor reservations on the subject at the beginning rather than be surprised by them later, at some cost to the film.

Audience

The objective of a film cannot be discussed in isolation. It always goes together with a consideration of the audience for whom the film is intended. You must know from the beginning something about your audience; either the sponsor tells you or you find out for yourself. You need to know who makes up the audience, how it can best be reached, and whether it is broad or narrow. The answers to these questions will influence your whole approach to conceptualizing the film. Writing for television is generally quite difficult because the audience is so broad. When doing a general documentary for television, you may have to assume that you are writing for all groups between the ages of fourteen and seventy-five, for all levels of education, and for people from all varieties of social and religious backgrounds.

What are the things you need to know about your potential viewers and related matters?

First, you need to define *the general composition of the audience.* Who exactly are the people who are going to watch the film? What are their ages? What are their politics? What are their religious beliefs? Is it a city audience or a rural audience? Is it sophisticated or unsophisticated, educated or uneducated? Is it an audience of professionals or manual workers? Obviously, you won't be asking all these questions all the time, but you will definitely be asking some of them, because the answers to the questions will help you speak directly to the audience instead of above it, below it, or around it.

Next, you need to know in what *context* the film will be shown. Will it be shown in a school, a church, or a university? Is it going to be shown on television in prime time or at an obscure midnight hour? If it is going to be shown on prime-time television, you might have to tone down your treatment unless you are working for HBO or PBS. If it's going to be shown in the early hours, then you may have a small audience, but you might get away with a much more revolutionary and radical approach to your subject. Is the film going to be used for fundraising at a massive dinner or is it going to be shown in a small village hall? Is it intended for a specific audience in one country or will it be shown around the world? Is it going to be shown in a television series or in isolation?

You must be certain to define *audience feeling* about the subject. What attitudes do they hold on the topic? Is it completely unknown to the audience or is it a familiar subject? Do they have any fears or resistance to the subject? Do they hold any taboos about it? Are there any prejudices with which one has to cope, or is the subject outside the normal experience of the audience? Are they likely to approve of the philosophy of the film or will they resist it? The practical ramifications of these questions are very important. For example, if you are making a film about birth control, it is vital to know whether your target audience is Protestant or Catholic, conservative or liberal. In short, you should understand the culture and beliefs of the audience you are trying to reach and influence. Unless you understand these elementary points, the film can be technically well made and yet fail to deliver its message.

Approach

Some of the inevitable questions that come up in the first discussion are, What approach are you going to use? How are you going to do it? and, What are the interesting elements? At that point I try to say as little as possible, especially if the film's topic is a new subject for me as a writer or if I do not really know the sponsor. I want time to become familiar with the subject before I jump in.

In working out an approach, it helps to look for certain elements and qualities in the subject. One way in is to start by exploring the following:

Are you dealing with a really good story?

Does it contain diverting situational or personal conflicts?

Can you find strong and charismatic characters involved in the story?

Is it easy to define possible areas of focus?

Does the story involve character and situational change, either immediate or over time, as seen, for instance, in Michael Apted's documentaries *7 Up* through *49 Up*?

There are other jumping-off points, but the above five represent the five strongest lead-ins and matters for overall consideration.

There may be questions at the back of your mind, but the sponsor or commissioning editor will want something very concrete, or at least a hint of how you would approach the subject. If you have been thinking about the topic for years, you should have no trouble with this question, as you have probably already thought of a way to do the film. The difficulty occurs when the subject is new and you know nothing about it.

Sometimes I just play for time. On major documentaries I try to make a strong case that I need to research and absorb the subject before I can guess at an approach. However, when they ask, "How would you do it?" you have no option but to plunge right in, even though you know you may junk the idea as soon as you exit the room.

One of the first times that question was sprung on me was when I was doing a news piece, and the director of the museum where I was filming asked me out of the blue how I would do a general film on the museum. At that stage I knew nothing about the museum except for having walked around it once. My spontaneous answer was that I thought we could look at the museum through the eyes of two eight-year-old children. It seemed to me that at their age there was a curiosity that would add freshness to the way the museum was observed. This would break the standard intellectual catalog approach to museum filming. In the end I didn't get the film. Would silence have been better? I don't think so.

Conversely, a friend of mine did get a film because he ventured a fresh approach at the right time to people with a receptive imagination. And again it was a case of jumping in while knowing nothing about the subject. The Vermont State Bureau of Taxes wanted to encourage people to pay their local taxes. David knew nothing about taxes but suggested a scenario where his hero dreams of leading a revolt against tax payment. Everybody supports him. He becomes the local hero, but suddenly there are thieves everywhere as there is no money for the police; likewise, there are no hospital services and no schools. The hero wakes in shock and pays his taxes. It was a very funny idea and powerfully put across the essential idea that taxes are necessary to make the social order work smoothly.

One difficulty that frequently arises is trying to get the sponsors to abandon an approach that they have been nursing for months but that you feel is wrong. For example, they may want the film to star the managing director, who is also the chief shareholder, but who would, in your opinion, be a total disaster for the film. If the idea is no good, then it has to be killed early, but tactfully.

Leaving all discussion of approach until the research has been done is great in theory, but difficult in practice. This is particularly true of television quasi news documentaries, where the time between idea, research, and filming is often so negligible as to be nonexistent. In reality, you start thinking about approach from the beginning, and later research either reinforces your original hunch or shows its deficiencies.

Limitations

The objects of the first discussion are to distinguish the possible from the impossible and to bring a sense of reality into the planning, such as budget costs, time, and technical matters. You might think that this kind of discussion should just be between the sponsor and the producer, but as it seriously affects the script, I believe the writer should be involved as well.

Cost Limitations

One has to know at an early stage all the cost limitations, because the size of the budget largely determines what can and cannot be done. The grandiose designs of the sponsor (or yourself) may require $100,000 and so be absolutely impractical if $20,000 is the maximum available. The script must be capable of being executed within the confines of the budget. This is golden rule number one.

Most people who work in television documentaries have an excellent idea of realistic costs. This knowledge is rarely shared by companies or charitable organizations who want films about their enterprises or projects. Sponsors are always shocked by the cost of filmmaking, and my heart no longer sinks when they say, "What! $30,000! We were sure it wouldn't be more than $5,000. Maybe we should do a slide show instead."

You must have a good sense of film costs before entering any discussion with the sponsor. In assessing the feasibility of doing your script, even at the earliest stages, you should be considering days of shooting, length of editing, stock costs, and so on, not to mention a living wage or small profit for the writer-director. So, you must think about all the expenses in order to tell the sponsor what your beautiful idea will cost and in order to see whether the film can really be brought in on the budget suggested by the sponsor or backer. Thus, golden rule number two: do not accept a budget that will be inadequate for your film concept. If you are given a budget limitation, then your script (but not necessarily your imagination) must be limited by that fact. You ignore this rule at your financial peril.

One of the problems of dealing with costs at this point of the proceedings is that you may also be at the bid stage. If you are the only filmmaker being considered for the project, and if the sponsor came to you with their idea, then you are in a relatively good position to argue for the best budget under the circumstances. What is the best budget? You should try to get a rough sense of the organization—whether it is wealthy or desperate, whether it lives from profits or donations. Once you have this picture in mind you will have a good idea how to make your bid.

When there is competition for the film, things are trickier. When other people are bidding for the same film, the question becomes how to make a reasonable bid that will keep you in competition with everybody else and yet will leave you enough to make both a quality film and a profit.

Time Constraints

It is also vital to discuss timing at an early stage. Are time considerations going to be of importance to any aspect of the film? If so, they should be discussed early. For example:

- Does the film have to be finished and ready for screening on a certain date, such as the annual meeting of the sponsoring organization or a political or historical anniversary within a country? If so, is there enough time to make the film while still maintaining quality?
- How do seasons and climate affect the filming or the completion date? Have you taken into consideration that you will be filming at the time of the heaviest snows or that the rainy season will prevent your helicopter shots?

- Are you dependent on one individual, group, or situation for any length of time, and will a change in the availability of someone or a change in the situation jeopardize the film?

If you are wary of these restraints, then think twice before you go ahead. If you still feel apprehensive, drop the idea. You'll feel better in the long run. Let me give you an example.

A few summers ago I thought that I had hit on a great idea. It struck me that John Houseman, the professor hero of the series *The Paper Chase*, had in his real life as writer, producer, and director seen almost every major change in film, theater, and television in the United States between the years 1940 and 1980. He had worked with Orson Welles on *Citizen Kane*, had produced *Lust for Life* with Kirk Douglas, and seemed to have known everybody and worked with every type of mass media. Knowing this, I thought we could do a fascinating film looking at forty years of change in the media and tie it all to Houseman's recollections and reminiscences. Houseman was agreeable and enthusiastic. What stopped me in the end was Houseman's age. When I met him he was already eighty-three. I knew it would take about eighteen months to raise the money and get the project moving, then another eighteen months to film and complete. Could I rely on Houseman's health for three years? It seemed to me too big a risk, and I dropped the project. Houseman died six months after we met.

Film or Video?

One major issue must be sorted out at the start: does the sponsor want a film or a videotape as the final product? This will also be a question for you even if no sponsor is concerned. The answer really depends on purpose and use rather than on technical considerations. You might prefer video

- if the program is intended mainly for home or office presentation;
- if the audience will have to go back and forth in looking at the film or if they will want to stop on one point for discussion or need to rewind quickly;
- if a tremendous amount of shooting has to be done and you are wary of cost—here the low cost of videotape is of tremendous help;
- if you want to make many copies yet keep the cost down;
- if you want very elaborate effects and think they can best be done electronically;

- if you need to work very fast, change magazines frequently, and also check your results as you shoot by using a monitor;
- if you need to keep your camera as inconspicuous as possible for political or other reasons (Ellen Bruno's film *Satya*, about Tibetan rebel nuns, was shot with a small one-chip Hi8 camera, and new digital cameras are fantastic in terms of compactness and quality).

You might prefer film

- if the sponsor wants a theatrical screening to impress people or if you are thinking primarily of a hall or theatrical presentation. The common use of LCD projectors these days somewhat diminishes that argument, however;
- if the quality of the photography is an important final consideration.

In fact, all these arguments are open to question because of the swift pace of change in video technology.

Feasibility

Before starting a new project, I hold a discussion in my head concerning the project's feasibility. Occasionally I get the most fantastic ideas and then realize they are not very practical. Often, extremely careful thought is required before saying yes to any idea.

Recently, a producer friend of mine told me he was considering doing a film on the intelligence services of the world and asked me to help him with it. It sounded like a splendid idea, and he had already made two films on international terrorism. If anyone could pull it off, it was Mike. But as we started to think through the project, a number of problems started surfacing. Yes, it was easy enough to talk about spies, about the blowing up of the Greenpeace ship by France, about the Israeli intelligence seizure of Vanunu, about John le Carré, about the KGB men who had defected and the problems of the CIA and so on—but was that enough? The film was about intelligence, not spies and not thriller writers, though these elements would appear.

The real question was whether or not we could penetrate in any meaningful way the intelligence systems of the world—the CIA, the British M15 and M16, the Israeli Mossad. I doubted it. We could perhaps get interviews with people such as Peter Wright, the former British agent and author of *Spy Catcher*, and in 1997 a whole heap of public evidence had been revealed about the methods of the Israeli Mossad, but I still didn't think it was enough. For the program to have bite, we needed real inside interviews. Instead, the most we could get would be old stories and tales of incidents based on hearsay, innuendo, and wild guessing. We could do an interesting film, but it wasn't the one I wanted to make. A year and a half later most of the information we had wanted had in fact become available, but by that time my friend had moved on to other things.

Generally I hate abandoning good ideas. If the subject is intrinsically interesting, then sometimes an alternative approach or a slightly different slant will show you a way in. Again, what at first sight seems a doubtful or unpromising idea often gets realized through sheer determination or imagination. A while ago, Roger Graef, a noted cinema verité filmmaker, wanted to make a film about the decision-making processes of big business in England. This necessitated entry into the most intimate boardroom discussions of the largest corporations, such as those controlling steel and oil. "You'll never get the necessary permissions," everybody said. "All decisions of big business are made by fat rich men in elegant boardrooms in secret." Graef persisted, and against all odds he got three of the largest corporations in England to give him permission to film their boardroom meetings over six months. The resulting series, *Decisions*, was one of the most fascinating ever to appear on television.

Sometimes it looks impossible, but it can be done.

ORDER OF PROGRESS

I have suggested that the logical development of your film begins with the initial idea and then moves into meetings and discussions that lead into the real long-form proposal. However, the order is often reversed, and you have to submit a detailed proposal before meeting with the sponsor. There are few rules, and each case is different. But for the purpose of this book I have assumed that the discussions came before the proposal. So, on to the proposal.

4

WRITING THE PROPOSAL

It is clear enough that everything starts with the idea, but what comes next? Proposal or research? Are we back to the conundrum of the chicken and the egg vying for seniority? Or maybe the example of Siamese twins offers a better guide for us, because in practice proposal and research are totally intertwined and march forward together. Therefore, if this chapter comes before research, it is only for convenience, as both proceed in tandem.

The two questions regarding proposals are *what to write* and then *where to send* your brilliant effort if no first approaches have been made. In this chapter I want to deal with the former, while leaving the matter of destination until chapter 23, "Staying Alive." For argument's sake, however, let's assume you have spoken to someone and your initial idea has had a warm reception. You have met with the potential sponsors or the television department heads, who like your ideas but want to know more. Now you have to write a formal proposal that will define your thinking in much greater detail.

A proposal is, first and foremost, a device to sell a film. It may serve many other functions, such as clarifying your own thinking or showing your friends what you want to do, and it will provide information useful to all sorts of people. It will show your working hypothesis, your lines of inquiry, your point of view on the subject, and all its dramatic possibilities. But its central purpose is to convince someone, probably a television commissioning editor or some organization head, that you have a great idea, that you know what you want to do, that you are efficient, professional, and imaginative, and that you should therefore be given the contract for the film against any competition and be financially supported in your endeavors. Proposals are all used extensively to sell film ideas at film markets, but I want to leave a longer discussion on that topic until later.

Sometimes a proposal is called for after a film has been awarded to a producer. However, for the next few pages I want to discuss the general writing of the proposal when its prime purpose is to get your foot in the door and sell the film.

STYLE AND MAIN TOPICS

The best rule is to aim for simplicity, clarity, and brevity in your proposal. Brevity may not always be possible, but it is a worthy ideal. Proposals for the National Endowment for the Humanities or the National Endowment for the Arts are often hundreds of pages long, but they are special cases. Few commissioning editors or sponsors have the patience to read long proposals in detail; a concise proposal contained in two or three pages is much more likely to get their attention. Recently I have been told by commissioning editors that they really don't want to see more than one page. One page! That's frightening, so you aim to get your message across as quickly as you can, and as dynamically as you can, and then if necessary amplify.

What is implied in the above, of course, is that sometimes you may have to write two, three, or even four different proposals for the same project. The first, short, is to gain the interest of a television station and to get them to give you a promise of airtime, backing, and some basic support. The longer, unfortunately often encyclopedic, proposal is to get your major funding from various national councils and foundations. And in between you will write other proposals of various lengths to go to all the agencies and groups in the middle.

What should the proposal discuss and how should it be organized? There are no absolute rules, but it helps to remember that a proposal is usually written with a specific person or organization in mind. I usually include the following items in my proposals:

1. Film statement
2. Background and need

3. Approach, form, and style
4. Shooting schedule
5. Budget
6. Audience, marketing, and distribution
7. Filmmaker's biography and support letters
8. Miscellaneous additional elements

Film statement. The statement formally declares that you are making a proposal and usually suggests a working title. It indicates the length of the film and briefly defines its subject matter and audience. It probably includes the basic assertion or target statement mentioned earlier. Only a few lines are necessary, as indicated by the following examples:

University Blues
This is a proposal for a sixty-minute video film on the future of Oxford and Cambridge universities for general BBC television audiences.

Because We Care
This is a proposal for a forty-minute 16mm film on St. Winston's Hospital to be shown to potential donors for fund-raising.

Background and need. The section on background and need reviews briefly any information necessary to acquaint the reader with the subject. This section lets the reader see why the topic is interesting and why such a film is needed or would be of interest as entertainment or information for a general audience. Here you must pay attention to the words *need* and *interest*. There are so many topics out there begging to be made into films, and your job is to persuade the commissioning editor that your film is so dynamic and vital for the audience that it just must be made.

Some years ago I wanted to do a film about nineteenth-century American utopian movements and started writing the proposal with a friend, Brian Winston. We called the film *Roads to Eden* and included the following sketch with the proposal:

The most sustained and widespread efforts to remake the world took place along the expanding frontier in North America, mainly in the nineteenth century. Literally hundreds of communities with thousands of members were established, and the vast majority of them sought salvation through rigorous and what they thought of as ancient Christian practice.

The discovery of the New World and the birth of modern utopianism occurred during the same quarter of a century. The one deeply influenced the other, and the New World immediately became a place in which tradition and history could be restarted and remade.

The potency of America as a ready-made site for social experiment survived undiminished by failures, lunacies, or frauds for the next three centuries.

Inspired with a vision of early Christian life traceable back to the communes of the Essenes, enriched by the monastic tradition and the example of primitive (mainly German) Protestant sects, the American Christian radicals set about building their Jerusalem. Out of a flurry of activity major groups emerged: Mormons, Shakers, Amish, Oneidans, Ammonites, Rappites, and Zoarites.

Brian and I took some time to establish the background, but we were making a proposal for an hour-long major network film, which we also hoped would be the basis of a series. We assumed most people would like the idea of a film about utopias but would know nothing of their histories; thus, the detail.

When we had finished sketching in the background, we set out our reasons for wanting to do the film, and why the audience really *needed* the series.

In this film or series we will look at the past in order to ascertain where we might possibly go in the future, for the dream of a better world is not dead, only diminished.

Thus, a series of questions underlies the film. How can we make a better life for ourselves, our families, and our children? What can we learn from the past about sexual mores, family structures, and social organizations? What do the visions and struggles of the utopians tell us about our own future?

The background sketch can be short or long. You must ask yourself whether the reader has sufficient information about the central situation and premise of the film to make a reasonable judgment about it. And have you provided enough information to intrigue the reader to go further? The background information should be a lure to fascinate the reader, to make him or her say, "What a marvelous possibility for a film."

Approach, form, and style. I have already mentioned that I am wary of defining approach, form, or style before I have researched the subject, as the research usually suggests the best way into the film.

Yet in most cases, at least a tentative approach will be asked for at the proposal stage. If the original suggestion came from you, an approach will definitely be required. This is the part of the proposal that most interests the reader. Your ideas sound fascinating and appealing, but how will you carry them out in practice? Where is the drama in your story? Where is the conflict? Where are the emotions and the character development? This is where you must be down-to-earth. If your approach or structure is tentative, then say so, or indicate two or three approaches you would like to investigate further.

The question of form and structure is discussed in detail later, but a few words might help now. In most television documentaries, the chosen form is usually that of the *general essay* or *illustrative story*, and the style ranges from the objective to the anecdotal or the personal. In the early 1970s, Thames Television in England put out a marvelous twenty-six-part series on World War II called *The World at War*. What was refreshing about the series was that it ran the whole gamut of styles and structures. One film would be an academic essay, while the next would be highly personal, telling the story of the war almost solely through the voices of the soldiers.

A few paragraphs back I set out the background for the utopia film. That was the easy part. But what approach should we use? It could be done, say, in essay style:

> The film is set up chronologically as we tell the story of the communities from the seventeenth to the late nineteenth century, from the Shakers to the Zoarites. The film will include all the main communities but will concentrate on the Shakers. It will be built around drawings, contemporary pictures, old photographs, and contemporary footage and will be told through a strong central guiding commentary.

This may sound a bit dry. Perhaps we could try a story form and an alternative structure:

> We will look at the utopian movement through two central charismatic characters; the leaders of Harmony and New Harmony. These two colonies were situated in southern Indiana. The first was a religious colony founded by the grim authoritarian preacher Emmanuel Rapp, from southern Germany. Eventually, the colony was sold to the Scottish idealist Robert Owen, who wanted to found a workers' utopia.
>
> We will film exclusively at New Harmony, which is today still faithfully preserved as in the days of Owen and Rapp. Besides filming on location, we propose using old diary extracts and the writings of

Rapp and Owen as the binding narrative. The film will look at these communities through the lives of their leaders, who could not have interpreted the meaning of *utopia* more differently. However, we will also try to recapture the feelings of the community members of the time. The style will be evocative and poetic rather than didactic.

In the early 1980s, Canadian filmmaker Michael Rubbo made a film called *Daisy* about plastic surgery. I never read his proposal, but from seeing the film I could imagine Rubbo setting out the proposal something like this:

Why do people go in for plastic surgery? What are their fears and expectations? We wish to show something of the history and practice of plastic surgery to the general public.

We think the best approach to a film of this kind is to follow one individual for six months, covering the period before, during, and after the operation. And we have found exactly the right person.

Daisy is an employee of the Canadian Film Board, an open, cheerful, and outgoing woman in her early forties. Though still extremely attractive, Daisy feels that plastic surgery will improve her looks and general social well-being. She also thinks it will help her find a husband.

Daisy's experience will provide us with the spine of the film. However, we will also branch out from time to time to show the history of plastic surgery, the way it is practiced in present-day Montreal, and how it exists as a thriving business.

Even without major research you can often take a pretty good stab at the approach you would like to take and the tentative structure of the film.

Some years ago I was asked to consider doing a film on the British prison system, a subject I knew very little about. My initial feeling, before I had undertaken any research, was that this should be a people film rather than an essay film, a personal film from both sides of the bars. In my first outline proposal, I suggested a film around the experience of five individuals. The first two would represent the administration in the person of a guard and the warden. The other three characters would be prisoners: one about to serve his first six-month sentence, the second a lifer, and the last someone who had served five years and whom we would follow in his first three months of freedom. I was fairly sure that I could find these character types and that the different experiences of the five over half a year would provide an illuminating and moving picture of the prison system.

I set all this out in the proposal and also indicated that there would be minimal narration; instead, the film would hang on the thoughts, feelings, and comments of the five "stars." I was a bit worried about the extended shooting time and its effect on the budget, and therefore I sounded out the sponsors before I wrote the proposal. They agreed to provide a decent budget, and I was free to explore the above approach. Had the budget been a small one, I would have cut down on my characters and shooting time or would have opted for an essay film that could have been shot in two weeks.

Where possible, I like to indicate early on whether there will be formal narration, direct dialogue, or a great deal of voice-over. I also occasionally say something about visual style if I think that will be a major element of the film.

Shooting schedule. The shooting schedule is an optional item in the proposal. You include it when time is of the essence: for example, when you have to capture a particular event or shoot within a particular season of the year. You also put it in when you want to protect yourself, so that you can turn to the sponsor and say, "The proposal says very clearly we would need six months, so don't tell me now that I have to do it in three. It just can't be done."

Budget. I usually include an approximate budget in the proposal. However, I try to put off committing myself on paper until I have had a word with the sponsors. I don't want to scare them off until we have talked about cost and I have received some feedback. Obviously, if you are sending a proposal to a foundation such as the National Endowment for the Humanities or the Rockefeller Foundation, you will have to provide at least an outline budget proposal.

Audience, marketing, and distribution. A discussion of audience and distribution is another optional item. If a sponsor has requested a film to train factory workers, or if a television station has requested a film for a certain documentary series, then you will not have to say anything about distribution in the proposal. However, when you are trying to sell a sponsor or a foundation on your idea by saying that there will be massive demand for your film, then you have to prove your claim, at least on paper. You also have to talk about getting the film to this massive public. This section of the proposal therefore sets out in detail the possible channels of distribution for the film. A section on distribution is invariably required for a major proposal to a foundation.

Below is the section on distribution from Jill Godmilow's proposal for *The Popovich Brothers.* The film took as its subject a Serbian musical family in Chicago. While it explored their music, it also looked at the sense of family, traditions, and close bonding of the whole immigrant community of which the Popovich brothers were just part.

We believe that filmmaking and film marketing are two halves of a full circle. A film that never reaches its audience is little different from a film that never gets made. It just costs a lot more.

We have two major goals in the distribution of *The Popovich Brothers*. The first is to make it available to the Serbian community on all levels: to the churches, to the local lodges of the Serb National Federation, to high school systems with a large number of Serbian students, to other Slavic groups, and to universities which have community-developed ethnic studies. Our experience thus far indicates tremendous interest and support for this project in the Serbian community, on a local and national level.

Besides the Serbian community, there are four general distribution markets for this documentary film:

1. *Television:* Television sales—commercial, educational, and foreign—constitute the independent documentary's widest means of exposure to a mass audience and its most immediate and least expensively obtained source of income.

   a. The commercial networks can buy up to thirty minutes of footage at $1,000 per minute and recut and narrate it for use as one segment of their program.

   b. PBS, the national educational network, is also in the market for quality independently produced documentaries.

   c. Foreign television sales.

2. *Print Sales:* Museums, public libraries, and university libraries have begun to buy films for their permanent collections. They are used for public screenings as well as borrowed for home use.

3. *Rentals:* Every nondramatic film must find its particular rental market, its own special-interest groups. *The Popovich Brothers* has a good market potential in areas such as music, dance, American history, ethnic studies, social anthropology, Slavic languages, and ethnomusicology.

4. *Theatrical:* The fourth general area of distribution for *Popovich* is theatrical. It is a limited market but an important one. The success of a theatrical campaign for a film like this one depends to a great degree on being able to open in New York, with the accompanying critical response and public excitement which can create a name for a film.

I have set out Jill's proposal at length because it is one of the best examples I have seen of lucid proposal writing. *The Popovich Brothers* was eventually made, received wide acclaim, and was followed by other films by Jill Godmilow, such as *Far from Poland*.

Filmmaker's biography and support letters. It helps toward the end of the proposal to give a short biographical description of yourself and the other principal filmmakers involved in the project. You should also affirm your track record by adding letters of recommendation or praise for your previous work. You may also include any support letters from individuals or organizations for your idea and any letters from television stations showing an interest in screening your film.

Additional elements. Your idea is to sell your project; therefore, you add anything that you believe, within reason, will help people to understand your concept and get the proposal accepted. This includes any illustrative materials such as maps, photos, and general drawings. It includes names of academic personnel who are acting as your advisers. And it may include a full revenue plan if your documentary is intended as a commercial proposition for theatrical release.

You should also very seriously consider doing a video teaser when you are thinking of making a long film for television. By this I mean making a five- or ten-minute video that dramatically highlights what your film is about. This obviously entails some expenditure and some shooting before your film is properly under way, but this preview can be one of your strongest selling tools. Thus, though your proposal about the history of Yosemite is very strong, it takes on even greater strength when supported by your video that shows the power and magic of the place. And though your proposal on a history of the U.S. Marine Corps is attractive, it will get an even better reception when supported by a strong visual backup.

Another practical reason for the video is that fund-raising for independent videos is often done at parlor meetings. Without a film, these can be very dry affairs, indeed. With a film or a trailer the situation is entirely different. You clearly show what you are going to do and how well you can do it, given the chance, and generally the response is much stronger.

EXAMPLES

Depending on the objectives of the film, the same subject might require two entirely different proposals. Let us imagine we have been asked to put in two proposals for a university film. One is to be a standard documentary for general television audiences, the second a film to raise funds for the campus; the working title for both films is *Tomorrow Begins Now*. Below, I have sketched out the main differences between the two proposals.

Film A	Film B

Introduction

A half-hour film to *explore* the changing university.	A half-hour film to raise money for the university.

Background

The changing university over the last twenty years. Ideas change. Communities change.	The changing community. Education today. Desperate need for a new kind of university. The answer as provided by our university.

Objectives

A reevaluation in the eyes of the public of the role and purpose of a university. For general television audiences.	To raise money for the university. For showing to small interest groups, dinner groups, and friends of the university.

Focus

The film is about a group of students. We set out to explore their world.	The complexity of a university and the need it fills in a community. Also the future requirements of the university.

Format and Style

We follow three students for six months as they become involved in different social, educational, political activities. The style is personal and intimate.	We follow two students and two professors through a typical day. The film is an overview of and university activities rather than an analysis of the pros and cons of the university. We intend to stress the building program and the intake of students from culturally deprived backgrounds.

Narration

As little as possible. Use the students' voices instead.	We will use a standard expository narrator with occasional voice-overs by students and faculty.

	Technique
Cinema verité	Basic directed documentary style

	Point of View
We view the students as basically idealistic and an admirable force for good.	We see the university as a vital force element in our growing nation, an element that must be supported if we are to survive.

The proposal for film A above follows in broad terms the film *The Berkeley Rebels*, made by Arthur Barron for *CBS Reports*. In 1965, CBS had told Barron that there was a lot of trouble at the Berkeley campus of the University of California; they suggested that he explore the situation in terms of the students' goals and see what kind of film he wanted to make. Barron spent a month at Berkeley, returned to CBS, and wrote out the following preparatory notes. These notes are not exactly a proposal but show clearly the kind of film Barron wanted to make.

Focus. This film is not about the University of California; it is not about the class of 1965; it is not about the demonstrations which have taken place at California. These are all elements in our story but the film is basically about something else. It is about a selected group of students. Call them "activists," the new radicals, or "green baggers." This picture is about them. It seeks to explore their world. It seeks to answer these questions: Who are they? What do they want? Why are they important? It seeks to reveal the mood, posture, and attitudes of a new and different generation of committed students.

Point of View. We do not state a point of view directly but we do have an attitude about these kids, and hopefully it comes through. It is this: despite their faults (intolerance, immaturity, a tendency to see things in black and white, rebellion for its own sake, a certain disrespect for law and order), these kids are a positive and admirable force in American society. They are idealistic, brilliant, vocal, and alive. They are willing to say, "The Emperor wears no clothes." They are generous, compassionate, and moral. They take America's promises seriously. They are, in short, our conscience.

Style. This is a highly personal film. It is intimate. It is emotional. Its style is human revelation rather than reportage. It is told subjectively rather than objectively. It is more a diary than an essay, more an autobiography than a report, more a drama than journalism. Its goal is to enter the world of these kids rather than observe and report on it.

Narration. The rule here is to use as little as possible. Ideally, the story will be told completely in the words and voices of our kids. First person all the way. We intend to use a CBS reporter merely to set the scene, to indicate that (distorted or not) this is the way these kids see the world, and to conclude.

Format. The film is in three acts. Each act corresponds to an underlying cause of agitation and disaffection among the students. Act 1 follows Kate Coleman, a senior who will graduate in June. On a personal level it is the story of her satisfactions and dissatisfaction with California. On a broader level it is the story of the achievement and failure of mass education. Act 2 follows Ron and Sally, two un-married students who live together. In this act we reveal these kids' attitude to authority, responsibility, their parents, the older generation, and individual morality. The message of this act is this: our kids feel the adult world is corrupt and morally bankrupt; they believe they must decide what is *moral* for themselves. Act 3 is "Mike and the New Politics." Mike is a grad student who teaches math. As we follow him we gain insight into the political mood and stance of his generation. Mike's politics are different in important ways from my generation which preceded him. We show how and why this is so, and we reveal what it means to youth today and in America.

The notes conclude with a description of the film techniques that Barron intends to use. They include actual scenes, fantasy scenes to reveal "inner states in an unusually imaginative and dramatic way," and staged scenes in which the students are directed and told to do something.

George Stoney is another excellent filmmaker, noted for such films as *How the Myth Was Made,* about Flaherty's work on *Man of Aran,* and *All My Babies.* Stoney is also well known as one of the produc-ers of the highly acclaimed *Wasn't That a Time,* about the musical group the Weavers. One of the most interesting of Stoney's films is the dramatic documentary *A Cry for Help,* made to assist police forces in coping with the problem of suicide. The following extract from Stoney's proposal illustrates his technique:

> What is the average policeman's attitude towards suicide? We have made some efforts to discover this. Fifteen police departments held roundtable discussions on the matter following a set of questions designed by Dr. Rowland. We have personally interviewed police-men in ten other departments. Our inquiries have gone far enough to suggest that attitudes on suicide in the abstract vary quite widely

among policemen as among laymen generally being affected by such fundamental things as family background, religion, education, etc. However, the average policeman's attitude towards the individuals involved in such incidents has been made startlingly clear.

In tape after tape one hears them talk about "sympathy bidders." In interview after interview they have made no effort to conceal their hilarity and disgust in telling us about the "repeaters" or the "nuts who call up."

Happily, we have found a good many policemen who have a great deal more understanding than this. Much of the material contained in the script has been developed with their help. However, it is to the average policeman that our film is directed.

What is our aim? The primary goal of the film is to save lives by emphasizing the importance of suicide threats and attempts.

While the film will be prepared primarily as a training film for the police, it should have instructional value for clergymen, social service workers, physicians, and in fact the public in general.

Emphasis should be on specific situations and how to handle them, but these should be generalized as far as possible and emphasis should be on attitudes.

The film should enhance the learning of the police officer so that he will handle suicide situations better. This can be done without making him a psychiatrist. Yet it is necessary that the policeman be a student of human nature. In fact, he gets very good at understanding people. With such qualifications, and with some training, he can be a very helpful person.

Structure sketch. Although the attached treatment will result in a film which we hope will be a single dramatic unit, it can be divided for purposes of subject matter analysis into four sections:

1. Ways of preventing suicide and suicide attempts in jail.
2. Emergency rescue procedures outside jails.
3. The role of the police in prevention.
4. The policeman's personal attitude towards people who attempt suicide; how this can hurt or help him in dealing with them.
5. Understanding "the cry for help."

The film's first section deals with suicides and suicide attempts made by people who are in police custody. This is a problem almost every policeman will accept as part of his responsibility, and here we can give him some fairly simple instructions.

The film's second section tackles a more difficult problem: suicides and suicide attempts made by people not in custody. The second section of the film undertakes these things:

1. To present suicide as a statistically important problem in the overall well-being of the community.
2. To stress the importance of responding to these cries for help as literally matters of life and death.

In part 3 the film begins to deal more directly with the policeman's role in preventing suicide. To help develop in our viewers an understanding of people who attempt suicide we sketch four case histories, moving from one to another as our analysis demands.

Just before starting on the revision of this book, a friend of mine, John, asked me to write a short proposal for a film about Joseph of Arimathea. The film was meant to be the third in a series tentatively called *Journeys of Faith*. John stressed that the proposal had to be short and dynamic. This was the result.

Joseph of Arimathea: The Life and Legend

> And did those feet in ancient times walk upon England's mountains green . . .—William Blake, *Jerusalem*

> Of course Jesus lived in England. And who brought him? Joseph of Arimathea, of course.—Cornish popular legend

We are in the Holy Land, 37 A.D. Jesus of Nazareth is dead, executed, in Jerusalem. His followers have gone underground. Rebellion is in the air. As Roman bands sweep across the land a small group of Christ's followers secretly prepare to flee the country. They gather at the port of Caesarea.

Jesus' mother is there, with Mary Magdalene, Philip, and Lazarus. But it is the leader who stands out . . . Joseph of Arimathea, the man who took Jesus' body and laid it in the tomb. He takes few belongings but cradles a precious cup to his body. Only he knows it contains the blood of Christ, and history will call the goblet and its contents the Holy Grail.

So begins the strange voyage of Saint Joseph of Arimathea, a trip that takes him and the Grail to the west of Britain, to the founding of Christianity in England, and to the birth of stories that will link Joseph to King Arthur and his knights, and even to the voyage of the Mayflower to America.

But how many of the escapees know other Joseph's secret . . . that he has already been to Britain with Jesus in the savior's boyhood.

Shot in Israel, Europe, and the West of England, this one-hour documentary takes us from the turbulent first century to a pulsating, still-mystic modern Britain. Starting in a period of Roman repression and pursuit, the film transports us through a savage Europe to a Britain of pagan sacrifice and druids and to a time of sweeping religious changes.

While expert historians examine the truth behind the legend that Jesus once lived in Cornwall, vivid reenactments and location shooting illustrate the amazing life and travels of Joseph of Arimathea . . . the man behind the myth, and show how his shadow still touches England today.

According to eastern sources Joseph was a rich tin merchant, the uncle of Jesus and took the young Christ with him on a trading expedition to the tin mines of Cornwall. In the Bible he is portrayed as a secret disciple of Jesus, the man who took down Christ's body from the cross and laid it in his private tomb. Other stories also declare that he collected the blood of Jesus in two silver vessels . . . the Holy Grail.

Following King Herod's persecution of Christ's followers Joseph, the two Marys and other friends flee to Europe to spread the gospel. They follow the route, well known to Joseph, of the Hebrew Phoenician tin traders . . . Cyprus, Crete, Marseilles, central France, and Cornwall.

The story seems wild, but legends abound, recounted by Gregory of Tours and others of the Virgin Mary's arrival in Marseilles, and of Joseph's visit to Limoges.

Invited by a Druid priest to the west of England, Joseph sets out by boat with twelve followers for Cornwall . . . a propitious choice. He knows the area well from his previous visits, and Cornwall and Somerset are outside the territories occupied by Caesar's Roman legions.

From the local ruler Arviragus, Joseph receives the isle of Avalon as a gift. Here he plants a staff grown from Christ's crown of thorns, builds a small mud and wattle church, and starts propagating the message of Christ. It is a dangerous life among hostile pagans with the Romans never far away . . . but gradually England's first church takes root and prospers. In 79 A.D. Joseph dies and is buried in Avalon, with the Holy Grail. Later Avalon will be called Glastonbury.

So go the legends that expand with time. The Grail is supposedly buried in a well near the church. The descendants of Joseph and his followers become the forebears of King Arthur and his Knights. Avalon (Glastonbury) now becomes the resting place of Arthur. The Holy Grail disappears to Wales or elsewhere. The Pilgrim fathers setting out from Lincolnshire make a sudden stop at Plymouth. Do they take the Holy Grail with them to America?

Joseph of Arimathea is a classic history mystery with local myth and folklore supporting the strangest of stories. Jews exiled by the Romans are supposed to have worked the Cornish tin mines. Jesus is said not only to have visited England but to have spent the missing years of his youth in Cornwall, preaching and building a small church. Ancient stones are exhibited with the Christ and Joseph story shown in pictogram. In Cornwall's mining area "Tunic Crosses" are shown with a cross on one side and the image of a young man on the other. And for some Avalon is no dream but is situated on the hill outside Glastonbury.

Today Glastonbury is a modern town of some 10,000 inhabitants. In winter it is quiet, but in summer it sports a rock festival, folk gatherings, and Morris dancers. While hundreds of visitors crowd into the cathedral trying to figure out its connection to Joseph and King Arthur, dozens of others celebrate memories of old Druidic rights in the surrounding woods.

The film, set largely in and around modern picturesque Glastonbury, sets out to examine and unravel the truth behind the legends. Who was the real Joseph of Arimathea? A gospel writer's fantasy or a man of flesh and blood? Did he really bring Jesus to England? Was he a simple merchant or a Christian visionary with a mission? And in spite of skepticism was he really the bearer of the Holy Grail? In the end the viewers will be left to decide on the true nature of this cult figure and all the enigmas surrounding his life.

Some years ago I worked with a wonderful filmmaker, John Fox. John was always shooting one film, writing a second, and planning a third. Projects came and went. But his central dream was a two-part series about Death Valley for presentation by KCET, California. The project was very expensive, so for funds John went to many of the major U.S. national funders and foundations as well as private corporations. Because of the complexity and scope of the project and the multitude of questions expected from the funders, the proposal had to go into tremendous depth and detail. Below I have set out (in abbreviated form) the parts of his proposal dealing with story, appeal, rationale, and approach.

Death Valley: An American Mirage
Why This Series
Death Valley occupies a unique place in American culture. Its name, familiar to every American, brings to mind images of barren deserts, 20 mule teams, of torturous heat, and of circling vultures. It has been portrayed in feature films and was the subject of long running series on both radio and television from the 1930s to the 1970s. Yet for all that, the real story of this valley remains almost entirely unknown.

There is no place in the world like it. Located on the border between California and Nevada, it is a spectacular wasteland of rippling sand dunes, rugged canyons, and landscapes hewn from primeval rocks . . .

For hundreds of years Death Valley was home to Shoshone Indians who extracted a living from its forbidding terrain. The rhythms of their life were disrupted, however, in 1849. In that year the valley was "discovered" by pioneers on their way to the California gold fields. The forces that transformed the continent were brought to bear on this one valley with such extraordinary results that by the beginning of the 20th century the valley had obtained something of a mystic stature for most Americans . . .

The valley became famous, however, less because of what it was than because of what Americans could dream it to be. Stories about Death Valley, true ones and untrue ones alike, struck a chord deep in the American psyche and continued to fascinate the public well into the second half of the 20th century. For most Americans Death Valley became a place more of myth than reality.

To understand why Death Valley rose to such prominence in popular culture and became wrapped in such a theatrical aura, the programs will explore both the history of the valley and the shifting dreams of America. In the interplay between the real and the imagined lies a story of the developing character of the nation. For most Americans, Death Valley was a desert illusion, a mirage that first arose in the days of the Gold Rush and grew until it enthralled the entire country. We will present the story of those Americans whose lives helped shape, and were shaped by, that mirage. Their ambitions and their struggles, and their successes and their failures are at the heart of this unique case study of American life.

Filmic Approach
Though they have never before been assembled into a single comprehensive body of work resource materials about Death Valley abound, documenting the colorful personalities and dramatic events of the

valley's 150 year history. Lyrical in story-line, with a wealth of original and archival imagery, and a humanistic perspective, these programs will tell the history of Death Valley through the actual and dramatized words of many of those people who were an essential part of the story.

One constant theme and "voice" for the valley will be the Shoshone Indians. While pioneers and others invaded the valley, beginning in 1849, the Shoshone remained a constant and stable presence. They never knew their home as a "valley of death" and their view of this wilderness will provide a foil for the wild tales, outlandish schemes and assaults on the valley made by outsiders . . .

The series will take full advantage of published accounts, and will draw from many published collections of photographs, illustrations and documents. It will also use personal letters, diaries and artefacts from family and private collections. Archival film footage audio recordings, and early motion pictures will also help bring the past to life.

A celebrity narrator/host will provide the voice-over spine of the story, and a star cast of actors will provide voice-over readings. Interviews with historians will be interwoven with the narrative to provide to provide an interpretive context.

Film crews will photograph original historic locations, many of which look today almost as they did fifty, or a hundred or a hundred and fifty years ago. The views of Death Valley are stunning, snow capped mountains, rock strewn gorges . . . and aerial photography will emphasize these breathtaking expanses . . .

Scale models of such ephemeral towns as Rhyolite and Skidoo will be built, carefully lit and shot with snorkel lenses to take the viewers through the living streets of what are now ghost towns. The Santa Fe railroad has offered the producers use of their working steam engines to illustrate the famous train race of Death Valley Scotty.

In writing his filmic approach, John also added a note on cameras, film, editing formats, and how he saw the film fitting into high-definition television (HDTV) broadcasts. He also dealt briefly with the use of sound through popular music—ragtime, jazz, big band—in the series. Finally, in a separate section, John provided a very detailed and compelling description of the narrative line and fascinating stories that provided the backbone of the films. It was clear that the proposal had taken tremendous time and effort to put together, but in the end it provided a wonderful platform for the idea and worked as a superb sales pitch.

For years I have been following the work of a good friend of mine, Jan Krawitz, and have always admired the professionalism of her proposals and the craft and artistry of the subsequent films. What follows is a very abbreviated proposal for her latest and very moving film *Big Enough*.

16mm color film, 53 minutes

Background

In 1981, I co-directed *Little People*, an Emmy Award–nominated documentary that aired nationally on PBS and the Discovery Channel. In the film, dwarfs of varying ages and professional backgrounds reflected on their struggle toward self-esteem and equal opportunity in a world that persisted in seeing them through the lens of stereotypes—circus clowns and sideshow attractions—from an earlier age. More than a dozen dwarfs, self-described in the film as "little people," shared a part of their daily lives through interviews and observational scenes, juxtaposed with activities filmed at the annual convention of Little People of America, attended by 600 dwarfs. Their candid insights offered an unusual and sometimes disturbing perspective on the average-sized world.

In the two decades since *Little People* was released, there has been a sea change in society's understanding of disability rights and our acceptance of diversity. In 1994, the gene for the most common types of dwarfism was identified, thereby introducing the prospect of the eradication of the dwarf condition. The discovery of these genes thrusts dwarfs into the middle of the medical, social and ethical debates surrounding the brave new world of genetic technology. Because dwarfism has historically been viewed through the medical model of disability, dwarfs today are concerned about health policies that identify their condition as a birth defect. They fear the possible emergence of "eugenic" public health policies whereby widespread prenatal testing could result in pregnancy termination by women who learn they are carrying a dwarf baby. Dwarf activists argue that short-statured people contribute to the complexity of a heterogeneous culture. Dwarfs embody America's ambivalence about what it means to be different.

Big Enough takes an ethically complex question and situates it in a concrete human story. The film revisits some of the original "characters" from *Little People* twenty years later and poses an unasked question: What would our culture lose if the condition of dwarfism was eliminated and we faced a future in which there were no dwarfs.

The lingering paradox is this: as society becomes more acceptable of diversity and disability, scientific research has introduced the prospect of eradication of the dwarf condition.

The film is multi-layered—its complexity created by the interweaving of contemporary stories and "back stories" of the five main characters. Their experiences will be linked by the themes of acceptance vs. ostracism, aspirations vs. unfulfilled dreams, the desire for family—concerns that are common to many people, regardless of stature. The dwarfs who appear in the original film have their current stories amplified and sometimes contradicted by footage shot twenty years ago. I draw on both "outtakes" and footage from the original *Little People* to represent the past. Looking at their lives through the prism of "then and now," *Big Enough* includes new "characters" who are connected to the original "little people" through marriage or birth.

The issues are topical, the voices passionate, the temporal challenges unique, and the range of material eclectic.

Characters

MARK TROMBINO was a spunky 11-year old boy in 1981. At 31, Mark is still three feet three inches tall, but his features have matured. The voice of the boy he once was—matter-of-fact, a bit lonely but confident of his ability to find his way in the world—is still discernible as we see him with his wife, ANU SINGH, an Indian dwarf he met at a Little People of America convention.

KARLA EASTBURG, at 16, had plotted out her future. She planned to marry a little person and have a career in medical technology. At 36, after years of failure in jobs and frustrated by the physical limitations imposed by multiple surgeries, she has been defeated by life. But she finds support in her relationship with JOHN LIZZO, an average-sized man with whom she has been involved for the past ten years. John is five feet ten, and Karla is three feet three inches.

LEN SAWISCH was a 30-year-old dwarf activist whose acerbic wit in *Little People* provided insight into the dwarf experience. Today, Len lives with his average-sized son BRANDON, 22. At five feet eleven inches, Brandon is the "other" in their household which includes Len's short-statured wife, LENETTE, and daughter, JOELLE. In recent years, Len has put his dwarf activism behind him. In his words, he "retired" from being a dwarf several years ago although he continues to share strong opinions about the issues confronting his community.

RON AND SHARON ROSKAMP were newlyweds in *Little People*. They now have two teen-aged children, ALISHA, 12, and ANDREW, 17. Both of their children are short-statured and have the unique perspective of "second-generation" dwarfs raised by dwarf parents. Both Ron and Sharon were born into average-sized families. The positive sense of self-worth experienced by Andrew and Alisha contrasts sharply with the ongoing battles that Ron and Sharon have waged as they attempt to find their places in an average-sized world.

Treatment Sample
[The following has been shortened by me because of pressures of space. —A. R.]

PROLOGUE
It is early morning and the sky is overcast. A pick-up truck, hauling a small fishing boat, backs up to a boat ramp on a quiet river. Two men—one white, one black, both of them dwarfs—climb out of the truck. Cut to 1981, with Len Sawisch, a 30-year old psychologist and activist, leading a consciousness-raising seminar. The audience laughs as Len delivers his talk about dwarf cultural heritage with the timing of a stand-up comedian:

> *I enjoy my interactions with other minorities, especially Blacks. They say, "For 200 years, my people were sold as slaves." Shit, for thousands of years, my people were given away as gifts!*

Back at the boat ramp, Len, now 50, and his friend Butch, laugh affably as they use a specially adapted winch to lower the boat into the river. In voiceover, Len says:

> *I retired from being a dwarf seven years ago. I gave a better part of my life to the movement and it was a great ride. I enjoyed it tremendously. But now it's time to go fishing.*

A GENERATION LATER
In 1981, Mark Trombino was a plucky 11-year-old on the cusp of a difficult adolescence. The diminutive boy sits at the edge of a wading pool, dangling his feet in the water, and muses:

> *There are some advantages to being little, but not too many [pause]. When you play hide and seek, it's a lot easier to hide.*

At 31, just over three feet tall, Mark is now a man who came of age as dwarfs joined a larger social movement that celebrated diversity and pressed for tolerance and civil rights. He has not grown much larger in 20 years but his features have matured. The voice of the boy he once was—matter-of-fact, a bit lonely, but confident of his ability to find his way in the world—is still discernible as the man speaks:

> *I think I'm a pretty normal guy. I'm 3-foot-3-and I wouldn't want to change the way I am. I think I have an advantage in job interviews because people remember me.*

Recently married, Mark is doing laundry this morning with his wife Anu Singh, an Indian dwarf he met at a Little People of America convention. Two inches shorter than Mark, Anu stands on a step-stool, clutching a long-handled "grabber" with which she raises a wet sweatshirt out of the washing machine. She swings the sweatshirt over to Mark who releases it and tosses it into the dryer. Now seated side-by-side in the living room, Anu and Mark talk about their plans to start a family. Mark says that if they become pregnant, their wish would be to have a dwarf baby like themselves.

[The sections following the above have been deleted because of space, for which I apologize to Jan. I have resumed the treatment where Krawitz describes how she sees the practical progress of the film. —A. R.]

EPILOGUE

Back at the river, Len—who retired from being a dwarf seven years ago—starts the motor. He and Butch head across the river as a light rain begins to fall. In voiceover, Len says:

> *When I think back on the first documentary, it represented a real closure point because it took all of my concerns and put it in a neat package. When you can get a handle on the dwarf experience, you can set it down and move on to other things.*

Project Status and Completion Timeline
Pre-Production: Spring 2000
Production (New Jersey, Virginia, Michigan): Summer–Fall 2000
Syncing/Edge-Coding: Winter 2001–Spring 2001
Interview Transcription/Outtakes Cataloging: Summer–Fall 2001
Editing, Music, Sound Mix: Winter 2002–Fall 2002
Estimated Release: Fall 2002–Winter 2003

Key Personnel
Jan Krawitz (producer/director/writer/editor) was producer/direc-tor/editor of *In Harm's Way* (1996), *Mirror Mirror* (1990), and *Drive-In Blues* (1986), and co-director and co-editor of the Emmy-nominated

Little People (1982), all of which were broadcast on national PBS. She is Director of the Graduate Program in Documentary Film and Video at Stanford University where she has taught since 1988, and she taught film production for eight years at the University of Texas at Austin. Krawitz holds a B.A. in Film/Photography from Cornell University and a Master of Fine Arts from Temple University.

Ferne Pearlstein (cinematographer) is a documentary filmmaker and cinematographer based in New York City. Pearlstein has been cinematographer on more than twenty documentary films. Her works include *Raising Nicholas* (Sundance), *Secret People* (about a leprosarium in Louisiana, nationally broadcast on PBS), and *Imelda*, an ITVS-funded documentary about Imelda Marcos.

5

RESEARCH

The proposal that was based on your preliminary research has been accepted. You have talked it through with the television commissioning editor. You clearly know what the film is about and what it is meant to do. You have thought about audience. The contract has been signed and you have gotten the go-ahead. The next stage is researching the subject *in depth*. As a researcher, you need to combine the penetrating brazenness of the good journalist with the painstaking attention to detail of the Ph.D. candidate. You must be observer, analyst, student, and note taker. Over a period that can be as short as a few days or as long as a few months, you must become an expert on the subject of the film, a subject you may never even have known existed a few weeks before—not easy, but always fascinating.

The one thing that dictates your research is your working hypothesis. You've already stated that your film is a look at the 82nd Airborne Division in the days immediately before and after the Gulf War, or about blacks in the military in World War II. Again you may have stated that your film is an inquiry into California mental hospitals, the early life of Michael Jackson, or that it deals with British screenwriters and actors in Hollywood. These brief statements of your subject should be your guide. And within the limits of your subject, you are going to try to turn up everything that looks dramatic, compelling, or interesting.

This may seem a trifle obvious, but focusing your mind on your central film question helps you eliminate an enormous amount of junk material and saves you immense time. It saves you from doing research that intrigues you at the time, but ultimately contributes little to the film. Research can be broken down into four sections: (1) print research, (2) photograph and archival research, (3) interviews, and (4) on-the-spot involvement with the subject on location. In practice, you are likely to be involved in all four forms of research at the same time.

PRINTED MATERIAL

Within the limits of time, budget, sanity, and common sense, you should try to read as much as possible about the subject. Your aim is simple: within a very short time, you want to become, if not an expert in the field, at least a person with a superior knowledge of the subject. Print research can involve scanning databases, checking bibliographies and print sources, and reading books, papers, magazines, trade journals, articles, diaries, letters, and even congressional records and transcriptions of court trials. If material is highly technical, complex, or filled with jargon, you should get somebody to help you understand it. Obviously, if you don't understand the material, you won't be able to say anything sensible about it in the film.

Of course there are problems all along the way. You will often read much too deeply, making it difficult to isolate the valuable or relevant material. You will get sidetracked by irrelevant but fascinating stories. After a while, however, you will learn to scan and distinguish the important facts from the obscuring details. Another problem is that much of the material may be out of date or presented from a biased or self-serving point of view. Take care to check the date of the material and the credentials and background of the writer. When I suspect that the material comes from a highly interested and partisan source, particularly in films of a political or controversial nature, I try to check the biases of the informant as well. I also double-check statistics, remembering that old adage, "There are lies, more lies, and statistics."

There is one point that I think is terrible important, especially in investigatory films, and that is to go back to the original sources for your information. Do not be content with second- or thirdhand reports. If you are doing a film on World War I, don't just read a few history books. Instead, start digging out government documents, wills, diaries, and contemporary newspaper accounts. If you are doing film on government policy, you should start digging into official records, state papers, memoranda, and the like. This is not easy, but it is necessary.

Since its inception, the Web has also proved itself a fantastic tool in research. For myself, I don't use it for basic research, but I find it very useful for turning up potted biographies, for example, or for tracing obscure documents and detail that would have been hard to find or taken hours to trace elsewhere. Thus, when I did a film on Hitler's Germany I needed to find out details about the ranks of the SS, and how they matched U.S. Army rankings. I also needed to see the exact organization of the RHSA, Hitler's security forces. Using the Web, I found the information in seconds.

PHOTOGRAPHS AND STOCK FOOTAGE

Your sources for photographs and stock footage are fairly obvious. Depending on the film, your sources may be government archives (such as the British Imperial War Museum, the German Bundesarchives, or the National Archives), local and press archives such as Sherman Grinberg, film archives such as Pathe, or television archives such as the CIIS archive in New York and ITN in London. You may be searching through local libraries, private collections, family albums, and attics, or looking at old videos shot by the industry you are investigating. Bear in mind that you are looking at the old films and photographs both as sources of information and as possible visuals in the film. If your objective is the latter, then you should inquire fairly early about permission to use the materials. But more on that subject later.

Once you have a general source for your material, it is not always easy to locate what you want. Old archives are often arranged haphazardly and, though you know there is gold around, it may be difficult to find, but the computer revolution has helped. Most archives list their collections by film title, by subject, and occasionally by filmmaker. If the film archive is good, a film's title card (under the old card index system) should list the subjects of the principal scenes; for example, "Hitler reviewing his guards in Nuremberg. Peasants in costume. Hitler's hotel at night. Torchlight parade."

Obviously, the better the archives are indexed, the easier it is to find material. Until recently, hunting through archives was an abominably difficult job. Today, with computer indexing, conditions have vastly improved. The trick is to feed into the computer the right names, subject, and place. Thus, if I were looking for footage on World War II conferences, I might feed in *Yalta, Roosevelt, Churchill*, and *Stalin* to make sure I got material in which all three politicians appeared.

For a wide subject, such as Kissinger's Vietnam participation, the computer, although keyed to search only for *Kissinger* and *Vietnam*, will spew out dozens of entries. The same goes for *George W. Bush* and *football*.

Even in the computer age there are problems. Films can often be indexed improperly when the archivist fails to recognize the importance of certain materials. Thus, the material you want may exist, but it may not be indexed. For example you may be looking for war criminal X in German archives first indexed in 1947. But if Captain X only came into prominence in investigations in 1960, he may appear on much of the stock footage but be unidentified in the files.

In short, archive research often depends as much on intuition, on asking and probing, as it does on hunting through the files.

I've mentioned the importance of the Web in print research, and the same goes for photos and archival footage. First, most good archives have copies of their photos available on the Web. This means you can sit at home and do a first survey by downloading pictures from the archive. The second point to note is the growth of specialist archives, which have their lists and occasionally viewing clips available over the Web.

INTERVIEWS

Your objective in research interviews is to talk to as many participants and experts in the field as possible. Again, as in print research, you have to make some shrewd guesses. Because time is limited, you try to assess which people are the best—the most important for you, the most knowledgeable, the most open—and you allocate your time accordingly. You are looking for people seriously involved in the subject, but who are they? They can range from technical experts and authorities to the ordinary people who have undergone the experience documented in the film. For example, if you want to look behind the scene at the Greek Olympics, you might find yourself talking to security men, suppliers, members of the Olympic committee, first-aid workers, and builders. Your perspective and the breadth of your subject will dictate to whom you talk, and your questions will obviously range from the general to the specific, depending on the topic.

When I meet potential witnesses or informants, I like to outline the project to them in general terms, but I rarely go into too many details. I want to intrigue them into helping me, and I try to tell them honestly why obtaining their cooperation and making the film is important. This introductory meeting serves both to obtain information from them and to audition them for a possible appearance.

Generally I try to do this face-to-face, rather than through a researcher, so that the personal bonds are established early on. In many cases, however, this is impossible, and you will have to rely on your researcher. I avoid two things in these meetings. First, I take everything down by hand rather than use a tape recorder. I know many people rely on tape recorders, but I find they add a very subtle barrier, at least in first meetings. Second, I make no promises about filming a particular person or a particular scene.

Approached correctly and sympathetically, most people will be willing to talk to you about your research. Occasionally, however, you will run into difficulties if the subject is personally painful or controversial. Do you then go ahead or do you back off? Everyone has to sort out that dilemma out personally. Several years ago, I interviewed Sue McConnachy, one of the principal researchers for the television series *The World at War*. She experienced some difficulties in talking to Germans for the film because she was investigating not just memory and experiences but also possible participation in war crimes and atrocities. Her comments were very interesting:

> Initially it was quite difficult to get people to open up. However, once the Germans agreed to see you and talk it was all much fresher than the English people's reminiscences because it hadn't been told before. They'd never been asked or questioned about the war by the younger generation. There was a feeling that whereas it was acceptable for dad in England to talk to the kids about when he was in Africa, India, or wherever, it wasn't acceptable in Germany.
>
> The problem was getting to the shadow figures and the possible criminals. This was often done through a series of contacts. One was in the position of being given confidential information which one was not supposed to broadcast or pass on. You were only allowed to go and see these people on the understanding that you gave nothing away.

Now once you'd got into a position of trust, once you'd got on to the circuit, you were handed on from one to the next. And it was almost an impossible situation as a researcher (and as a human being) because I was dealing with people who, in the period of their lives that we were talking about, had not operated with the same code of behavior, morals, whatever you call it, that I by nature and upbringing operate on. (Alan Rosenthal, *The Documentary Conscience* [Berkeley: University of California Press, 1980])

About the time I met McConnachy, I also spoke to Peter Watkins about the making of his famous antinuclear-war film *The War Game*. Among other things, the film discusses civil defence procedures in England and the psychological aftereffects of the dropping of a nuclear bomb on a civilian population. Watkins commented:

The more films I do, the more I research. It's a growing pattern. I tend to put more and more emphasis on the solid basis of research. With *The War Game* I had to do a great deal of original research because nobody had collated all the information into an easily accessible form. . . . There is an extreme dearth of literature about the third world war. What literature there is is stacked up on the shelves of the American Institute for Strategic Studies and is never read by the public. So it was an extremely esoteric subject for a filmmaker to delve into and quite hard to find basic facts.

As far as research went and talking to people, you have to differentiate between people in general and government bodies. The experts, professors and so on, were extremely cooperative and very interested. A few were a little skeptical of an amateur blundering into their domain but they freely supplied what little information they had. The government bodies were different. In general they said no. (Alan Rosenthal, *The New Documentary in Action* [Berkeley: University of California Press, 1971])

The Home Office, responsible for internal affairs and security in England, refused to help Watkins in the making of the film. In fact, it not only refused information but also withdrew all official help and tried to hinder the research by preventing the Fire Service and the police from giving Watkins details of their plans in the event of a nuclear holocaust. He noted that "the only group that helped me voluntarily at that time was the Fire Service, which appeared to me to be the only group in England that had a realistic approach to the effects of a nuclear attack. They were the only (semi-official) group willing to talk to me. And they did it unofficially. Officially there was a complete clamp-down."

Reliance on only a few interviewees for anything controversial has its dangers. In those cases, it is best to interview, or try to interview, a broad range of people so that you can contrast opinions and estimate how much of what you are being told is biased or partisan. Obviously, you have to rely on common sense. You are not aiming for balance, but you are aiming for the truth, and it could be that the extreme, one-sided view just happens to be the truth. During interviews you will ask both easy and awkward questions. Naturally, your technique will differ from subject to subject; sometimes you may have to play the probing investigator, but more often you will ask commonsense questions that any interested person would bring up.

In a technical film you may want to accumulate facts, find out about problems, systems of work, difficulties, successes, side effects, and results. In a human or portrait film you will probably want to find out about human experiences, memories, change, thoughts, and the consequences that certain actions have wrought on people's lives, and so on. Often the interviewing will be difficult or painful as you touch on emotions and sensitivities. You are not just collecting facts about a subject but trying to gain a perspective that goes beyond the facts. An adjunct to this is that you always have to keep in mind whether you want the emphasis to fall on facts or on emotions, because each may pull you in a different way.

It is also important to be open to stories and to think about how they can be used. Remember that the stories you have may be more powerful than any facts you dig up. Let us assume you are doing a film about refugees from Hurricane Katrina. You could say, after your research, that thirty thousand people were evacuated and four thousand homes destroyed. But it is better if you can also use personal anecdotes: "I was at home. The wind smashed everything. First the upstairs roof collapsed, then the wall. Finally the wind lifted my bed and threw it, with me in it, into the garden."

As usual, a warning: there is a tremendous difference between interviewing someone about the current scene and the past. In both cases you have to be aware of bias, but in talking about the past you also have to be aware of the pitfalls of memory and romanticism. Sometimes, of course, the events of the past are etched more strongly on the mind than are the events of yesterday. But not always. Whether driven by love or hate or age or even romanticized recreations, as in the recent Leni Riefenstahl film biography *The Wonderful, Horrible*

Life of Leni Riefenstahl, the memory can be a strange, distorting mirror. So beware.

LOCATION RESEARCH

Finally, you should experience the subject in situ, on location. You go to see the factory at work, spend two weeks getting the feel of the university, take the plane trip, ride with the police in their patrol cars, watch the daily life in a small Vermont village, accompany the theater director to rehearsal, and watch the new tourists stream through Saigon. All the time you are trying to soak up the subject and get as close to it as possible.

Research is vital to most good films, and yet it is a difficult subject psychologically. This is because you know that only a fraction of the material you are accumulating will ever be used in the final film. As a colleague of mine, Jim Beveridge, once put it: "Research is like an iceberg. Seven-eighths of it is below the surface and can't be seen."

Research is also a tantalizing mistress because she is constantly showing you new possibilities and new direction for your film. You think *you* are the boss, and research the obedient donkey you ride on, but before you know it she's kicked up her heels, resisted the reins, and taken you to a totally undreamed of destination. Two years before writing this book, I did a film on Adolf Eichmann, a Nazi war criminal and high SS officer. The film was to be a view of his life based on the diaries Eichmann wrote in jail in 1962. But while researching, I found to my astonishment he had written a secret and contradictory set of memoirs in 1957. So it was oops, halt, and rethink the whole basic premise of the film.

DEFINING LIMITS

People often go astray in failing to define suitable limits to their films. If your goal is clear, then you should be all right, but you may have problems if you approach a very broad topic—drugs, juvenile delinquency, international terrorism—with no guidelines. What do you do when the subject is seemingly limitless? You have to do some preliminary research and then make some quick choices. Using your common sense, you select boundaries, and within those boundaries, you then select three or four promising areas for further research and development. The boundaries do not have to be arbitrary. You will be guided by what you yourself are interested in, by current public interests, and, as always, by what is feasible and practical. Thus, you don't decide simply to do a film on drugs; you decide to do it on drugs and the young, or drugs and their sources in the Far East, or drugs and big business. Once your subject's scope has been limited, you can go ahead.

The trouble is that even with the most rational head in the world, you sometimes try to do too much in one film. In the end, your ambition may let you down, whereas a more modest film would have worked well. This happened to me on a film I did about automobile accidents. It was clear that the subject involved three diverse elements: people, including drivers, pedestrians, and accident victims; vehicles; and roads and road engineering. I could have concentrated on any one of those topics, but I decided to look into all three. I saw all the films, read all the books, talked to experts, and wrote to dozens of people around the world. And all the time new topics of interest kept opening up. I found out about a correction course for dangerous drivers. I was told about a society for bereaved families. I obtained photographs showing cars of the future. A psychologist told me of hypnotic experiments on aggressive personalities.

I accumulated a mass of fascinating materials, yet the film came out a mess. My cardinal mistake, which was obvious in hindsight, was trying to cover the three topics of driver, vehicle, and roads instead of limiting myself to just one. The research had been great fun, but I didn't know when to leave well enough alone; as a result, I seriously weakened the film.

POSTRESEARCH

After you've done most of your legwork, give yourself a breather. Let the materials drift around your mind a bit without any conscious sifting on your part. This helps clear away the debris and allows you to see what is really important. What often happens is that the research reveals alternative paths and strategies for you. New and unsuspected material has come up. New characters have emerged and it is very possible your original thesis has to be requestioned, as in the case of my Eichmann film. In short, this is a good time for a total reexamination. Before, you merely suspected what the film could be about. Now you know, and can, if necessary, refocus your central questions and inquiry before you plunge into the film itself.

6

SHAPING THE FILM

Note: In the scripted film shape and form are mostly determined before shooting. In cinema verité films, in very many cases, the shape is determined after filming. This chapter mainly concerns the problems of the scripted film, while the approach to cinema verité is discussed at length in chapter 18.

After the research, you still have to answer a few questions before tackling the draft script. Your main concern is how to shape the film into a logical and emotional whole that has tremendous appeal for your audience. Here you are concerned with four topics: approach, style, form, and structure. The topics often overlap, and it is sometimes difficult to separate them. Form runs into structure, and can you really distinguish approach from style? Because of this overlap, the topics may be covered in any order, but I find it easiest to think about them in the order given here.

APPROACH

When all the mist has cleared away, there are usually two main choices for the overall approach: the essay or the narrative. My feelings in this matter are simple. An essay is fine, but it is hard to maintain viewer interest in such a piece if it exceeds thirty minutes. You can talk generally and interestingly about Arab or Iraqi nationalism for half an hour, but if you want an hour-long film you should be doing the story of bin Laden or Saddam Hussein. I also believe people really enjoy a story, especially one that has drama, conflict, strong characters, reversals, life threats, and so on. Here, I follow the old belief that truth is stranger and more interesting than fiction, and that part of the documentarian's function is to tell those fantastic real-life stories.

My first tendency, therefore, in thinking about a film is to see whether a good narrative approach is possible. Obviously, some of the best films combine both approaches, with a good story illustrating an abstract, intellectual idea. Mike Rubbo's film *Daisy*, mentioned earlier, is an amusing essay on the history of plastic surgery and its practice today. The essay, however, backs up the personal story of Daisy and her hopes and fears as she faces major plastic surgery. Another great film that combines both approaches is Dennis O'Rourke's film *Land Mines—A Love Story*, which tells the personal story of an Afghan woman, Habiba, while making a wider comment on the whole use of land mines.

When I have to confront what is obviously a broad essay topic—say, crime in the next ten years—I prefer to look at the general through the particular, finding a few cases that highlight the key problems of the subject. Helen Whitney did just that in her film *Youth Terror*. Although ABC assigned her the broad topic of juvenile delinquency, her film concentrates on the experience of a small group of teenagers in Brooklyn, New York.

Yet there is a dilemma in all this, an unresolved tension between the story film and the investigative essay. Looking at problems through individual stories and attractive characters makes for an entertaining film, but it may do so by sacrificing deeper, more meaningful information. Sometimes you find that you have told a great story, but the film itself has become too narrow, with the major problems only superficially treated. Another difficulty in the case-study film is that viewers may perceive the individual story as typical, whereas a more balanced consideration of the subject might reveal it to be idiosyncratic.

In order to succeed, most films driven by topics, such as terrorism or poverty in America or the use and abuse of vitamins pills, need a *key*, or *handle*, an angle from which to tell the story in the most interesting, riveting, and entertaining fashion. Otherwise the essay tends to fall flat. The key may be a character you have come across in research. It may be the oldest member of a factory now being shut down; it may be one of the soldiers who led an abortive raid; or, to quote a BBC film, it may be three women whose lives are driven by the need to consume vitamin pills.

One example of a key or handle comes from my film *Part of Them Is Me.* The task of the film was to tell how various youth villages in Israel provide homes for immigrant orphans while preparing them for life in a new country. A good subject, but ten films had been made on youth villages in the past five years, so it was difficult to find a new approach. During the research, though, I found that the villages were the participants in a new arts program. Once a month a music teacher came to the villages and taught the children various aspects of music. One day I saw David, the music teacher, at work. He was about thirty-five and very charismatic. When I discovered that David had grown up in one of these villages himself twenty years before, I immediately saw him as the natural key. If we told the film through his eyes, we could cover the history of the villages through his childhood memories and his travels as a teacher.

As a rule, I like to see whether a character will give me a slant on the film. A character can provide warmth, empathy, and identification. Most of us are naturally inquisitive; we like to delve into people's lives, into their ways of thinking and modes of work, their problems and triumphs. Characters can also observe things, do things, have things happen to them. That's why people are the ideal film key. A character may also function as the key in a sponsored or industrial film. Such characters are often fictional, sometimes comic creations who help focus the situation through their problems and inadequacies or through their superhuman capabilities.

Besides being the key or handle to the film, a chosen character, such as Habiba in *Land Mines—A Love Story,* can also give shape to what would otherwise be a formless current-events film. To give another instance, most of Pam Yates's and Tom Siegel's *When the Mountains Tremble*, a film about the civil war in Guatemala, recounts rebel life, village encounters, pursuits, and sudden death. To bind the film together, the directors call on an indigenous Guatemalan woman, Rigoberta Menchú, to tell the story of her family. Rigoberta is filmed in limbo in a studio and appears four or five times throughout the film describing the tragic fortunes of her family. Her vital, recurring presence gives the film its spine.

Another good example in which the focus on one character helps give shape to a rather loose, rambling film is Keva Rosenfeld's *American High.* The film illustrates a year in the life of a fun-loving California high school student body, and everything is covered from the proms and parties to classes in surfing and divorce. Much of it is very funny, but also too familiar to be very exciting. What saves the film, and transforms it into a very interesting piece of work, is the focus on a young Finnish student who is visiting the school for a year. We follow her amazed questioning of American norms and behavior, and they are her frequent comments to the camera that give the film life, sparkle, and a different perspective.

The trouble with this approach is that the use of a commenting character or central star may strike viewers as a gimmick or a cliché. We have seen so many films based on the memories of the old professor or the difficulties of the Vietnam veteran that it is hard not to groan when the film starts. But if the film is well done, we forget about the possible gimmickry and are held by the authenticity of the situation.

If you can find the right key, half your troubles are over. Consider *Wasn't That a Time!*, Jim Brown's film about the Weavers, a folk group extremely popular in the 1950s and early 1960s. Brown could have told the story as a disinterested outside observer, but he chose instead to portray the Weavers through the eyes of Lee Hays, the oldest member of the group. Irascible, irreverent, a man of tremendous charm and humor, Hays was cast as a storyteller, thus transforming a fine film into a superb one.

When the main focus of a film is people, there is usually no difficulty finding a key or handle, but you may run into trouble in films dealing with, say, abstract ideas, architecture, specific historic periods, or geographical locations. The danger is that you may string together a series of film ideas without any imaginative force. Sometimes the sheer power of the material will make the films work; more often than not, however, what we see in the end is a series of facts tacked together in some logical but unexciting order. Unfortunately, there are no simple solutions, no magic formulas. Instead, you have to struggle with each film until you find the key, and then if it is good, it often seems inevitable.

When Meredith Monk was asked to make a commemorative film about Ellis Island (the old entry point for immigrants to the United States), the solution must have seemed simple to the sponsors: give us a historical documentary based on facts, old photographs, and records, and throw in a little bit of recent film. Monk's solution was much more imaginative and far more elegant. She abandoned the records and instead recreated the atmosphere of historic Ellis Island using dance and short vignettes. She framed the film by following a modern tour group as they are shown around Ellis Island; this portion was filmed in color. Into the tour she inserted black-and-white "postcards" that suddenly metamorphose into an animated group of nineteenth-century arrivals, a scene of Greek immigrants dancing, or a filmed sketch (deliberately set up by Monk) of 1920s women painfully learning English while the teacher writes the word *microwave* on the blackboard. Viewers could have been bored by a dry historical record, but they were granted instead a marvelous documentary that vividly captured the spirit of the place. A potential failure was transformed into a success because the filmmaker had bothered to find an original and stimulating road into the film.

Some time ago I was asked to do a film about the area around the Sea of Galilee in northern Israel—an extremely beautiful spot, interesting because of its historic and biblical sites and its contemporary development. The film had vast potential, but I wasn't sure how to bind everything together. Then I remembered that an annual marathon circles the lake. That seemed the obvious key. The marathon would give a certain tension to the film, and as we followed the runners I could dart off into history or whatever I wanted.

An interesting variant on all the above, but still a definite *key*, is when the director becomes an interactive participant in the proceedings. Thus, Michael Rubbo often appears in his own films and, as in *Waiting for Fidel*, you can see him on screen affecting events and guiding them to their destiny. Michael Moore is an even more extreme practitioner of this technique, and *Bowling for Columbine* and *Fahrenheit 9/11* show what can be done with a strong personality and a little bit of chutzpah. But it is not a technique or approach for everyone.

Clearly, finding a key is a lot of work and doesn't come easily. Is the search worth it? Absolutely.

STRUCTURE

The question of structure has been tremendously neglected in discussions of documentary films. Not so with features. Of the latter, William Goldman wrote, "Structure is everything," and book after book on narrative film writing stresses structure, often with an emphasis on the three-act drama. Though documentary filming is very different from feature filming, I believe (as does Goldman), that structure is the key to good filmmaking. One sees too many films that are structureless, that amble along, showing an occasional interesting interview or compelling incident, but with no spine. There may have been an interesting key to the film, but somewhere along the way it was lost.

Just as every good book and play need a structure, so, too, does the documentary film. It should present an interesting, well-shaped story, with pacing and rhythm that lead to a satisfying resolution.

It may help to think of structure as being either *natural* or *invented*. From the beginning, one looks for a natural or, one might say, obvious and commonsense structure; one dictated by the material itself. I am talking about a form in which the nature of the material compels you and is so strong and obvious that this seems to be the only way the story could go. Here one of the easiest natural structures is the search structure, which is used widely not only in history mysteries, such as *The Search for the True Cross*, but also in personal films, such as *Family*, in which the Arab Danish filmmaker Sami Saif searches for his father.

Finding such a structure often seems like a gift from God. The classic examples of natural structure documentary are the films of Drew Associates, made at the start of the cinema verité movement: *The Chair, Jane*, and *On the Pole*. These films concentrate on an individual at a crux in his or her life. *The Chair*, shot by Don Pennebaker and Ricky Leacock, covers five days in the life of Paul Crump, a black man sentenced to death. At the time of the filming, Paul had apparently been rehabilitated, yet he faced execution in only a few days. The film follows his lawyer's last appeal to have the sentence commuted. We see Crump in his cell and discover that he has written a book; we watch Crump's lawyers in public and private action; we find that the Catholic Church supports leniency toward Crump; and we watch the warden as he tests the electric chair. What gives the film its tension is our knowledge that a final decision must be made in just a few hours. The suspense attains its highest pitch on the day of the decision: Crump's sentence is commuted, and he is transferred to another prison.

Jane, made in 1962 by Don Pennebaker, follows Jane Fonda as she rehearses a Broadway play that seems destined for disaster. We watch the public and private difficulties, the stress of the weeks of preparation, the tensions of opening night. The newspaper reviews come in the early morning and are murderous. The play is quickly abandoned and the actors separate. This film, like *The Chair*, seems to follow an inevitable progression from the statement of the conflict to the inexorable climax.

Most of the Drew Associates films depend on what has been called the crisis structure, a common literary and theatrical device. We are also familiar with this device from feature films, but despite its familiarity, it still works amazingly well. Another common structural device is based on the principle of great change over a relatively short time; such change is both interesting and filmic.

Ira Wohl's *Best Boy*, a good example of this type of film, covers two years in the life of Philly, Ira's cousin. Philly is a fifty-two-year-old man with a mental age of six. Philly's parents have always taken care of him, but they are now in their late seventies. Concerned about Philly's future after their parents' death, Ira wants to enroll Philly in a school for the retarded, where he can learn how to take care of himself a little better. The film becomes a riveting study in Philly's growing independence and self-assurance. The theme of change is underscored by contrasting shots at the beginning and end of the film: at the start of the film Philly is shown being shaved by his father; the last scene shows him shaving himself.

This ability to portray change is one of the gifts of documentary. The process fascinates most viewers, and when filmed in a natural and interesting framework the results can be superb. The most noted world example here is Michael Apted's brilliant studies of English children from *7 Up* to *49 Up*. Each film in the series was shot at an interval of seven years from the one before, and traces the lives and development of a dozen or more men and women over twenty-eight years from childhood to their mid-thirties. The films are moving, funny, sad, poignant, and inspiring as one sees how hope and promise are played out in each individual life. *Hoop Dreams* is another film that wonderfully illustrates the magical results possible when you can follow change over time.

Being myself very much interested in the processes of change, in 1994 I wrote a television proposal for a film about young Israeli women, who must serve two years in the armed forces. In the proposal, I suggested following three women through basic training: one the daughter of a rich city family, one from a rural family, and the third a recent immigrant. I intended to talk to them about their hopes and fears for the future before they went into the army, then follow them for five or six weeks after they joined the same unit. I wanted to see what happened to them away from home for the first time, transplanted into the hothouse environment of the army. I thought the army background would be fascinating, and we would probably see interesting changes in the women as they adapted to their new circumstances.

What pleased me enormously was that the film seemed to have an obvious and very workable structure. The first part would focus on the period before the army: the waiting, the hopes, the fears, and the preparation. The second part would concentrate on the induction and the shock period of the first two weeks. In the third part the women would go on a brief leave, and in the fourth part they would complete basic training and disperse to their units. The subject was exciting; the proposal was exciting. But a glitch developed: television workers went on strike, and when work resumed the proposal was lost in budget cutbacks.

One of the more difficult problems for documentary filmmakers is finding structure where there is no obvious approach. Even if you have found a good handle to the film you can face this problem. The previous chapter discussed a proposal for a film about a university whose object was simply to portray the university to a general audience. A film of this sort has no natural structure; depending on the writer, it could go in almost any direction.

In such a case we have to plunge in and make some arbitrary decisions. For starters, we decide the film will concentrate on two students, two professors, and an administrator, giving us a human approach and contrasting perspectives of the university. While these characters lead us into the film and offer themselves as constant and easily identified figures, the film itself could still go different ways: it could be built around a day at the university, or it could follow key university events, lectures, sports rivalries, examinations, and graduation ceremonies. Another approach, one well suited to a fund-raising film, might use the homecoming celebration to contrast the university's past and present. In this case, the film might begin with the preparations for homecoming; identify typical new students, graduating students, and alumni; develop their individual stories; and conclude with the homecoming dance at which all the characters are present.

Given the right scriptwriter and director, any of these approaches could work, but one structural device, that of "a day in the life," does present problems. When this technique first appeared in the symphonic films of the 1920s, such as *Rien que Les Heures* and *Berlin*, it was comparatively fresh, but since then there have been perhaps too many days in too many lives. Now the technique must be used with caution. Occasionally, though, it can still be potent, as it is in *Royal Family*, which Richard Cawston made for the BBC. *Royal Family* is both a narrative about the British royal family and an essay on the function of the monarchy within the British constitution. Its form is quite simple: the first part presents an imaginary typical day in the life of the queen, while the rest of the film takes her through a typical year. The structure is not a masterpiece of intellectual invention, but it works extremely well—and that's the whole point. Given the intense curiosity about the life of the queen, particularly her private life, it was a case of the simplest, most obvious structure being the best.

Another example of a well-structured film built from very loose and amorphous material is *City of Gold*, made for the National Film Board of Canada by Colin Low, Wolf Koenig, and Roman Kroitor, with commentary by Pierre Berton. In 1956, while doing research in the Dominion Archives, Low discovered a collection of glass-plate photographs of Dawson City, center of the Klondike gold rush of 1898, taken by E. A. Haig. Together with Kroitor and Koenig, Low planned a film about Dawson City based on these photographs, which covered all aspects of life in the boomtown. But what was to be the framework?

The solution provided by the directors and writer is beautiful. The film moves from the present to the past then back to the present, inscribing a circle that gradually completes itself. Beginning in Dawson City of today, we see a small restaurant, old-timers lounging around, and small boys playing baseball in the park. From there the camera directs us toward relics of the past—an old engine, a landlocked riverboat, a boarded-up window—and the commentary recalls the days when they were new.

Almost imperceptibly, the film moves from location photography of the present into the past, as seen in Haig's photographs. The transitional shot is that of the foreboding, icebound Chilkoot Pass, which the gold miners had to conquer before heading to Dawson City. At first we think we are looking at the pass; only when the camera moves into the figures of the miners do we realize that we are looking at a photograph. Using the photographs, the film then recounts the journey downstream to Dawson City and the crazy life that awaited the gold-hungry miners. We see how gold was panned and we follow the fortunes of the lucky and the disappointed. We look at Mounties, prostitutes, bartenders, and Dawson City on carnival day.

Then, almost unnoticed, the film moves from past to present, and with a shock we realize we are back in Dawson City today. The film closes with what almost looks like a repetition of the opening shots. The boys are still playing baseball, and the old men are still talking on the porches—but it's not quite the same. We have awakened from a dream, but now our perceptions are haunted by the memories of the past. It is a very satisfactory ending and more. The return to the present completes the circle, and we sense that perfect form has been achieved.

There is usually no one perfect approach to a film; all sorts of ideas can get you to the same goal. Often I like to play around with two or three ideas, debating the pros and cons of each before making up my mind which to use. Thinking about alternatives is not just an intellectual exercise; it also helps you to cheek the flaws in each strategy.

Some time ago I was asked to do more or less the same film for two organizations in two successive years. Each organization supported a hospital and wanted me to make a film that could be used for fund-raising. I found the handle to the first film after about a week of research. The hospital I was dealing with was rather grim and old. Though most of the staff members were locals, there were also about fifteen foreign doctors working there. I thought maybe that was the clue. I debated a couple of ideas and eventually decided the best approach was to build the film around three expatriate doctors from North America. One was a top surgeon who had been working at Mount Sinai Hospital in New York, where he had probably earned about $200,000 a year. The second was a middle-aged doctor from Phoenix who specialized in geriatric care, and the third was a young doctor from Toronto who cycled to work and wanted to specialize in family medicine.

My meetings with the doctors in the few weeks of research raised a number of questions in my mind. Why had these doctors given up prosperous careers to move to England and work in a shabby hospital? Answer: because they believed in the work. They thought the hospital was vital to the community and believed that the overall challenge more than compensated for the lousy pay and the poor conditions. From there, matters went smoothly. I would tell the doctors' stories in their own words: why they came, what drove them, why they were enthusiastic about the hospital. The doctors were very warm and likable, and I hoped that their example and dedication would inspire the potential donors to give.

Having found the handle, it was then easy enough to find a structure for the film, which we eventually called *Because We Care*. The first part shows the doctors arriving at the hospital and going about their duties. During this part we are introduced to the doctors and get a feel for the hospital and the patients. The middle part of the film, intended as a breather, shows what the doctors do with their private time. We filmed them at home with their families, shopping or camping. The third section, which shows the doctors at work in serious situations, digs a little deeper into the doctor-patient relationship. The film concludes with a quick look at building operations and the planning of a new hospital. The director of the hospital appears at this stage, talking directly to the camera. His function is to make explicit what had only been implied up to then: that the hospital really cares about its patients (a point proved to me over and over during research). The final scene could have been propagandistic, but the preceding scenes had provided a strong basis for the director's sentiments.

Because We Care had no narrator, relying entirely on voice-overs. My second hospital film, *For the Good of All*, depended heavily on narration, but it seemed to work just as well. It was filmed only a year later and also had a fund-raising goal, but it took a totally different approach. My sponsors wanted a film that dealt with research, teaching, and care. I felt that was too wide a subject range and suggested instead that we concentrate on the care and healing aspects of the hospital. After a few discussions the sponsors agreed that we should focus on four areas: oncology, neonatal care, eye surgery, and cardiology. That still left the questions of approach and form. So I suggested to the sponsors that we look at the hospital through the eyes of the patients. We could use their voices to reveal how they felt about their illnesses and the hospital treatment. However, feeling that this material alone would not suffice, I also wrote in a few general scenes with standard narration. After some work I thought that the approach was right but that we still needed something else to give a boost to the film. The answer was a framing device in the form of an outdoor symphonic concert featuring Isaac Stern and Jean-Pierre Rampal. Shots of the orchestra serve as interludes between the separate stories. At the end of the film the featured patients appear in the mass outdoor audience as the orchestra plays the 1812 Overture, with cannons roaring and fireworks exploding. It was all a little hokey and contrived, but it provided a splendid, upbeat spirit to the ending that the sponsors loved.

STYLE AND IMAGINATION

Four men see a beautiful woman on a hill and instantly fall in love. All want to court and marry her. One writes her a letter, plods up the hill, and lays it at her feet. The second rushes toward her and garlands her with flowers. The third stands on his head, then dances for her, while the fourth hires a plane that trails the message "I'll love you forever!" Each is exhibiting his own particular style in accomplishing his objective. One is thorough and plodding, another dynamic. The third tries comic relief, and the fourth adds a little imagination to the whole business.

Style is as important in documentary as in love, and it may be straightforward, comic, experimental, elaborate, fantastic—whatever you want. In brief, think of where you want to go, what you want to do, and then find the most appropriate style to reach the objective. But watch out for baffling boredom, the dull discourse, the esoteric essay, and long-winded piffle. For many people, documentaries are synonymous with everything that is tedious. What hurts is the amount of truth in that comment. Today, the form seems to have settled into familiar patterns, with too many documentaries that are excruciatingly dry. This is unfortunate because there is no need at all for documentaries to be like that.

Many filmmakers seem to think there is a standard pattern for making documentaries. Nonsense. What should dominate your thinking about style (and many other things) is the knowledge that there is no prescribed, hallowed way of making documentaries. Grierson's group understood that in the 1930s when their experiments in editing and sound revolutionized documentary. And Drew, Leacock, Wiseman, Rouch, and others understood it thirty years later when they turned the documentary movement on its head with their ideas about cinema vérité. More recently, Ellen Bruno's groundbreaking film *Satya: A Prayer for the Enemy*, showed how a poetic and lyrical visual style could be applied to the hardest of subjects—the political film. On another level, Marlon Riggs's *Tongues Untied*, about the problems of being both black and gay, illustrates how both theatrical elements and standard documentary techniques can fuse together to make a powerful plea for racial and sexual tolerance.

So where do you begin? For starters, give your style a bit of freedom. Remember, the only boundaries are those of your imagination. For inspiration you have to go no further than look at Bert Haanstra's classic short *Glass*. In an eight-minute love poem on the making of glass, he uses humor, jazz, sly jokes, invented sound, industrial techniques, studies on hands in movement, and a variety of experimental editing possibilities.

The style used in most documentaries is straightforward, realistic, prosaic. But think for a minute. You could opt instead for fantasy, humor, farce, parody. But if these latter elements are so good, why aren't they more widely used in the realm of industrial and educational films? One answer is that too many television stations demand news-style documentaries and frown on imaginative gimmicks and humor. I think they are misguided, and the limits they impose are to be regretted because imagination can invigorate even the dullest subject.

As a writer, it is useful to remember that you can choose from a tremendous number of tools. Some people argue that a documentary should consist only of sequences filmed from real life, archival material, or stills. This stricture has always struck me as nonsense. If you want to use dramatic or fantasy sequences, then go ahead. A few years ago, Carl Sagan's noted series *Cosmos* used every filmic trick the producers could think of. First, they designed a control cabin for a futuristic spaceship and used it as the main setting of the series. It was from this cabin that Sagan looked out onto different worlds. The series then played among the cabin, real locations, computer graphics, models, dramatic reenactments, and archival film. Purists may have quaked, but the series, done with verve and panache, became one of the most popular on American television. Above all, it showed what a documentary series could do with imagination and a decent budget.

In the past the U.S. commercial networks, whose forte was the news documentary, unfortunately tended to restrict their documentary writers and producers to a very plain, realistic style. PBS seems to be continuing that approach. Sometimes the writers have rebelled at the constraints and have tried to break out of the confines of the network method. One such writer was Arthur Barron, who talked to me at length about problems of style and imagination in *The Berkeley Rebels*, which he made for *CBS Reports*.

I didn't want analyses or objective reporting. I wanted to invoke the world of the students with as much dynamism and strength as I could. After a big of discussion CBS agreed to go along with this approach. The film was a mixture of things. On the one hand there was the simple, diarylike following of people. But then I tried deliberately shaping scenes to evoke a particular mood. For example, I tried a sequence which I called "Facts, Facts, Facts!" One of the criticisms of the university was that the kids were being fed information and facts but were not being taught wisdom or how to think. So "Facts" was to illustrate this point.

We had a bathtub filled with soap bubbles and suddenly out of this bathtub emerged a huge, bearded student with water dripping off him. He looks at the camera and says, 'The square root of the hypotenuse is so and so," and then he sinks back into the water.

In another shot I had a guy racing down a hill on a skateboard and as he goes past the camera he screams, 'The Athenian wars began in . . .' For another evocation sequence I took a dog and gave him molasses candy to eat. As he chewed it looked as if he was talking, and we put a voice under the dog with a German accent. (Alan Rosenthal, *The New Documentary in Action* [Berkeley: University of California Press, 1971])

The small touches that Barron wanted to add were very funny, but in his own words, they "drove CBS completely up the wall." In the end the network deleted both the "Facts" sequence and the dog sequence. Humor and imagination were elements they felt very uneasy about. Luckily, the BBC has always been open to experiments, and one of their best recent sponsorship roles was to support Tony Harrison and Peter Symes's *The Blasphemers' Banquet.*

This film, a damning critique of Ayatollah Khomeini and Muslim fundamentalism, is interesting for both its concept and narration. Its gimmick is to invite you to join the poet, Harrison, at a banquet. At the table places are set for Omar Khayyám, Voltaire, Molière, Byron, and Salman Rushdie. These are the "blasphemers" whose courage has pushed the world out of religious darkness toward the light. The story of each one's historical difficulties is told by Harrison on and off camera against a background of theatrical pieces, Paris demonstrations, auction parlors, ranting politicians, Khomeini's funeral, and fundamentalist rallies where Rushdie is burned in effigy. From time to time we return to the simple restaurant, the Omar Khayyám, where the banquet is being held, and also look at the city of Bradford, England, today, where fundamentalism is daily becoming stronger.

The magic that binds the whole piece lies in Tony Harrison's narration, which is written in sparklingly witty verse and comments dryly and acidly on the abominations of religious fundamentalism of all kinds. But wait a minute! Using verse and poetry for documentary— didn't that go out with Pare Lorentz and *Night Mail*? Yes, the verse is strange, but its very strangeness, together with the concept of the banquet and the film's humor, creates a much stronger and effective polemic than one usually sees in most political documentaries.

For me the most interesting and exciting experiments in style, and a wonderful example for filmmakers, are those illustrated in the films currently being made by the English director Brian Hill in cooperation with lyricist Simon Armitage. In a trio of films starting with *Drinking for England*, Hill has been experimenting with a new form, the musical documentary, which is totally different from a documentary with music. Hill's method is best illustrated by a quick glimpse at his film *Feltham Sings.*

Feltham is a prison or closed institution in England for juvenile offenders. Much of the film is made in standard documentary style. Offenders are seen at work, at play, and asleep. And both warders and offenders are interviewed by the director in the usual way and questioned about their thoughts and observations. Suddenly, however, the offenders break into rap song, commenting on their plight, with each verse tending to be shot in a different prison location. The effect is startling and brilliant.

Hill's method is to interview the offenders and warders and then send the transcripts to his lyricist Simon Armitage. Simon then re-arranges the thoughts into a set of rap lyrics that, when sung by the offender or warder, convey the feelings of the singer with a possibly more lasting and penetrating effect than the usual straight interview. The singing scenes are very carefully orchestrated and designed by Hill, with the singer (offender or warden) also being helped by a music coach. The result is dazzling and seems to me the most stunning and entertaining innovation in documentary in the last ten years.

Below are some abbreviated extracts from *Feltham Sings* of one of the film interviews with Paul, a teenage inmate sent down for burglary.

I've had enough of it. I have to fucking go to the toilet in front of an-other man. Do you see what I'm saying? That's not right. I don't like that going to the toilet in front of the next man. You want to go to the toilet in your own house, in your own bathroom, you know what I mean? I just want to be a normal person.

I knew I was going to come to jail, from, like, early age, like. I'd been going and visiting like my uncle in jail and my big brother in jail for years, you know what I mean? So, like, I kind of half knew what I was expecting when I come here. But like, it's still a bit of a shock, you know what I mean . . . It's just dirty, it's freezing cold, no TV, no nothing. So you're bollocksed. Because I can't read either, like, I can't even read a book.

From when I was, like, say 12, I was smoking puff. Yeah. And once I turned, like, 13, 14, I started taking Ecstasy, trips, speed, like all the time, like every other day. Started smoking crack from then. Life's fucked.

Got completely drunk, beat up some boy, got covered in blood . . . So he's got a knife. I took my girlfriend down stairs and there's two little boys playing cricket, so I took the bat off them, for something to hit him, but he'd run off, like.

These interviews appear in the film, but also appear as rap lyrics written and transformed by Simon Armitage as follows:

Brother did time, mother did time
Uncle did time, now it's my turn
All my crowd been crooked from the start
It's hard going straight if you've got a crooked heart
Four square walls and three square meals
A bed and a telly, it's a pretty square deal
First day home and it all goes wrong
Boomerang boy is back to square one
Ain't no picnic, ain't no holiday
Not for a kid that's born in Holloway
Monday's a bad day, Tuesday's a sadder day
Let me out tomorrow, but I'm back again.
Your ma says she'll visit, then suddenly she can't
So you're sat for an hour in the corner like a cunt
Wanna be a chef, wanna be a stuntman
Don't want to sit in the corner like a cuntman
Wanna go far but it's hard to get ahead
If the car that you drive is a four-wheel bed
If your cradle or your cot is a prison cell
It's your office and your toilet and your grave as well
I might be a tich
But I can handle myself
I'm a one man menace to the national health.
I done puff and speed
And trips and crack
And smacked someone up
With a cricket bat.
Stew in your room, angry as a bastard
Throw a few punches at the pillow and the mattress
Drugs on tap, stop you getting twisted
One red line means you've buggered up the piss test.
Ain't no picnic, ain't no holiday
Not for a kid that's born in Holloway [Women's Prison]
Monday's a bad day, Tuesday a sadder day
Let me out tomorrow but I'm back on Saturday

Though Hill's work is brilliant, not everyone has been able to accept where he is going, and many film festivals have rejected his films. This inability to see where and how imagination and humor might work in a documentary seems to be not just a problem for festival organizers, but also for many television executives and sponsors. Maybe that's the reason so many documentaries lack spark. In effect, the executives are saying that serious and important subjects can be treated only in a heavy, dull way. That's sheer nonsense, whether one is talking about documentary or features.

Stanley Kubrick's *Dr. Strangelove* was a brilliant farce, but at the same time it offered a devastating critique of nuclear strategy. Putting it simply, humor can enliven even the most serious documentary, perhaps saving it from drowning in its own profundity.

One of the best examples of humor enlightening a subject can be seen in the series *Connections*, written by James Burke for the BBC. The series was really a history of technology, and the binding theme of all the stories was the strange and unexpected ways in which change has been brought about. Burke's sense of humor was exhibited both in his offbeat, throwaway commentary and in the visual jokes he inserted in his scripts. In *Distant Voices*, one of the films in that series, he discusses early experiments with electricity: "A flamboyant French friar called Nollet, who gave private courses in electricity to beautiful women, decided to run a charge through multiple monks to see if the effect would produce an uplifting experience. It did!" The visuals accompanying the narration show six monks joining hands and then receiving a communal shock from an electrical jar. Thus shocked, the monks jump up and down very solemnly in slow motion; in fact, they appear to be skipping to music, and the effect is quite hilarious.

Many feature films use the device of the running gag, and it also works quite well in documentary. In 1998 I had to do a low-budget film on sports for television. The film, essentially a sports survey, was informative and full of action, but it needed something to bind the separate sequences together. As a solution I wrote in four or five short scenes that utilized the services of a slightly plump friend of mind. In the first scene he plays an enthusiastic football fan who is content to watch everything on television. Later, in a sequence dealing with automobile racing, we see him in a close-up in his car, battling with the wheel. When the zoom opens we see that the car is being towed by a pickup truck. Another sequence features marathon walkers and concludes with an exhausted Dave in baggy, short pants thumbing a lift. I realize that these weren't the world's most marvelous gags, but they worked well in the context of the film. They also did something else: they told us silently that we shouldn't take sports too seriously.

Ross McElwee's film *Sherman's March* also uses the running gag, but in a slightly different way. The pretense of the film is that it is an investigation into Sherman's destructive march through the South during the American Civil War. In reality, it is a very personal and funny look at McElwee's search for love and sex among southern women. Thus, though the main film follows McElwee's encounters with a variety of strange and wonderful women, the film occasionally touches base with the running gag: the idea that we are somehow interested in Sherman's march.

Occasionally a few well-selected graphic images can add humor and zip to a film. The best example I know of here is Agnieszka Piotrowska's film *The Bigamists*. Working with designer Julie Innes, Piotrowska inserts a series of very funny images throughout the film that comment on the subject of bigamy. Thus, playing cards images are semianimated so that the queens are now carrying babies. Occasionally a queen winks at the audience. In another image we see a cartoon blond weep while three husbands wait in the background. In yet another graphic cupid hovers with an arrow while different suitors hover around a bride. Here Piotrowska's deftness of touch lightens a subject that in reality is often sad and tragic.

Imagination and humor are tremendously useful elements for helping odd sections of films, and they can do wonders when they inform the picture as a whole. When this happens, as in *The Road to Wigan Pier*, the basic film can be turned into a small work of art. Made for Thames Television by Frank Cvitanovich, *The Road to Wigan Pier* deals with labor and mining conditions in England in the 1930s; it is based on George Orwell's book of the same name. What one expected from the title, and from knowledge of Orwell, was a serious historical documentary using Orwell's text over stock footage of miners, coal pits, crowded factories, and slums. And that almost exactly describes the first half of the film.

I say *almost* because Cvitanovich does two other things that alter the feel of the film. The first departure from the expected approach is the insertion of six or seven industrial ballads between portions of the stock footage. The songs, sung in different mining locations by an English folksinger, comment humorously on Orwell's text, turning the film into a documentary musical rather than just a historical study.

The second surprise comes close to the end of the film. We have been following a history of the 1930s and expect the film to conclude with war breaking out in Europe, marking the end of an era. This expectation is shattered when the narrator suddenly asks, "But what of your dream of socialism, Mr. Orwell?" The scene abruptly shifts to a modern but empty television studio. The folksinger then appears, seats himself at the television control board, and studies the monitors. They flicker, and various British prime ministers appear on the scenes, ranging from Baldwin and Chamberlain to Churchill and Wilson. One after another, in sequences lifted from electioneering speeches, they promise Britain prosperity and a glorious future. However, the footage is edited in devastating fashion. When one politician states, "Britain never had it so good," he is answered by a politician on another screen exclaiming, "Rubbish!" when a Labor prime minister says the workers are going from strength to strength, a Conservative prime minister answers, "Utter poppycock and nonsense." Finally, when Harold Wilson talks about Britain's New Jerusalem, an edit cut makes former prime minister Edward Heath respond, "Shut up, belt up, and go home." It's a wickedly funny, satirical sequence, and we occasionally cut back to the folksinger in his cloth cap, watching the screen and grinning at all this political balderdash.

The film then abruptly takes another turn as the folksinger dashes down endless corridors of computers and revolving disks. As he pauses, computer reels spin, cards spill out of machines, and various anonymous voices proclaim the appalling state of industry and labor conditions in the 1970s, implying that little has changed since Orwell's day. The conception of this last sequence is brilliant, changing a good documentary of mild interest to the general public into a very strong comment about present-day England.

EXAMPLES

Stuart Hood's *Crisis on Wheels*, a discussion of the automobile and its function in the scheme of things, is another very funny and imaginative documentary. Given the subject, Hood must have been tempted to fall into all the standard traps and make the expected film about mass production, automobile economics, car design, accident prevention, and sales. Hood neatly sidesteps the obvious, building the film around five or six slightly offbeat essays concerning cars. The first section deals with the car as the idol of worship, and I have set out an extract below:

Visual	Audio
A car radio in close-up.	The object of veneration in suburban avenues on Sunday morning.

A car is being washed.	[Music: *Holy! Holy! Holy!*]
A man kneels down and wipes the wheels.	An indispensable utility for all but the poorest. An object of affection—a member of the family. The good car—cherished and loved by all.
An automobile show with beautiful women seated on the tops of cars.	This religion has its priestesses and handmaidens. It also has its golden idols that require a daily offering of human sacrifices.
An advertisement of a car being put on top of a mountain.	The objects of veneration are set up for adoration and worship on pinnacles and high places.

One of the most amusing scenes in the film is called "The Car as a Home Away from Home." The section targets the massive traffic jams seen with increasing frequency around London's suburbs. To make his point about our growing inability to deal with traffic congestion, Hood imagines a scenario in which the traffic jam becomes absolute, and people grow accustomed to living in their cars for weeks on end. The scene was staged in Slough, a medium-sized town near Windsor Castle, and the text is given below. The visual side is only suggested in outline, but it is not very difficult to imagine.

Visual	Audio
A staged traffic jam of immense proportions.	Over on Clifton Street in Harpenden, a town located just outside of London, it's still saturation point. No use offering anyone here a tow home. This jam started three weeks ago and it still hasn't moved an inch. Now that abandoned cars are liable to instant destruction, these drivers have decided to stay put. And most of them actually prefer their home on wheels.
	The women volunteers cope magnificently with morale, and early
People serve tea between cars.	morning tea is the brightest spot of the day.

Paperboy.	The jam may not suit everyone, but the paperboy is delighted. With everyone so close he can get through his rounds in a fraction of the time.
Postman delivers mail.	The postman had a hard job at first coping with the number plates instead of name plates, but now the traffic-jam community is easing his task.
Mrs. Stacey's car.	It's been a long weekend holiday for Mrs. Stacey. Now her fifteen-horse-power home is the smartest in the street. The kitchen is in the back, there's a telephone, and the television works off the car battery. At teatime Mrs. Stacey links up to the exhaust, lights the fumes, and pops on the kettle for a quick cup of tea.

It's marvelous stuff, and once again it shows what wit and imagination can do for a subject.

One film that continues to strike deep chords within me is *Berkeley in the Sixties.* It not only is very good but also brings back nostalgic memories of being a graduate student at Stanford in those turbulent years. While preparing the second edition of this book, I ran into one of the authors of *Berkeley in the Sixties*, Steve Most, in Berkeley itself. Steve had been brought in to write narration for the film, and over dinner he told me of the tremendous problems involved in trying to find a shape for the finished work. As the problem of form and structure is one of the key topics of this book, I asked him if he would mind jotting down a few of his thoughts. The extracts below come from Steve's subsequent letter to me:

> *Berkeley in the Sixties* was the seven-year odyssey of filmmaker Mark Kitchell. He collected archival film and interviewed participants of events that marked the generation that came of age in the sixties. What unified the material was the subject; the order that Mark followed was chronological. However, these events—the free speech movement, the antiwar movement, the Black Panthers, the appearance of the hippies, the rise of Reagan, People's Park—were very different in kind and in feeling.

The rough cut that I first saw when Mark asked me to consider writing the narration lacked characters who could provide a link, other than reminiscence, between the episodes in the film. There was no story line, no unifying theme. And unfortunately the emotional sequence of the episodes had a depressing effect, for one went from the exhilaration of the free speech victory to the defeat over People's Park, which resulted in one death and a great success for Governor Reagan. Why let the audiences feel that the "sixties" ended in failure—although there were failures—and that perhaps nothing was gained from that decade of activism except for illusions that did not stand the test of reality. Who would see such a film, and what would one have to gain from it?

I gave this critique to Mark Kitchell, Kevin Pena, the associate producer, and Veronica Selber, the editor. They listened and at the end, agreed. And because I had a solution to this problem, I took the job.

As I saw it, this was the story not so much of the events that occurred in Berkeley in the 1960s as of a generation that came of age in those years. The narrator then needed to be someone who was there, and who could also speak as a representative voice of her (and our) generation. Susan Griffin's double role, as an actor in the free speech movement and as narrator, also pointed to a solution to the problem of the ending. For the political experience gained during the 1960s had enduring and positive effects, some of which did not become evident until the 1970s: namely the growth of a women's movement, among others, and a sense of freedom and power that she and others carried through their lives, a sense that the world can change and that anyone may play a part in those changes.

Here, then, was a theme that the film could communicate from one generation to those to come. We tried—and still try—to change the world for the better. We have done what we could, falling short of what we hoped to accomplish. No generation can do it alone. It is for others to learn from our experience and to carry the work forward . . .

Generally speaking, when I work on a film I apply the craft I have learned as a playwright, dramatic storytelling, to the documentary medium. One thing dramatists learn to do is to begin in medias res. While Mark Kitchell had wanted the film to begin with an illustrative narrative about the 1950s, or later, with Clark Kerr's lecture about the multiversity, I advocated something more effective, like the anti-HUAC protestors being hosed down the steps of San Francisco's City hall in 1969, thereby receiving their "political baptism." That became the opening after Kitchell tested his ideas in front of an audience and, to his credit, recognized the need for a dramatic, rather than didactic beginning.

The narration of *BITS* was a three-way collaboration. Sometimes the producer wrote the first draft; in every case, he critiqued what I wrote. The narrator, Susan Griffin, joined us after the picture was locked to choose the words and phrases that best conveyed her voice as a poet and sense of things as a witness to history. The editor was indirectly a collaborator, joining in the discussions that advanced our thinking. I think that we are all pleased with the result.

As did Steve, I faced a similar problem with form in a film I did a few months before I met him. In December 1992, the Israeli Foreign Office put out a call for a film on the Middle East *after* peace. This was long before the Oslo accords between Israel and the PLO, or the return of Jericho and Gaza, and the film's topic was obviously a highly optimistic act of faith. I decided to submit a proposal, but I had to support my entry with a fairly detailed statement of approach and treatment.

The problem was that one had to make a film about events that *had not yet happened.* My first move was to research several subjects: economic development, agriculture, tourism, water sources, arms control, and refugees, just to name a few. That was the easy part. The hard part was to come up with an imaginative framework for the film; one that wouldn't just rely on experts talking and pontificating.

The solution was to set the film in the future, actually in the year 2004, and have a reporter look back on ten years of peace. The reporter would actually be on assignment in the desert to cover a ten-year anniversary meeting and celebration of the first peace signing. As he waits he recalls everything that has happened in the last ten years; events that are "re-created" on screen by a fusion of documentary, faked newsreels, and dramatized segments. Below are a few extracts from the first treatment.

Picture	Idea or Commentary Line
We are in a desert. A reporter is obviously preparing for a broadcast. We sense activity behind him. An assistant comes up with a film clapboard, calls "Take one," and marks it. The reporter now addresses his audience, as if in a live broadcast.	REPORTER *(rough commentary outline)*: Today we celebrate ten years of peace between Israel and its neighbors. It's fitting that

	this simple ceremony is here, because the original treaty was signed at this spot 10 years ago. Audiences will remember that that was the culmination of years of work . . . But what a day that was . . .
Rejoicing in mosques, churches, and Western Wall.	Today delegates from Lebanon, Syria, Jordan, Saudi Arabia, and Israel are revisiting this spot to renew and reaffirm the commitment to peace made a decade ago.
We see cars with diplomatic flags emerging through the desert haze.	
Figures emerge from car.	Looking back we are all amazed at the changes. Given the social, economic, and cultural benefits of this last decade, how could we have been so foolish as to wait so long?

An assistant runs up and bangs the clapboard. It is the end of the take. Obviously we have been watching a film rehearsal. We are still in the desert. The reporter wipes his glasses, sits casually on a table, and again addresses the audience, this time much more informally, almost as a personal chat.

	REPORTER: Yes, just a film. Just a created scene. But a utopian fantasy? No! What you have just seen could well be true in a few years time. The elements for change, the elements for peace are in place.
	But we've talked so long about war we've forgotten what peace might be like, what it might bring.
The diplomats' cars are seen. Close-up of flags.	What we'd like to do in this film is stretch the imagination a bit . . . take a Jules Verne or

H. G. Wells trip into the next
few years and try to envisage
what this world, what this
turbulent Middle East would be
like with a real peace, what it
would be like in say . . . 2000,
the year 2004, or in 2010.

The treatment then went on to review a little bit of the history of the wars and battles in the region (illustrated with archival footage) before we moved into the documentary fantasy. I enjoyed writing the script, and it was accepted with enthusiasm. The sponsor, however, then got cold feet. It was too controversial a subject. A good script, but maybe for production "next" year. And that's the way it goes.

7

BEGINNING THE FIRST DRAFT

You are a few weeks into the film, and things are beginning to clarify in your mind. You have decided to do the film as story plus essay. You think that you have found the right approach and structure, and you are beginning to see a possible opening, middle, and end. Great! Now all you have to do is sit down and write your first draft. This may take the form of either a draft shooting script with ideas only or a draft shooting script with commentary. In the first case, you will merely set out the ideas you want to accompany the visuals. In the second case, you will actually write a preliminary commentary, even though this may well change as the film progresses.

A draft shooting script with the ideas sketched out might look like this:

Visual	Idea Line
Jerusalem seen from the air.	The concept of Jerusalem as the highest ideal. It is perfection. St. John's vision. Mention Jerusalem as religious center.
Crowded Jerusalem streets. People struggle against a mass of cars.	Jerusalem of here and now. Discuss its reality. A city of

	twenty-five thousand. The everyday problems.
Presenter comments.	Commentator expresses the dilemma of modern Jerusalem. So many tensions in the present. The need to balance the spiritual and the practical. Then state where the film is going.

A draft shooting script with commentary might look like this:

Visual	Audio
Jerusalem seen from the air.	When he left Palestine in 1920, the British governor of the capital said, "After Jerusalem there can be no higher promotion." For him, as for millions of others, There was no counterpart to Jerusalem in the history of the West. Jerusalem was the center of two faiths, and holy to a third. It was the light, the guardian of ideals, the eternal city, the symbol of perfection.
Jerusalem seen on the ground. Crowded streets. People push against cars. Chaos.	But as well as the Jerusalem of the mind, there is also the Jerusalem of reality. There is the modern city developed in the last century, and the ancient city where twenty-five thousand people still live and work within medieval fortress walls.

Which of the two forms should you choose? The answer is usually forced on you by the circumstances and by the nature of the film. Most sponsors like to receive a full commentary script even though they know it will most likely change at a later date. Seeing just the visuals or a list of ideas means little to sponsors. By contrast, it is very easy to understand the film through the commentary. Even a television documentary department, familiar with all sorts of presentations, may require a draft commentary script before letting you do a history or personality film. And the same may be true of foundations to which you have applied for a grant. For many films, however, it is quite clear that you will only be able to write the commentary at the end. These may be political films, news documentaries, or any films that are constantly evolving or that are essentially built in the editing phase. In such cases, the best you can do is set out the ideas you want to use to guide you through the film and write the commentary when the editing is finished.

When I have the choice, I prefer to write a first draft (for my eyes only) using the idea form and then rewrite the script with commentary for presentation. This double work is not strictly necessary, but I find that it helps me focus my ideas.

SCRIPT FORMATS

From the examples given so far, you probably have a good idea of what the standard script format looks like. The usual practice is to divide your page into two sections, with the visuals described on the left side of the page and the audio portion (commentary or ideas) on the right, as below.

Visual	Audio
Ascot race track.	
Horse enclosure. Elegant people seen in fancy suits and dresses watching.	Once this was known as the sport of kings. And you came because you had wealth and leisure and wanted to show off your mistress.
Other working-class types, drinking beer and eating hamburgers and dressed in jeans and old trousers.	Now the sport of kings has become the pastime of the proletariat.

As you can see, although the commentary is fairly detailed, the visuals are only sketched in. What you are trying to do is give the director a broad idea of what you want from the visuals, leaving the rest up to him or her. Obviously, some pictures will call for more details. Thus, for a scientific or medical film you may have to describe precisely the handling of a technical shot. But usually a brief suggestion is enough. A rough sketch will also suffice for "idea" scripts. Usually I don't bother to set out my ideas in long, elaborate sentences—just a few words to suggest the main ideas.

Does the script have to follow the divided page format? Not really. It's just that we're used to this convention. However, if you want to write your visuals across the full page and follow that with the commentary, then go ahead. The only criterion is clarity: will the ideas in the script be clear to those working on the film? If they are, then you have no problem.

GETTING STARTED

Before getting down to the draft, it's useful to recap once more what you are trying to do for the viewer. You are going to open secret doors for him or her. You are going to invite the curious viewer in to observe secret goings on or to look at familiar situations in a different way. You are going to show wonderful visual things, and at the same time you are going to provide fascinating entertainment. These are the essentials you should never forget.

When you do actually start writing the script there are probably some general thoughts that have been with you sometime. You've got a feel for an interesting story and its contradictions and for characters and their conflicts. You've thought about story threads. And you've thought about structure, situation, and meaning, and how everything changes over time. So you're ready to plunge in. That's the best situation. Or you sort of know where you want to go but are still a little confused how to begin. In both cases, it may help you to jot down a few notes under the following headings:

main ideas
logical progression
visualization
opening
rhythm and pace ·
climax

This kind of analysis works well for me, though many of my friends plunge straight into writing without any such breakdown. It has become second nature for them to consider all these things in their mind, so they do not need to formalize their thinking. It is important to remember, though, that every scriptwriter, formally or informally, consciously or unconsciously, has to consider most of the issues set out above.

Your first goal, in a non-verité film, is for the script is to present your key ideas in the most interesting, emotionally compelling and fascinating way. Furthermore, you want them to be seen as a whole rather than as a diverse collection of fragmented thoughts. And you want the ideas to move forward through the film with an easy and seemingly effortless logic and progression.

The problem boils down to this: what ideas will you use and how are you going to present them? Your research has churned up a hundred ideas and questions. Now you are going to have to sift them, focusing on some and eliminating others, always keeping in mind the main goal of the picture. If, for example, you started researching the film *University Challenge*, your overall list of questions and ideas might include the following:

What Is a University? What Does It Represent?
originally for religious and legal training
status: Oxford, Cambridge, Harvard, Yale
difference between universities and junior colleges
a waste of time
a focus of resentment for nonuniversity people
a generator of ideas
a featherbed life for pampered faculty
a hotbed of political unrest
a marriage market
the ivory tower
a center for intellectual stimulation
abundant sex

Another point you might be investigating for the film is university research. Again you may have set yourself a question:

Research: What and Why?
pure
applied
necessary for promotion
esoteric
immense costs
waste of taxpayer's money.
used by the military
research one field opens up another

In trying figure out what's in a film, I work on the first premise that there are no bad ideas. So I brainstorm; I pour all and everything out on paper. Your task after that is to winnow out your ideas, concentrating only on those you deem of major importance. In the process, some great ideas will be thrown out, but that can't be helped. From the list above, perhaps only three ideas will find their way into the script. But ideas are never considered in the abstract. You should also be considering "characters" for your film. These are people whose lives, actions, and behavior illustrate the affect of ideas on human action. Thus, in *The Berkeley Rebels*, the university is portrayed as a center of political activity, illustrated in the film through the story of Mike.

At this point, it is useful to keep your audience in mind. Will they be interested in or able to understand all the issues you want to deal with? How much detail should you provide on each idea? Should you go into depth? Many executives at the American networks tend to believe their audiences are idiots capable of understanding only a few ideas, and those only if they are presented in the most superficial way. I disagree. I think most audiences can quickly grasp a great number of ideas, even complex ones, provided the film is attractively made.

It is also useful to remind yourself at this stage that no matter how many ideas you have, there must be one binding thread running through the film. Often this idea will be framed in the form of a question that the film will attempt to answer. Are universities good or bad for the country? Has George W. Bush been misjudged by history? Was the second Gulf War necessary? Was Irving Berlin the greatest popular composer of the century? Who was the real Hemingway? Is Madonna's quest for faith genuine? Does this sound familiar? It should: this statement of the main idea was the first thing you did when you wrote out your proposal all those months ago.

After you have decided on the main ideas, the next task is to arrange them into logical blocks or sequences that lead easily and naturally from one to the other. By *sequence* I mean a series of shots joined by some common elements—a series of ideas, a visual setting, a series of actions, a musical motif—that makes one or more specific points. The shots in a sequence may be unified by the following:

- *A central idea*: We see children playing football in a park, a woman throwing a javelin, a professional baseball game, a wrestling match. The sports motif is the obvious unifying element, but the central idea that the writer wants to make might be that sport originates from war.
- *Setting*: We see the Rocky Mountains. Tremendous mountains, waterfalls, and streams; immense forests; impenetrable jungles. Here the common element is the setting and the grandeur of nature.

- *Action*: A student leaves her house, goes to the university, greets her friends, has coffee, then finally enters class. All the actions up to the class entry have a certain unity; a classroom shot would probably begin a different sequence.
- *Mood*: War has begun. Tanks are advancing. Women are weeping. Destroyed buildings are seen in silhouette. Men are talking in groups. A small boy wanders forlornly along a street. Here, the binding element is not just the start of war (idea) but also the gray, bleak mood of the people and the setting.

Obviously, there are more categories and they overlap considerably. Ideas, actions, setting, central characters, mood—all these things may join together to unify a sequence. Another way of looking at it is to think of groups of ideas, images, character actions, and information that suggest a totality, a unified block. This will give you the sequence, and later you can see where the sequence fits into the whole. You must continually ask yourself:

What is the *point* I want to make in this sequence?
What can I *show* to make that point?
What are my *characters* or participants doing?
How will *sound*—whether music, dialogue, effects, or commentary—help make the sequence more effective?

The above can be illustrated by a simple example. We have seven shots making up a sequence showing different students arriving at the gates of a university. The *point* I want to make is the variety of the students in ages, races, and looks. The seven varied shots adequately *illustrate* that point. What are my characters doing? Talking in different languages. All this is possibly accompanied by bright jazzy music indicating the students are happy, and the university might be fun.

In practice, in an essay or historical film, you will probably be using your narration to unify the sequences and show the viewer where you want to put your emphasis. In a cinema verité or observational dialogue-guided film, ordering sequences can be much harder, and those problems are discussed later in the book.

When you start thinking about putting your sequences in some kind of order, keep two points in mind. First, remember that there is a tremendous difference between film logic and mathematical logic. The former is much more elusive, emotional, and insubstantial. It is a logic that is often felt through the gut rather than through the head. I recently saw a film about the world-famous cellist Jacqueline du Pré, who died very young. The writer-director might have started the picture with du Pré triumphant in concert and then gone back to her childhood. Instead, the film opens with Elgar's cello concerto heard over soft, warm shots of autumn, with views of the sun sparkling through red and orange leaves. The director had opted for a gentle, poetic opening and it worked, even though the real entry into the subject was somewhat delayed. The second point is that the progressive logic of the ideas has to parallel the visual and emotional development of the film. Emphasis on one at the expense of the others can ruin the film.

The simplest and most natural ordering of ideas is chronological, but you might also want to consider a spatial development. The main thing is to find an order that gives a sense of growth. In his excellent book *Film Scriptwriting*, Dwight Swain suggests thinking about movement from the simple to the complex, from the specific to the general, from the familiar to the unfamiliar, from problem to solution, or from cause to effect. The important thing is the suggestion or illusion of inevitability, of natural movement.

The chronological progression is the oldest form of storytelling. It is the most frequently used method because it satisfies our natural curiosity to see what happens next. If we are introduced to a gifted child, we want to know what becomes of that child in adulthood, or what becomes of Philly when he goes out on his own in *Best Boy*. We want to know what happens when the sheltered girl who has been confined to her family circle takes her first room alone. We want to see the nun in the cloister, and then follow her progress when she gives up her vows and returns to the secular world. Jon Else's Academy Award–winning film *The Day after Trinity* tells the story of Robert Oppenheimer and the events leading to the creation of the atomic bomb. The basis is the simple chronological story of Oppenheimer's life from childhood to maturity to the supervision of the Los Alamos atomic project. Similarly, Don Pennebaker's *Jane* starts with Jane Fonda arriving for her first Broadway rehearsal and concludes with the arrival of the reviews after the disastrous opening night.

In *Tongues Untied*, one of the most moving films ever made to deal with racism and personal identity, Marlon Riggs digs deep into himself to chart his gradual discovery of his own homosexuality. This progression is confronted by hostility on all sides, until a young white boy shows him that love and feeling can overcome racial barriers. The film is about evolution, both political and sexual, and is quite simply a superb human document.

Another progression is the crisis, conflict, and resolution structure discussed earlier in reference to *The Chair.* At first glance, this progression looks similar to the chronological structure, hut there are quite a few differences. For example, one of the familiar strategies of the chronological film is to show the development of character or the growth of a career in politics, business, or the arts, such as that of Oppenheimer in *The Day after Trinity.* The same may happen in a conflict documentary, but in the latter case, we are generally more interested in the conflict resolution than in the character change.

The action in *The Chair* takes place over five days; time passes, but there is no character change. Instead, the tension concerning Paul's fate propels the film forward. Will he live or die? We are waiting for the answer. In *Mooney versus Fowler,* by James Lipscomb, we follow the lives of two extroverted football coaches and the struggle between their two teams for the local championship. Once the game is over and the conflict resolved, the film ends.

A good example of another film based on the progression of a fight is the BBC film *Whose House Is It Anyway?* In England, most people cherish the myth that their home is their castle, sacred and inviolable. But evidently it isn't. If the local council has a good reason for wanting a house, it's theirs. Billy and Gordon Howard had owned and lived in Rose Cottage for years, but one day the local council placed a compulsory purchase order on the house and assumed ownership. The eccentric bachelor brothers, aged sixty-five and seventy-three, refused to recognize the validity of the purchase order, saying that when the bailiffs came they would shoot them rather than give up their birthright. The conflict is established in the first few seconds of the film, and the next hour shows us the stages and progress of the fight. It is a subject that touches all of us, and we are immediately drawn into the film, curious to see how the conflict will be resolved.

The chronological progression and the conflict progression are the two most common documentary threads, followed closely by the search motif, or the hunt for the solution of the mystery. Thus, the popularity of the Discovery Channel series that investigated everything from the origins of the Dracula story to archaeologist Schliemann's search for Troy.

James Burke's series *Connections* (mentioned previously), is really a variation on the search theme. Instead of filming a deliberate search, his aim is to show us how technological discovery is often achieved in the most unexpected ways. His films progress from surprise A to surprise B and so on. Watching the series is like watching a magician astonish an audience, pulling wonders out of a hat. Burke's secret is to stimulate our curiosity into following a strange series of technological changes. For amusement, I charted the progress of ideas in Burke's film about the invention of rocket propulsion:

1. The film opens. Burke stands in a modern factory and talks about the many uses of plastic.
2. This leads him to talk about plastic credit cards replacing money.
3. The film slips into a discussion of financial credit.
4. That subject takes us back to the fourteenth century. While the film shows us knights and ladies playing around in castle grounds, Burke starts telling us how the *new idea of credit* in those days helped finance the small army of the Duke of Burgundy.
5. Because of credit, the army can grow from a few thousand to sixty thousand—that is, credit allows bigger armies.
6. As armies grow new weapons come into fashion. The pike is used in a new way, but then it gives way to the blunderbuss, which gives way to the musket. Then the pike joins the musket in the form of the bayonet.
7. We return to the idea of the ever-growing army, now two hundred to three hundred thousand soldiers strong. But armies need food.
8. Armies like that of Napoleon grow so large that they cannot live off the countryside. They need food that can be eaten even if not fresh. This leads to the development of canning.
9. This in turn leads to ice-making machines, which in turn inspire the invention of chemical and gas refrigeration and refrigerators.
10. The growing emphasis on food preservation leads to the invention of the vacuum flask.
11. The principle of the vacuum flask allows gases to explode in a vacuum. Do this on a large scale and you have the invention of the German V-2 rocket by Wernher Von Braun.

One is a little staggered at the end of the film to find that food for armies has led to rocket propulsion. You wonder how the trick was done. The answer is the fascinating but "logical" thread of ideas that Burke has woven for the viewers.

Burke's film was built up of about eleven sections that seem to lead inevitably from one to the other. I say *seem* because on close examination we can detect a terrific sleight of hand. But what do you do when the film has no superficial logic? The answer is to build up blocks of associated ideas, and then segue smoothly, with the help of visuals and commentary, from one distinct section to another.

When I did a film about automobile accidents, I knew I wanted to concentrate on four things: the accidents as they happen, the reactions of the victims, the causes of accidents, and road engineering. There seemed to be no compelling arguments for placing one topic before another. So what were the reasons behind the final arrangement of the script?

I put road engineering first because it raised some interesting issues but lacked the emotional interests for a film climax. On the other hand, I thought I could get some highly moving and dramatic material on drivers that would work well toward the end. The section on cars would then slip into the middle. The script was written that way until I turned up some fascinating material on cars of the future that I thought would lead easily into the question of where we will go in the twenty-first century. That seemed a good way to end the film, so I reversed the sections on cars and drivers. The first and very rough draft of ideas and sequences was as follows:

Visual	Ideas
Cars on road	The trauma of the accident
Crash, police	
Ambulance	Title: *Always Someone Else*
Hospital patient's subjective view	Accident patients' reactions
Patients interviewed in hospital	

Accident Background

Urban congestion	City crowding
Masses of traffic	The problem of movement
Inside police lab; police tests at scene of accident	How police investigate accidents

Why Accidents Happen

Bad road engineering, death spots, blind spots, discussion with road engineer	*(a) bad road engineering* The state of the roads
Talk to bus and taxi drivers	*(b) the driver*
Training course for bad drivers	Not taking care
Training new drivers	
Specialist training	Driver training
Bad visibility	Pressures on drivers

Crowded car, bad road signs	
Rain, family pressure	
Sports-car racing, big cars and beautiful women	Cars an extension of the driver's psyche; the psychology of cars and driving
	(c) The car itself
Impact test on cars	Building the car
Cars on test courses	Car safety faults
Safety belt tests	New safety measures
Innovative car designs	The car of the future
Cars with reverse seats and periscope mirrors	
Animated film with new cars and well-designed, car-accommodating cities	The world of the future
Wreck of cars in a salvage yard	Need for concern now

What I have set out above eventually grew to cover fourteen pages. Very much a first sketch, it nevertheless set out clearly how the visuals and ideas would work together. I knew that later scripts would require much more detail and that the shooting itself would suggest new patterns and variations. However, I needed to put some ideas on paper so that I could react to them and see whether the order made sense, at least in theory.

It is also worthwhile to point out that certain sections were included not because I thought they were logically necessary to some thesis I was developing, but because I thought they were visually interesting and might be fun to shoot. The scene in the police accident lab, for example, did not contribute much in the way of ideas, but it was a marvelous place to poke around and look at lie detectors, secret camera units, methods of metal testing, and so on. The jazzy sequence, with a beautiful blond on top of a Rolls-Royce, also was not strictly necessary, but I thought it would provide a certain visual contrast.

What is important is that the first draft suggested a tentative order and connection between sequences that were really quite disparate. It was a beginning. In the end, the editing suggested quite a radical reordering, but that's a story for the editing chapter.

I stress the notion of sequence connection because without it your essay and ideas film can fall flat or fail to reach its full potential. This is one of the few criticisms I have of *Tongues Untied*, a film that I have already mentioned that I admire greatly. In *Tongues Untied*, many sequences are quite brilliant, but they often seem arbitrarily juxtaposed, one against another. In the end, this undercuts your emotional connection to the work.

TYPICAL PROBLEMS

In looking for logic in your scriptwriting, you will often find yourself being pulled in different directions by the variety of possibilities. The most common problem is trying to decide whether to proceed chronologically, intellectually, or spatially. What is all this about in practice? Let's consider a chronological progression versus an intellectual progression.

You are doing a film about World War II and want to bring in the subject of civilian resistance. Your general story has taken you to 1942. You then find several stories you want to use about resistance: one in 1942, one in 1944, and one in 1945. In terms of ideas, you probably want to tell all the stories in one sequence to prove a certain point about resistance. But that will carry you to 1945, whereas the main part of your film will have only reached 1942. So you have a problem.

In the same film you are showing the D-day invasion of June 1944. Your idea line suddenly pulls you into a discussion of other successful and less successful attacks in the war, such as the Dieppe raid and the Italian invasion. Do you branch out and show those incidents, or do you stay with the scenes on the Normandy beaches?

There are no easy answers, but it helps to ask yourself a few questions: Will what you are doing confuse the viewer? Will it aid or spoil the dramatic and emotional telling of the story? Will it affect the overall rhythm of the film? In nine cases out of ten you'll find it best to keep within a chronological progression and to stay with one physical location until the information about it is exhausted. There are exceptions, but these guidelines seem to be the most helpful in practice.

Another problem in writing the first draft film is to *overload* it with too many sequences. There is suddenly so much to say and you want to put everything in. I would suggest you resist this impulse and really question the place and worth of everything you insert. I know there will be second drafts, and I know you can eliminate sequences in editing, but it is worthwhile trying to get everything right the first go around. Overloading is, in fact, the second problem of *Tongues Untied*. It simply tries to do too much, with the overloading eventually reducing the power of the rest of the film. The rule here, then, is that less can be more.

8

COMPLETING THE FIRST DRAFT

VISUALIZATION

You have worked out a story line and idea line. Now comes the fun as you start considering how to put over your ideas visually. Every sequence has a point or a number of points that can be put over by visuals, by commentary, or by a combination of both. Your aim is to find the most powerful way to use the joint forces of both picture and word.

As the film proceeds, it makes a series of assertions: today, the car is God; the famine in Ethiopia is tragic beyond all belief; marriage is out; the youngsters of today are crazier than their parents ever were. These statements need illustrating in order to prove their truth. They can be illustrated in comic or serious ways, but they must be proved. So one of your first jobs is to choose the pictures that will prove your points in the most imaginative and interesting way.

The writer and director share the job of visualization. The writer will suggest the action and visualization but knows that the director, on location, may add to or alter the suggestion or think of a better way to put over the idea. But the script visualization is always the starting point and is usually a tremendous help to the director.

In my automobile accident film, one of the points I wanted to make was that the car often becomes an extension of one's personality. It can represent power, sex, virility. In the film the point was made visually as follows:

Visual	Audio
Very low shots of the road surface rushing past. The road blurs at speed. We cut to racing cars speeding around a track. Women wave the cars on.	In my car I feel like a real guy. There's power in my hands. My girl's at my side. Put my foot down and I can get to Monterey in an hour. In my car I get really turned on. You're just not a man without a car.
Cut to a man looking through the window of a car showroom. Inside, two beautiful women in bikinis are sitting on the hoods of a Mercedes and a Ferrari—and smiling.	

The commentary was in my own words but based on a number of interviews I had done during research. What I wanted from the visuals was not a parallel of the commentary but a visual sense of the meaning behind the commentary. What the visuals had to do was express the machismo that drove the man who was talking.

In another part of the film I wanted to talk about all the pressures on the driver. My notes show my first thoughts on the subject. Pressure could be shown by the following sequence:

1. A mass of road signs that block one another and give confusing directions. The driver's brain is overloaded with information.
2. The windshield is blurred and rain lashed.
3. Inside the car, kids scream and nag.
4. The traffic is getting very heavy. The roads are icy and night is falling.
5. The oncoming drivers are using their brights, and the lights are dazzling, going in and out of focus.
6. It starts to snow.

Sometimes you need visuals to illustrate a process or an evolving action, and that's quite simple. But sometimes you need to find visuals to illustrate something a little more abstract or a little less obvious, and here you can often really be creative. In our proposed university script, we might want to make the point that today's students are tremendously politically involved. We might write the scene like this:

Visual	Audio
A student lies on the grass and reads a book beside a river.	Once the student lived what was almost the life of a monk. Solitary and studious, devoted and disciplined.
Student riots in Paris, 1968. Student anti–Gulf War riots in 2004. Students battle with the police.	That idea seems just a little bit strange today.

Here, the whole argument is made visually, with the commentary providing the lightest of frameworks. This point needs stressing because it is one of the most important things in script writing: you can write with words, and you can write with pictures, but very often the pictures will make your point much more powerfully.

I wrote earlier that there were few laws for scriptwriters. I was wrong. There is one immutable law: the good scriptwriter must be visual as well as verbal. Failure to attend to the visual side of things accounts for many boring documentaries.

One of the pleasures of visualization is the fun you can have finding the pictures to match an open text. Let us assume that we are making a film about the brain and need to put over a simple statement in the commentary: "One of the main differences between humans and animals lies in the development of speech. We have it and, except in a primitive way, they don't. And what we do with it is incredible." This comment is very simple to illustrate, and we could do it in a hundred ways. A random choice of visuals might include the following:

Chaplin singing a nonsense song
a man on his knees making an eloquent proposal of marriage
an Italian and a German yelling at each other in their respective
    languages
Al Pacino reciting "To be or not to be"
Hitler haranguing the masses
a baby talking to a doll

Just for fun we might want to finish off the sequence with the line "Language is golden, but thank God we can turn it off."

I leave it to you what visual we use there.

Visualizing Sequences

For many documentaries, maybe the majority today, you shoot a developing scene and write a commentary, if necessary, later. Your visuals are "given" in the sense that you are following things as they happen. But a lot of the time in documentary, particularly in essay or historical films, you have to plan. What we did above was plan shots to illustrate commentary lines, but more often you try to visualize entire sequences. Again, your task is to think of the best situation to flesh out the script idea and then describe the elements of that situation in as much helpful detail as possible. That may mean writing notes regarding setting and characters, including the characters' dress and actions. This is standard practice for the "invented" industrial film, but it is also useful for the film based on more or less real situations. This is particularly true when you have researched a story and know what's likely to happen. Your writing helps the director see where to put the emphasis in a scene and what you want to get out of the scene.

An old script of mine called *A Certain Knowledge* illustrates some of the above points. The script dealt with a four-day encounter between two groups of teenagers from Los Angeles, one black, one white. The object of the film was to show that stereotypes could be broken and that suspicion and antagonism could give way to friendship if only some of the mental barriers could be removed. I wanted to go for a simple observational film, but the sponsors wanted more. They argued that the film was not simply a documentary but had the specific purpose of encouraging other schools to participate in the encounter. To that end, they wanted realistic situations written into the script.

Obviously, I had to isolate the situations, known from the past, that would reveal the initial antagonism and then indicate the change of attitudes. I explored the basic four-day program and suggested the following for the script: First, I wanted either a basketball game or a volleyball game close to the beginning, with whites against blacks. This would set up the concept of opposition, and such games often took place. Later in the film I wanted to repeat the scene with racially mixed teams. I also suggested a closed-circuit video session in which we would show clips of police brutality against blacks in the South and other clips of Malcolm X and Louis Farrakhan railing against whites. Here I suggested recording the on-the-spot reactions of the two groups for use later as voice-overs against the video viewing. I also wrote in an open discussion to follow the viewing session.

For the latter part of the film I suggested a home visit, blacks in white families and vice versa, to be followed by a half-day hike in rugged terrain. My thinking here was that the home sessions might be awkward and tense and that we could use the hike to break the tension. The hike also served another purpose, and I wrote in some notes for the director regarding its shooting. I asked the director to concentrate on filming groups where one helped the other across rocks, where hands were stretched out in assistance, or where they sat on the grass and ate and sang together.

I wanted the visuals to be very positive but realized there was a danger of the film becoming saccharine and unreal. To counter this, I suggested we put in a number of voice-overs in the last sequence. While some would indicate a positive change in attitudes among blacks and whites, a number would still be skeptical and doubt the lasting quality of the friendships and the value of the long weekend.

Sometimes you may really want to surprise with your visualizations. When I did a film a few years ago called *The Hunt for the Treasures of God*, the first line went as follows:

> For two thousand years the world has been intrigued by an archaeological mystery. What happened to the fabled treasures of the Jerusalem temple? Are they beneath the desert of Israel? Buried under Egyptian sands? Or maybe even locked in some ruined Templar castle in the south of France?

To back up the scene visually I shot two figures at dawn, clothed in Arab galabias, burying some mysterious objects in the earth as the sun came up. The figures were silhouetted against the red sun and russet hills and the scene presented, or so I hoped, the perfect visual support for the text.

Visual Resonance

No matter how many years I've been working, I still find it enormously helpful to study the work of other documentary directors. Looking back, I find one director above all others has influenced my thinking: Humphrey Jennings, the classic English documentary director of the early 1940s.

Jennings's greatest film is often thought to be *Listen to Britain*, and it can serve as a veritable textbook on visualization. The film provides a sound and visual portrait of Great Britain in the middle of World War II. What gives the film its power is the emotional resonance of its visuals. Again and again in *Listen to Britain*, Jennings and his collaborator, Stewart McAllister, choose shots that have not just an immediate meaning but also cultural and emotional resonance. It is this hidden effect that makes the Jennings and McAllister films so powerful, and you can see it at work in the playground sequence from *Listen to Britain*:

1. A middle-aged woman is in her bedroom looking at a photograph of her husband in uniform. We hear the sounds of children singing.
2. The woman looks out of the window and sees, in long shot, a group of seven-year-old children doing a circle dance in a school playground.
3. Cut to close-ups of the children dancing in couples.
4. The sound of the children singing merges with the sound of a Bren gun carrier (an open half-track vehicle with a light machine gun mounted next to the driver). We then cut to the Bren gun carrier rattling through the narrow streets of an old English village.
5. As the Bren gun carrier passes we see more fully the ancient thatched roofs and the Tudor style of the English cottages.

The images are open to many interpretations, but given the purpose of the film—to boost morale in wartime Britain—I think the intended resonances are very clear.

- The woman looking at the soldier's photograph sets up the idea of the loved ones who are absent but who are protecting us.
- The children represent the protected, but also stand for the future.
- The Bren gun carrier asserts the immediate protection of the British way of life.
- The background of the village, with its Tudor gables and thatched roofs, suggests the wider culture and history that is being protected. It also recalls an earlier crisis, when Elizabethan England stood alone against the Spaniards and defeated them. The parallel to England and Germany in 1939 is clear.

The sequence lasts only forty seconds but engenders a whole series of emotions and responses that build throughout the film.

The importance of resonance is worth keeping in mind in any documentary writing. Every visual you use may have both an immediate and appropriate surface meaning and an additional emotional resonance that can add tremendous depth. I am not talking here of obvious symbols—the American flag and so on—but of scenes and sequences rooted in cultural memory: the Saturday Little League baseball game, Christmas shopping, high school graduation. Used well, such scenes can evoke powerful memories and moods that can obviously be of enormous help to a film.

There is, however, one point to keep in mind when going for the resonance effect. The emotional echo of a scene may be specific to a certain region or culture and may be meaningless to other audiences. Jennings's work, which is so powerful in the English context, comes over as far weaker in the United States. Nevertheless, resonance is a tremendous addition to a filmmaker's bag of effects.

THE OPENING

The opening of the film has to do two things very fast. First, it has to catch, or *hook*, the viewer's interest, and second, it has to define very quickly what the film is about and where it is going. These are good artistic rules and also good practical rules in a world in which documentaries are seen primarily on television and have to compete with many other programs for viewers. The only real exception to both these rules is when you are dealing with well-known, presold subjects. If I were doing a film titled *Sherman: The Greatest General*, *The Real Elvis*, or *George Bush: The Early Years*, then I might ignore the two golden rules. In all three cases most viewers would know something of the subject matter once they heard the title. Knowing what to expect, they might not mind a slower introduction. This is exactly what occurs in the film about cellist Jacqueline du Pré.

The opening hook should play into the audience's curiosity. You present an intriguing situation and say, "Watch me! You'll be fascinated to see where we're going to take you." For example, as the film *Lotan Baba: The Rolling Sadhu* opens we see an Indian man dressed in red shirt and shorts, with hands and feet bound, rolling over and over very fast along a narrow dirt road. Indian women in vivid saris look on and clap, while a crowd of men smile and laugh in approval. We see this and say to ourselves, "What on earth is happening?" Then the commentary tells us: "This is Lotan Baba and he's going to roll two thousand miles from his village to the shrine of a goddess in northern India." This seems to us an incredible and crazy feat. Why is he doing this? So we are hooked and go on watching.

Sometimes the hook is more gradual. Let us imagine, say, a film that opens with a very serious, middle-aged man dressing up as a woman. In another film a rather prim and proper teenage girl is seen loading her revolver and then shooting at objects in her basement. Immediately we are struck by the strange, even bizarre, quality of these situations. We want to know who the man is and what he is doing. Is he an actor, a transvestite, a spy? And what about the girl? Is she practicing self-defense? Does she want to commit suicide? Is she about to kill her parents? Is she the best revolver shot in the state? What is she going to do?

At this point, the curiosity is piqued, the imagination stimulated. We want answers to our questions, so we decide to stay with the film for a while, but only so long as there is a payoff from the first two or three shots. They had better be leading somewhere interesting. Thus, the core assertion assures us that we are going to be treated to a fascinating topic that we would be utter fools to miss or ignore.

The hook does not have to be as tremendously dramatic as the two just suggested. In fact, sometimes we can play against the very ordinariness of the situation. For instance, a quiet man is seen in a library reading a book. He writes something down and then takes another book from the shelf. Another film opens with a frail woman chatting with a middle-aged Indian woman. Neither of these scenes is visually very interesting; in fact, they are rather boring. But they take on a completely different dimension once we add commentary. Over the visual of the man, the commentary might go as follows: "He plays chess and football. He has a wife and two daughters. Not one person in a thousand would recognize him, yet he has saved millions of lives. His name is Professor Jonas Salk." And the other scene might be accompanied by the following commentary: "She's seventy-five. She lives in two small rooms and earns the equivalent of $2,000 a year. Yet beggars bless her, parliaments have honored her, and presidents carry her picture. Her name is Mother Teresa."

In these cases, most viewers would know that Salk discovered a vaccine against polio and that Mother Teresa was awarded the Nobel Peace Prize for her work with the poor of India. Even if they did not know these things, there would probably be a certain intriguing ring of familiarity about the names, so the core assertion accompanying the opening would not have to do very much. But most times the assertion and the hook have to be well fused and balanced, working hand in hand with one another.

Let's look a little closer at the *core assertion* that sets the film on its way. Sometimes the assertion appears in the form of a statement:

> At first they were heroes, and America worshipped them. Then they were villains and the world abused them. They were the most famous parents the world has ever seen. One fathered the atom bomb, the other created the hydrogen bomb.

Tonight in *A Is for Atom, D Is for Death*, we discuss the careers of Robert Oppenheimer and Edward Teller and what their discoveries mean for the world today.

Obviously, there is a bit of hyperbole in calling them the world's most famous parents—after all, what about Adam and Eve?—but it is the kind of exaggeration that is acceptable in script writing.

In contrast to the above, we find many central statements presented in question form. Using that technique, *A Is for Atom* could have opened this way:

> When they split the atom, they promised a brave new world. Fifty years after Hiroshima, has the promise dimmed? Will nuclear physics bring destruction or deliverance? A new universe or an abandoned planet?

Sometimes you might want to make the opening question deliberately provocative and disturbing: "He came as a prince of peace, yet his followers rampaged, massacred, and destroyed in his name. They said Jesus inspired them, but was that true? Were the Crusades a holy mission or the last barbarian invasion?" These opening sentences, whether statement or question, establish clearly where the film is going. They are the written counterpart of the visual hook, but if the visual hook dangles the promise, then the statement has to guarantee that an hour's viewing will fulfill all expectations.

Below I've set out for you one of the most intriguing openings I've seen recently. It's from Agnieszka Piotrowska's film *The Bigamists* and is a model of concise tantalizing writing.

Debbie's picture	How would you feel if your husband was somebody else's husband?
Will's picture	How would you feel if you were that husband?
Another couple	And why would you ever have four husbands at the same time?
General weddings	Thousands of people get married every year. In Britain two weddings a week are bigamous, entered into illegally with one of the spouses already married.
	Bigamy, which used to be a hanging offense two hundred

years ago, is still considered
a criminal punishable by prison.
Given that divorce is so easy
these days and that it's perfectly
permissible to cohabit without
the blessing of marriage, I
wondered why so many people
still do it.

If you examine these lines carefully, you'll see that Piotrowska has been extremely brief but very very clever with the few lines she's used. First she involves you, the audience, with a very blunt, slap-in-the-face question, "How would *you* feel if *your* husband was also somebody else's husband, or if *you* were that husband?" Immediately she pulls you personally into the film. She then titillates your interest with some amazing facts. "In Britain, two weddings a week are bigamous," and that bigamy used to be a hanging offense. Didn't know that, did you! Having aroused your interest, she then invites you to go on a journey with her when she says, "I wondered why so many people do it." And of course you are by this time wondering the same thing, and want to go with her, especially when she tells you later, "The landscape is full of dark secrets."

If the film is about some charismatic figure, a historical personality, or even a fictional central figure in a sponsored film, it helps to introduce these characters very early and to hint at the conflicts surrounding them. You want to dangle all the goodies in front of the viewer and get their mouths watering over the intrigue and passions that will be presented to them in the next hour.

While revising this book, I was asked by German television to do a film based on the secret diaries of a Nazi war criminal. By chance, both he and the young Hitler lived in the same town, Linz, in Austria. Because of this I wasted a week or so drafting an opening that compared the fate of the two. Then it struck me I was totally blind. A fantastic opening was already there, waiting for me, in the diary pages.

Visual	Audio
Very slow montage of war and victims, death camps and corpses	*Eichmann Prison Memoirs* I have seen hell, and death, and the devil, and the senselessness of destruction. I have seen the horrors of the operation of the machinery of

	death and I have seen those who supervised the work and its execution.
	It was the greatest and most terrible dance of death of all times.
Gradually super photo of Eichmann in his prison cell	NARRATOR: So spoke Adolf Eichmann—SS officer, war criminal, and one of the major figures responsible for the murder of nearly six million Jews in the Second World War. Who was this man?
Title over Eichmann writing in his prison cell: *Eichmann: The Secret Memoirs*	

Here I reckoned the words *hell*, *destruction*, and *terrible dance of death* would intrigue an audience who was immediately told that this man was a central character in the celebrations of the devil. We were in, and we were in fast.

By way of contrast it is interesting to look at the start of *The Day after Trinity*, a life of Robert Oppenheimer directed by Jon Else and written by David and Janet Peoples and Jon Else.

Visual	Audio
Main title over back: *The Day after Trinity*	NARRATOR: In August 1945 the city of Hiroshima was destroyed in about nine seconds by a single atom bomb. The man responsible for building the bomb was a gentle and eloquent physicist named J. Robert Oppenheimer. This is the story of Robert Oppenheimer and the atomic bomb.
Haakon Chevalier reading from a letter	HAAKON CHEVALIER: Stinson Beach, California, August 7, 1945. Dear Oppie: You are probably the most famous man in the world today, and yet I

	am not sure this letter will reach you.
Photograph of Robert Oppenheimer	If it does, I want you to know we are very proud of you. And if it doesn't you will know that anyway. We have been irritated by your reticence these past years.
Blast and fireball from the Trinity atomic test preceding Hiroshima	Under the itchy surface we knew that it was all right; that the work was progressing, that the heart was still there, and the warm being we have known and cherished.
Slow zoom in on Oppenheimer photo	I can understand now, as I could guess then, the somber note in you during our last meetings . . .
Hans Bethe sync	HANS BETHE: You may well ask why people with kind hearts and humanist feelings — why they would go and work on weapons of destruction.
Oppenheimer as a child	NARRATOR: When Robert Oppenheimer was born in 1904, the atomic bomb was not even science fiction. He was educated at the ethical cultural school in New York City, and mastered Harvard's curriculum in three years, summa cum laude.
Oppenheimer at Harvard	He spoke six languages and had difficulty deciding whether to be an architect, a poet, or a scientist. But it was his love of physics which led him to England . . .
Göttingen University	and Germany in the early 1920s, where the atom was beginning to yield its secrets to Einstein, Rutherford, and Bohr.

Here we have a very quiet but effective opening that is also extremely carefully constructed. The first statement beginning "In August 1945" sets forth the basic assertion: we are going to follow the story of the man responsible for building what was, until the early 1950s, the most devastating and destructive weapon in the history of the world. The film could then have proceeded easily with the narration cut that begins, "When Robert Oppenheimer was born in 1904," but it doesn't. There would have been nothing terribly wrong with such a continuation. It's a competent progression that gets you straight into the story of Oppenheimer.

Instead, the filmmaker goes from the opening statement to an excerpt from a letter. Why? Isn't this just a delaying tactic? Not really. The letter is a bold but beautiful touch. It takes us straight to the soul of Oppenheimer and humanizes him; it tells us that the creator of the atomic bomb had feelings, that he could be moved and grieved. Having shown that the man has a soul, Bethe's short comment then poses a question that will haunt us throughout the film. That done, the narration can take over and move the story forward.

One useful device is to start off with a short statement and then add a provocative comment from one of the participants in the film. The comment may be angry, even furious. Sometimes it is defiant. The common element is the passion with which these emotions are expressed. We are touched by people and their passions—whether about marriage, war, suffering, or happiness—and we want to hear more and learn more. *Haunted Heroes*, produced for the BBC by Tony Salmon, offers an excellent example. Its subject is Vietnam veterans who have abandoned society. The opening provides just enough narration to define the subject before the director inserts an interview extract that completely grabs us.

Visuals	Audio
Aerial shots of valleys, lakes, mountains	*Music* NARRATOR: Hidden in the forests and the mountains of the American wilderness are men haunted by the echoes of a forgotten war.
Trees and lakes	Lonely and tortured, they live alone, exiles in their own country.
Steve hacking a tree	Protected from people, they

	survive on skills learnt in the jungles of Vietnam. *Music out* These woods are sanctuary for men like Steve.
Medium shot of Steve	STEVE: I live on a black-and-white level. I live on a life-and-death survival time. And when I'm confronted in a stressful situation, there's always a chance I'll go too far. I generally turn to the woods for peace of mind and to calm down and cool out. I'm not especially afraid of society.
Close shot of Steve	I'm more afraid of what I will do in this society. Basically if you have a knife, some string, and maybe . . .
Steve carrying ferns to shelter	an axe and the clothes you are wearing, that's pretty much all you need. Also pick a place that is secure.
Steve inside shelter	Not only are you not getting wet, but the wind's not hitting you and you have a full view of the area, and if you camouflage properly, nobody can find you.
Title: *Haunted Heroes*	*Music*

In 1980 Robert Kee, a well-known English journalist, appeared in and wrote the commentary for the BBC series *Ireland: A Television History.* The fourth film in the series deals with the great potato famine of nineteenth-century Ireland. The opening is quiet and understated, yet the power of the words and the significance of the events that led to the great Irish migration to the United States make the opening moving and effective.

Visual	**Audio**
A dark Irish landscape. Hills. Valleys. A church bell tolls. Various	ROBERT KEE: A few of the names of Irish men, women,

Irish names are called out.

and children who died in the great famine in Ireland between 1845 and 1849. There were many hundreds of thousands of them altogether.

The names of only very few are known. The vast majority of deaths, perhaps as many as a million, went unrecorded.

Sync: interview with Mrs. Dunleavy

MRS. DUNLEAVY: My mother used to tell us about the famine and all the people that died because there were no potatoes. Well, of course I don't think you'd die if there were no potatoes. I think the English were in some collusion to get rid of the Irish from their lands, you see.

Hills; sun turning dark; clouds sweeping over the land

KEE: As with many great disasters in human affairs, there was no unmistakable signal that this one was at hand. It had been a fine hot summer, but there was a sudden . . .

Rain and lightning

break in the weather at the beginning of August 1845, with showers of sleet, lightning, and heavy rain. Reports from the counties spoke of potato crops of the most abundant yields. Then, on the eleventh of September 1845 . . .

Freeman's journal

SECOND NARRATOR: We regret to state that we have had communications from more than one correspondent announcing what is called "cholera" in potatoes in Ireland, especially in the north.

| Robert Kee to camera | KEE: Why was this such particularly disastrous news for Ireland? Well, because one-third of the entire population of Ireland depended wholly on the potato for survival. The Irish small farmer lived off his potato crop, so that even at the best of times life was a struggle. It had become increasingly a struggle in the past forty years because during that time the population of Ireland had doubled from four to eight million. |

Kee's style is spare and straightforward. He has a strong, emotional story to tell and relates it in an unobtrusive way, letting the events and the facts speak for themselves.

RHYTHM, PACE, AND CLIMAX

A good beginning takes you into a film with a bang, with a sense of expectation. The problem then is how to sustain that interest for the next half hour or hour. A lot of the problem is solved if you have provided yourself with a solid structure for the film. Even so, there will be pitfalls that can be avoided if you have thought a little about *rhythm*, *pace*, and *climax*.

These are obviously not just elements of documentary films, but elements that every writer—whether novelist, playwright, or feature filmmaker—has to worry about. How often have you heard someone say, "Well, the book runs out of steam halfway through," or "It started dragging and then never seemed to end." This complaint of a low, dragging film is, unfortunately, too often made about documentaries, particularly documentaries that are determined to give you every detail of a process, every fact about a person, whether interesting or not.

And the problems occur in the best of films. *Harlan County*, by Barbara Kopple, rightfully won an Academy Award a few years ago. It was a courageous film about a Kentucky miners' strike for a decent contract. The first two-thirds of the film were brilliant, but then it became repetitive, discursive, losing all its energy. Here there was one glaring central problem: the film had a natural ending that Kopple ignored.

The result was that after the natural climax, the film began again in a more boring way and seemed to go on and on forever. Points made earlier in the film were merely repeated in different circumstances without adding very much to the viewer's knowledge. My view is that Kopple, in her obsession with her subject, had ignored or forgotten the basic rules about rhythm, pace, and audience demands.

What do we mean by good rhythm and pace? Quite simply, that a film should have a logical and emotional flow, that its level of intensity should vary, that its conflicts should be clear and rising in strength, that it should hold our interest all the time, and that it should build to a compelling climax. Unfortunately, it is easier to point out the problems than it is to offer all-embracing solutions. Here are just a few of the most common problems:

- Sequences go on too long.
- There is no connection between sequences.
- Too many similar sequences follow one another.
- There are too many action scenes and too few reflective scenes.
- There is no sense of development or logical or emotional order to the sequences.

Are there any hints about rhythm and pace? I can offer just a few, very personal ones. First, get into the film fast. Establish what you are going to do, then do it. Second, build the film with a *variety* of scenes and a gradual *crescendo* of climaxes.

Allan King's *A Married Couple* is an excellent example of a well-paced film. *Couple* deals with three months of a marriage crisis between Billy and Antoinette Edwards. Halfway through the film we see an extended party. Billy is wandering around with a camera, ignoring Antoinette and taking photos. Antoinette is sitting next to the fire and pointedly suggesting to a New York visitor that they could become lovers. The scene sets up a tremendous distance between Billy and his wife. The next scene, however, shows Billy and Antoinette in bed together, with Antoinette weeping on Billy's shoulder. As the audience we imagine her thinking, "Why do I have to do these things, make passes at other men? I really do love my husband." The conjunction of the two scenes is perfect.

The film also illustrates the value of establishing a series of rising climaxes. During the months of shooting, Billy and Antoinette were involved in three or four violent quarrels. In the most vicious of the arguments, which came near the beginning of shooting, Billy basically threw Antoinette out of the house. Though this was the second argument chronologically, it was the most powerful of the four, and King placed it as the climax of the film.

Lotan Baba: The Rolling Sadhu is another useful example to note as regards pace. The film starts, as I've mentioned, with a hook that shows Lotan Baba rolling along a dirt road. The scene is exciting and fast. We then cut to a slow paced scene in Lotan Baba's village that introduces us to Lotan and his background. This then gives way to a fast-paced interior evening scene of prayer in which people are praying, dancing, and whirling around in a semitrance in front of the statue of a goddess. The prayer scene then cuts to morning, where Lotan Baba is seen meditating in silence. The juxtaposition of these four differently paced scenes absolutely grips the attention and projects you beautifully into the main film.

This need for variety between the scenes is a point that bears repetition. We see such variety in feature films, and it is just as important in documentaries. What we need is variety in the types and tempos of the scenes. *Butch Cassidy and the Sundance Kid*, written by William Goldman, was one of the most successful "buddy" movies ever made. Part of the success was due to Goldman's marvelous sense of structure and his masterly sense of variety and tempo. The film is full of sequences of action, pursuit, and gunslinging, but even these get boring. So in the middle, Goldman inserts an idyllic scene of Paul Newman riding his girlfriend around on his bicycle in between the trees, while the music plays "Raindrops Keep Falling on My Head." It's a light, funny scene that allows us to breathe and relax before we return to the chase.

The third hint is to put in a *definite ending* or *resolution*. These words of advice seem obvious but are often ignored. You do so at your peril. Many films, especially crisis films, have natural endings. When the end is not so clear, many documentarists shove in the montage ending, doing a fast recap of the major figures in their film. Sometimes it works, but it usually seems to me a confession of failure. If you have built your script logically, then the ending should be obvious: the completion of the school year, the graduation ceremony, or the medical recovery. If you really have no ending, then I suggest a sequence that is fun and visually striking: the high school dance, the celebrations at the end of the war, the boats arriving, the planes vanishing into the sunset. Finish with a flourish, and let them know the film is over. In *The Chair*, Paul Crumps's execution is waived, and we know the film is finished. In a more open-ended piece like *Best*

Boy, the film concludes with Philly shaving himself. Such an act would have been impossible for Philly when filming commenced a few years earlier, and symbolizes both closure and a new beginning

What do we mean by a good *climax*? Well, just that. The film should give us a sense of finality of completion, of catharsis (to use the old literary term). This seems obvious but isn't, and I've seen documentary after documentary that trail away with no sense of an ending. I know there is a deeper problem here. Life doesn't wrap up easily; not all stories have a neat beginning, middle, and end, and there is a grave danger in implying that it all concluded nicely. The Irish problem goes on and on after we finish our story of the pursuit and capture of the IRA man. The problems in Afghanistan and Bosnia continue after the refugees cross the border or the UN troops arrive. And they don't live happily ever after. I acknowledge all this, but I still insist that the particular story of the film must have a strong sense of conclusion.

All this is easier to write about than it is to do in practice. You are often uncertain about where the climax comes, whether the obvious ending is the best ending, or whether you can spare the time to wrap up the story. In 1993 I made the film *Special Counsel*, a documentary drama about the making of the 1979 peace treaty between Egypt and Israel and the public and private personalities who helped resolve the conflict. There were tremendous battles and conflicts along the path to peace, and in one sense it was very easy just to end the film with the signing of the peace accords on the White House lawn in March 1979.

That provided a very effective ending, but I felt there were still too many questions left unanswered regarding the fate of people and issues mentioned in the film. I therefore added a ten-minute section showing the actual Israeli withdrawal from the Sinai Peninsula and the battles to evict settlers forced to leave under the terms of the treaty. I also showed what happened to the main players of the film: the assassination of Sadat, the election defeat of President Carter, the death of Moshe Dayan, and the award of an honorary doctorate to one of the private but significant participants in the drama. It was a difficult choice, because this section might have been anticlimactic. I think it works because there was both a psychological need for the information and a physical need to cool down after the rush of the great events.

What is the part of the editor in solving all these problems? As I have argued, it is the job of the writer to establish the essential solutions to problems of pace, rhythm, climax, and ending. Obviously, the editor also plays a major part in establishing pace and rhythm. The rhythms and solutions that you, as a writer, put down on paper may not necessarily work when translated into the realities of filming. So, as often happens, the writer, editor, and director must work together to find an answer. However, the writer should not try to avoid tackling the problem in the first place; if you fail to provide the basic skeleton, you end up just dumping the problems in the editor's lap. But the editor must have the initial blueprint, something to react against. With that blueprint in hand, the rest is comparatively easy.

DRAFTS AND CHANGES

The scripts we have considered above are final narration scripts and have to be looked at with a certain amount of care. They look good, but they may have gone through enormous changes since the first draft. Another point to bear in mind is that whereas a text such as that of Kee's on Ireland could largely be written before production, the link narration of a film such as *Heroes* is definitely postproduction. The draft outline of *Heroes* probably only hinted at how it should begin; it may have appeared as follows: (1) We open with a statement about Vietnam veterans living alone in the forests, surviving on skills learned in the war; (2) we then cut to a comment by one of the veterans describing that life and showing us how he lives.

Scripts also change enormously from first to last draft, and tentative beginnings and text may change radically as you search for the perfect film. They may also change tremendously in length, particularly in films on historical subjects. In *Adolf Eichmann: The Secret Memoirs*, my first draft script for the hour-long film was seventy-three pages long. I had put in everything I thought could possibly be in the script. My attitude then, as now, is you can always cut, but it's not so easy to add. The final script—taut, spare, and effective—was twenty-three pages long.

TREATMENTS

A treatment is a simple narrative outline of your film, written when you've completed the research phase. It presents much more information than your sketched-out proposal, but it is not yet as detailed as your shooting script. You are not required to do a treatment, and most of the time you won't bother with them, but they are useful exercises for sorting out your ideas when dealing with long, complex political or historical films. You should also note that very often sponsors will demand to see a treatment after they've given you the go-ahead, and most foundations will ask to see a very detailed treatment once you've completed your initial research phase.

The treatment fleshes out all your first thoughts and is supported by all the ideas we've discussed in the last two chapters. Its length can be anything from an informal few pages to almost book size (required for some proposals for the national endowments). Generally, the purpose of the treatment is to show and illustrate

- The way the story develops your film thesis and conflicts;
- The key sequences;
- Who your main characters are;
- The situations they get caught in;
- The actions they take and the results for them or society;
- The focus at the beginning and the end;
- The main action points, confrontations, and resolutions;
- The sense of overall dramatic buildup and pace.

To illustrate what a really good treatment looks like, I've set out below a few pages from *Perilous Journey.* The treatment was written by Jon Else, for a major foundation grant, and is a description of how he saw the opening film in the series *The Great Depression.*

Synopsis

As we begin in 1914, this film appears to be a fond celebration of the partnership between Henry Ford, his polyglot assembly line workers, and "the great multitude" for whom they make motor cars; but nothing is quite as it seems.

Ford demands extraordinary control over his workers, both on and off the job; the agrarian America liberated by the Model T gives way to an industrial landscape of mammoth factories like Ford's River Rouge works. 1920s American nativism and racism begin to surface; the benevolent capitalist becomes the repressive autocrat and his once meek employees resolve to demand control over their own destiny.

Finally, the center will not hold. The stock market crashes and economic troubles of the 1920s come home to roost. With tens of thousands of auto workers unemployed, the people of Detroit free fall towards the rock bottom of the Great Depression; and we end in March of 1932, when marchers die in a hail of gunfire outside Ford's River Rouge factory.

This tragedy centers on the losing struggle to preserve an impossible past, and on the lost opportunities of an industrial utopia gone sour. It is a story of power and powerlessness. What began with Ford's very real and extraordinary achievements, with optimism and absolute confidence in the American system, ends with rigidity, shattered faith, fear of revolution, and an industrial system in hopeless collapse. Through the eyes of those who manufactured and purchased Ford's cars and trucks, we reveal the nation's hopes, fears, and determination on a journey toward economic disaster, and we see in the wreckage a tiny glimmer of hope for the real potential of America.

Prologue: Series Tease
The film opens with a five- to ten-minute overview of the Great Depression, relying heavily on music, anecdote, and strong visual images, drawing on material from all eight programs. The program will introduce the often-heroic ordinary people who form the backbone of the series, and will give a glimpse of our main series characters: FDR, Joe Louis, Eleanor Roosevelt, La Guardia, Upton Sinclair, Dorothy Healey, and men like Harry Hopkins, "who spent five million dollars in his first two hours on the job, and who put three million people to work in six weeks." We will introduce the major themes, the expansion of democracy and multiculturalism, and we will plant a few "ticking bombs" on the table: Can American democracy survive while dictatorship blossoms around the world? Can government respond to the crisis in time? Will rising awareness of race bring us together or rip us apart?

There will be familiar icons in a new light—"Okies" who turn out to be African Americans, FDR standing with braces, surprising outtakes from Dorothy Lange's *Migrant Mother*, and some extraordinary contrasts in style (President Hoover vs. General Smedley). Most of all, the series tease will alert the audience that this is not the tired, depressing old "Great Depression" they think they know and understand.

Our narration makes it clear that these people on the screen are our parents and grandparents, our own aunts and uncles. In their America, the America of the 1930s, something went terribly wrong ... a bad dream ... a nightmare or plague. Their world, their wonderful new modern industrial world, collapsed on them, and they didn't know why.

Out of work, out of money, out of food, they had nowhere to go and nowhere to turn but to their families, their communities, and the kindness of strangers. No one knew when it would end, or how it would end, or even if it would end. No one knew what to do.

But somehow, in the hardest of times, with America slipping away, our parents and grandparents found it in themselves to fight their way out. They came together in struggle and conquered their fear. Hope drove them to unknown levels of heroism, drove them to take hold of their own destiny, to take hold of their government and make it work for them.

It didn't always turn out exactly right; some people got left out, and there was unfinished business, but by the time it was over they did better than just survive, they invented a new America.

Act 1—Fordism: 1914–1918
Seq. 1: Intro Henry Ford and Model T. Henry Ford is climbing a tree, shinnying right up the birch like a lanky farm boy. These are home movies from the summer of 1914, filmed on a camping trip in the northern Michigan woods with Ford, his family and friends. Ford was born 51 years ago (the same week as the battle of Gettysburg) and he loves the simple, wholesome outdoor life of his farm upbringing as much as he hates big cities, Wall Street, disorder and laziness. This shy, self-educated, pure and simple Yankee mechanic is a devotee of Thoreau, a vegetarian, and father of the Model T automobile.

Henry Ford has set out to "democratize the automobile" (which until now has been a plaything of the rich), and his simple, reliable Model T has gone down, down, and down in price until it now costs less than a team of good horses. We learn from retired farmers just how empowering the humble car is, how it frees the tillers of the land from dreadful isolation and physical labor. We discover from women who grew up on the plains how the Model T expanded their horizons, allowed them to go to school, and how it brought mental health and comfort to their grandmothers' fearful isolation, courtesy of Henry Ford:

> We traded a horse for a Model T automobile . . . there were eight of us brothers and sisters went to school at the same time. But you had to work on the farm, you had your chores to do. To get it all done we *drove* to school; otherwise we would have just stay out there a million miles from nowhere. It was just wonderful. [Else adds in his notes that dialogue is from preinterviews; and pilot interviews, and in several cases is constructed from quotations in books and articles listed in the bibliography —A. R.]

In the old newsreels and publicity films the Fords putt-putt their way through rivers and streams, forests and deserts, and up the steps of half the state capitols in America. We see Model T rodeos, Model T polo, Model T farming, and Model T camping. Henry Ford's motorcar is transforming America and has, almost by accident, made him the richest man in Michigan.

And so this beautifully written treatment goes on for another forty-two pages. It reads like a very picturesque and graphic essay, and at the end one is absolutely clear about the ideas and mood of the film, where it is going, and how it is going to get there. The treatment also contains a bibliography and working notes that support the observations of the film. However, even after all this work, there will still be many changes in emphasis between this treatment and the final script.

PART TWO

Preproduction

9

BUDGET AND CONTRACT

The production contract, the agreement between you and those who are giving you the money to make the film, formalizes the terms under which the film is to be made. It is usually drawn up on the basis of your proposal before the script is written, but many organizations prefer to pay for a script and then, if they like it, commit themselves to the actual production. For the sake of convenience, I am assuming your sponsor is of the first type: that they like the proposal and they want to proceed with the film.

So far, you have probably only discussed money in very vague terms. But now that you are going to sign your life away in a formal agreement, you must carefully budget the film; otherwise, your contract may not provide sufficient money to make a decent film according to the approved script.

In reality, you will have thought about the production budget, at least in a general way, from your first moments in considering the film. But now is the moment of truth. My own procedure is as follows. First, I draw up a detailed production budget, trying to cover all contingencies from which I get a sense of the cost of the film. With that figure in mind I deal with the formal draft production contract, arguing terms and conditions. Because I have a very concrete idea of the needs of the budget, I am now much less likely to make mistakes in the terms I require from the sponsor.

THE BUDGET

In budgeting, we often face a number of conundrums. Do you budget according to script, or do you script according to budget? And how do you prepare a budget, which is normally demanded very early by commissioning editors, when you haven't done the main research? There is no absolute answer to these questions, as the conditions under which you make each film will be different. Only one thing is important: your budget must be as complete and as accurate as possible. This point is more than important; it is vital. If you make a mistake in budgeting, committing yourself to making a film for what turns out to be an unrealistic sum, you're likely to finish up bankrupt. My answer is to put into the budget every single need I can think of and then a few more; I always overbudget rather than underbudget. You may lose a few films if you are bidding in a competitive situation, but it's worth it in the end. A decent budget will save you many a sleepless night.

Below are the major items that appear in most film and video budgets; this list should serve as a good first guide. If something occurs to you that does not appear here, then add it, as you'll probably need it.

    A. Research
       1. Script research, including travel and hotels, books, photocopies, library viewing expenses
       2. General preproduction expenses, including travel, meetings, etc.
    B. Shooting
       1. *Crew*
          Cameraperson
          Assistant cameraperson
          Sound person
          Lighting technician
          Production assistant
          Driver and/or grip
          Production manager
          Makeup artist
          Teleprompter operator

2. *Equipment*
   Camera and usual accessories
   Special camera equipment, such as fast lenses and underwater
   rigs
   Tape recorders and microphones
   Lighting
   Teleprompter
3. *Location expenses*
   Vehicle rental
   Gasoline
   Crew food
   Hotels
   Airfares
   Location shooting fees
4. *Stock*
   Negative film
   Tape cassettes
   Developing film and making work print
   Reels of quarter-inch tape
   Audiocassettes
   Magnetic tape, including quarter-inch transfer
   Leader and spacing

C. Postproduction
   1. *Editing*
      Editor
      Assistant editor
      Sound editor
      Editing room supplies and equipment, including video off-line
   2. *Lab and other expenses*
      Sound coding
      Sound designer
      Music and sound transfers
      Opticals and special effects
      Video window dubs
      Making titles
      Narration recording
      Sound mix
      Negative cutting
      Making optical negative
      First and second answer print

On-line video editing
Release print—theater, television, videocassette dubs, etc.
Making DVDs

3. *General*
Office expenses, rent, telephone, faxes, photocopying, etc.
Transcripts
Music and archive royalties
Errors and omissions (E&O) insurance
Insurance
Legal costs
Dispatch and customs clearance
Voice-overs
Translations
Advertising and publicity
Messengers
Payroll tax provisions

4. *Personnel*
Writer
Director
Producer
Narrator
Associate producer
Researcher
General assistant

D. Sponsor station overheads
E. Company provisions
   1. Contingency
   2. Company profit

Ninety percent of the above items occur in most documentaries. The other 10 percent depend on the size and finances of your production. If the production is small, there may be no associate producer or general assistant, and you may also find that you are not only writing and directing but also doing all the research.

Two notes. First, the crew is normally budgeted per day, and the editor and assistant per week. So your cameraperson might appear in the budget for fourteen days at $300 per day, while your editor would be figured for ten weeks at $1,000 per week. Equipment rental is also budgeted per day. Second, stock, both film and magnetic sound stock, is usually estimated at so-many-cents per foot—for example, twenty thousand feet of film stock 7291 at $0.18 per foot.

Besides the above, a few other items occur from time to time, and they are worth noting in your checklist:

computer graphic images (CGIs)
graphic design
studio use
actors
special wardrobe
special props
donations and presents

Most of the items in both the main and miscellaneous lists are obvious, but others require some explanation because a miscalculation about them can have grave effects on the budget. I have discussed a few of these items below in more detail.

Stock and ratios. It is extremely important to sense at the beginning how much film stock you are likely to require for your shoot. A film that can be preplanned to the last detail and has fairly easy shooting may require a ratio of only five to one—that is, if you want a half-hour final film, you need to shoot only two and one-half hours of film. A more complex film, however, may require a ratio of twelve or fourteen to one, which is fairly standard for major television documentaries. If you are going for verité, emulating the films of Fred Wiseman, Ricky Leacock, or the Maysleses, then you may be in for a shooting ratio of forty or fifty to one.

At the moment of writing, it costs about $350 to produce a twenty-minute work print, so you must be accurate as to what ratio you want to use; otherwise, your budget will be terribly inaccurate. I budget generally on a ratio of ten to one if most of the shooting can be thought out in advance.

If you are doing a videotape documentary, you have far fewer problems, since your forty-minute videotape will cost $30 or less, or $6 for mini-videocassettes, compared with $350 for shooting on film.

Equipment. Some people own their own equipment. I don't, though I share two editing computers and screens with a partner and am thinking of buying a Sony HD camera. Generally I prefer to rent the equipment according to the needs of the particular film; sometimes I might want to film with an Aaton, sometimes with an Eclair. Even if you own your own equipment you should put a cost for it in the budget. This helps you at the end of the year to assess whether the equipment has really paid for itself.

Crew and shooting time. One reason for doing a decent script before shooting is that it helps you predict the shooting time needed. These days the minimum cost for a crew and equipment is somewhere in the region of $1,500 a day. If you want the best cameraperson and the fanciest equipment, your costs may go up to $3,000 a day. If you have underestimated the number of days needed for shooting, you will be spending anywhere from $1,500 to $3,000 out-of-pocket per day. So again, overestimate rather than underestimate.

Be sure that you know exactly what you have agreed with the crew. Is the arrangement for eight, ten, or twelve hours per day? Can you make a buyout arrangement, offering them a flat fee whatever the length of the shooting day? What arrangements have you made about travel time? Is the crew to be paid anything on their days off when they are forced to be away from home? Do you have to deal with a union? What are you paying for a location scout? These questions must be resolved; otherwise, you will think you are paying one rate, but you will end up with an unexpectedly inflated bill at the end of the day.

The trouble is that you are dealing with a lot of imponderables. The only useful guideline, then, is to err on the generous side. This is also true about editing, as it is often impossible to say whether the editing will take eight weeks or ten.

One way around some of these problems is to agree with the sponsor on the number of shooting days and editing weeks and get them to pay extra if it goes over. This approach is discussed at greater length in the section on the production contract.

CGIs. Computer graphic images are being employed more and more in documentary films, particularly in docudramas and films dealing with history. I don't particularly like CGIs, but many commissioning editors have fallen in love with this new technology. That's fine, but you must note that CGIs are very expensive, so budget accordingly.

Graphic design. It is also becoming more and more fashionable to employ some fancy graphic designs in your credits or in the film itself to jazz up your film. In the past this was frowned upon by purists. Today the attitude seems to be "what works in James Bond films can work for us." Used wisely, there is no doubt that good graphic designs can enhance a film, and here I would refer readers back to Agnieszka Piotrowska's fascinating film *The Bigamists*, which I discussed in previous chapters. But graphics are expensive. So be warned!

Mixing film and video. What is becoming increasingly common is to shoot on film and then transfer to video for the initial editing process. If you plan to do this, you must be sure your budget covers all the transfer work.

Royalties. Royalty payments may be necessary for the use of recorded library music, certain photographs, and film archives. Most of the time that you use ready-made recordings you will have to pay a fee to the company that made the recording. The fee is usually based on the length of the selection you use, the geographic areas where the film will be shown, and the type of audience for whom the film is intended. The rate for theatrical use or commercial television use is usually higher than that for educational purposes. Occasionally, you may be able to arrange the free use of a piece of music if the film is for public service purposes.

If you are unsure of the final use of the film, it's best to negotiate the rights you want and fix a sum that will be payable if you alter the use. My policy is to get everything fixed in one go before the film is made; if you try to negotiate later and the seller knows you badly want the rights, you may be in a bad bargaining position. In other words, make a provisional clearance that will stand you in good stead if you need it.

The position with photographs is slightly different. If the photographs are not in the public domain, you will have to make an arrangement with each individual photographer. Newspapers are usually fairly good at letting you use photographs for a small fee, whereas individual photographers will be much more expensive. It makes sense to hunt around for options on different photographs or to find photographs in the public domain. The extra trouble may save considerable sums later.

The main thing is that you must obtain permission before use. I know that many people don't, pinching from everybody and paying nothing. It seems a stupid policy, one that ultimately works against the film and the director. On the one hand, you lay yourself open to a lawsuit, and on the other, you may find that a television station will not accept a film unless you can produce written permissions.

Most of the above comments also apply to stock footage or film archive rights. Like music and photos, the cost of the rights will vary according to the purpose and destination of the film. A few years ago most archive rights were comparatively cheap; battle footage from World War II could be had for a few dollars a foot. Today, though, film archives have turned into big business, demanding immense sums for archival clips. It is not unusual to find an archive asking $50 to $60 for a final used foot; this figure translates to $100 for three seconds in a completed film or $2,000 to $3,000 per minute of screen time. Thus, if your film deals with history or a well-known personality, you may have to budget a huge sum to cover archive rights. In a film I did about World War II for a New York educational television station, our archive payments came to more than $30,000.

Part of the answer is to hunt for film in the public domain, such as film held by the National Archives. Where this is not possible, and where people are not willing to charge you nominal sums because your film idea is so great, you just have to budget adequately.

Even though archives usually publish a price per foot at which you can obtain their material, you may find it expedient to talk personally with the management. If management particularly likes your film, it may arrange for you to have the rights at a reduced cost. Sometimes the management will acknowledge that students aren't millionaires or big television corporations and will make allowances. It doesn't always work, but it's worth a try.

In negotiating use of rights, you must remember that price varies according to territories demanded and length of use. Thus the price for rights for the United States alone and for three years will probably be less than for worldwide rights for ten years. You must also consider final use. Do you want rights merely for television, or also for cinemas, home videos, educational purposes, DVDs, and so on. The rule is to make sure you've acquired the rights for what you need.

Having said that, I should mention there has been a growing rebellion against the exorbitant costs being demanded these days for rights. This rebellion has been translated into action by academics such as Pat Aufderheide who argue that in many cases payment for rights is unnecessary. The basis for their argument is the evolution of a legal doctrine called "fair use." The terrain as yet is rocky and unclear. For more on what is happening in regard to copyright, and when and when not to pay, I would strongly recommend Michael Donaldson's excellent book *Clearance and Copyright.*

Errors and omissions insurance. Errors and omissions insurance, or E&O insurance, as it is generally called, is basically insures the filmmaker against being sued for breach of copyright or for libel or slander of someone in the film. It provides payment for a legal defense against a court action. However, it is very expensive and can cost between $5,000 and $8,000 to purchase for a one-hour film. While the need for E&O insurance is usually ignored in films made for Europe, it will be demanded by all U.S. and Canadian broadcasters in coproductions and in film purchases. The way out of this expensive demand is to try to get the big coproducer to foot this bill. Sometimes this works. Sometimes it doesn't, but there is no harm in asking. For those interested, there is a very good discussion of the whole nature of E&O insurance in Michael Donaldson's book cited above.

General insurance. We have insurance because of Murphy's law: what can go wrong will go wrong. Having insurance helps you face chaos and catastrophe with a certain equanimity. Insurance should cover equipment, film, crew, properties, and third-party risk. It should also cover office and equipment, errors and omissions, and general liability. Within reason, your coverage should be as wide as possible. You should insure the film during the shooting and up to the striking of a master negative, paying particular attention to faulty equipment and damage arising during processing. The usual compensation covers the cost of reshooting.

However, insurance will not cover faulty original film stock. Therefore, be absolutely certain to test your stock before shooting. Nor will insurance cover damage and fogging by airport X-rays. This is a severe hazard these days, and insurance used to be available. Unfortunately, most companies have now deleted such coverage. The only answer is to have the film hand checked (not always possible) and/or carry the film in lead-lined bags. Most airport authorities seem to be more aware these days of the dangers of X-rays to film stock, and most machines state that they are safe for film up to 1000 ASA. That may be so, but my heart always trembles until I see a processed film without damage.

Sometimes you may need bad weather coverage, but cost can be exorbitant. Usually I don't bother.

I always insure sets and properties as well as film equipment. I don't insure crews unless we are going on an overseas assignment. I also cover third-party risk in case the filming damages any property or any person. I didn't do this until one day my lights melted a plastic roof and almost set a school on fire. That was the only lesson I needed.

It is possible to be too cautious and find yourself paying out enormous sums for risks that are hardly likely to occur except in someone's imagination. You can usually safeguard against this by going to a reliable specialist film-insurance broker.

Most insurance companies these days are unwilling to insure one individual film, preferring to work only on a yearly basis. The answer is a cooperative in which the insurance costs can be shared among various friends who between them will have several films going during the year.

Translations. Though you will probably be making your original film in English, you may sometimes find you are also involved in shooting abroad and interviewing in a foreign language. If you think this is indeed a possibility, then you have to allow for translation services in your budget. You may also want to make foreign translations of the total film for sale to foreign countries. This too has to find a place in your costing.

Advertising and publicity. What filmmakers often forget is to allow for postproduction advertising and publicity. The completion of the film itself is only part of the process. Later you will want to enter it into film festivals, make advertising and publicity brochures and posters, and take the film to various film markets. All this requires money, so make sure that an allowance for such items appears in the budget.

Legal matters. At some point in your film, either in the negotiations with the sponsor or later, you may need to seek legal advice. This becomes particularly important if you are negotiating a split distribution deal or foreign sales. You may also need advice on the basic contract between yourself and the sponsor, even if there seem to be few complications. It is therefore advisable to allow at least a token sum for this in the budget. Under the same argument, you may wish to write in a sum to cover bookkeeping costs.

Whether you do the contract yourself or use a lawyer there are two or three key commonsense points worth keeping in mind as background before entering into the contract.

- Check who you are dealing with and research their reputation. This is of particular importance when dealing with distributors.
- Make sure you have a clear chain of title to all intellectual property.
- Make sure you understand the contract and the meaning of terms and conditions like *net profit.*
- Try to limit your representations and promises. A television station will try to make you warrant that your soul is pure. Try and add the phrase "to the best of my knowledge" if you can get away with it.

Personnel. Payments to the writer, director, and producer usually appear as lump sums, though the director may also be paid by the week. What should they be paid? There is no fixed rule, though many people pay the writer about 5 percent of the overall budget and the director about 12 percent. A lot depends on the bargaining position of the parties. If the writer is a member of the Writers Guild, then you will have to pay at least union scale, and the same is true if the director is a member of the Directors Guild of America (DGA). The situation becomes complicated if you want a DGA director, as you may have to sign a contract with the directors union and also employ a DGA assistant.

Payment to the narrator varies according to his or her fame and bargaining power. A half-hour narration might be as low as a few hundred dollars or as high as a few thousand. If you want the best or the most well known, then you have to pay accordingly. If you have a really prestigious public service film, you may be able to get a "personality" to do your narration for free or for a token sum donated to charity.

General overheads. Overhead can amount to a surprisingly high proportion of your costs, and adequate allowance should be made for it in the budget. Thus, you must think about office rent, telephone bills, administrative help, transcripts, messengers, duplicating services, and any general help you will need. If you are shooting abroad, you must add not only general travel costs for the crew but also possible costs for film dispatch and customs clearance. Even if you bring the film back home by yourself, the customs authorities may require an agent to clear it with them. So that's another item on your list.

Station overheads. If you begin working with a PBS station to back your film, many will want to add an overhead of 21 percent or more to the budget. This theoretically is for all the help and publicity they will give you. However, the catch is that they will also usually charge you for room space, editing, and so on. So try to find out what you are getting for that 21 percent. It is an awfully big chunk of the budget, which you will do most of the work raising, so see if you can lower it.

Contingencies. However well you budget, you may find that the film costs are running away with you. The usual problems are that you need more shooting days than you thought or that the editing goes on longer than you reckoned. But the problem can be something else entirely. A few years ago, for instance, the Hunt brothers tried to corner the world's supplies of silver, and for a few months the price of silver rose astronomically. As a direct result, film stock prices also suddenly rose. This meant that contracts signed before the rise did not adequately cover the real price of stock.

The contingency element in your budget shields you from the unexpected; it's a hedge against overruns. I usually budget about 7.5 percent of the total budget as contingency. This sometimes leads to arguments with sponsors who fail to see why a budget cannot be 100 percent accurate. In that case, I usually omit the contingency but specify in my contract with the sponsors a fixed number of shooting days and a fixed amount of stock. If more time or more stock is needed, then I get the sponsors to pay for these items.

Obviously, you have to use a certain amount of common sense and discretion in all this. It's no use arguing your rights, feeling your position is totally justified, and then losing the contract. This means that the contingency sometimes becomes mostly a matter for internal consideration: you budget and then add the 7.5 percent to see what a really comfortable budget should be. You then know both the preferred and the bare-bones cost for the film.

Profit margins. Should you put in a figure for company profit, and if so what should it be? People, and sponsors in particular, have a funny attitude on this score. They reckon that if you are the writer, director, and producer, then you should be satisfied for the amounts paid in these roles and should not ask for a company fee. This is nonsense and applies to no other business. If I run a garage, which is mine but registered in a company name, I expect both to be paid as manager and for the company to make a profit. The same reasoning is absolutely true in filmmaking. You may spend half a year making a film and the other half writing scripts, chasing down other projects, and trying to get various ideas off the ground. Meanwhile, rent has to be paid, taxes accounted for, and electricity and telephone bills settled. It is only the company profit element written into your film that allows you to exist the other half of the year.

That answers the first part of the question, but what should the profit margin be? This is hard to answer, but 15 percent is certainly within reason. However, that 15 percent is taken on the total budget without the contingency. Similarly, the contingency is taken on the original budget without the profit margin.

Videotape. There are a few differences, most of them fairly obvious, between the budget for a film and for a videotape. Clearly, stock costs are different, and items such as developing and printing will disappear. Major budget differences appear in postproduction. On some things you will save—no negative cut, no first answer print—but other costs can be exorbitant. On-line editing, cost of a Betacam or one-inch work, and special effects can be very expensive, so check those elements thoroughly before signing on the dotted line.

Budget example. Up until now, I have tried to provide you with a broad overall view of what to expect and what to put in a film budget.

However, in order to let you see how this works in practice, I've set out a detailed budget in the appendix. This was the estimate for a major network film, *Peace Process*, with everything budgeted down to the last dollar.

THE PRODUCTION CONTRACT

Once you have done a realistic budget breakdown, you are in a good position to negotiate or finalize your contract with the sponsor. You may have made an informal agreement with them, but it's better to have a short memorandum in writing that records the basic terms of the agreement. This is much safer in the long run. It's also wise to exchange contracts before you begin shooting, though a surprisingly large number of people plunge into the film on the assurance of a mere handshake. I wouldn't unless I knew the sponsor extremely well or if there were some compelling reason for starting in a rush, such as a necessary but onetime film event. And remember one essential rule: this is a negotiation process, and you get what you bargain for.

As I mentioned earlier, you may be dealing with the production contract before script or after script. The contract may run to three pages or thirty, but in reality there are only a few points to consider, with all the rest being elaboration. I have set out below the main elements of most contracts and have tried to bring to your attention some of the points that you should consider in detail.

Definition of length and purpose. The contract will generally define in its first few paragraphs the kind of film you are doing, its object, its maximum length, and the gauge in which it is being shot. So it may read, "This is a one-hour, 16mm color film on the treatment of deafness for use in specialist schools," or it may say, "This is a half-hour videotape on frog jumping for educational television." These first few paragraphs may be surrounded by *whereas* and *wherefore*, but that's just legal jargon that you need not worry about. The main thing is that you understand clearly what you are contracting to deliver.

Time and manner of delivery. The sponsor will try to get you to commit to a specific delivery date. Here you have to be careful because of the immense number of things that can go wrong and cause you to miss the deadline. I prefer to put in a definition of intent rather than commitment: "The filmmaker will endeavor to deliver the film by such and such a date," or "The filmmaker understands that the film is due for presentation on July 15, 2008." Avoid being penalized for late delivery. This is important, since even with the best intentions in the world, there may still be delays. Normally, the sponsor understands why the film is delayed and is sympathetic, but not always. So watch out.

The contract may also specify how many prints are to be delivered. I usually designate one, with any others to be paid for by the sponsor. I also ask for the sponsor to pay for the combined reversal internegative (CRI, used in making multiple prints).

If you are doing a videotape, the sponsor will probably require not just a VHS but a number of Beta masters and DVDs. You should also double-check whether copies have to be delivered in any foreign formats, such as PAL or SECAM, if you are working in the States.

In some contracts, the sponsor asks for all the rushes, original tapes, and negative to be handed over at the conclusion of the film. This is fine in most cases, but if you have film that may be valuable in the future as stock footage, try to hang on to the negative.

Personal responsibility. Some contracts may demand that certain people do specific jobs; this usually concerns the writer and the director. The clause is fair enough, especially when the film is the very special baby of one of those two. However, you should allow yourself an escape hatch in case of unforeseeable factors such as illness.

Film cost and payment schedule. The agreement should state clearly both the overall sum that the sponsors will pay for the film and the times of payment. In most cases, payment will be made in stages, and you should try to ensure that those payments come at convenient times. A typical payment schedule on a $100,000 film might look like this:

1. $10,000 on signing the contract
2. $10,000 on script approval
3. $30,000 on commencement of shooting
4. $20,000 when shooting is completed and editing starts
5. $10,000 on approval of fine cut
6. $10,000 on completion of mix
7. $10,000 on delivery of print

Sometimes the number of stages is reduced to only three or four, which might be (1) signing contract, (2) commencing shooting, (3) approval of rough cut, and (4) delivery.

One vital matter is to try to get the contract signed and some money paid before stage 2 script approval. Unless you do this, the sponsor can hold you over the barrel with its approval, asking for more and more script changes before you have even signed a contract. This means, in practice, that you are doing a tremendous amount of work without any formal guarantee or agreement, and the tension will drive you crazy. Here I talk from bitter experiences, having suffered through six drafts of a 110-page script for German television before the contract was signed. A good rule is first the signatures and then the work.

There is, of course, a rationale behind the timing of the payments: you should have all the necessary money at hand when you need it. Your big costs are going to be shooting and editing, so you need money in advance to cover these stages. You also need money for your own salary and living expenses; thus, I like to receive about 20 percent by the time the script is approved.

One common bugbear is the sponsor who procrastinates on approvals. This can happen on approval of the fine cut or of the final narration. Unless you are careful you can find yourself in an exasperating situation, waiting weeks for payments while the sponsor plays around with small changes. One way around this is to put in specific dates as well as film benchmarks for payment. Thus, you could specify $10,000 payment on approval of the fine cut or on February 5, whichever comes earlier. The sponsor may or may not agree with this point, but it's worth battling for.

Can you ask for extra payments besides the principal sum? No. The contract usually stipulates a total fee for the delivery of the film, and once that sum is on paper, that's it—thus the importance, as I have stressed before, of very accurate budgeting.

If I am doubtful about the number of shooting days or if the sponsor argues for the inclusion of something that I am not sure about, I try to put in a clause covering additional payments. The clause might read, "The sponsor (the television station) will pay for any additional days shooting at the rate of $1,000 per day and will also pay for any film stock used on that day at cost." I am not fond of this kind of additional clause, and neither is the sponsor. But sometimes it may be the only way to safeguard your neck and your pocket.

For videotapes, you have to watch very carefully to see if the sponsor wants you to employ all sorts of cute video and CGI effects. They may, as I have mentioned, turn out to be horrendously expensive, and you want to be sure your contractual sum covers this. If you think the sponsor may suddenly dump on you the idea of high-cost digital-video effects (DVEs) when you are nearing the end of the film, then protect yourself with an item regarding extra payments.

Approvals. The contract should stipulate someone who can act as the sponsor's agent and give approval at various stages of the film.

Try to make sure that this is someone who understands the film and whose judgment you value. In most cases, the person giving the approval is the person with whom you have been dealing from the first discussions of the film, but not always. Sometimes the sponsor decides that some top executive has to give approval. From then on it's all a matter of luck. Get somebody who is intelligent and sympathetic and understands a little about film, and you're home free. Get the opposite—and it happens—and you're in trouble. So keep your fingers crossed, or better, insist that the person giving approval is someone you know.

Insurance. I have listed insurance as an item in the film budget itself and one of the responsibilities that you, as filmmaker, have to take care of. Sometimes, however, you can get the sponsor to take care of both general and E&O insurance or at least to share responsibility. Many companies and television stations have insurance policies that may cover your filming. Your task is then to make sure the company includes your film on their insurance list. Even if that is not the case, the sponsor may have so much at stake in your film that it will take out insurance on the film itself, up to the making of the master. This will still leave you to insure crew and equipment, but it will save you quite a lot of money.

Ownership. The best position is for you to try to own the film. You need to establish from the start what rights you have in the film, and ultimate ownership is best. Contrariwise, the television station will usually try to ensure that it owns the film because, of course, it's worth money. Even though you are the contracted producer-director, you may be able to argue that the sponsor should share eventual ownership with you. There are also questions of ancillary rights and extra payments for foreign sales. The DGA, for example, has stringent clauses regarding residuals that directors must receive on certain distribution deals relating to their films.

If you enter into a coproduction deal with a PBS station, then the station itself will probably have a standard contract. This usually calls for joint raising of production funds, for an equal share of the profits, and for each PBS member station to show the film four times within three years.

Miscellaneous contract clauses. The above items take care of the most important points, but there is no limit to the things people will dream up to put into a contract. So what else can arise?

Contracts are drawn up by lawyers who try to protect their clients from every catastrophe, real or imagined. Their answer is to put in the necessary, the unnecessary, and then some. There may be a discussion of publicity. You may be asked to take stills. You may be requested to refrain from immoral conduct. You may be asked not to hold yourself out as an agent of the sponsor. You may be told that though the film is being made and edited in England, it will be governed by U.S. law. You may be told that all notices to the sponsor have to be written in red ink and hand delivered to the office before ten o'clock in the morning.

I have already stressed the points that are vital for you, the film-maker. As for anything else the lawyers write in to the contract, look it over carefully and try not to laugh at the more nonsensical points. Then use common sense. If you feel that an obligation is unfair, reject it. You may have to explain your objection at some length, but don't accept the clause just because someone has written it in.

Remember one thing. At this point the sponsors want you to make the film as much as you do, so don't be afraid of arguing controversial points with them and looking after your own position. If you don't, no one else will.

Finally, if a lot of money is involved and you feel uneasy about your obligations or uncertain as to what you are really committing to, get yourself a lawyer—not one who merely sells real estate, but one who understands something about the entertainment business. It's costly, but the advice will probably pay for itself in the end.

Coproduction and distribution contracts. You are likely to encounter both of these kinds of contracts as your film career progresses. Both involve special issues that are outside the scope of this book and are issues on which, for self-protection, you should seek the advice of a film lawyer or very experienced producer.

10

PREPRODUCTION SURVEY

Once you have signed the production contract, you are ready to begin the film. You are now in for a period of work that can take anywhere from two months to a year or more and that falls into three distinct sections: preproduction, production, and postproduction. This chapter deals with the problems and tasks you are likely to encounter during the preproduction phase and all the arrangements you have to make before shooting. It assumes the outline or script has been approved and you can move into action. This is a tremendously important period. Time and effort invested here in coherent planning, which is the essence of preproduction, pays off immensely when you come to the actual shooting.

During preproduction you have to attend to the following matters:

reviewing people and location
selecting the crew
selecting equipment
drawing up the shooting schedule
obtaining permissions
dealing with problems of foreign locations

Preproduction is also a good period to look a few more times at the outline or the script. When you began writing it, your key consideration was that it be accepted by the sponsor; you are now beyond that stage, and you should probably reconsider the script as a plan of action. Preproduction is a useful time to stand back and ask yourself, "Does it really say something? Does it have vision? Conflict? Interesting characters? Does it have a point of view? Are the main ideas still valid?" This questioning is not a once-and-for-all process. It should be something that goes on (at least subconsciously) through all the film stages. But the preproduction period is an especially good time to do this because you can still change a lot of things, whereas once you start filming such changes become much harder and more expensive.

REVIEWING PEOPLE AND LOCATION

During preproduction, try to revisit all the filming locations and talk once more to the main people who will appear in the film. The location review (on which I often take the cameraperson) helps, first of all, to refamiliarize you with the subject matter. A few months may have passed since you did the scouting and research, and things may have changed. The review also helps you sort out practical questions, such as parking and security. You are also now looking at locations from a slightly different perspective, with a director's eye rather than a writer's eye. What will be the best shots? From which direction does the sun come up? Should you plan to shoot that building in the morning when it's in shade or in the afternoon when it's sunlit? What is the sound situation like? Do the rooms echo or reverberate? Is there exterior sound interference from noisy traffic or schools getting out?

This is also a time to meet again with your key film participants and anyone else who is going to help you. The meetings serve both a psychological and practical purpose. First, it may be beneficial to talk over the film in a little more detail with your on-camera interviewees and explain to them what you want to do. It's a time to put their minds at rest about how difficult it will all be and about how much their lives will be disturbed. This is also a time to get to know them better: to explore who they are, what they will say, how they might appear on camera, and if anything new and important has happened to them since you last met. You should also work on establishing a real trust between yourself and the participants or the interviewees. I cannot stress enough how important this is; it has always seemed to me that documentary directing is more about trust than about finding the right camera positions. You should also use this time to examine scheduling possibilities. When are your participants free? When do they do those particular operations at the hospital? When do the main business meetings take place? What is the actual date of the school graduation? Whom should you contact when you come to film? How many days in advance should you notify that contact person?

One particular point that calls for your attention is future lighting options. For example, it was only while doing a preproduction recce that I noticed that the hospital where I wanted to film used electrical outlets totally different from those normally used. Had that been overlooked, we would have been in serious trouble. Remember to check how much power is available and how accessible it is.

SELECTING THE CREW

A tremendous amount of any film's success depends on the selection of the crew. Pick the right crew for the job and you start with a tremendous plus. Select the wrong crew and you're headed for disaster. You need to consider three factors in selecting your crew: size, function, and temperament.

Size

Should you use a large or a small crew? My own preference is for the smallest crew possible, at least when shooting intimate human situations. A large crew can get in the way of the subject matter, distancing people and disrupting privacy and human connections. Most people are tremendously wary of filmmakers. So, when you come into someone's home asking questions of a personal or painful nature, the fewer people around the better.

What is "a few"? I would say director, cameraperson, assistant cameraperson, and sound person. Often, in intimate situations you can get the assistant cameraperson to do lights. If that's impossible, then an electrician or gaffer can complete the crew. If you really want to cut down the crew, then you as director can handle the sound. Similarly, the director can take over the job of production manager and the driving can be shared. If that's impossible, the production manager and driver should keep their distance during the filming.

Very often, in these days of excellent mini digital video cameras, I do some of the preliminary shooting myself, with just one extra person to do sound. In that way, I can do an initial advertising promo for the film very cheaply. But when we get into full production I simply try and get the best cameraperson I can.

Obviously, cutting the size of the crew doesn't always make sense. If you have a big production job, with a lot of organization and on-the-spot problems, you will probably need to add a production manager, general assistant, grip, perhaps an extra electrician, and a driver.

One thing to sort out right at the beginning of the film is whether it is being done with a union or nonunion crew. Sometimes you may have an option, but if you are doing your film for television or within a television station, you may not have the option. If you are doing the film with a union crew, then you must familiarize yourself with the appropriate union rules. These cover working procedures, hours, breaks, food allowances, and the like. They also often cover travel conditions, such as first-class seating for flights over a certain distance.

If you are acting as producer, then the choice of the crew will be in your hands. If you are director, with a producer over you, you must make sure that the crew is selected, as far as possible, according to your directions and instructions. Here the battle is often for a crew of the right size, with the producer trying to save money by giving you an inadequately small crew or low-cost personnel who are not equal to the job.

Function

Naturally, you want the best people for the crew, with scope and responsibilities for each job clearly defined. I try to work again and again with the same people whose work I know and trust, but this can't always be done. When you are taking on unknown personnel, try to check them out with people who have worked with them. Try to find out both the professional factors and the human factors. Can they do their jobs not just competently but creatively? What are they like under stress? What are their best points and their faults? If I am taking on a new cameraperson, I want to see examples of previous work and talk to other directors who have worked with him or her. And invariably I will want to sit and chat with the prospective camerapeople to get my own overall impression before committing myself.

Problems with personnel have occurred when I have worked for television companies and have had to accept staff camerapeople. Sometimes they have been terrific, but a few times I have had camerapeople who were bored, burned out, and just waiting for retirement. In those cases, the film suffered by having to use someone who was uninterested in the film and the job.

The functions of the different personnel are usually well delineated. The *sound person* looks after the sound quality of the location recordings. He or she needs to be an expert on equipment and microphones and also a person of taste and sensibility, with a sensitive ear for what is being recorded.

The *assistant cameraperson* is usually picked by the principal cameraperson, since the two must work closely. Among other things, the assistant will check equipment, lenses, and filters; will change magazines and keep the camera clean; and will generally set up and carry the equipment. As the key assistant to the cameraperson, he or she will often act as focus changer on difficult scenes and will assist with lights on a small shoot.

The *electrician*, or *gaffer*, is in charge of the lights, a job that carries both heavy artistic and technical responsibilities. Although it is the job of the cameraperson to define the lighting style, on a documentary film the gaffer often has considerable leeway for decisions. Gaffers may be told specifically what lights to rig and where, but they may also be told very vaguely, "Key light from here, back light from there," and be on their own to carry out the job. Besides being experts in lighting styles, gaffers must also know everything about kinds of lights and their maintenance and about electrical systems. Does the small house have an adequate power supply? Should a special electrical board be brought in for the filming? What will the use of twenty-five kilowatts of electricity do to the stage lights in the concert hall?

Besides letting the cameraperson choose the assistant cameraperson, I also consult with him or her on the choice of a gaffer. The two will be working hand in hand, and if the gaffer knows the cameraperson's style and method of work, that's a great help to the production.

The *grip* is the muscle of the group, with the task of helping with all the heavy jobs. Grips may carry equipment, help with the lights, or drive. They handle the odd jobs and may be called on to help in many undefined capacities. On a small production, the assistant cameraperson may also function as a grip; on a larger production, that will be a separate job.

I rarely take a production manager (or PM) on a small shoot; instead, I do most of those jobs myself. But when the job is quite arduous I do take a PM—if the budget allows it and if the extra person doesn't disturb the shooting. The PM is the general manager of the shoot. Together with the director, he or she draws up the shooting schedule and points out any problems that may be involved in the plan. The PM will handle advance preparations; take care of travel, hotels, and food; and look after the money. One of the tasks of the PM is to spot impending difficulties and to troubleshoot when they happen. The PM goes into action when the camera breaks down, when the rental company doesn't have the right van, when officials get difficult, and when the spare stock fails to arrive. Obviously, the PM should be someone who is highly intelligent, organized, and fast—a man or woman of action. These super people do exist, and they are worth their weight in gold.

Choosing the right cameraperson is your most important crew-selection decision. Though the film's success depends on many people, the cameraperson's work is crucial. Together with the director, he or she is responsible for shot selection, lighting style, and all the camera movements. It goes without saying that the cameraperson has to have a creative eye. But he or she also needs to have fast reactions for news- or verité-style shooting and the strength to carry and use a heavy shoulder camera if there will be extensive handheld shooting.

In recent years films have often credited the "cameraperson director," and some of the best documentaries have been made by this double-functioned personality. But is the combination of cameraperson and director good policy? In some films it not only makes sense but also may be the only way to get the film made. This is particularly true of cinema verité and observational cinema. On *Salesman*, Al Maysles had to be both director and cameraperson, and the same was true when Jon Else shot his film about the DeBolt family of California. I prefer, however, except as I have said in preliminary shooting, to have the two jobs done by different people. When a cameraperson's eye is on the lens, he or she cannot usually be aware of all the nuances in a situation. The director has more distance, is less involved, and can be more aware of the overall scene rather than the particular detail. The director can also listen more carefully and see how the conversation is going to affect action.

I don't believe that there is one ideal cameraperson, but I do believe that there is an ideal person for each film. However, the cameraperson who is ideal for film A may be disastrously wrong for film B. It's all a question of style and situation. Some years back I shot a film on art and artists. We had ample shooting time and a very controllable film situation. We also had a heavy lighting job. For the lighting cameraperson I chose a friend of mine called Robert. Bob was marvelous at composition, provided he had plenty of time, and he was also an artist with light. Exactly what I needed. Six months later I shot a sports film and Bob was the last person I thought of contacting. On the sports film

I needed someone who was fast and decisive, someone with both news and verité experience, someone who would essentially be picking the shots without my help. Although he was a superb cameraperson, Bob just didn't have the skills or the temperament for that situation.

More than any other crew relationship, the director-cameraperson relationship is that of partnership. Together they will plan the style of the film, and once the filming starts they become almost inseparable. Sometimes there will be difficulties and divisions of opinion between the director and cameraperson (more on that later when we discuss directing), but the more the two understand each other, the better the film will be.

One last point: it makes sense to take the cameraperson on a location scout before filming starts. The cameraperson's eye will be able to spot production difficulties, and he or she will also be able to advise you on the kind and amount of lighting you need for the shoot.

The *producer* is the head of the overall film team, but not usually a member of the crew. His or her function is to raise money for the production, get it off the ground, and look after the business side of things. All of this is discussed in detail in chapter 23, "Staying Alive."

Temperament

Making a film tends to be an all-consuming operation, at least during the shooting. For many people, nothing else exists during that period except the film itself and the other members of the crew. Although this is particularly true for features, it also describes the conditions on many documentaries. During filming, whether for one week or seven, whether in New York or New Guinea, your crew tends to become your family. Therefore, when you choose your crew, it is worthwhile to look at their temperament as well as their skills. I always hope that the filming will be interesting and fun, and I want people to join me on the crew who share that attitude.

Often the filming is done under tremendous pressure, in frightful conditions, and far away from home. All that tends to bring out both the best and the worst in people, so you should look for people in whom the first comes out and not the second. I am generally wary of morose, silent types, however good their professional skills. On location, I want someone with me who is cheerful and bright and has at least an elementary sense of humor. I don't necessarily need someone who is going to be my bosom friend for life, but I do prefer people with whom I can comfortably relax and have a drink at the end of a difficult day.

Though I think informality is necessary among small crews, it is also extremely important that there be a clear working structure, that everybody knows what they have to do and when, and that the ultimate decisions are made by you, the director. You are the leader, and this is something that should never be forgotten. As leader and director, you have to exercise patience, sanity, and equanimity as you make sure that your team is pulling together as a group.

One thing that is always interesting to see is how the separate individuals gradually bond into a cohesive team. That usually happens on the third or the fourth day of shooting, or after some mishap has been solved and can be laughed at. When that bond comes, the film stops being just work and becomes a real pleasure.

Sometimes, however, even with the best-selected crews, tension suddenly arises. And it can happen for all sorts of silly reasons, such as one member of the crew feeling that a second isn't pulling his or her weight. Once you become aware of that tension, it needs to be settled immediately, or it festers. Usually a private talk will do the trick; if not, try to get the matter out into the open, discussed, and assigned to the past.

SELECTING EQUIPMENT

Although this is not a book about equipment, it is a subject with which every director must deal, so a few short notes are appropriate. Equipment choice should be a matter for crew discussion rather than the sole decision of the director. The function of the director is to tell the crew all he or she can about the film's style, shape, difficulties, and objectives, and then make decisions about equipment with them. The goal should be to use the simplest but most effective equipment compatible with the nature of the film and the size of the budget.

In selecting a camera, you need to discuss whether your shooting is basically static or mobile and whether a lot of handheld shooting will be required. Will you need a single-frame option or variable speeds? Do you require special lenses? What about filters? Does any of the shooting require dolly tracks? And since you are going into the jungle, should you perhaps take a spare camera? Also, try where possible to take a video monitor. This is very useful when shooting to check the shots and invaluable at the end of the day when you want to view rushes.

You will also need to discuss stock. Since you have gone on a preliminary recce with the cameraperson, he or she will know whether to recommend normal or high-speed film, Kodak or Fuji, and whether to work in negative or reversal. The cameraperson will also know whether your preference is for shooting with available light, whatever the conditions, or whether you want plenty of light to give a feature quality to the production. Again, that discussion will influence the choice of stock.

The sound person needs to know who and what you want to record and where. Given that information he or she can choose a recorder and, very important, the appropriate microphones. If you are going to film a concert, the sound technician will know to bring microphones of types X and Y, and if you want to do interviews without a boom, he or she will also know to bring microphones A and B.

Lighting equipment must he thoroughly planned in advance because it is often too cumbersome or bulky to be replaced in a hurry in some remote outback. In most cases the lighting will he chosen by the director, cameraperson, and gaffer in consultation. Lighting is the bane of most directors because it takes so much time to set up and can be such a pain once it's standing. I like to go for the simplest and the least heavy. This often leads to arguments with camerapeople who fear for the quality of the filming. My counterargument is that I want to go in fast and film the family while they are all fresh and haven't waited hours for the crew to get ready.

Equipment always goes wrong; that's why I go for the strongest, the simplest, and the most reliable. I also try to cut down on all the extras that the technicians swear they need to bring, but which experience has proved to be unnecessary. On the other hand, certain items always seem to be scarce—spare lamps, connection cables, and pin boxes. Here, I bring more than is necessary and have never regretted that decision.

DRAWING UP THE SHOOTING SCHEDULE

When all the preliminaries are over, you are finally ready to draw up the shooting schedule. This is normally the joint work of the director and the production manager. The main responsibility is the director's, but the PM is there to double-check all the ideas, to ensure that the schedule is feasible, and then to put the first scheduling decisions into action.

The shooting schedule is a plan of work for the shooting. Theoretically, it should take all the problems involved in the shooting and solve them in the simplest, most practical, and most economical way. The schedule tells you what to film, whom to film, and when and where this should all take place. Before you can do this you need certain information at your fingertips. Assuming you have fourteen days of shooting starting June 1, you will probably need to know

anticipated weather at your locations
people's availability (checked out on your second visit)
distances between locations
any public holidays
any special happenings such as school graduation, summit meetings, and sports events

With this information, you can begin to break down the script and juggle the shooting to maximize shooting freedom.

The first thing to do is to go through the script and list all the filming that has to be done in one location and the people involved during the filming. You may finish up with something like this:

New York:	Leon's house, scenes 3, 5, 21, 33, 45
	Leon's office, scenes 7, 10, 18
	Mayor's office, scenes 9, 24
	Joe's party, scene 1
New Jersey:	Diana's garden, scenes 2, 8, 14

Of course, the numbering of the scenes may just be shorthand for Leon's study, his children's' room, kitchen, garden, and so on.

You will go right through the script in this way, listing who is in each scene. At this stage I also like to list all the photographs and any stock footage that I will need. My list will also include any special requirements for a scene, whether technical, such as special lenses, or practical, such as ordering drinks and food for a party. In a complex history film you may want to lay out your preproduction list slightly differently and I've discussed that at more length in chapter 20.

Once you have the script breakdown, you start adding other considerations, and then the complications start. Personally, I like to start off the shoot with a few easy days. This allows the crew to assess one another's pace and working habits and allows you to see how the equipment is performing. With this in mind, you start drawing up your daily shooting list. At first this is very tentative because you have to juggle so many elements. Let's say on your first day you have five scenes in mind. If you want to see whether it's feasible to do them, what questions should you be asking?

If we want to start in the office at ten, what time will we have to
leave the hotel?

How long will it take to set up lighting?

Once the lighting is up, how long will the shooting take?

If we finish at eleven, can we be at Lincoln Center by twelve?

When should we break for lunch?

Can we do three scenes by five o'clock, get the stuff from the hotel,
and be at the airport by seven o'clock to catch the seven-thirty
flight to Atlanta?

Will the crew eat on the plane or expect a meal in Atlanta?

We will probably be working from 8 A.M. until 10 P.M. Is that too
long for a first day?

Depending on your answers, you may stay with your first tentative
schedule or juggle it to allow more freedom. Your considerations each
time are fairly simple: how much time do you need for preparation,
lighting, meals, breaks, travel, and shooting. If you are unsure of the
way your crew works or the difficulty of the scenes, it's best to be
pessimistic rather than optimistic, allowing more time rather than
less time for the shooting and allowing for a worst-case scenario. I
am always wary of beautiful schedules that look magnificent on paper but fail in practice. Something always goes wrong on a shoot. A
camera breaks down; an interviewee suddenly has an urgent appointment. You overcome these difficulties in two ways. First, you make
your schedule flexible rather than rigid: if you suddenly cannot film
Diana in the morning, you can substitute the library sequence and
film Diana in the afternoon. You allow alternative sequences in case
of rain. Second, every third or fourth day you should leave a couple
of hours in the schedule totally open for fill-ins and emergencies.
If there are no crises, you will always find something to film, but if
you have lost time or lost an interview, then the open periods in the
schedule come as a godsend.

Observation films or evolving action films are the most difficult
to schedule. Here, you may only be able to sketch in an approximate
schedule for a day or a morning, but anything tighter often gets lost.
You have to allow for emergencies, for changes, and for the unexpected. The only advice is stay loose, and stay patient.

OBTAINING PERMISSIONS

If you have not done it before, you must, while scheduling, begin to
consider the question of permissions. Are there points in the shoot-

ing where you will need permission to work? Have you discussed that permission, and do you have it in writing? If you are interviewing people in their homes or offices, then their word is probably enough (but watch for higher "officialdom" wanting to get into the act). Most public places, however, such as parks, museums, railways, and official institutions, require written permission.

One thing to watch is that you have asked for all the necessary permissions and not just some of them. For example, a few years ago I wanted to film a concert rehearsal. I spoke to the manager of the theater and the manager of the orchestra and all was well. When I came to film, however, the orchestra at first refused to participate. No one had asked their permission directly or explained the filming to them. In the end, we went on with the shoot, but there were a few anxious moments.

Another point to check is that, as far as possible, your permission is flexible regarding date and time of shooting. Sometimes you arrange to shoot on a Monday and then have to shoot on a Tuesday. Obviously, you try to tell the authorities in advance this will happen. Sometimes you can't, and then it's tremendously frustrating to find yourself confronted by some petty official who takes pleasure in wielding power and stands by the letter of the law that you have permission only for Monday.

You should also consider the *personal release form* under the heading of permissions. This is a piece of paper, signed by a film participant, allowing you to use the footage in which he or she appears. Normally you orally ask permission to shoot, and then get the signed, written release when the shooting is completed. Such a release is usually a matter of safety rather than necessity. Few states or countries have rules about privacy, and filming someone on the street is not a basis for legal action. If such a person wants to take you to court, he or she must prove harm. That's normally quite difficult, but it can happen. You shoot a man kissing a woman who turns out not to be his wife, and he then claims your film implies that he is an adulterer. But that's the rare case. So why does one bother with a release? For safety's sake!

The release stops someone you have filmed from making trouble for you at the most inopportune moment. You have filmed a woman talking very frankly about her boss. A week before broadcast the interviewee gets frightened and goes to court to stop the broadcast, claiming that she has been harmed and never gave her permission. The judge cannot possibly hear the issue in one week, but in order to protect the plaintiff's rights issues an injunction to stop the broadcast until the case has been decided. The plaintiff's weapon, used to obtain money or out of genuine fear, is the injunction, because in practice she could probably never win the case. Showing the court the release form stops any threat of an injunction against the film.

Some people insist that you should pay one dollar for the release to make it legal. I don't hold with that argument. The dollar is necessary as consideration if your whole aim is to make a contract. But what you are really doing is getting proof of agreement, which is different. My own feelings are that offering money leads to more complications than it solves, and I have never done it.

Many people use releases on every occasion. I don't. If I am filming a street scene, I don't usually get releases from passersby or from the people I talk to casually. Again, if I am filming in a home and it seems clear that the interviewee has given permission (otherwise why would they appear?), I don't ask for permission. This has been my practice when I film privately, and so far I have never come to grief. Most television stations, however, will insist that you produce releases for every interview; they prefer to err on the side of caution. You will also need to produce the permissions when trying to get E&O insurance when selling your production to a U.S. or Canadian television station.

Obviously, it's valuable, perhaps even necessary, to get releases when you are filming in a very tricky, painful, or potentially embarrassing situation. For example, I always ask for releases when filming in hospitals, schools, or prisons. In those situations, you may really be at risk without the releases. Even with releases you sometimes have to beware. Fred Wiseman obtained permissions from the superintendent of prisons and commissioner of correction when filming *Titicut Follies*, yet he still ran into trouble.

If you are doing a commissioned film for a television station, it will most likely provide you with its standard release forms. When I am doing a film on my own, my general rule is to keep the release as simply worded as possible; for example, "This is to confirm that I, Jane Smith, have given permission for the interview filmed with me today to be used in a film called *Great Modern Ladies*, to be made by Jack Thompson for showing on television and other outlets." Signed, dated, and address given by Jane Smith. My rational for the simplicity is that the more details you put on the form, the more problems you raise in the mind of the signee. In many years of practice, I have had few problems with this simplified system.

You usually don't need permission to shoot in unrestricted public places. Many cities, however, require that you receive police permission if you want to film in the streets and want to put down a tripod. The theory is that you could tie up traffic or cause a nuisance. The permission also soothes the cop who approaches and wants to know what you are doing. Many times you don't have time to get permission so you just shoot, and nobody will give a damn. But you are at risk, so the time spent getting permission is usually time well spent.

SHOOTING ABROAD

When you want to shoot abroad, a tremendous number of extra problems arise, from different weather to extricating yourself from a revolution, and you must try to consider all the difficulties in the preproduction stage. Your aims are to shoot all you need, stay healthy, and come back with all your footage and all your crew. In most cases you won't have a chance to retake, so your planning has to be especially good. The first thing to do is to hire a special production manager familiar with all the ins and outs of the country you are going to and to listen to him or her very carefully. Your main questions will involve the following:

What can you shoot and do you need permission?
Will officials (government or otherwise) expect to be paid off for
    their help?
What is the political state of the country?
Are there war dangers?
Are certain people or subjects off-limits for filming?
Do you have to declare what you are shooting?
Is your film open to censorship?
What is the weather like?
Are there health dangers? Are there good medical facilities?

In other words, a good part of your questioning will relate to bureaucratic practices and the political situation in the country you're visiting. A second series of questions relates to stock, equipment, and crew:

Is raw stock available?
Are there good labs?
If equipment goes wrong, can it easily be replaced or repaired, or
    do you need to bring spares?
How does local weather affect film stock?
Are there facilities for sending the stock home?

My experience shooting in Eastern Europe used to be that most of these countries insisted that you have a government official with you during all of the filming. Some countries also insisted that you use a local crew. Since the end of the cold war, things have become quite a lot easier and the bureaucratic formalities less irksome.

The question of home or foreign crew is also important in budgeting. If, for example, you are an American shooting in England or France, it may be worth your while to pick up a local crew rather than bring one from home. But check your costs beforehand. In Poland my Warsaw PM, working for the then-communist government, wanted to charge me for two days of time, at $400 a day. All just for checking the camera. I told him that was fine and understandable for a socialist country, but unfortunately coming from capitalist America I had to justify my expenditure. He saw the point, and the item was dropped from the bill.

One of the main questions you will be faced with is customs arrangements and getting film and equipment in and out of the different countries. Here, forewarned is forearmed. Many countries make tremendous problems when you try either to bring in film and equipment or to take it out. Rules and regulations are often produced out of thin air, and confronted with them you feel like committing murder.

Your two best solutions to these problems are a highly efficient local agent and a PM who knows everything and everybody, and a *carnet de passage*. A *carnet de passage* is a customs document that you obtain in your own country, usually from your local chamber of commerce, for a small sum. It has a page for each country you are going to visit and lists in detail all the equipment and stock you are carrying. When you arrive in a country, the local customs will check your baggage and stamp the form, and will do the same when you exit. The forms act as a guarantee that you won't leave film or stock in the country, thus relieving you of the necessity of paying duty when you enter or leave. The *carnet* also serves another useful function: it relieves you of most of the problems with customs when you return to your own country, as it proves that all the equipment not only returned with you but also departed with you.

A word on excess baggage: this problem always confronts you, whether you are filming abroad or in your own country. Given the amount of equipment you are carrying—camera, tripods, lights, and so forth—you almost always finish up very heavily loaded. If you are traveling by train or car, that doesn't matter. But if you are traveling by plane, extra weight means extra payment. When you know this, talk to the baggage master before the flight. Point out the frequency with which your company or the television company uses the airline. Bring a letter from the airline's public relations division promising you help for a small mention in the film. In other words, anticipate the problem and use every stratagem to get the excess payments reduced or even ignored.

If shooting time and travel time are difficult to assess at home, they are doubly difficult overseas. This is particularly true of Africa, India, the Far East, and South America. Trains due to depart in the morning depart in the afternoon, if at all. Often you can't get a guaranteed departure on a plane, and even then the plane develops strange ailments, like ducks flying through the engine, which happened to me in India. If you are aware in advance that such problems will happen, you can prepare your shooting schedule accordingly. Your headaches may be no less, but your emotions will be calmer.

Once you have thought through all your problems, you are in a position to prepare the final shooting schedule. When this has been done, give a copy to every member of the crew and discuss it with them to see whether it really is practical or if you have left out anything. Besides saying what you will film and where, the schedule should also contain all the travel information regarding planes, hotels, and the like, and all the addresses and telephone numbers of where you will be and local contacts. As you can see, a tremendous amount of thinking and energy will have been expended before the shooting schedule is finalized. Believe me, it's worth every drop of effort. Plan well, and half the battle is over.

PART THREE

Production

11

THE DIRECTOR PREPARES

First of all, you have to take risks.—Dennis O'Rourke

The purpose of this and the following two chapters is to look at the attitude and working methods of the documentary director, offering a few hints to ease a path that is difficult but ultimately tremendously rewarding.

Up to production and location shooting, many of the director's responsibilities could, in theory, be shared. When shooting starts, however, the full responsibility for the film falls on the shoulders of the director. His or her job is to create or find the pieces that will come together in the editing to make a complete film. If a director fouls up in a feature film, it may be possible to reshoot. If a documentary director makes a mistake on a onetime event, there may be no film to speak of. So, the responsibilities are quite high.

It is not so difficult to define the image of the documentary director, which has changed tremendously since the days of Robert Flaherty and John Grierson, as it is to clarify the role. In certain films, the role of the documentary director will be similar to that of the feature director: setting up shots and telling people how to move and what to do. The similarities to the feature director's role are, however, superficial. The substance of documentary differs vastly from that of features, since you are dealing with reality, not fiction. Because the quest of the documentary director is different from that of the feature director, different qualities are called for in directing. While both share the necessity of understanding film language and film grammar, the vision, purpose, and general working methods of the documentary director differ radically from those of the feature filmmaker.

DEMANDS ON THE DIRECTOR

What are the demands made on directors? What kind of people should they be, and what skills should they have?

First, the director must obviously have excellent technical skills. This kind of knowledge is absolutely essential. Most books that purport to give instructions on directing are really talking about technical problems of shooting and maintaining continuity. I assume that the first thing film students do is read these books, so I don't want to waste much time going over familiar territory. I prefer to use this book for discussing how one *thinks* about film. However, it seems worthwhile to set out a checklist of technical points and elementary directing.

- *Camera movement*: We are talking here of pans, tilts, crabs, tracks, and dollies. You should know what they are and what motivates their use.
- *Continuity*: The main problems here are maintaining correct screen direction between shots and proper continuity between sequences. Any good book on editing will tell you all you need to know. What is vital is to understand how screen direction changes once you cross the main axis of filming.
- *Motivating the viewer*: This is the first rule in directing. You guide your viewer into almost demanding certain shots. A man raises a knife and looks down. Obviously, the audience wants to know who he's looking at, so your next shot is the victim.
- *Cutaways*: These are shots that help you condense time and shift point of view in a sequence in which you might have a problem with screen direction. Most beginning documentary filmmakers tend to take too few. They realize this error when they come to edit. You also need to understand the importance of reaction shots and the way they comment on the main scene.
- *Shot impact*: Are you paying attention to the emotional impact of the shot, such as moving in close for intensity and emotion?

And do you remember those old guidelines about shooting from below when you want a character to dominate the screen and from above when you want to diminish him or her?

- *Lenses*: Do you know the impact on the film of using different lenses, such as the long lens to slow down action and pack things together? The close-up lens is useful when you are shooting from a tripod, but be wary of it when you are shooting from the shoulder. For shoulder shooting that continually changes direction, I would recommend you stay with a wide-angle lens.
- *Sound*: This may sound like heresy, but I don't wear earphones when I am doing the sound myself, nor do I use a boom. The rationale is simply to keep the filming as simple as possible so that anyone being filmed is not overwhelmed or put off by your technical paraphernalia. Later, of course, during a break, I do check the sound.

All of these points are elementary but worth review. My own attitude about technical matters and guidelines for directing is simple. First, I want to know as much about the subject as possible because the rules reflect long experience. Once I have the knowledge, I can decide whether to stay with the rules or break them. Second, I want to know as much about technical matters as possible, because only then am I really in command and not subject to the whims and wishes of my crew, however much I love them. The more you know about filming, whether technical or human, the better position you will be in as a director.

In addition to technical knowledge, the documentary director must also have the vision and attitude appropriate to the genre. And here I very much believe in taking risks and being willing to jump outside of the boundaries I've earlier fixed in my head. The point is that although we use the word *directing* for both features and documentary, half of the time we are talking about two different things. Many documentaries can be written, set up, and shot as if they were features. But a sizable number of documentaries require an entirely different mind-set and mode of work and an immersion in the subject that doesn't happen in scripted features. And there begins the problem for the director. In these documentaries—and they are not confined to news, current affairs, and cinema verité—there may be no script at all, and hardly anything that you can plan in advance. With luck, you begin the film with a series of notes and a rough idea of where you want to go and how you want to proceed; you plunge in and hope for the best. Things will happen unexpectedly. Characters will reveal themselves in different ways. Sudden conflicts will emerge. New story lines will become apparent. You discover the film as you proceed. As events unfold, you try to understand their significance and grab their essence. You try to see the important details and how they will build to a significant whole.

This is what half the world of documentary filmmaking is like, and it resembles feature filmmaking as much as a lion resembles a mouse. More important, it makes tremendously different demands on the director. Given all that, what do we require of the director?

What Is Required of the Director?

Clarity of purpose. Some directors, like the superbly talented Dennis O' Rourke, director of *Land Mines—A Love Story* and *The Good Woman of Bangkok*, tend to plunge into their films without much prethought. They are sure of their talents, have a sense that the chosen material can lead into all sorts of interesting directions, and just jump in. But those are unusual cases. As a fledgling director, it is better to be absolutely sure where you want to go and how you want to get there. You must know clearly what you want the film to say. In short, you must be sure of your focus. If the focus isn't there, the film is heading for trouble.

A friend of mine made a film about her family, which had five thousand members. The family had come to California four generations previously and had helped develop the state. The family name had become a household word, but this fame was not always welcomed by the family members. A few of them felt burdened by the name and history and wanted independence. My friend Jane came to me when the family was planning to hold a massive reunion in San Francisco, which she wanted to use as the backbone of the film. That made sense, but as Jane continued talking I grew more and more uneasy because she resisted committing herself to a definite focus.

The film was potentially interesting in many ways: it could have been a story about maintaining family links in the late twentieth century; it could have been a story about the development of California; it could have been a story of two or three European immigrants who made good. But it had to be one story. Jane refused to see that this was a problem that had to be resolved before filming; instead, she just plunged in, shooting a bit of this and a bit of that. Once editing started, it was clear that there was no point of view and no rationale behind much of the shooting. In the end, the film was passable and fairly entertaining, but if Jane had made some stronger decisions in the beginning, it might have been superb.

Style. As with purpose, it is important for the style of the film to be established at the beginning and then maintained consistently throughout the work. The style may involve action, flashbacks, humor, or satire. It may be moody, poetic, or evocative, or bright, harsh, and ultrarealistic. The main thing is that the style should be consistent and that the director should be aware of what he or she is doing. Obviously, you can take risks and change style midway, but this often confuses the viewer. Novelists like John Fowles do this all the time; *The Magus*, for example, changes style and direction half a dozen times. Such changes are a much riskier proposition in film, although they can be done, as in *Tongues Untied*, which treads a risky path between comedy and tragedy, and between theater and documentary.

One of the best examples of a sudden change in style appears in a film I mentioned earlier, *The Road to Wigan Pier*, by Frank Cvitanovich. Three-quarters of the film evoke the 1930s by using George Orwell's text and archival footage. The last quarter of the film shows the film's symbolic worker-singer watching television footage of British politicians. It's a drastic shift in style, but it works because the underlying theme is strong enough to sustain the change of place and mood and because the film itself suggests from the start that its style is experimental and humorous.

The lessons are simple. Consider at length what style you want before you begin filming and then stick with it. If you want to break or change your style, think through the pros and cons very carefully. What you should avoid at all costs is shifting styles without reason.

More and more these days, I am reducing my own style to the minimum. I tend to eschew multiple shots and fast cutting and to go for a long, steady medium shot in which many things are happening in the frame. But that's just personal. You, of course, will establish your own style—trendy, zip, flash, moving, tilted—and if you are happy and the final effect is good, that's all there is to it.

Ability to listen. As we know from so many books, many feature directors tend to talk rather than to listen. The image of the old Hollywood director Otto Preminger, for example, was that of a martinet who commanded rather than directed and who would listen to no one. Perhaps that will do for features, but it just does not work in documentary. The documentary director must maintain authority and command, but above all else, he or she must be able to listen: to observe, absorb, and pay attention. This stricture applies to both people and scenes. You are trying to understand complex human be-ings, their behavior and motivation, their pain and their happiness. On a wider scale, you are trying to understand a scene, a group, or a society. You are trying to understand so that ultimately you can pass on your observations to a general audience. In order to do this, you have to listen. You have to expose yourself. Sometimes you have to show your own vulnerabilities. There is no other way.

Decision-making ability. Decision making is the essence of direct-ing. The difficulty in documentary is that many of the decisions have to be made with little preparation and no forewarning. Decision making for documentaries that can be prewritten and preplanned is relatively easy. The exploration of a university, for instance, calls for decisions of a fairly simple type. You know in advance whom, where, and when you want to film, and then direction becomes basically a managerial and technical job. You make sure that you have enough shots to edit and that you have pulled the essence out of the scene.

The difficult decisions come in unplanned films, in which no event can be foreseen and the situation is constantly changing. There, you need your wits to establish immediately what is important and where or on whom the camera should be focused. Everything is unexpected, and you have to be able to move and roll in any direction. Such situ-ations don't demand much intelligence to shoot, but they do require the intelligence to shoot the right thing. And that only you can know. The cameraperson may consider the burning house and the wreckage the important elements; only you can tell him or her that the real story lies in the indifference of the onlookers.

All the points we have been discussing now begin to come together. If you know what you want the film to do, and if you have thought through its central point, then you have a clear guide to your decision making. If you have not done that homework, then you have no basis for your decisions.

It goes without saying that most of the time your decision mak-ing has to be done at speed. If you are uncertain what is happening, then consult the crew and listen to their opinions. What is fatal is abandoning the decision-making process and just hoping that your crew gets something. They will sense the indecision, and you will be lucky if it does not negatively affect their attitude toward you for the rest of the film.

I have stressed the necessity of knowing where you want to go with the film, but sometimes something happens during filming, some-thing completely out of your hands, that negates your original idea.

When this happens you have to make some fast decisions in order to save the film. Here the decisions are very hard because you may be bending the film ninety degrees in order to salvage something. That happened on Mike Rubbo's film *Waiting for Fidel*, made for the National Film Board of Canada. Rubbo's mission was to accompany two Canadians to Cuba and film their interview with Fidel Castro. In the end, though, Castro was never available, even though the duo waited around several weeks. With the central idea for the film aborted, Rubbo turned his cameras toward the two Canadians, one a right-wing media millionaire, the other a left-wing politician. The film became a study of the two men's views and conflicting personalities, set against the background of Cuba. This was not the original film, but it was a salvage job par excellence. And it worked because Rubbo had the courage to decide on a new direction in the middle of filming and reconcentrate his energies on a more feasible subject.

THE DIRECTOR'S EYE

Many books list qualities required by a director. By the time you have tallied off wisdom, intelligence, patience, an IQ of two hundred, and a summa cum laude from Harvard, you realize that you are looking at the requirements for God and not for a mere humble documentary director. The one serious asset I would list besides basic intelligence, patience, and a capacity for hard work is a good visual eye. Film is a visual medium, and the good director is one who knows how to use all its potential.

This point may seem so obvious as to be trite, yet the custom the last few years has been to treat documentary, in many cases, as if it were radio with pictures. Thus, we see interview after interview, all filmed in the most boring way and interspersed with meaningless visuals that seem to have been put in merely to pass the time. It seems to me at such times that the director has forgotten the very basics of the medium. Obviously some all-interview films do work, but in many interview films, one senses a director who is more interested in the polemics of the printed page than in the excitement of a visual medium.

So the director must have a good eye. We accept this as a given in feature films and look to the work of John Ford, Josef von Sternberg, Sam Peckinpah, Terrence Malick, Oliver Stone, and Ridley Scott, for example. A good sense of what is visually important is just as essential in documentary, but the eye is subservient to purpose. You first determine what you want the film to do and say, and these decisions will then determine the visual style. You can work the other way, determining a visual style regardless of subject matter, but that can be a recipe for disaster: witness the later work of Ken Russell.

You fix your style and discuss it with your cameraperson. Again, the more the cameraperson knows about your thoughts and feelings, the closer he or she can interpret your approach on film. When you actually shoot the film, there are a few obvious things the cameraperson should know or be considering. What should a particular scene do, and what is its place in the film? What is the mood of the scene? Is it to be frenetic, calm, dramatic, poetic? Is the scene to be viewed from a distance, or is there to be a participation effect?

This last point is extremely important. If you are shooting on a tripod, your shots will normally appear to be calm, third-person observations of the events. You will be the aloof spectator at the political meeting, the outside observer at the college graduation. In contrast, shooting from the shoulder and moving with the action enhances the first-person, participatory quality of the scenes. Instead of observing the crowd at the disaster, you become one of them, moving in their midst. You will, of course, have to decide whether you want to aim for the third-person or first-person point of view.

Finally, the cameraperson will also want to know the degree of intensity you want in your shots. Are you going to go for close-ups or extreme close-ups, or do you prefer to maintain a greater distance from the subject?

When I talk of a director having a good eye, I am actually talking about two things. First, I mean that he or she should have a good sense of framing and composition and should be able to see the best angle from which the story can be told. But "a good eye" also signifies a sense for the telling detail. Sometimes that significant detail is written into the script. Thus, you shoot the employees busily at work, and then the script tells you to shoot the boss with his feet up on the table perusing a *Playboy*. However, many of the most telling sequences happen without any warning, and the job of the director is to see their significance and get the camera to film them. I mentioned earlier doing a film on a music teacher and his work in various villages. For the last scene of the film, I had the teacher telling the story of Stravinsky's *The Firebird* to some eleven-year-olds and then conducting an imaginary orchestra as the ballet music swelled upward. Suddenly, I noticed that while David, the teacher, was waving his arms with the imaginary baton, a very sweet eleven-year-old in the first row was carried away and was conducting alongside him. It was a nice shot in itself—the two of them conducting, arms just inches apart. But it was more, because the shot accidentally symbolized the continuity of the generations. Had I tried to set up the shot, it would have looked very kitschy, but happening naturally, it was tremendously useful.

Again, we return to the theme of the director hunting for the symbolic shot. The technique can be overdone, but used well it can be highly effective, because in a few seconds it encapsulates what the film is about and what you want to say. The most famous example comes from Humphrey Jennings's masterpiece *Listen to Britain*. All the shot shows is a small man in a dark suit carrying a helmet and gas mask and walking jauntily along a street. But the street is bombed out, the windows of the shops shattered. In itself, the shot is nothing. But what the shot symbolized to British audiences was the courage of the ordinary Londoner to face life in spite of the worst the Nazi bombing could do.

THE DIRECTOR-CAMERAPERSON RELATIONSHIP

The relationship between the cameraperson and the director is probably the most crucial working relationship of the whole film. If the cameraperson fails to capture the material in the way the director wants, the very basis of the film is flawed.

As mentioned earlier, the first task is to find the right person for the particular job. Once you have found that person, you must get him or her to understand and translate your vision to film as accurately as possible. Of course, there's more to it than that. You hope that the cameraperson will take your vision, add his or her own creative skills and imagination to the dream, and make something superb that neither of you could have done singly.

Visions are abstract; scripts are concrete. Therefore, the first thing to do is give the cameraperson the script or the proposal to read and digest. The next thing is to discuss what you hope to do with the film. The script will offer a partial explanation that will be amplified by your discussion. This is also a time to discuss style, objectives, and difficulties, and to answer questions. Some questions will relate to your filmic ideas, and others will be practical ones about equipment, time for shooting, crew, and lighting. You must gradually build a relationship of openness and trust, a relationship in which each person values and respects the other's creativity and judgment. And this relationship and trust had better be there, because half the time you will be entirely in the hands of the cameraperson, who will be working without your control.

Generally, I like to work with a familiar team and with a camera-person who has been on location with me before. When I am going to work with a new person I like to do three things: I want to see examples of previous work, I want to meet over a drink and get a sense of the person behind the work, and I want to talk to people who have worked with him or her in the past.

Most camerapeople will bring you a demonstration roll if you ask for it, but it has to be viewed warily. The demo contains his or her best work, the best extracts, which may not be typical. That's why you should check with a few people who have worked with the applicant to see what he or she is really like. The personal meeting is necessary because you need to get a sense of personality and temperament. No matter how good the technique, if the person is dour and morose, or lacking a sense of humor, he or she will find no place on my crew. Equally important, you need to assess whether the cameraperson is open to direction. Some are all sweetness in the beginning but then refuse to take directions on location. They become prima donnas, demanding the sole right to select what is being shot and how it is being shot. Usually you can sense this attitude in the first meeting or through your background check. When I face an attitude like that, I just get rid of the cameraperson.

But this does raise another point: who selects the shots? The simple answer is that you both do, with the director retaining the final judgment. If I am working with a new and unfamiliar cameraperson, I will, at least in the beginning, select most of the shots and also check the shots through the viewfinder. If I am working with an old friend whose judgment I trust and who knows my style, I will let him or her choose the shots and I merely check the viewfinder when the framing is crucial.

Let the cameraperson know clearly what you want from the scene and what specific shots are vital to you. While shooting a riding scene, I might say, "I want some wide shots of the woman riding against the trees, some close-ups—real close—of her coming toward us, and some cutaways of the spectators. You can also give me close-ups of the horses' hooves by themselves, and a few shots of the other riders waiting their turns." If I know the cameraperson well, I might leave it at that, but if he or she is unfamiliar to me, I will probably set up a few shots to demonstrate the kind of framing I want. I will also be very precise on crucial shots—for example, specifying that in the close-ups I want the subject's head to fill the frame.

Usually I leave a good deal open to the cameraperson's judgment after telling him or her what I am looking for in a scene. Most camera-people are creative artists in their own right, with years of experience and a superb visual sense. Most probably they neither need nor want a director breathing down their necks the whole time. I also like them to feel that I am open to any suggestion of how to improve the scene.

Keep one thing in mind: however much you trust the cameraper-son, the responsibility is yours. You must be aware the whole time of what he or she is doing, and you must not hesitate to ask that the shot be done over again if you think it has not been done properly.

From time to time, problems arise even with the best of camera-people, and you have to be prepared to argue them through. In some cases the cameraperson gets overwhelmed with the beauty of a par-ticular shot and fails to see (a) that the shot doesn't convey what you are looking for or (b) that the shot has nothing to do with the film at all. I was doing a film on architecture and wanted to shoot the fancy new wing of a certain museum. My cameraperson came up with one of the most artistic shots I have ever seen. The museum was framed through branches, with beautiful patterns of sky above. The only problem was that you couldn't see the building for the branches. This being so, there was no point in turning on the camera.

Not only do you have to guard against shooting beauty for the sake of beauty, but you sometimes have to remind the cameraperson that, unlike stills, the shot doesn't stand by itself. It has to be edited into a sequence, and if it doesn't contribute to the sequence, it's useless.

Occasionally the battle becomes one of art versus practicality. Most camerapeople will try their utmost to give you memorable and artistic shots, but if they take too long, the shot may not be worth the effort. As a director you know that, but trying to convince the cameraperson to relinquish the shot is something else. Why bother to argue? Because time is money, and the effort spent on one shot reduces the time you can spend on another.

A few years ago I was directing an industrial documentary for which I needed a six-second shot of someone working with a laser. In this case, my cameraperson decided to go to town on the sequence. He set up inkies (very small lights), soft lights, and reflectors, gener-ally having a ball. But all this took an hour and a half, and when I told him it wasn't worth it for a six-second shot we almost came to blows. My argument with him was simple. We had a great deal to do in very little time, and the laser shot was not terribly important to me. Given the circumstances, I didn't want to waste an hour and a half on an artistic six-second shot. I preferred a simple shot that could be executed in fifteen minutes. He knew rationally that I was right, but his sense of artistry was terribly offended and he wouldn't talk to me all the next day.

Another problem concerns fatigue. Even under the best of conditions, shooting can be a tremendous strain. Very often, a lot of physical activity is called for, as well as high concentration. Ultimately, this affects the cameraperson's performance, the energy dissipates, and the shots lose any flair or distinction. Focus and exposure will be all right, but the ultimate result will be very flat. This situation usually occurs on the fifth or sixth day of a continuous shoot, and you can often predict that it's coming. When it happens, the best thing is just to pack up for the day and get a good rest.

Most of the remarks up to now relate to the way the director and the cameraperson handle the controlled sequence, but many documentaries involve shooting developing, news, action, or intimate sequences. In many of these cases, the cameraperson has to act alone, so where does the director fit in? As director, the main thing you have to do, as I've stressed before, is indicate in advance how you want a scene shot and where the emphasis should be. The more the cameraperson knows what you want from a scene, what the point is, and where the emotional center is, the easier it is to shoot it.

In 1969 Richard Leiterman shot *A Married Couple* for Canadian director Allan King. This was an intimate family portrait shot verité style over the course of a few months. King was rarely present at the shooting but analyzed the rushes every few days with Leiterman so that the latter knew fairly precisely what King wanted.

In cases like this, the director's job is to get the fullest preliminary information possible, think it through, and pass on directions to the cameraperson. Occasionally, the director is present during the filming but is wary of disturbing the cameraperson. Here it helps to work out a few directional signs, such as a light tap on the shoulder for zoom in, two taps for a zoom out. If I want the cameraperson to pay attention to a particular shot or to some evolving action, I wait until the current shot is finished and then whisper directions in his or her ear.

The guiding rule for working on uncontrolled sequences is simple. Assess as fast as you can the essence of the scene, let your cameraperson know that, and make sure you get it. At the same time, keep in mind that you will have to edit the scene, so be certain that you have enough shots to enable you to do so.

12

DIRECTING THE INTERVIEW

We use interviews at two stages of the film: during basic research and during the filming itself. The problems arising during research have been dealt with earlier. This chapter deals with preparing and conducting the film interview.

BEFORE THE SHOOTING STARTS

At some point, you will have lined up a list of potential interviewees for the film. It probably doesn't include everybody you want, but it is the best you can come up with given the circumstances. Once you have decided who you want to interview and they have agreed to appear, it's vital that someone meet with the interviewees and go over the nature of the interview and the way the filming will be conducted. And the right person to do all this is usually the director and not an assistant.

There are a number of objectives to this meeting. The most obvious is to get to know the interviewees better and to explain, without all the pressures of the camera, what you want from the interview. It's also a time to let the interviewees get to know you and to put to you any questions about the film or the interview. In short, it's a time to build confidence between the two of you.

What is important at this stage is that you establish a few ground rules. These rules may cover anything from the way you want the interviewee to dress to questions that are off-limits. Such rules are generally minor, but occasionally they can be very important. For example, the interviewee may want a list of questions in advance and may agree to answer only those questions. Is this a limitation you are willing to accept? Again, the interviewee may demand to see the interview at the editing stage or may want to have the right of censorship afterward. You may or may not agree to all this. If any of these things are likely, it is much better to discuss them before you come to the filming than at the filming itself.

This preinterview "getting to know you" does not have to be terribly formal. Obviously, half the time it will be conducted at home or in the office, but I have also gone fishing with the interviewee while discussing the filming, and in another case I discussed matters while helping strip an engine. The time taken in the preinterview session can also vary. It can be half an hour over a business cocktail, or it might be a matter of days. There are no rules. The simple object is to know the interviewee well enough to get them to relax with you, and trust you, so that you can get the maximum out of the meeting on film.

The most important thing in interviewing is to know what your objectives are and what you want to get out of the film session. You may want some very specific answers to very specific questions. Again, your main aim may be just to get a general feeling of the person, his or her attitudes, mind-set, likes, dislikes, prejudices, and so on. You may want someone to talk generally about a mood or a situation. You may want interviewees to detail their childhood, their divorce, the importance of their research, or their reasons for committing a murder.

The main thing is that your questions must have focus and direction. This means that you must do your homework. Normally, this will have been done in the research or the preinterview meeting. But if your filming is actually the first meeting, then make sure you know as much about the interviewee as possible. Know who the people are; where they come from; their likes, dislikes, political attitudes, and biases. Obviously, this is the ideal. Many of the documentary interviews you do will be spontaneous, with no time for preparation—in which case you just plunge in. When possible, though, your questions should be thought out in advance. The interview itself may lead in all sorts of directions and open up interesting new paths of inquiry. That's fine, but make sure you have the main lines of your questioning preplanned.

Your choice of location for the interview depends on two factors, which you hope will mesh easily. First, you want to choose a site for the shooting at which the interviewee will feel totally at ease. This could be their home, work, or any quiet place. You have to be a bit careful because the most obvious may not always be the best. The father of five who is unemployed might be ashamed of his home and feel more comfortable talking to you in the park. The businesswoman may feel awkward talking to you in the office, where she knows people will tease her afterward, and may prefer the comfort of her home.

The second point to consider is the importance of background. If the story is about research, then you probably want to go for the laboratory background. If you are talking about the development of the modern university, then a dynamic campus backdrop is probably better than a dull home location. Some stories will impose the location on you. Thus, you take the general back to the French beaches to tell you about the D-day invasion of the Normandy coast, or you take Andre Agassi back to Forest Hills or Wimbledon as he tells you about the tennis triumph of his life.

At this stage, you are asking yourself three things. Will the background add to the mood and drama of the story? Will the interviewee feel at ease in the location, with the possibility of numbers of people around to interfere and distract? And is there any danger of the background being so strong that it distracts from the interview?

Wherever possible, I try to do the interview outside on location. This often eliminates lights, which make people nervous, and I think it gives them a certain physical looseness that is often missing in a room interview. Other advantages of the exterior location are that interview cutaways make more sense and you can have the interviewee participate in the scene. I also like to get the interviewee to walk and talk at the same time, instead of filming him or her sitting passively in an armchair. This is difficult and doesn't always work, but it can add dynamism to the scene.

Should other people be present during the interview? Every case is different. The only criterion is whether another person's presence will help or hinder the interview. If somebody is talking about the end of a happy marriage and is obviously upset and on edge, I would sense that the interview should be done with no one else around. If someone is talking about the loss of a father in a war, it could be that in this case the interviewee needs the comfort of a family member whose eye she can catch and whose hand she can hold.

However much you have discussed the film, people are always wary about being interviewed. Yes, they have talked to you before about their experiences, but that was in the privacy of the home. Now, suddenly, four or five other people are present. There are lights. There is a rather large camera on a tripod. There is a person going around taking light readings, and someone else who wants to affix a small microphone to the subject's clothes. In this situation your main task is to make the interviewee feel relaxed. I try to do this by introducing the crew, briefly explaining what all the technical equipment is about, and then taking five or ten minutes to chat over a cup of coffee or tea.

The warm-up is the culmination of what you have been trying to do in all the previous meetings—that is, make the subject feel that he or she matters, that you are concerned and involved in what they have to say, and that you care about their opinions. You are trying to build empathy between the two of you, and the more the other person feels this, the better the interview.

Normally, you are the one trying to put the interviewee at ease, but this won't always be the case. Sometimes you'll be interviewing presidents or prime ministers or the like, and it may be your turn to feel awkward or shy. Even in such cases, I'm not sure the rules change that much. The main danger here is that you may become too deferential and back away from the hard, awkward questions. In most cases it will be easy to create an atmosphere of trust, because the interviewee knows that you are on his or her side. However, with the political or controversial interview, trust may not come so easily. In the difficult cases you have to convince the interviewee that you are interested in his or her point of view and that you are going to be fair and nonjudgmental.

Besides breaking the ice, you should also use the warm-up time to let the interviewees know how the session will be conducted, reviewing the main topics and letting them know that if they make a mistake you have plenty of film and can shoot the question again.

GROUP INTERVIEWS AND VOX-POP

There may be times when you want to conduct a group interview. Or a situation may arise where you see that there may be specific advantages in interviewing four or five people in one go. For example, you may be shooting in a school, or at an army base, or in a factory, and have realized that the presence of two or three people discussing the same question may stimulate a variety of interesting and possibly contrasting answers. Your function here is fairly loose, and you have to roll with the discussion. Sometimes you may want to keep throwing in questions. Is the senate corrupt? How can we bring people back to the land? But more often than not, once the discussion is flowing, you may want to stay well clear.

As you will probably keep going without pause, your problems in such a situation tend to be technical. Is everyone reasonably well lit? Does the mike pick up everyone who may speak? Is the cameraperson well situated so that he or she can reframe and refocus very fast? The human problem is then to stop everyone from talking at once. Sometimes I ask the members of the group to just take a breath before he or she responds to someone else's answer or offers a different opinion themselves. Sometimes when I see someone dying to go, I'll just nod to the cameraperson where to direct the camera. As a general rule, I find it better to let things flow rather than interrupt and lose spontaneity. This means that your framing in general may suffer, but you maintain liveliness and spontaneity. You may lose a gem of dialogue here and there, but if it was a real diamond you can always ask for a repeat.

Vox-pop (or vox populi, which means "voice of the people") is a method whereby you ask different people in the street the same question, hoping to get a very broad variety of responses. In theory, it broadens your responses to certain issues and shows where your film or central character stands in relation to burning or interesting public questions. However, personally, I am very distrustful of the technique. I think it is really just a flashy news technique with little depth and of little value to a serious documentary filmmaker. My advice is to stay clear.

CONVERSATION AND MONOLOGUES

These days, where it has become the accepted practice for directors like Michael Moore and Mike Rubbo to appear in their own films, you may be involved in simple conversations as much as formal interviews. This is particularly true in making documentary soaps or when you are involved in an investigatory film. Here everything I've written about putting the interviewee at ease now applies to yourself, except that you are now very definitely in the role of performer. You have to make a good impression on camera and be confident, but you also need to be aware that you very much have to lead the conversation and lay down the tone of the scene. As it's likely to be totally spontaneous and unrehearsed, the conversation or confrontation can go off in all sorts of wild directions. That's fine, but make sure the topics that really concern you get brought into the conversation.

Now as everyone knows, and as I discussed in more depth in chapter 18, cinema verité films tend to dispense with formal interviews. At least that's the way it seems on the surface. However, in reality, the interview is often replaced by the monologue that carries the film. Here I'm referring to a situation whereby the film's main character goes off on a rant as to how he is, what he wants, how he sees life, where he's going, what he thinks of marriage and women, and so on. One of the best examples here is the opening of Michèle Ohayon's film *Cowboy del Amour*, in which a lanky seventy-four-year-old Texas cowboy, Ivan Thompson, tells us who he is and the kind of work he does:

> You know, I was married to an American woman for seventeen and half years. She spoke perfect English. I never could understand her. I was kind of tired and lonely for a woman, so I ran an advert in a Mexican newspaper, "Gringo looking for a Mexican wife," and I got back some eighty responses from some really pretty girls. They were doctors, secretaries, salesgirls, and they were dressed really nice. So I said to myself this would make a really good business so I should be doing it for the public.
>
> I introduce American men to Mexican women for marriage. I've been doing it for sixteen years. I know there's a lot of Mexican women who want American men and I thought it would be a natural meeting.

All the above is spoken directly to the camera as we see Ivan saddling a horse, seated at his desk in front of souvenirs, or driving through his hometown. The film then cuts to Ivan taking a young man across the international bridge into Mexico, and again he is still speaking direct to camera.

> I'm taking Rick across the border into Mexico to fix him up. He's paying me $3,000 and I reckon it will be worth every penny of it. He's pretty good looking and younger than me and I'm still getting fixed up. Depending on what gauge his pulse is I know who to fix him up with, and from what I seen he can have a young one.

The above recitation is very funny, but the point is that it didn't just happen. Although Ivan is a natural entertainer and raconteur, Ohayon had obviously spent a terrific amount of time with him getting to know him, interviewing him for basic voice-over material, and had also told him, "At every stage try and tell us what you're thinking and why you're doing what you're doing."

FILMING THE INTERVIEW

In the above sequences, Ivan talks to us from his horse, from his office, and from his car. All is very informal. However, one also has to learn how to set up for the formal interview. Here there are essentially three basic setup possibilities.

1. The interviewee looks, or appears to look, directly into the camera.
2. The camera catches the interviewee obliquely, so that he or she seems to be having a conversation with an unseen person off camera, left or right.
3. The interviewer is seen on camera with the interviewee so that we are quite clear who the second person is involved in the conversation.

Each of these setups has its own rationale.

Position 1, in which the interviewee looks directly into the camera, adds a certain authority to the interview. In effect, the subject is making direct contact with the viewer, and the straight-on look tinges the shot with the magisterial conviction we associate with the World War I posters that proclaimed, "Uncle Sam wants you!" It's the direct-contact pose that politicians give us when they want to assure us that they are our friends and not a pack of liars.

Position 2, the oblique angle, relaxes the quality of the interview, making it less authoritarian and more anecdotal, informal, and friendly. This is the interview position I prefer. For a very intimate but nonauthoritarian feeling, you can make the angle less oblique and sit or stand very close to the camera. This avoids the glaring, in-your-face contact with the viewer but makes the connection very sympathetic.

Position 3, the two-person interview, is used mostly for news or when a documentary series is being conducted by a famous host such as Bill Moyers, Ted Koppel, or the late Edward Murrow. The two-person setup is also used when you are deliberately aiming at or expect a confrontation.

When considering which position to choose, keep one elementary point in mind: how far do you want the viewer to be drawn into the film? Normally this is a function of the tightness of the shot and the directness of the approach. If the shot is tight and direct, the viewer will usually be more involved than when the shot is oblique and the subject framed in a looser way. Once you have decided which approach you want, direct or oblique, then arrange the seating accordingly. If you want the interviewee to appear to be looking straight at the audience, then you, as interviewer, should sit slightly to the side of the camera lens. If you want the oblique shot, you should move further away from the camera.

Though much documentary filming can be left to the cameraperson's judgment, I think you are wise to check the suggested interview frame. Does the person appear as you want them to appear? Are the clothes in order? Is there anything disturbing in the background? If the interviewee gesticulates frequently, is the frame wide enough to take in all the gestures? It is also necessary to tell the cameraperson not just what frame you want at the beginning of a shot, but whether you want any camera movement in the middle of the answer. You have to indicate that at the beginning, because after your question is asked all your attention will be focused on the interviewee and not on the camera.

The experienced cameraperson who has worked with you for some time should know roughly what to do even without your instructions. He or she will know that you can afford to take a camera movement in or out on a change of topic, that you probably want to vary the size of the subject in the frame with different questions, and that you probably want to zoom in slowly on an intense answer.

Besides considering whether you want the interviewee to appear directly or obliquely in the frame, you also have to consider how you want the interviewee to appear. Do you want the interviewee to appear formal or informal, serious or funny, relaxed or uptight? Because your very framing will induce a certain attitude of acceptance or rejection on the part of the audience, your capacity to manipulate the interview, deliberately or accidentally, is very high.

Susan Sontag's 1974 film *Promised Lands* is largely dependent on two interviews, and it is interesting how Sontag directs those sections. One interviewee is filmed in an open-necked shirt, sitting very relaxed on a sofa in a pleasant living room. His gestures are wide and open, and even before he speaks we like him and trust him. The second interviewee is filmed in a dark suit and tie, standing up with his arms folded in front of dead-white sterile walls. We feel an instant dislike for the man although he has yet to say something.

The lesson is simple. Your interview is not going to make its impression merely by what is said, but also through all the film techniques you use, from closing in on bad teeth to making the interviewee look like Dr. Strangelove. So be careful!

During the filming, all your attention and eye contact should be on the interviewees. You are the person they are talking to, and you must make them feel you are interested and completely with them. You are the friend to whom they are unburdening their souls about the revolution, the battle, their first love, or their last fight, and you'd better be interested if you want anything to come alive on the screen.

One thing you have to do before the interview starts is decide whether your questions will be heard after editing. If they are to be cut out, you must ensure that the interviewee gives you statements that are complete in themselves. If you ask, "Where were you when John Kennedy was assassinated?" and he answers, "Walking with my girlfriend along Fifth Avenue, wondering whether we should get married," then the answer, without your question, will make no sense by itself. Instead, you should have told the interviewee that you need a self-contained answer, for instance, "The afternoon Kennedy was assassinated I was walking with my girlfriend along Fifth Avenue in New York." Should you interrupt an interviewee? I try not to, even if I realize the answer won't help the film. If the answer is going nowhere, I try to terminate it gently. Sometimes I try to warn the interviewee in advance that I may want to cut occasionally if I think we are going down the wrong trail. But I say this with caution: although most interviewees will understand the necessity to cut here and there, others may find their pride offended and turn off. Many interviewers set out with an elaborate list of questions to which they keep referring during the interview. I hate that technique because it breaks any spontaneity between the interviewer and the subject. Instead, I try to get the questions well planted in my head and take everything from there. When the interview ends, I glance at my list to make sure that I haven't missed anything vital. I also ask the interviewee if there is something I've left out that seems important to him or her and that they would like to add.

What do you ask first? It's best to start with a fairly simple question that will ease you into the interview but that will require more than a one-sentence answer. For instance, "Tell me where you were and what you were doing when you heard the news that you had won the lottery, and what was your first reaction?" or, "What was the reaction of your friends and family when you came back from Vietnam? Were they sympathetic to what you had been through, or did they blame you for all the killings? How did your girlfriend react?" I have in fact put several questions here, but they are all just variants of the question, What was it like when you returned? Putting the question in different forms allows various ways into the interview.

Keep the questions clear and down-to-earth rather than philo-sophical. Don't ask about the problems of humanity in the twentieth century; instead, ask what it felt like to be thrown out of work on a day's notice after forty years. Also, don't bother too much about the order of your questions unless there is something you particularly want to build up to, because you will do all your final ordering in the editing room.

Remember that you are not just looking for facts, but trying to bring out emotions, drama, and a story. You must therefore encour-age the interviewee to give you details of sights, tastes, recollections, smells, feelings. Usually the more specific the interview, the better it is. If you ask, "What was it like being a child in World War II?" the interviewee might answer, "It wasn't very nice. We didn't have many things. My father was away and then I was sent away. When the Ger-man planes came over we went into a family shelter." That's vaguely passable, but not really very good. With a bit of encouragement, you might elicit the following:

> We didn't have anything. No sweets, no meat, no eggs. I didn't even know what an egg looked like because they gave us dried eggs. The only bananas I saw were made of wax in the fruit stores. My father was away in Africa fighting, so they sent me to stay with an old farmer in the country. He had this shelter, we called it a Morrison shelter, and it was like a table, but made of steel. When the German bombers came over six of us slept under the table, like sardines.

A good method is to start with straightforward questions and move into the more complex and emotional questions. In a program on divorce, you might start with questions about the couple's first meeting, the attitude of the parents, and the difficulties of the first years. When you are well into the interview you can try the riskier questions: "Tell me about the night she said she was leaving."

One of the most difficult things to assess is how far to press the questions when you are getting into intimate and sensitive areas. One way to overcome this difficulty is to acknowledge from the start that you might be venturing into dangerous areas and that if the questions are too painful or too sensitive, you will leave them aside. But you may risk self-censorship if your questions are too restrained from the start.

Silence itself can be a tremendous prod and encouragement in an interview. Rex Bloomstein, an English filmmaker who specializes in films about prison life, uses this technique to great effect. Rex has interviewed single murderers, mass murderers, and all types of criminals from the gentlest to the most violent. He gets them to say the most amazing things, and his weapon is silence, as on the following interview from his film *Lifer*:

> I saw the old woman lying in bed. When she wouldn't give me the money I hit her with the brick. [Rex stays silent for ten or fifteen seconds and the prisoner continues.] Well, actually she looked like my mother, so I hesitated at first, and then she said, "Call yourself a man, you're just a child," and that's when I hit her. I'd already bruised my knuckles on my girlfriend earlier that evening, so that's why I used the brick.

Another filmmaker who knows when to keep silent is Kate Davis. Her 1988 film *Girl Talk* is about the experiences of three teenage girls who leave home. Davis established a tremendous bond of confidence with the girls, so the interviews are fresh, intimate, and tremendously poignant. Many of the interviews are quite long, more like monologues than interviews, but they clearly show Davis's ability to get her subjects to talk. As an example, I have extracted Davis's interview with one of the girls, Mars, as she talks about her life and her work in a striptease club:

> He asked whether I wanted to stop by a mutual friend of ours 'cause he wanted to pick up some cocaine. I said sure and he asked me whether I wanted to go up. . . . He parked the car and we went up and he had six of his friends waiting for me. I remember them like having sex with me. I don't remember them hurting me, like physically beating me up. I guess after the third or the fourth one I passed out, and when I came to they had put me in his wife's running path in the park and left me there. She loaded me up in her car and took me to a hotel room and one of her friends was a doctor and he checked me out. She got round-the-clock nurses and bodyguards for me. Three weeks later my eyes got to where I could see. They were still all black and blue, but they weren't swollen shut anymore.
>
> She asked me if I wanted lawyers. I told her about my stepbrother and how when my mom had gone to court they had said that I had led Michael on and it was my fault . . . that you couldn't put the star of the track team on trial for rape.

Though you know where you want to go, strange things happen once the camera turns on. Some people freeze, and others become very free and eloquent. In the latter case, you may find an area opening up you hadn't even dreamed about. If it's interesting, take a chance and go with it. The freshness of this new area may well compensate for any problems you have fitting the answers into your well-laid film plans.

It's useful when you've finished to ask your subject if there is anything you have missed out on, or whether there is something they would like to add. At that point, they are warmed up, know roughly where the film is going, and may surprise you with a story, anecdote, or observation that you hadn't considered and that is helpful for the film.

If you know or suspect that a question can be answered in a better way, and the circumstances seem appropriate, don't hesitate to go back and ask the question again. While making *Year of Decision*, about the 1967 Arab-Israeli war, I asked Israel's foreign secretary Abba Eban to describe the cabinet meeting when the decision was taken to go to war. His first take was cold, dry, emotionless, and dull. I then asked him to try and reach inside himself and tell me more about the atmosphere and people's conflicting emotions. How did he and the others feel, knowing their decisions, though justified in their eyes, would result in the deaths of hundreds if not thousands of young men? This time the take was wonderful; it was alive, warm, and compassionate.

PROBLEMS AND CAUTIONS

Good interviewing is the hallmark of the best documentarists; indeed, some have taken interviewing into the upper realms of filmic art. In England, one of the best practitioners of the form is Alan Whicker, whose series *Whicker's World* was essential and delightful viewing for years.

Whicker was the urbane, soft-spoken, dark-suited interviewer who could go anywhere and ask the most outrageous questions. He got away with it because his questions were witty and down-to-earth, and wherever he went he seemed to show a genuine interest in his subjects. He had the knack of establishing immediate contact, disarming his interviewees, and getting them to talk in the most intimate and frank way about anything from hippies, sex, and drugs to Kentucky race horses or millionaires' yachts. Like Bill Moyers, Whicker was the participatory interviewer who would do anything and try anything. He would ride in a cross-country hunt and then interview the master of hounds, asking the hard questions about foxhunting as a blood sport. What characterizes Whicker and Moyers is that their questions are straightforward, not convoluted gush. This leads me to the following cautions.

- *Caution 1.* Stay away from gush. Many interviewers think they have to demonstrate a knowledge of higher physics that would leave Einstein gasping. Gush is not only unnecessary, it's also very off-putting.
- *Caution 2.* Keep the question simple, which is not the same as asking a simplistic question. In a program on the atom bomb, you could ask the following: "Everyone knows there are tremendous intellectual and moral problems arising from the creation of the atom bomb. But then mankind through the ages has been beset by moral dilemmas. Bearing in mind the quantum leap of evil that Hitler represents, and also remembering the power and influence of Japanese militarism after the Meiji Restoration, was Oppenheimer spiritually and theologically correct in forwarding the Manhattan Project?" As I say, you could ask something like that—but I would resist the temptation. It's dreadful rubbish. Instead, you could simply ask, "What were the pros and cons of making the atom bomb, and do you think our attitude about atomic weapons has changed over time?"
- *Caution 3.* Keep your questions open rather than biased toward a particular answer. I go crazy when someone opens a television interview with, "Don't you agree with me that . . ." or "Wouldn't you say that Roosevelt was the greatest politician of the century?" Occasionally you may want to be deliberately provocative or play the devil's advocate, but it's a tricky business and best avoided until you are fairly experienced.
- *Caution 4.* Avoid interrupting the interviewee. This is one of the cardinal faults in interviewing and tends to show that you are uninterested in the answer. It also wrecks the pace of the interview and is apt to throw the interviewee off stride.

INTERVIEW ETHICS

In addition to the four cautions above, there is also the matter of the philosophy or ethics of interviewing. Here we are concerned with questions of sensitivity, fairness, politics, and propaganda.

In documentary films we use people. Our rationale is that we are using them for a higher purpose—to expose corruption, to right wrongs, to promote the public welfare, and so on. And in the name of the public good, we delve into people's lives, invade their privacy, and expose their souls. At the same time that we are digging into all this corruption and sin, or simply examining history or telling a good story, we are also using people's lives to make our living. And we know that in many cases the juicier and more sensational a story we can tell, the more exciting and profitable our final film will be. My statements may seem extreme, but an interview can affect a person's life; it can have long-term effects outside of the film, and the interviewer must realize the responsibility thus entailed.

I'll give a short example. You interview a farmhand and coax from him or her a story about the terrible conditions on the farm. You retire to your comfortable motel, and a few months later your film breaks the story. You are hailed as the wonder reformer, a great crusading journalist, but as a result of the interview the farmhand gets the boot.

Another dilemma, touched on earlier, is the legitimacy of digging into wounds and resurrecting pain. Again, we often pretend that we are doing something for the public good or because of the public's right to know, when in reality we are doing it out of the knowledge that exposed pain makes for great journalism.

Sometimes the question at issue is not how to conduct the interview but how to use the interview in the finished film. I would argue that when you interview somebody, as the director, you have the sole right to decide whether to use an answer or to leave it out of a film. But if you use it, then the real substance of the answer must be conveyed, even if it is slightly abbreviated. It also goes without saying that in the film itself you want to portray the whole person and not a series of distorted pictures.

Sometimes, however, the shoe can be on the other foot. This happens when the filmmaker is being consciously or unconsciously used by the interviewee to make a political or propaganda point. A witness in a film tends to receive the stamp of your authority and approval. In effect, he or she is elevated to the rank of authority. Usually that's fine and all the witness's statements are true. But occasionally the statements are incorrect, and there the troubles begin. By my estimate, this problem of the unvalidated authoritarian witness creeps into 50 percent of well-intentioned American and English political documentaries.

PROBLEMS AND POWER RELATIONSHIPS

I've discussed the necessity for trust between director and interviewees and film participants, and usually there is no problem. Occasionally, however, the interviewee or film subject may feel put on. Occasionally that anger is expressed. More often it is suppressed and can build up and create a rift in the relationship. One example of this can be seen in Michael Apted's recent film *49 Up*. Here, after years of being interviewed in Apted's previous films in the *7 Up* series, one of the women participants suddenly tells Apted he's often never listened to her and what she really wants to say, and instead has selfishly pursued his own agenda.

Very often, the truth is that the participant or interviewee is a difficult character around whom you have to tiptoe with caution. This is what happened when Faramarz K-Rahber was making *Donkey in Lahore*. In the film a young Australian, Brian, falls in love with a Pakistani girl called Amber. Subsequently Brian becomes a Muslim, changes his name to Aamir, and goes to Lahore to pursue his romantic quest, which is made very difficult because he can never be alone with Amber and always has to talk via a translator. This pursuit of love takes two to three years, during which Brian is filmed and interviewed at great length by K-Rahber. This is how the director described the process to me:

> Interviewing Brian is and was tremendously difficult. One of the problems was his momentary moods. Sometimes even asking him a simple question is a big deal and almost impossible. He hasn't refused directly to answer my questions so far but he's often made it very difficult for me.
>
> He's also said that at times I have "ordered" him to do this or that for the camera, something I very rarely do in documentary unless I am desperate. I asked him for an example and he said when I had used the translator to push him and Amber to talk about divorce. He continued, "You pushed me to talk about that because you felt the situation is great for your film. As a result of that push we talked about it [divorce] and then we ended up having a verbal fight again! You were just thinking of the film and not us."
>
> I tried to explain to Brian that my suggestion for such a conversation was not just for the sake of the film, but it was an opportunity he had always dreamt of. I told him, "You've always wished for this kind of situation, to be able to talk to her without the presence of the other family members." I also said that "Obviously I am making a

documentary and those kinds of moments are very interesting for me." At the end I told him that so far I've been doing my best not to ask you to do anything in order to keep the situations comfortable for you. (Conversation between Faramarz K-Rahber and Alan Rosenthal in Australia, September 2005.)

Can one draw any lessons from all this? I think so. One lesson is that you have to be extremely sensitive to the moods and foibles of everyone around you and anticipate and deflect growing resentment. A second idea to hold on to and think about is that the agenda of the participant or interviewee may be very different from yours. Because of this you may need to act in a way that satisfies some of their expectations, because if you don't the film may implode around you.

Anu Trombino and Mark Trombino, in *Big Enough*.
Photo used with permission of Jan Krawitz.

Mark Trombino, director Jan Krawitz, and Anu Trombino, during film ing of *Big Enough*. Photo used with permission of Jan Krawitz.

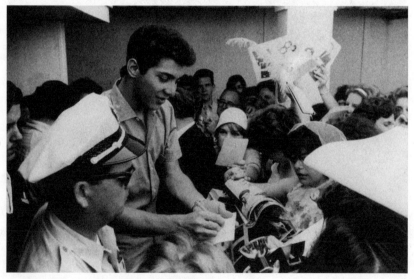

Paul Anka and his fans, in *Lonely Boy*.
Photo used with permission of the National Film Board of Canada.

Paul Anka, in *Lonely Boy*. Photo used with permission of the National Film Board of Canada.

Looking for the yellow streak, in *City of Gold*.
Photo used with permission of the National Film Board of Canada.

City of Gold. Photo used with permission of the National Film Board of Canada.

Ivan Thompson and client, in *Cowboy Del Amour.* Photo used with permission of Michèle Ohayon.

Ivan Thompson and his billboard, in *Cowboy Del Amour.*
Photo used with permission of Michèle Ohayon.

Michèle Ohayon, director of *Cowboy Del Amour*. Photo used with permission of Michèle Ohayon.

Graphic designed by Julie Innes for *The Bigamists*.
Photo used with permission of Julie Innes.

Title graphic for *The Bigamists*, designed by Julie Innes.
Photo used with permission of Julie Innes.

Graphic from *The Bigamists*. Photo used with permission of Julie Innes.

Habiba and Shah, in *Land Mines—A Love Story*.
Photograph by Dennis O'Rourke; copyright Camerawork Pty. Ltd.

Director Dennis O'Rourke. Photograph courtesy of Dennis O'Rourke.

Cannibal Tours. Photograph by Dennis O'Rourke; copyright Camerawork Pty. Ltd.

John and Fahimeh, in *Fahimeh's Story*. Photo used with permission of Faraway Productions Pty. Ltd.

Fahimeh, in *Fahimeh's Story*. Photo used with permission of Faraway Productions Pty. Ltd.

13

ON LOCATION

Much of the approach to directing people on location has already been covered in the section on interviewing. In this chapter I will try to fill in the gaps, covering the more intricate situations.

In shooting you aim for one thing, *maximum naturalism*: your key objective is to get people to behave in the most genuine way in front of the camera. Luckily, that problem is much easier to solve these days than it was in the past. Television and the mass media have become an integral part of our public lives. We are all too familiar with the camera crew in the street, the vox-pop interview, the filming in the park, the cameras at the football games, and so on. At the same time, professional video cameras have become smaller and less intrusive, and cameras and video equipment have also entered our private lives. At least one member of the family has a video camera, using it not just for weddings and parties but also for experimental filmmaking.

This increasing familiarity with the filming process undoubtedly makes the documentary filmmaker's task easier. But there are still problems, since the documentary film is intended for public exhibition, not private, and because you, the filmmaker, are an outsider, not an insider. Documentary filmmaking often intrudes into private lives. We are saying, "Give us your lives. Trust us, and let us put it on the big screen." And for the craziest of reasons people agree, and we arrive with loads of equipment and cigarette-smoking strangers and say to them, "Fine. Now *just act natural!*" The amazing thing is that, for the most part, they do. What's the secret?

A great deal depends on the *bond of trust* established between the director and the participant. The deeper the empathy and the greater the ease between the director and the people in the film, the better the final result is. This is particularly true of most verité and deeply personal films. This doesn't mean that the filmmaker and the subject have to be buddies, but it does mean that time spent getting to know each other pays off in the end.

The second part of the secret is that people look most natural when they are performing some action, usually familiar, that takes their minds off the camera. In the Canadian film *Lonely Boy*, about the career of singer Paul Anka, we get a few natural scenes and a few terribly self-conscious scenes, and it's easy to see why. In the natural scenes, Paul is always involved: he is rehearsing on the piano; he's rushing to change clothes; he's signing autographs or driving a bumper car. In the self-conscious scenes, he is usually sitting with a friend or a manager, and the director has obviously said, "Well . . . er . . . just talk about anything." Paul is clearly conscious of the camera a few feet away, there is no motivation for the dialogue, and the scenes fall absolutely flat.

The best action scenes arise easily from the natural flow of the film: the mother sending the children to school, working around the house, attending to the garden, visiting the neighbor; a man dealing with an intricate job and then relaxing over a beer in the local bar. The action should be relevant, should advance the film, and should also reveal something about the characters. And, to repeat, it should be something the character feels comfortable doing.

A while back I was doing a film on aging and the distances that can grow between marriage partners after fifteen or twenty years. We shot one scene in the living room, with the husband reading and the wife knitting. It was dreadful! The scene made the essential points, but it was static, awkward, and boring. I then asked the woman what she was most happy doing. Gardening! So we filmed her among the roses. The husband was happiest alone in his room, building model airplanes. We filmed that, too. Later we added a voice-over of them explaining how they retreat to their private worlds for satisfaction. We also used scraps of them talking to us as they gardened or built, and that worked perfectly. I had tried the same thing previously in the living room and it had been a dismal failure.

A common fault in documentaries is to have people engaged in actions that say nothing about them or the film. For example, a woman cooks for five minutes while the voice-over tells us she believes in women's rights, was married at seventeen, and divorced at nineteen. So what? The picture is irrelevant to the development of the thoughts and seems to have been put on the screen purely to pass the time.

PREPARATION

In preproduction for both scripted and cinema verité films you will have already sketched out what you want to shoot. In most shoots you will also have sat down with the participants and told them clearly what they're getting into. That sounds easy in theory, but it can be tricky in practice. Craig Gilbert, director of the verité series *An American Family*, on the Loud family of California, claims he explained everything in detail to the family before any cameras came in. However, in her own book on the filming, Pat Loud claims she didn't have a clue what he was talking about, but went along out of goodwill.

At all costs, try to avoid pressuring the people in your film. The more relaxed they are, the better. Are they comfortable with the mikes? How do they feel about a lavalier? Are the lights too harsh for them? Yes! OK, then see if you can soften them. The calmer the atmosphere around the shooting, the better the results are.

Your participants must know plainly what demands are being made of them. That means they must be aware of the schedule, the hours of filming, and how long you will want them. Overestimate rather than underestimate. If you want someone for a morning, don't say an hour. If you want them for a week, don't say a day.

If dress is important to the film, be as clear as possible about what you want your participants to wear. Thus, you may want your principal character to wear a light-blue sweater in most scenes so that he or she will be clearly identifiable. If you are working in someone's house, assure them that everything will be left clean and neat at the end. Check the power supplies so that you don't plunge the whole neighborhood into darkness by overloading the electricity. And tell them not to worry about food or drink or meals, as you will be supplying everything.

Occasionally, though not very often, your participants may want a fee for appearing in the film. This is more pertinent to the "personality" documentaries than the average social documentary. If a fee is involved, make sure that both sides agree on how much it is and how it is to be paid. Also, be sure that the exchange of money does not contravene network rules.

If you have the time and the money, try to spend an acclimation period with your subjects without filming. Allan King did this with tremendous effect when he made *Warrendale*, one of the pioneer cinema verité films. *Warrendale* was shot in a home for emotionally disturbed children in Toronto, and King and his cameraperson William Brayne wandered around the home for a few weeks with an empty camera before turning a foot of film. The time taken getting to know the children and letting them get used to the cameras paid off in the tremendous naturalism and authenticity achieved by the film. This period of "getting to know you" and "relaxing with you" pays off tremendously in the end, and I try to do it more and more in my own films. Believe me, it is well worth the time and the effort.

Occasionally you may want to reorder the setup in which you are filming, just to make it easier to shoot. I try not to do this too often because people may feel uncomfortable with the arrangements. So, you weigh the pros and the cons before making such a decision. The converse of this is to stop your participants from cleaning up the filming area and transforming interesting backgrounds into ordered sterility.

Some, but not all of the above, applies to verité type films in which you are following conflicts and breaking action. When you plunge straight in, a lot of the rules go by the wayside. But not all. Consider what advice is applicable from the above and use it when appropriate.

As you do more and more filming, certain kinds of problems keep coming up again and again. The most common ones deal with privacy, areas of questioning, involvement or noninvolvement of children, and payment. In recent years many participants have also begun asking for the right to see the rushes and for the final decision about whether the material can be used. I fully agree with the right to see the rushes, but I will not go ahead with the filming unless final-use decisions are in my hands only.

Each film will necessitate certain ground rules, and they must be established before you turn on the camera. True cinema verité often demands almost a wall between the film subjects and the participants. When I interviewed photographer Richard Leiterman about how he shot *A Married Couple*, a very intimate portrait of a problem marriage, he told me, "We went in with a kind of ground rule that we would have no communications with them. We put up an invisible barrier between us."

Ground rules obtain everywhere and are particularly relevant for much institutional filming. A little while ago Roger Graef made the series *Decisions* for Granada Television of England. The films dealt with crucial decisions made inside various British oil and steel companies. The intimate corporate scenes Graef wanted to film had rarely been filmed before, and Graef obtained permission only after rigid ground rules had been established. These rules included the following:

- No scoops. No information was to be released in advance, and no one was to be told about any information obtained during the filming.
- The filmmakers would only film what they had agreed to cover.
- No lights would be used, no interviews filmed, and nothing would be staged.
- The companies were left with the right of veto over confidential material.

ATTITUDE

In a novel I read recently, one of the principal characters is a documentary director. At one point he goes to a hospital where he puts on a terribly sympathetic air, is shown around for two hours by the head nurse, and generally agrees with her that the hospital is well run, efficient, a model of its kind. When he comes back to film he selects two utterly atypical wards and emphasizes their dreary, dirty, almost-horrific quality. Unfortunately, the story could be true. Many directors work their way into situations by guile and then, in the interests of cheap drama, falsify the story and betray the people who have trusted them.

When we film people, we are using their lives to earn our living. Their motives for participating vary from a kindly desire to help, to a desire for publicity for their organization, to a genuine desire that their experience, their pain or joy, will enlarge someone else's vision. When everything else is said and done, there is a heavy responsibility on the director's shoulders. If, at the end of the film, the director and the participants are still friends, then there's not too much to worry about.

LOCATION CHECKS

So far, we have talked about handling the interview and working with people in different situations. In doing so, we have begun to suggest certain rules or approaches for location shooting, but a few things have been omitted. This section summarizes what you should be doing and thinking about on location. You will have to make some of these decisions on the spot, but many of them should be thought out before you leave for filming.

Schedule. You made up an overall schedule at the preproduction stage, but changes may have been made since then. Before you go out, make sure everyone on the shoot has an up-to-date schedule indicating where and what you are shooting, and the amount of time you are allowing for each scene. Make sure, too, that the list has the names of the participants and where they can be contacted as well as the name, address, and telephone number of your hotel.

Equipment check. Make sure your equipment is in working order before you leave your base. This is particularly necessary in the case of video equipment, as the cameras are notoriously temperamental and batteries run out very fast. Sound equipment should also be thoroughly checked, particularly in regard to synchronizing functions. It is also good practice to check your cables, particularly power cables to the cameras and the sound. When possible, you should take spares. Finally, check that you have all your special equipment, and in this I would include any permissions you might need on the shoot.

Shooting list. Run over the shooting list with your cameraperson. Does it still make sense in regard to the weather, mood, and so on? If, for example, you think it's going to rain, try to think of alternative locations before you go out instead of waiting until catastrophe hits. Also, run over the shooting list in your own mind. Do you have a well-formed sense of the way you want to shoot the scenes? Do you know where you want to begin and roughly what your first setup will be?

ON LOCATION

Filmmaking is a cooperative and consultative process, but it is not necessarily a democratic process. On location, you are the boss. You can consult, you can ask advice, but you are the one in command who has to decide what has to be filmed and how everything should be ordered and carried out.

Your first problem on location is usually not what to film (that has already been decided in most cases) but how to film the sequence. Where should your camera go? What should it frame? Should the camera pan with the people coming out of the building, or should it get them in a fixed frame with a close-up lens? You will be settling all these decisions with your cameraperson, clearly defining what you want from the shot. Sometimes he or she will choose the frame; sometimes you will. Most of the time, you will be standing close enough to the cameraperson to whisper instructions and to have an accurate sense of what the camera is doing.

Sometimes your instructions to the cameraperson will be loose; sometimes they need to be very specific. For the film's opening scene it may be enough to say, "Give me plenty of medium shots and close-ups of the students going into the university. Also try to give me a variety of types. I'm particularly interested in trying to give the impression that we have students from a dozen different countries." Another time you may say, "I want a very tight zoom into that window," because you know that in the film you want to cut from the outside of the building to a class in progress inside.

Both you and the cameraperson will be looking for the best way to express the scene, but you have to be the guide, because you know much better than anyone else exactly how the scene will be used in the finished film. You also know more than the cameraperson does about the mood you are looking for. Discussion of this matter will help, and you should also indicate very specifically the kind of shots you want. For example, you are filming in a prison. The film is about men who have been forgotten by society, about harsh treatment, about antagonism and broken lives. Obviously, the mood you are aiming for is one of separation, isolation, and oppression, so many of your shots will be low angle. The harsh lines of the prison walls are emphasized. The barbed wire on the walls dominates the frames. The guard with the rifle is silhouetted. By way of contrast, you film the prisoners from above, isolating them as tiny figures against the bleakness of the prison exercise yard. And most of the time your camera is on the tripod as you take fairly long, calm shots.

In another film, you are shooting automobile racing trials, and you are aiming at a completely different mood. This time the dominant word is *exhilaration*. You instruct your cameraperson that you are interested in movement, in low, long-lens shots of the cars coming directly toward you and sweeping around the curves. You want people running, jostling, calling. You want close-ups of watches, eyes, and flags. You tell the cameraperson to get inside the action, to prowl, to be part of the scene, and you suggest that most of the people shots be done from the shoulder.

One of the things that must be kept continuously in mind is the final editing process. So a key question, always, is whether or not you have enough material to give to the editor to build a decent scene. In particular, do you have enough cutaways so that you can alter your point of view or cut out of a scene easily? This failure to take cutaways is one of the most common problems among beginning filmmakers.

Another essential thing is to maintain a clear logging of the sequences and shots for both the camera and sound when working in film. Normally this will be done by a slate that will record camera roll, sound roll, sequence, and shot. Sometimes you will use an electronic slate. Sometimes you will use an old mechanical clapboard, which by hitting the slate will also give the editor the sync points for both camera and sound. Every time the cameraperson changes a roll, the soundperson should indicate that on the audiotape as well.

In some situations you will not have the luxury or the time to slate the scene properly, and you have to be careful that under pressure you don't lose sync. One way around this is to hold up fingers indicating take one or take two, and then slap your hands together. The effective sync mark will be the point that your palms make contact. Another way is for the sound person to tap the microphone on camera, the moment of contact again being the sync point.

One of the advantages of video is that you avoid the hassle of postproduction syncing, as you are automatically in sync, but logging and identification is still very important for every cassette and for every new scene. I usually keep this brief. I make just a few notes to guide myself, knowing I can log the scene properly when I look at the material in the editing room. You should also check that you are generating a time code on your tapes, and that the numbers you have selected for your cassettes don't overlap.

When shooting interviews on video, I usually go to manual operation, but tend to use a wide-angle lens on automatic focus for evolving action. That's pretty good for most of the time, but you need to remember that on automatic your camera will tend to take its focus from the verticals in your frame. In video interviews, I try to take the mike off the camera, as such attachment can interfere with the sound. However, as mentioned, I try to avoid a boom. Given the amazing light sensitivities of modern video cameras, I also try to avoid bulky lights a much as possible in interview situations. This is to make the participants relax. Instead, I'll look around the room and maybe use a few of the existing room lamps to give a sidelight or backlight.

Besides dealing with the dynamics and mechanics of the filming itself, the director also has to think about the human dynamics of the crew. If the crew is fine, the filming benefits; if not, the filming suffers. As director, you will set the tone of the filming, and whatever you say or do will affect the crew. If you're a martinet, you can antagonize them; if you're unsure of yourself, the crew loses confidence; and if you're generally inconsiderate, the crew will get its own back. On the other hand, if there is confidence, if there is a smile, if there is consideration for the work done and the professionalism shown, then the crew will work wonders.

It sounds easy, but it isn't, and this is because so much of the work is done under pressure and so many things can go wrong. The three qualities that seem to me to be essential for the good director are patience, humor, and calmness. Everyone knows things will go wrong—that the weather will be foul, that cameras will break down, that planes will be missed, that cables will be lost, that food will be lousy, and that tape recorders will go out of sync. But if you can remain calm and humorous under those tensions, then things will be all right. Not immediately, but soon. And when you do continue, the problem and its solution will become part of the bonding between the crew.

One thing the director must be aware of is relations among the crew. Sometimes rivalries and antagonisms develop during the shooting, and they can be deadly to the film if they are not caught and squashed. I find it helps to spend a few minutes with each member of the crew after the day's filming. Are they satisfied? Were any problems overlooked that I should have known about? Is the equipment working all right? Is there anything we could do better tomorrow? Are they enjoying themselves? The objective is simple. You start off with a crew, but you want to finish up with a team. And there is a great deal of difference between the two.

As you have gathered, much of the director's work consists of foreseeing a problem or solving it as soon as it happens. This problem solving does not have to be individual. It can, and often should be, a communal process. The camera motor has gone crazy. The sound person doesn't feel well. You have taken a wrong turn and are four hours behind schedule. You have been given the wrong lights. The equipment van has broken down. When these things happen, and they happen frequently, discuss them openly. Your crew is there for you to consult, and their opinion and advice matters. But, in the end, you're the one who has to make the decision. With directors as with presidents, the buck stops with you!

At the end of a hard day's filming it's tempting just to turn off, but one thing must still be done before you wrap. Review what you have filmed and ask yourself whether you are satisfied or whether you have neglected anything important. If everything is fine, you can complete the wrap. If it isn't, then do the missing filming immediately or fit it in to the following day's schedule.

When the equipment has been packed, check that all the cassettes or film cans and film tapes are labeled and safely stored. Then go and have that drink, because you deserve it!

PART FOUR

Postproduction

14

EDITING

Many people regard the shooting phase as an end in itself. It isn't; it merely provides the raw materials for the film. The real building process takes place during postproduction, which is supervised for the most part by the editor. The director still acts as the captain on the bridge, but the editor now becomes the chief mate who does 90 percent of the work. Sometimes the work will be supervised by the director; sometimes it will be independent of the director. The most important thing is for the director and editor to understand each other and to function as a team as they complete the film.

Besides the overall command of the editing room, the editor's work will include screening rushes, having the film and sound synchronized and coded, having transcripts made, supervising the editing itself, discussing music and effects, laying in narration and other sound tracks, and supervising the sound mix.

The work of the videotape editor differs slightly from the above, though not very much. For the sake of convenience, I have dealt with videotape editing procedures at the end of this chapter.

This chapter discusses the way the editor and the director work together. It's not about the technical side of editing, which is outside of the scope of this book. For those who want to know more about the craft of editing, I strongly recommend Roger Crittenden's *Film Editing*, while the classic on the aesthetics of the subject is Ken Dancyger's *The Technique of Film and Video Editing*. I also like Walter Murch's *In the Blink of an Eye: A Perspective on Film Editing*. Murch discusses feature editing but his advice is also very good for documentary filmmakers. On the ever-changing subject of technology and video editing, one of the clearest books on this complex subject is *Videotape Editing*, by Steven E. Browne.

THE DIRECTOR-EDITOR RELATIONSHIP

Most directors of any worth are also apt to be competent editors. Many, like Fred Wiseman and Mike Rubbo, edit their own films. So, given that the director (who is in most cases also the writer) knows the most about the film, why not let him or her go ahead and edit it as well? One answer is sheer fatigue. The shooting process tends to be such a debilitating and demanding period that often there is no energy left to supervise the equally arduous task of editing. A second answer, perhaps more important, is that editing is best done with a fresh eye. And that's something an independent editor has and the director lacks.

Like it or not, the director brings a tremendous number of hang-ups to editing, one being his or her familiarity with the agonies and trials endured getting the footage. The director sometimes falls in love with material regardless of its worth. The independent editor, however, sees only what is on the screen. Everything else is irrelevant. Consequently, he or she is often a much better judge of the value of the material.

The good editor can also be a tremendous creative stimulus to the director. The editor is there not just to carry out technical directions but also to advocate better ways of looking at the film and new and different ways of using the material. He or she is there to support what is right, challenge what is wrong, and put new energy into the whole process.

Finding the right editor is crucial to your success because documentary editing is so much more open than feature editing. In documentary, there is often no story, no script; the director dumps a bunch of rushes into the editor's arms and demands that he or she find the story. Creation and invention are vital to the very nature of the documentary editor, while such qualities may not be so necessary for the feature editor.

As a director, I find that working with a talented editor is one of the most dynamic and stimulating parts of filmmaking, and most films are better for having that person around. History bears this out over and over again. Roger Graef's films for Granada Television are superb, but their excellence owes much to the editing of Dai Vaughan. We talk of the poetry of Humphrey Jennings's films, yet again, much of their success is due to editor Stewart McAllister.

The relationship between the director and the editor can be tremendously fruitful, but it can also be quite hard. In essence, you have two strong characters dissecting, analyzing, and arguing about the film for days on end. When you agree it's fine, but when you disagree the air can get quite hot. Yet when you finish, you usually have something finer and better than if each had worked separately on the film.

FIRST STEPS IN THE EDITING ROOM

In the best of circumstances, one sees the "dailies," or rushes, during shooting. When the shooting is finished, I like to go over all of the rushes with the crew so that together we can analyze what happened. The editor is best left out of the group viewing; this is a time to look back, whereas your screenings with the editor prepare for the march forward.

After the group screening, the first task is to get the rushes synchronized (or *sunc up*, in film vernacular) and sent out for coding. This is usually the work of the assistant editor. Not all directors code their films, but I find it very useful. Coding is the process of putting identical edge numbers on the rushes and on the 16mm magnetic sound track. This ensures that you can easily match sound and picture, and it also makes it easier to preserve and arrange trims. If you are working in video, you need to have window dubs made. These are copies of your original tapes that show the time code on a screen.

While syncing and coding is going on, the editor will also be preparing five or six logbooks for future use. One will contain the original script, the editing script, and any script changes. The second is the log of the rushes, which will show the code number, length, scene number (if available), and subject matter of the rushes. A typical series of log entries might look like this:

Code	Scene	Length	Subject
AA1–22	3	40 sec.	Students enter university
23–51	6	55 sec.	General shots of art class
52–65	9	20 sec.	Students in corridors

The function of the rushes log is to help you locate material quickly. How you write it and how you subdivide it is up to you. Some people like exact descriptions of every individual shot, noting close-ups, medium shots, and even what people are wearing; all I need is a general description of a series of linked shots.

A video log is very similar to a film log but will be set out as follows:

Beta Source
Reel 1

#1	Sc. 4	01:00:00–01:19:00	Exteriors church
#2	Sc. 7	01:27.00–02:06:00	Interior classrooms
#3	Sc. 9	02:15:00–03:25:00	Close-up of student faces

I like to set up a third log dealing only with stills, but many people list the stills in the rushes log. One reason for separating the two is that you may have to pay copyright fees on the stills, and a separate log can also include all the information on sources and fees. The fourth log is that of the archival material ordered for the film. It is set up similarly to the rushes log, but like the stills log, it should include source and any copyright fee. The fifth log contains all the film transcripts, which we will discuss below. The sixth log lists all the music you will use in the film and its sources. It is also helpful to include a list of sound effects in this log, as that makes the final sound work on the film that much easier.

What you are doing with the logs is setting up different working aids. In the beginning it may seem as if a lot of time-consuming effort is involved, but as you go on with the editing you will see that the logs are invaluable.

The way you proceed once the material is synchronized, coded, logged, and boxed depends on the kind of film you are doing. If your editing is based on a fairly tight script, you will work one way; if the film is verité or only partly scripted, you will take a slightly different tack. For the next few pages, I will discuss editing methods on the assumption that there is a basic script at hand. The problems of verité and the unscripted film in general are dealt with at length in chapter 18.

APPROACHING THE EDITING

The editing room is organized, but now begins the problem. How do we begin shaping the film? Well, if you have some semblance of a script, which I have been advocating up to now, no problem. The script will show you a beginning, a middle, and hopefully an end. And you just plunge in. But if your editor doesn't have a script or a good set of guiding notes, and this may be the majority of cases, then you are in for a few weeks of very hard work. The burden of saying where this film is going and what it is about, which should be the director's, then falls squarely on the editor. The editor, in essence, then becomes the writer of the film. He or she may delight in this, but it is an unfair and unnecessary situation.

But in such a situation, what do you begin to look for? The following are a few suggestions that may help:

- *Story*: This is your first and most impelling commandment. Find the most compelling story in your material. A philosophic essay will gain you brownie points, but a compelling story will gain you viewers. What is your story and where is it going?
- *Characters*: Find the strongest characters to carry the story. What are their quirks, their foibles, their distinguishing traits, either endearing or off-putting. Find all these things and use them.
- *Focus*: Establish your focus and point of view.
- *Conflicts*: Find what they are then bring them out.
- *Simplify*: Don't tangle up or complicate your film lines.

All these elements obviously go hand in hand. Material has been handed to you about a research trip in the desert that went wrong. David and his ingenuity in fixing the jeep and finding water save the situation when all seems lost. Here you start from the end and work backward. How do we establish David earlier? Can we find material in the earlier footage of neglect, of wastage, of warning signs? Were their earlier conflicts between David and the group leader as to how the expedition should be conducted?

I am being oversimplistic in all this, but again I want to emphasize the basic points. You can only begin editing when you clearly see the story, the characters, their goals, and their conflicts

There are also three other points about editing that may be helpful to keep in mind when approaching the material: space, nonlinearity, and the shooting of stills.

Space

Try to allow the viewer space to move into the film rather than bombard him or her with action and provocations the whole time. Allow space for viewer reaction. Allow time for the viewer to create his or her own film. In *From Mao to Mozart*, we see a series of funny, amusing, and touching sequences in which Isaac Stern instructs Chinese violin students. The scenes are crowded with movement and dialogue. The film then glides into a three-minute train journey during which little is said. But the journey, with the Chinese landscape flashing past, allows the viewer to muse on the meaning of everything that has gone before.

Nonlinearity

With documentary we deal with the real, but we also deal with imagination. Occasionally it is worthwhile to break from reality to deal with feeling, with spirit, with thoughts and sensuality, with movement, with beauty. A child watches a concert. Let's break from the concert and fly with her thoughts to the clouds, to the rivers, to the breakneck horse ride, before we come back to settle on her face. Pudovkin's films were full of these kinds of shots and sequences. Some were very kitschy. Not all worked, but when they did they were unforgettable.

In a recent documentary of mine, *Stalin's Last Purge*, I very much wanted a sense of fear, tension, and suspense to underlie and pervade the film. Eventually, I achieved this by the editing in of night snow-storms, rustling curtains, defocused lights, and dark and menacing shadowed windows. The point is that these shots edged around main scenes. They didn't provide linear information but helped immensely in creating a mood of menace and terror.

One of the most beautiful and spectacular editing sequences in documentary, and one that clearly breaks from simple linear progression, is the dramatic diving finale in Leni Riefenstahl's *Olympia*. At first, Riefenstahl appears to be interested in the diving in order to tell us who wins. Gradually, however, the sequence turns into nothing more or less than an aerial ballet of shapes and movements played out in silhouette and slow motion against a darkening sky. The effect is stunning, and is still today, a lesson and example of what editing can achieve at its best

The Shooting of Stills

The director Rick Burns once said, "I like to make the viewer live in the photo." I totally agree with him. The task is to make the photos, the stills, come alive, and I think this is best done by involving the editor in the process. I very much believe that the editor should be consulted in the shooting of stills, and when possible this should not be done until editing has started. The stills don't exist alone. They exist as part of a sequence, and it is the meaning of the sequence that bests dictates whether the stills should be photographed, full frame, with a zoom-in, or with panned movement, and so on.

When I made *Out of the Ashes* about the Nazi death camps, I wanted a tragic sequence in which the victims are seen minutes before entering the gas chambers. It was my editor, Larry, who suggested that we film the stills with very intense slow zoom-ins to the faces, with the shots dissolving one into the other. The effect was very powerful and overwhelmingly moving.

In *City of Gold*, about the 1897 Klondike gold rush, the directors Roman Kroitor and Wolf Koenig want us to enter the heads of the miners. They are away from their families. They have come thousands of miles. Few have found gold. Yet they are somehow prouder and wiser than when they came. How do the directors let us know this? By letting their rostrum camera pan over a crowd of miners and then linger on a wistful face seen in profile. The camera then moves on, over the same photograph before lingering on another face, and another face. We cut to photos of miners looking straight into the camera. And magically we are with them. We can imagine what they are thinking and feeling, and all because of some excellent editing.

THE EDITING SCRIPT

Before doing any work with the editor, you should give him or her the original script to read, if such a thing exists. This will illustrate where you first wanted to go with the film and how you thought that could be achieved. The next stage is to screen the film alone with the editor. Preferably this should be done in sync, on a large screen (if working in film), so that you can feel the quality and detail of the shooting. Once you have absorbed the material on the large screen, you can review further on the editing table.

The aim of these viewings is to crystallize your own thoughts and impressions about the material. Is what you hoped for there on the screen? Has your central vision come through, or has something different emerged? Do you see new possibilities for the material? Which scenes work, and which scenes appear hopeless? Which characters seem to come alive on the screen, and which seem to die? What excites you in a completely unexpected way? Lest these impressions be forgotten, jot down a few notes or talk into a small tape recorder. Normally I don't do this until a second viewing. For the first viewing, I just want the material to wash over me, and then I can ask myself a few hours later what I remember.

The editor is also taking notes, and it can be useful to compare impressions. As mentioned before, the editor comes unburdened by any preconceptions about the material. He or she sees only what is on the screen and views it with the critical eye of the potential audience. In many ways, it is easier for the editor to see what is good or bad than it is for you, the director. After the viewing, sit down with the editor and listen to first impressions. Just as you asked yourself what works and what doesn't, what is important and what you want to bring out, now is the time to hear the first reactions of an unbiased observer. This is also the time to talk about style. For example, is your film going to be fairly straight and orthodox, or are you going for a fast, flashy, MTV-paced show?

The first screenings show you what you have—in reality, as opposed to in theory. Up to this point you have had only an intellectual concept of the film. Now the only thing that matters is the reality of the material, and there are bound to be shocks, both good and bad.

In 1988 I made a film about President Carter and the Israeli-Egyptian peace treaty of the late 1970s. The film was supposed to start with the restaging of a celebration party. On paper it was a great opening, but the party never came to life on film, and this was immediately apparent on seeing the rushes. The scene had to be cut.

About the same time, I interviewed Nobel Prize–winner Elie Wiesel for another film. Here I had the opposite situation. During the filming, Wiesel had given me the impression that he was tired and disinterested. When the filming was over, I felt that we had nothing usable. However, when we viewed the rushes, we saw that the man had a compelling power and intensity that the lens had caught but that we had been unable to see.

After a few screenings of the rushes, and after talking to the editor, sit down and review the script. Does it still make sense in view of the nature of the material? Should you lose scenes or change the order? Has any situation or character come out so well that you want to strengthen that element or that person in the film? Did the editor make any suggestions that you want to incorporate?

When the review is complete, your next move is to write an editing script. You don't just dump the material on the editor. You give him or her some clear written directions. The editor will use this script as a guide, and it will reflect what is *actually* in the material. The editing script is often almost identical with the shooting script, but for the reasons given above, you may also need to make considerable changes.

Different scripts have different purposes. For example, one of the aims of your very first script was to raise money for the film. Now, the one and only purpose of the editing script is to give the editor a solid master plan on which to build the film.

And the editing script is only that: a guide to lead you into the editing. As you work on the film, building the different sequences and searching for a rhythm, you may decide to depart radically from the editing script. But that happens only when you are far into the editing and have a chance to step back and see whether the shape is correct or not.

Most editing scripts look very much like shooting scripts—that is, visuals on the left and audio or idea line on the right. As the script is only for the editor's eyes, you can afford to add any notes or comments to the editor that you think will help. For example, an editing script on modern universities might look like this:

Visual	Ideas
Students streaming into the campus.	The university as the idyllic place of higher learning. A quiet retreat removed from reality.
Sixteenth-century university buildings.	The concept of the ivory tower.
Cambridge students with books.	Probably always was a false picture.
Riots at Berkeley and at Columbia.	Today, to be a student is to be a political animal. [Jim, I think we can get the riot footage from the National Archives. What do you think about also using footage from the French protests of '68? Or do you think that would be too esoteric for an American audience?]
Professor comments on riots.	[We have two good interviews that would fit here. Either Prof. Jones or Dickson. I think Jones works a bit better on camera.]

Unless the original script contained commentary, it's often easier to work with an idea line rather than a commentary line in these first stages. The writing of the commentary or link narration can usually wait until the editing becomes more focused and abbreviated.

Transcripts

If your film contains interviews or long dialogue sections, these should be transcribed as soon as editing begins—a tedious process, but an absolutely necessary one. My rule is to transcribe all interviews but to use discretion on interaction dialogue, where it may suffice merely to jot down the main topics people are discussing. Thus, while you transcribe everything the professor says on nuclear disarmament, you may simply note, "John and David discuss the merits of various sports cars, then start talking about holidays."

The simplest method of transcription is to have an audiocassette made from video, or the quarter-inch or DAT tapes or, failing that, from the 16mm magnetic track. The cassette then goes to a transcriptionist. You can transcribe from the magnetic tracks or video on the editing table or at the edit screen, but that tends to cause enormous delays.

Once you have the transcripts, you have to decide what to use and where. A few readings of the transcripts will tell you roughly what you want, but you have to make your final decisions watching the material on the table. This is necessary because how someone says something can be as important as what is said. The table viewing will also give you inflections that are missing from the printed page. When you read a transcript, you might at first think that you can use merely a portion of a sentence. However, when you listen to the interview you may realize that the voice at the cutting point is too high and has clearly been caught in the middle of something rather than at the beginning or end of a thought.

The typed transcripts go into the transcripts log, and I like to keep the filmed interviews themselves separate from the rest of the rushes. Once you have decided what part of the interview you want, mark it clearly in the logbook with in points and out points. A marked-up transcript log might look like this:

> New York was marvelous. Nothing I'd seen in Europe could touch it. And meeting Irving Berlin was the climax. [*In point*] He looked old and weather beaten, but there was a sparkle around his eyes. One evening we sat down with a piano and he played "There's no business like show business," and all the years dropped away. For a few seconds I glimpsed the genius who had written "Blue Skies" and "Alexander's Rag Time Band." Then he stopped, said he was tired, and went to bed. [*Out point*] The next day we went on.

The editing script should reflect the transcripts in whatever way is easiest for you. Thus, the editing script might refer to the excerpt above as "Mark Davis talking about Irving Berlin, interview three, page seven of the transcripts."

Obviously, it's best to get the transcripts completed before you write the editing script, but little harm is done if you have to put them in later. In that case, the editing script might just say, "Various interviews commenting on Irving Berlin at age eighty."

THE EDITING PROCESS

Before getting down to edit, it's worthwhile to keep a few elementary points in mind. You are making a drama and an entertainment. You want to hold people and not put them to sleep. And less is usually more.

The editing process is usually split into three stages: the assembly cut, the rough cut, and the fine cut. In practice, the stages blend into one another, so I am really using these terms as a quick assessment of where you are in the editing rather than absolute divisions of work.

The Assembly Cut

The *assembly cut is* the first assembly of your rushes. You take your best material, your best shots, and attempt to put them roughly in order according to your script. This is when you are trying to get a very loose sense of the whole film, whether it is organized well and whether the structure works. At this stage you are evaluating shots, selecting some, and cutting others. The selected shots will probably be inserted at full length, with no attempt to shorten them. You should be overly generous at this stage, using a variety of shots to make the same point and only later deciding which you prefer.

Your interview shots will go in with the corresponding sync sound track, but apart from that you will not bother with sound at this stage. Nor will you bother with rhythm or pace; the objective of this first cut is simply to give you a rough sense of what you have and an overall feel of the film once it has been put in some kind of order. At this stage, the film could easily be two or three times its final length.

The Rough Cut

The real work begins when you start working on the *rough cut.* Here you are beginning to talk about proper structure, climaxes, pace, and rhythm. You are looking for both the correct relationships between sequences and the most effective ordering of the shots within a sequence. You are checking whether your story is really clear and fascinating, whether your characters come over well, and whether the film has punch.

You should now be paying particular attention to structure. Is your ground plan for the film's development correct? Is there a smooth and effective opening? Is there a logical and emotionally effective development of ideas? Does the film have a growing sense of drama? Is it focused? Are the climaxes falling in the right place? Is your ending effective? Is there a proper sense of conclusion? Broadly speaking, this is where you leave all your theoretical ideas aside and instead concentrate on examining whether the film is really working and holding you.

Something else you are looking for at this stage is what I call *overloading*. During the scripting stages you probably packed your film full of ideas. That may have looked fine on paper, but during editing you may find that it's all just too much to take. You are overloaded. The audience also won't be able to absorb this much information, so you may have to dump a few of your choice scenes.

What soon becomes apparent is that the material itself will dictate major changes in your first editing ideas. For example, a few viewings might suggest that a sequence would work more effectively at the end of the film rather than at the beginning.

In my automobile accident film I had a series of interviews five minutes into the picture in which people talked about the effect of accidents on their lives. During the rough cut I realized that I had too much and cut out two of the interviews. One I abandoned completely; the second, in which a father talks about the loss of his son, I hung on to for later use, though I wasn't quite sure where. In the middle of the film I had a good sequence but realized as we edited it that it had no climax. The sequence showed cars racing along roads, cut to cars on a racing track, and ended with a man looking at bikini-clad women decorating sports cars in a lush showroom. Meanwhile, the commentary talked about the car representing power and masculinity. Looking at the sequence, I realized that it would work more effectively if we dropped the showroom, went from the racing cars to a rollover crash, and then cut in the interview of the father talking about the loss of his son.

You continually have to ask yourself, is the material really working where I have placed it? If not, why not? Here, the editor's eyes become extremely useful in breaking your preconceived notions of order and flow. Often the editor can suggest a new order that might have escaped you because of your closeness to the material.

During the rough cut you also begin to pay attention to the rhythm within the sequences. Are the shots the right length? Do they flow and blend well? Are they making the points you want? You also begin to keep an eye on length. Thus, if your final version has to be a fifty-two-minute film for television, your rough cut could be anywhere from fifty-seven to sixty-five minutes. In your fine cut you will adapt the film to required length. There are no hard-and-fast rules here; however, if your rough cut is way over the required length, it defeats the purpose of the fine cut, which should be a trimming and refining process only.

The Paper Cut

During the editing, a tremendous amount of rethinking and reordering is going on. In many cases even the editing script soon ceases to bear much resemblance to what is on the table. How does one cope and maintain order?

One of the best methods is to make a *paper edit* of the film. Each sequence is written out on filing cards that show briefly the points being made and the intros and exits. The cards are then pinned to the wall following the order of the first editing script. As the film goes on, a glimpse at the cards may suggest a new order. You can then juggle the cards to see what, in theory, this new edit would look like. If you follow through and reorder the film itself, the cards stay in the new order. Thus, though the editing script may be out of date, the cards always reflect where you actually are in the film. This paper edit is useful in scripted films, but it really comes into its own when you are working with verité and partly scripted material, where it becomes tremendously helpful in building dramatic structure.

When you edit films as a student, length probably isn't too important. You are told to do a ten-minute exercise and you turn in a cut of eight or twelve minutes. This is usually fine and nobody worries too much. When you work professionally you very much have to keep in mind the demands of your sponsor or commissioning editor. And these demands vary. German television may ask for forty-three minutes, while PBS requires fifty-six minutes. Again, if you are working on a feature documentary you should probably be aiming for ninety minutes. You should keep these demands in your head from the start and edit accordingly. If you ignore these requirements you are heading for trouble.

The Director-Editor Love Affair

The rough cut is a process of examining, building, and tightening that can take anywhere from a few days to a few months. And the editor's role in this is crucial.

Some people look on their editors as mere cutters, artisans who are there only to work under their control and put their great directorial decisions into effect. Such an attitude is the height of foolishness and stupidity. The good editor has honed his or her skills over the years and is probably just as good a creative artist as you are. So it helps to pay attention and learn. Most editors want to listen to you, to see where you are and where you want to go, but they can also bring something creative to the job. Sometimes they will propose radical departures from your original concept. The only criterion is artistry. Will such a suggestion improve or hinder the film? Most of the time you don't know until you try.

In my film on the children's village, I had a lovely sequence half-way through where the children attend the rehearsal of a major symphony orchestra. The sequence concentrated on the players, with marvelous close-ups of violinists, tuba players, and trumpeters, and some especially good shots of the conductor. At the end of the film the children watch David, their teacher, as he tells them about *The Firebird* ballet, puts on the music, and then mimes the actions of an orchestral conductor.

And that was where the film was supposed to end. Suddenly my editor, Larry, suggested that we intercut some shots of the real symphonic musicians, the violinists and the conductor, as the children and David listen to the ballet music in their school shack. Initially, I opposed this suggestion. I thought that the audience would be confused between the scenes in the middle of the film and the scenes at the end, that there was no logic behind the second appearance, and so on.

I was completely wrong. The intercutting gave the scene a magic and an extra dimension it never had in the original version. And this magic was entirely due to the creative input of the editor.

Narration

Although writing narration is covered fully in chapter 15, I want to mention a few points here that affect the editing process. As the rough cut proceeds, it often helps to write at least a tentative version of the commentary. You can record this yourself and then have it laid as a guide for the picture editing. This will help establish the logic of the film and the flow and length of the shots. If you don't want to go to the expense of a rough guide track, you can just read the commentary to picture. However, as you will often be absent from the editing room, a guide track that can be laid in is much better.

At this point there is a certain basic dilemma. Should the words dictate the picture or vice versa? I have always believed that when possible, pictorial rhythm and flow should be the first consideration, and that words should be written to picture rather than pictures adjusted to words. That's why I have argued for the first editing to be done to ideas rather than to a strict commentary. However, when you are making a film about politics or complex ideas, you may find that the commentary has to come in sooner rather than later, that you need to edit against specific words rather than ideas. In such cases write a fast commentary. There will be time to adjust it later, but it will be a tremendous help as the editor refines the material.

Music

Your film may or may not have music. In feature films we expect music everywhere, and the usual complaint is that there is too much. The music often drowns the film or leads the emotions so that there are no surprises. Documentary films tend to use less music, since it can break the illusion of reality. However, when used well, music can lift a film tremendously.

Most historical documentary series—unlike social realist documentaries—use music galore, so that Russian tanks go into battle accompanied by Tchaikovsky, while Polish partisans work wonders to the music of Chopin. Most people love it. Some people hate it. But it's all encompassing. The interesting thing, as a filmmaker, is to see and understand what the music is really doing for the film.

Triumph of the Will, Leni Riefenstahl's paean to Hitler and his Nazi thugs, uses music to tremendous effect. The film opens with Wagner's stirring "Ride of the Valkyrie," which sets the mood of expectation and exultancy. Later, the drums add passion and drama to the dark mystery of the torchlight processions. Finally, German folk songs add excitement and vitality to the early-morning shots of high jinks at the Hitler youth camp.

One of the best documentaries for learning about the use of music is still Humphrey Jennings's *Listen to Britain*, a sound portrait of Britain in World War II. It has no commentary, depending for its powerful effect on the conjunction of music, natural sound, and images. Within the film, Jennings uses folk songs like "The Ash Grove" and music-hall songs like "Underneath the Arches" and "Roll Out the

Barrel" to stress his faith in popular culture and the sense of the very Englishness of the scene. Later, he uses Mozart to stress the continuity of civilized human values threatened by Nazi barbarism. The Mozart scene actually begins with a Myra Hess piano concert at the National Gallery. But the music then continues, accompanying a series of public images. As the music swells, we see trees, a sailor, people boarding buses, the statue of Lord Nelson (England's savior against Napoleon), and a barrage balloon. Finally, and unexpectedly, the Mozart music underscores work in a tank factory, where it is gradually lost among the natural sounds of the machines.

Many filmmakers use songs in historical documentaries to give a flavor of the times, and that seems fine in moderation. Thus, the old union songs in *Union Maids* are quite effective, as are the folk songs in *The Good Fight*, a film about the Spanish Civil War. In *Stalin's Last Purge*, I used a number of songs popularized by the Red Army choral group. Ken Burns's very careful selection of contemporary songs and period music in his Civil War films adds immensely to the feel and success of the series. The dangers are that the music may be used as a crutch and that the viewers may weary of Pete Seeger and his banjo or the like. This tends to happen when your visual material is weak, or if the connection among subject, mood, and music is not appropriate.

Too often, music is used for emotional uplift alone. This is a pity, because it can also comment effectively, even ironically, on the visuals. One of the best films in the series *The World at War* was John Pett's *It's a Lovely Day Tomorrow*. The title was taken from a well-known song of the 1940s, performed by Vera Lynn. The film is about British soldiers fighting the Japanese in Burma, and the song is used sparingly to accompany shots of soldiers dragging through the mud in the monsoon rains. The song evokes a dreamy, wistful mood, a sense of regret and abandonment. But the music also suggests that there is no tomorrow, only the continuing shock and horror of today.

When should you begin thinking about music? Probably somewhere between the rough cut and the fine cut. A lot of your film may actually be cut to the rhythm and beat of the music; therefore, it's best not to leave the choice until the last minute. The best thing to do is take some songs or musical pieces you think suitable for the movie's theme and see what ideas strike you when you place the music on the timeline. This is called guide music. In the end, you may well change the music, but putting something in at an early stage helps you decide on the right rhythm for the shots.

Your music will either be specially written for the film or taken from prerecorded albums, tapes, or compact discs. My preference, where budget permits, is to have music written directly for the film. It's not just that the music is fresh, but you can aim for a unity that is hard to achieve when your music comes from all over the place. When you are using prerecorded music, the simplest way to deal with the whole business is to record your possible music choices on cassette and then play them against the picture. You will soon sort out what works and what doesn't. The effective music is then transferred to a 16mm magnetic track, while the other music is put aside. On video you can simply load your music into the computer from a CD.

Test Screenings

At some point in editing you will probably have to hold some test screenings. These might be for the sponsors or the executive producer, or to get the reactions of the intended audience. The aim of previews is to get feedback while you can still change the film. The best time for this is toward the end of the rough cut. A critically constructive preview can be tremendously helpful to the director, enabling him or her to see where the mistakes are and to guide the film closer to the wishes of the sponsor or senior producer. But you also have to be on guard against comments that are meaningless and even destructive.

On one occasion I held a preview of a university public-relations film with the university president and five of his junior colleagues in the cutting room. After the screening the president asked his juniors to react to the film. Their problem was that they didn't know whether the president liked it or hated it, and they wanted to show that they agreed with him. The result, which was rather funny, was that they all hedged their bets. "The film was fine, but . . ." "The issues were clear, the photography was good, but . . ." In the end, the president, to my relief, said, "I think it's great and we don't need any changes."

Most directors of any worth know the faults and problems of their films well before these screenings. But the one thing they lack is the reaction of a test audience to a teaching or training film. Previews here are essential. What you are trying to find out is whether the film is really achieving its goals in terms of altering or reinforcing attitudes. Ideally, these test screenings should be held in normal surroundings rather than in a screening room. If the sponsors are present, they should be at the back so that their presence does not inhibit discussion. In the end, the discussions do two things. First, they show you if you are reaching your audience. If you are, that's great. If not, you can begin to see where the problems lie. Second, such screenings often assuage the sponsors' fears. In private screenings with you they may have objected to certain scenes, characters, or language. In the test screenings they can see that the fears were baseless, with the result that you can go ahead as planned.

After the screenings, think through the criticisms. Some will be valid, others nonsense. It is useful to remember that the general tendency of these screenings is to look for problems, so don't be surprised if there is little praise. And don't revise just because a lot of people have said you should. They may be wrong, and you may be right. Make changes only if you think they are actually going to help the film.

The Fine Cut

During the fine cut you make the last changes to the picture and start adding or finalizing commentary, music, and effects. *Locking* the fine cut is the process of saying, "Enough. That's the film; that's its length, and that's the way it's going to go out." When you get to the fine cut, you will have expended a tremendous amount of time and energy on the film, and you will want to get out as fast as possible. You will have to resist this impulse, take a deep breath, and ask if the film is really working, and if not, what can be done. You should ask yourself for the last time if all the issues are clear, if any of the information is redundant, if the film has the right opening and ending, the proper rhythm, pace, and flow. Does it grip the emotions? Is it interesting to an outsider? Does it fulfill your intentions?

The three elements that begin to dominate at this stage are narration, music, and effects. Some narration and music may have been added while you were working on the rough cut, but both must now be finalized. This becomes a seesaw process: sometimes the narration and music are adjusted to fit the picture, and sometimes exactly the reverse happens. Only when the picture is locked do you add missing sound effects.

EDITING VIDEOTAPE

Most of the points I have made about film editing also apply to editing videotape. You use slightly different technical methods, but your mind-set is the same. This being so, I merely want to comment on a few points worthy of attention.

Your initial cut will probably be done off-line in a small, low-cost studio. The purpose of your off-line edit is to create an edited work print and an edit-decision list (EDL). A few years ago when that stage was complete you would move to an on-line studio to do your conforming and to add visual effects. These days, except for final sound editing, you can complete most of your film while working with just one edit system.

In order to edit effectively, either your videotape must be shot with time code or time code must be added before editing. The time code, as mentioned earlier, is a series of numbers that appear on the screen during editing that later will help you find the matching point in your original master tape. They also help you dub from one generation of tape to another.

With video, it helps to lay in the commentary very early. This is both because picture changes are slightly more complex than they are in film and because many video editors argue that such a procedure helps them work much faster.

Very often your first editing will be done from mini digital-video tapes or Beta cassettes that have been digitized into the editing computer. Once the picture has been fine cut, an EDL can be produced from the edit master. This is simply a list of all your edit decisions with time code numbers, printed out on a piece of paper, and stored on a floppy disk. Once the picture has been cut, you can start laying in more complex effects and doing a proper grading or on-lining of the film. Again, thanks to improvement in editing systems, most of this can be done on your general work computer without having to go into a specialized studio. Once the picture is finished and graded, the sound mix can be made, as described in chapter 16.

One final point to bear in mind is that while most European studios work with the PAL system, studios in the United States work with the NTSC format. If you have shot and edited on NTSC but your work is for Europe, you will need to go through a systems conversion. Once this was hideously expensive, but today costs have come down to the merely exorbitant.

I have been very brief here because video equipment and video techniques seem to change daily. But not to worry. Beyond all the paraphernalia, the art and the thinking behind the editing doesn't change drastically. If your thinking and approach are right, you can handle anything.

RANDOM ACCESS AND THE VIDEO FUTURE

When the Ampex Company first brought out videotape in 1956, the standard was two-inch-wide tape, or Quad. A couple of years later they brought out a videotape splicer that basically worked with razor blades. If the editor could find the frame line, which was quite a problem, he or she cut at the line and physically spliced material onto the end of the original tape. Today this seems laughable to us, but what we are presently doing may soon seem as prehistoric as technology in the 1950s.

When I prepared the first edition of this book, most video editing was still being done using a *linear* process. Each edit occupied a defined space, and editing was done sequentially. If you wanted to play around with a finished editing section, you either had to lose a shot of the length of the one you wanted to insert or go down another generation. This was primitive, but workable.

Today *nonlinear editing* has become the standard. Nonlinear, or random access technology, involves the use of computers, instead of using traditional videotape recorders, and uses digitized audiovisual information machines to enable fast access time and virtual fine cut. Put simply, this means that each time you edit, the following edits adjust immediately to take in the change. In a way very similar to film, shots can be added or removed instantly, without the need to reassemble a videotape.

At the moment, the machines most widely used for random access editing by the networks are manufactured by Avid, with the Avid Media Composer 9000 setting the standards. Unfortunately, they are hideously expensive, ranging from $15,000 to $50,000. Since the birth of the Avid, other companies such as Adobe Premiere, Media 100, and the very popular Final Cut Pro have come along offering systems at slightly lower costs.

The basic mode of operation of all the systems is relatively simple. Your starting point is provided by your original tapes or film transferred to tape. These tapes are then digitized and put into the memory of your Avid or Final Cut Pro, with the quality of your picture being affected by the memory capacity of the machine.

All your sound, music, effects, and narration can also be fed into the memory, and you are then ready for action. The system then becomes *film editing plus.* This is because the system allows you an incredible facility for playing around instantly with all sorts of combinations of picture and sound. If you are undecided about what to do, a variety of combinations can stored for review.

What all this clearly means is that the future of editing will be exclusively nonlinear. Whether this will make a significant difference to the shaping of documentaries is hard to tell, but one thing is certain. In the future, you won't be able to go far in filming without at least a minimum grasp of these new technological possibilities. The problem is that these technologies are becoming more and more complex to handle. One can only hope that creativity will not be displaced by mere technical competence.

15

WRITING THE FINAL NARRATION

As the film has been progressing through its various stages, you have probably been drafting a narration line, and perhaps even the tentative narration itself. Certain films, such as a historical documentary, require that you think about the narration very early on. Other films, heavily dependent on interviews and verité techniques, may allow you to proceed much further without thinking about the commentary. However, the moment comes when you have to write the definitive narration. That moment is usually just before or just after finishing the fine cut. It's a challenging task, but one which in the end is tremendously satisfying.

In the 1940s and the 1950s, almost every documentary was accompanied by commentary. In recent years, though, a school of filmmakers has emerged absolutely opposed to the use of narration. This opposition stems from various beliefs, from a dogmatic assertion that it is a Fascist practice (de Antonio's belief) to a feeling that pure verité has eliminated the need for commentary. In practice, there are some serious drawbacks to commentary that cannot be ignored. Very often, it tends to be authoritarian, giving the impression of the voice of God speaking through the mouth of Charlton Heston or Kenneth Branagh or Jeremy Irons. The tone can be patronizing, and if it is done badly, narration can seem like a horrendous lecture forced upon the audience. Finally, instead of stimulating thought and participation, narration can produce a deadly passivity that distances the viewers from the film.

However, I think there is a much more positive side to narration. For example, though pure action films and the verité efforts of Leacock and the Maysleses can work well with no commentary, the complex essay, historical, or political film almost always demands commentary if it is to have any level of seriousness. Narration can quickly and easily set up the factual background of a film, providing simple or complex information that does not arise easily or naturally from the casual conversation of the film participants. It can complement the mood of the film, and above all it can provide focus and emphasis. It does not have to judge what is seen, but it should help the viewer understand more fully the significance of what is on the screen.

Taking a rigid stance that no films should have narration or that all films should have narration seems to me rather restrictive. Certain films work well without narration. Others are tremendously enhanced by narration. The job of this chapter is to ensure that when you are required to write narration, you can do it well.

The broad function of narration is to amplify and clarify the picture. It should help establish the direction of the film and provide any necessary information not obvious from the visuals. In a simple but effective way, it should help focus what the film is about and where it is going.

I quoted earlier from Agnieszka Piotrowska's film *The Bigamists.* This is how her opening narration continues.

> Given that divorce is so easy these days and it's perfectly acceptable to cohabit without the blessing of marriage, I wondered who so many people still do it.
>
> Lies, love, passion, illegitimate children—this is the journey I am taking you on. It is a passage through an emotional landscape of dark secrets, and sometimes unbelievable pain.

The writing is simple but very effective in doing its job. It tells you where you are going and that the filmmaker is going to be involved as well. And it grabs you with words "landscape of dark secrets" and "unbelievable pain."

In my own film *Stalin's Last Purge*, I wanted the viewer to understand from the start that he or she was going to follow both a personal story and a series of state crimes. With that in mind, I wrote the opening as follows:

In January 1958 a man was found dead on a winter swept road in Minsk, Byelorussia. There were no witnesses. It seemed like a hit-and-run case.

But the dead man was no ordinary Soviet citizen. He was Solomon Mikhoels . . . the most famous Jew in Russia outside the Kremlin.

As director of the Moscow Yiddish theater his productions had become the focus of Jewish life and pride in the capital.

In the war Mikhoels had assumed another role, spokesman for Soviet Jewry and propagandist for Stalin.

Now he was dead . . . but was it accident or murder?

In the year following Mikhoels's death, numerous associates of his disappeared into the clutches of the secret police and Lubyanka jail. Thus, with the hidden assassination and midnight arrest began the fatal assault on Soviet Jewry.

Narration can also help establish the mood of the film, and it is particularly useful in bridging filmic transitions and turning the film in a new direction.

The first thing one learns in journalism is to let the reader know the five Ws: who, what, when, where, and why. This is often the function of narration when the visuals by themselves make no sense. Let's imagine the following scene:

A sun-swept hillside is covered with thousands of people of all ages. Their appearance is somewhere between that of gypsies and hippies. Some are cooking over campfires; others are playing musical instruments in the shade of hastily erected tents. In the center of the multitude is a grave surrounded by a brick wall. Fires are burning in the vicinity of the grave. All around the grave, old and young men are doing Greek-style dancing, their arms linked at the shoulder, while women press notes into the cracks in the grave wall.

By itself, the above scene is fascinating but incomprehensible to the viewer. It needs some narration based on the five-Ws approach to make it meaningful.

Once more it's May. And as they have been doing for the last six hundred years, the followers of Abu Jedida, miracle man and wonder worker, have come to this lonely spot in the Atlas Mountains to commemorate his death. Here, for twenty-four hours, picnic, passion, and prayer will intermingle until once more the crowds will disperse, leaving Abu Jedida to his lonely thoughts.

The narration lays out the essentials of the scene but doesn't describe everything. We still don't know why the men are dancing or why people are putting notes in the wall. However, it doesn't take much intelligence to assume that the first is a sign of fervor while the notes are pleas to Abu Jedida to grant favors such as a successful birth or marriage. These facts might or might not be explained as the film proceeds. The narration is simple, but there's the odd bit of flamboyant alliteration in "picnic, passion, and prayer." However, as the scene itself is fairly wild and colorful, for once the extravagant commentary can be excused.

The basis of writing most narration is finding interesting facts and presenting them in the most gripping or imaginative way to the viewer. Facts are the raw material of commentary. The writer's job is to use them judiciously to make the narration come alive and sparkle. Below we can see how Agnieszka Piotrowska introduces some fascinating facts in a very simple but effective way in *The Bigamists*.

> Bigamy, which used to be a hanging offense two hundred years ago, is still a criminal act punishable by prison . . .
>
> Most bigamists are men. There are very few women bigamists. Mostly we don't betray, we nurture. [So] when a bigamist woman is caught it causes a sensation.

The above is very good, but what is less clear is how far the writer should add value judgment to the facts. Some writers take a purist position on this matter, arguing that while it is permissible to draw attention to certain situations and present evidence about them, the final judgment must come from the viewer.

That's fine as a basic rule, yet there are times when the writer feels so passionately about a subject that his or her own commitment and point of view must be expressed directly in the narration. So Agnieszka writes "Mostly we [women] don't betray, we nurture." That kind of editorializing, which can be seen in the films of Edward Murrow or Bill Moyers, or in *60 Minutes* is problematic, yet it is probably appropriate to films calling for action and social change. But such writing usually has a tremendous impact and should not be used indiscriminately.

VOICE AND STYLE

Before you actually begin writing the narration, you must consider what voice and style are most appropriate for the film. You probably thought about all these things very early on; you must think them through before committing yourself to the word processor. Is your style to be somber and serious, or are you aiming at a lighter and more folksy effect? If you are doing a historical film, you will probably adopt the former. If you are doing a film on tourism or animals, you might prefer the latter. I say *probably* because there are no ironclad rules.

Again, you might want to try for a slightly humorous and offbeat style, the approach taken by James Burke in his series, *Connections*, about technological change throughout history. In program three, *Distant Voices*, Burke discusses the nature and purpose of the medieval tournaments, with their fights and jousting.

Visual	Audio
Slow-motion montage of knights on horseback.	*Burke*: The answer to shock was a stronger horse that could take all the punishment. And rearing big horses—as anybody who knows will tell you—ain't cheap. But the coming of the knight changed the basic structure of society.
Cheering tournament. Montage of horses, riders, spectators at castle.	The tournament was a kind of cross between the circus coming to town and a wild free-for-all, where half the time things ended in absolute shambles with whole towns getting burnt down. Things got so out of hand that even the pope tried to ban the fun and games. These were definitely not the days of courtly manners and fair play. But behind all the chicanery and dirty tricks there were two very good reasons for these affairs, and they both had to do with fighting on horseback. You see, the idea of cavalry was a new thing and you needed all the training you could get to

use the lance right. The other
reason had to do with the
prizes you won. You knocked a
guy off his horse at the tourna-
ment and you took everything
—his armor, his horse, his
saddle, the lot.

Burke's style is really quite amazing. It's loose, conversational, free,
and funny. He uses colloquialisms and slang, and is occasionally quite
ungrammatical. And it works superbly. It looks easy but is quite difficult to imitate. In essence, it's a style evolved by Burke to suit his own
personality. Burke presents the film and gives the image of a loose,
easygoing sort of fellow—so the language fits the man.

This is an important point, for very often you are writing not in
the abstract but for a particular narrator. Thus, if Dan Rather or
Ted Koppel were presenting the above film, your language might be
more serious; if Walter Cronkite or Jack Lemmon were presenting,
it might be a bit more folksy. If, however, you were writing for actors
such as Kenneth Branagh or Meryl Streep, then your narration could
go almost any way imaginable.

Other fascinating examples of experiment in narration style and
voice can be seen in *Feltham Sings*, which I discussed earlier, and
The Blasphemers' Banquet, written by Tony Harrison and directed
by Peter Symes. Harrison is one of England's most interesting poets.
In *Blasphemers' Banquet*, which I described earlier, he uses verse to
excoriate not just Khomeini and Islamic fundamentalism, but all
religious extremism that limits the spirit.

I've taken the following passage from the end of the film. What
makes it work is not just the verse, but the whole powerful combination
of picture, sound, and narration, excellently orchestrated by Symes.

Visual	Audio
Short cuts showing violent speeches of Rushdie. Close-ups of Muslim, American nun, rabbi, Northern Ireland Protestant priest, and yelling Baptist minister.	
Close-ups of shrieking followers of Khomeini, waving effigies of Rushdie. Close-ups of ravers, grown-ups, and children, waving razors over self-	Crowds yelling hate, and cursing Rushdie.

inflicted bloodied heads and
other scourged wounds.

We move into a slow-motion
mode, then freeze-frame on the
head of a Muslim child, bloodied
by religious frenzy.

The shouting diminishes to an
ominous silence.

Dissolve into blue, lapping water,
on which floats a Muslim pamphlet.

Then we hear a soprano sing, "I
love this fleeting life."

Cut to wine being poured in Omar
Khayyám restaurant.

Close-up of Tony Harrison, a laid
table, and chairs awaiting Voltaire,
Molière, Byron, Khayyám, and
Rushdie. Camera revolves around
Harrison.

HARRISON: There's me, and
one, two, three, four, five. Four
of whom can't come, they're
not alive. One couldn't come
because the fatwa führer has
forced him into hiding to
survive.

Other shots in the restaurant.

Right from the beginning I
knew you'd never make our
Bradford rendezvous . . .
The ayatollah forced you to
decline my invitation to share
food and wine

Harrison close-up

With poets blasted and blasphemers including Omar, now
a restaurant sign . . .

Empty chairs around Harrison.

The dead go down. Those under
threat are not at liberty to come
here yet. When you're free,
you're welcome.
Meanwhile I toast you on your
TV set.

The advantage of a good presenter, like Harrison or Burke, is that the presenter can personalize the experience. He or she is always talking directly to the viewing audience, enhancing contact and involvement. If the documentary does not have a presenter, as most do not, you have to decide what perspective you want to use—first, second, or third person. The essay or the film on history or science tends to use the formality and objectivity of the third person. The effect is rather distant and cool and runs the danger of being slightly authoritarian. Nevertheless, used well, the third person can be highly effective. As suggested above, the use of first and second person helps involve the viewer.

Here is an example of a film written in the third person and then in the second:

Third Person
One turns the bend and sinister mountains immediately confront the viewer. On the right a dirt track is seen to ascend to a black hilltop from which can be heard strange noises. Thus, the stranger is welcomed to Dracula's lair.

Second Person
You turn the bend and immediately confront dark, sinister mountains. On your right a dirt track climbs to a black hilltop from where you hear strange noises. Welcome, my friend, to Dracula's lair.

To my mind, the latter version, using the second person, is far stronger and more effective for this film; you want the viewer to feel, taste, and smell the atmosphere of Dracula's retreat. But there is another difference between the two versions. The first is essentially written in the passive voice and the second in the active voice. Generally, the active voice makes for more energetic and vital writing. And there is one more thing, which I want to stress. Writing in the second person can create a sense of dialogue and conversation, of commonality with the audience. It takes you, the viewer, into the film and gets you involved. So, in *The Bigamists* Piotrowska asks, "How would *you* feel if your husband was somebody else's husband? How would *you* feel if you were that husband?" Again, in William Wyler's classic war film *Memphis Belle*, the commentary puts the viewer straight into the pilot's seat as he takes off from an English airfield. "Four months ago you were a student of chemistry in Chicago. University. Now you are heading for Hitler's Germany." Such an approach may sound cliché, too simple. Maybe, but it works!

Your final option is to write in the first person, like Tony Harrison. This can be highly attractive for a number of reasons. It can be a gentler format that allows for a tremendous number of nuances. It's far less linear than the third person, and it allows you to be more experimental. And, of course, the more personal form makes for a more human and closer identification with the viewer. In short, the first-person *I* form breaks down the distance between the filmmaker and the viewer, which is one of the key objectives of good narration.

One of the best examples of first-person narration occurs in *City of Gold* (mentioned earlier), a film about the Klondike gold-rush town of Dawson City. According to Canadian critic D. B. Jones, "This was a film which needed an *outstanding* commentary, one that would work together with the pictures and the music to evoke the nostalgic mood that the filmmakers were after."

The filmmakers' solution was to have Canadian author Pierre Berton, who had himself grown up in the Yukon, write the commentary. Berton uses his own childhood memories of Dawson City and then contrasts them with his father's stories about Dawson City at the height of the gold rush; thus, the personal element of the film works on two levels. At first the narration is full of comments such as, "Every summer we used to play locomotive engineer, almost on the very spot where George Carmack picked up the nugget that started it all." The writing is poetic and warm, revealing a gentle, happy childhood. Gradually the father's memories take over. "Even when my father's memory began to fail, this spectacle remained. The Chilkoot Pass. You had to pack a ton of goods up this terrible forty-five-degree slope of sheer ice—a year's outfit. Without that, the Mounties wouldn't let you enter the Yukon. You couldn't stop to rest or it might be hours before they'd let you back into that endless human chain."

One of the reasons that *City of Gold* works so well is that it taps effortlessly into mood and feelings and memory. It is this ability to deal with feelings that I find so attractive about the first-person narrative.

A few years ago I was asked to write the narration for a film on the Yom Kippur War between Egypt and Israel. The film, *Letter from the Front*, was a string of hastily edited battle sequences, and I was brought in to write the commentary after the film had already been edited and mixed. The film had no story line to speak of, and my task was to write to pictures and sequences that couldn't be changed and went all over the place. My answer was to use first-person narration from the point of view of one of the soldiers. That way, the narration could dart all over the place and still reflect the inner tensions and feelings of someone in the midst of war. The following sample suggests my approach to the problem:

Visual	**Audio**
Soldiers lying alongside cars, in tents, absolutely tired.	You keep running, and when you stop there is this overwhelming tiredness, not just of your body but of your whole being. Where are your friends?

	Where are those you love? And you feel a terrible heaviness covering everything.
Soldiers playing football barefoot. Mountains behind them.	Okay, so now we have a cease fire. Big deal! Mind you, I'm not knocking it. It's good, but I don't quite believe in it, and the silence is strange.
Soldiers talk, write letters, sleep on the grass, etc.	Now I find time completely standing still for me. There's no yesterday and no tomorrow . . . no normalcy, no reference points. There's only the immediacy of this moment. We are all still mobilized, and plans, future, home life—all these things are vague and unreal. A lot of my mood has to do with the fact that we tend to share all our emotions here, both the joy and the pain . . . and of the latter there is quite a lot.

Often one has to lift the first-person narration from interviews. In 1992, Ellen Bruno journeyed to Tibet to interview Tibetan nuns. This is how her interviews were used in her subsequent film *Satya: A Prayer for the Enemy.*

Notes on screen:
China invaded Tibet in 1949. In an effort to impose communism on a deeply Buddhist society, over 6,000 temples were destroyed. Nuns and monks were forced from religious life and the Dalai Lama exiled. For years Tibetans practiced their religion in secrecy despite the threat of imprisonment.

Since 1987, a limited number of nuns and monks have been allowed ordination. Tibetan nuns have emerged from relative seclusion to lead public demonstrations against the Chinese occupation. They are demanding human rights, religious freedom, and independence.
Very soft voice of a woman narrator:
When I was a child there was so much darkness in Tibet that when someone died we couldn't say a word of prayer or light a butter lamp to show the soul which path to take.

My father told me that after the Chinese invasion everything turned to the opposite way. Monks and nuns were forced to marry but many kept their vows secretly. Buddhism is deep within us.

The Chinese say they have come to save us from the Ocean of Sorrow. That in communism there is equality, and we must learn the difference between happiness and sorrow . . .

We are frightened into silence. People disappear into the night. It is dangerous to tell anyone the truth of our suffering.

They want our land but they don't want the Tibetan people. The women in our village are called to be sterilized one by one. Those who refuse must pay a fine. They have no money so they have no choice.

As in *Letter from the Front* and *City of Gold*, we never see the narrator who is telling us both a personal story and a general story. Where *Satya* differs from the other films is that we are given direct interviews from time to time that break up the narration. As always, the narration doesn't exist alone, but it has to be considered together with picture and sound. In *Satya* the overall effect is simply stunning. As the narration begins, we see black-and-white video pictures of oil lamps, monks and nuns at prayer, empty streets, and close-ups of faces. All the Hi8 images have been slowed down, and occasionally bleed into one another. Alongside the narration we hear prayers and music. The overall effect is of a hypnotic, graceful, ethereal, dark vision that, in spite of its beauty, fully conveys the tragedy of the Tibetan people.

THE SHOT LIST

In order to write good and accurate narration you have to prepare a shot list. This means going through the film with a footage counter or seconds counter and listing the length and description of all the key shots and sequences. This is something that you (the writer) should do, rather than the editor, as each of you will view the film differently.

If your film is about a university, then your first few shots might consist of groups getting off buses, students talking to one another, a cluster of buildings, more students, the occasional professor, and then a drastic cut to a lesson in progress. Your subsequent shot list might look like this:

Seconds	Picture
10	Buses arrive at campus.
4	Students get off buses.
8	Groups of students talking.

5	A Japanese student close-up.
6	A Burmese student close-up.
8	Old buildings
7	New campus buildings
10	Group of students with guitars
12	University professors enter campus.
8	A professor looking like a hippie.
15	Science classroom.

The timings and groupings of the first few shots are obvious and probably would have been the same even if your editor had prepared the shot list. But why single out the Japanese student and the Burmese student? Because you suspect that at this point in the narration you may want to say something about foreign students, and these pictures are the obvious trigger.

You have also noted the hippie-looking professor for more or less the same reasons. You sense that while you may want to use the first few shots of professors to say something general about the faculty, the shot of the hippie professor may allow you to go in a different direction. Over the general shots you could say, "There are four hundred members of the faculty."

Then, as the hippie shot comes up, you continue, "The trouble is, these days you can't tell the faculty from the students." In other words, your shot list should not only help you make general statements but also give you the key pictures for making or suggesting specific points.

You proceed through the entire film in this fashion until you have a shot list of four or five pages. Then you can forget the hot and airless editing rooms, take your pages, and go back to the comfort of your home to write. You don't need the editing table or the screen any more. The two essential things you need, pictures and timing, are contained in the shot list.

At this stage, you know what you want to write and how to write it; you have only one problem—timing. That's where the timing section of the shot list becomes invaluable. It tells you that although you want to say something about the types of students who attend the university these days, you must be able to express everything in less than twenty seconds, as you only have twenty seconds of student shot. In fact, you probably have to express your thoughts in twelve seconds, as you want the film to be able to "breathe."

Some people count syllables or words, allowing themselves, say, eight words to three seconds. My own method is to take out a stopwatch and write two or three versions until I have my thoughts into the allowable time. This seems hard, but it becomes quite easy after practice.

One problem is that people read at different speeds. So while the narration may fit when you read it, your actual narrator may read much more slowly and ruin your timing. The answer is to underwrite rather than overwrite; also, keep in the back of your mind that you may have to cut certain words and phrases when you finally lay in the narration.

STYLE AND LANGUAGE

Who are you writing for?

A story is told of a broadcaster in the first days of radio who had a beautiful voice but kept stammering every time he confronted the cold, bleak metal of the microphone. His wife knew he loved his horse and solved the problem by putting a picture of his horse around the microphone. Henceforth, he wasn't talking to the anonymous masses, but to his horse.

When I work, I assume that I am writing for a good friend. He is sitting beside me watching the film, and in a simple but effective way I want to make the film more interesting for him. I'm not going to use pompous or superintellectual phrases, but straightforward and conversational language. However, I am going to turn my imagination loose, letting it go off in any direction that will make the film more dynamic and alive for my friend.

One thing I am definitely not going to do is describe what's on the screen. Your viewers don't need to be told that the woman is wearing a red dress or that the scene is taking place in Paris; they can see all that. But they may be interested in knowing that the dress was worn by Queen Erica on her wedding day and then never worn again after her husband was assassinated a few hours later. And they may look at the Eiffel Tower in a different way if you tell them that each year at least five people leap to their deaths from the top deck.

What I have been suggesting above are the two basic rules of narration: (1) Don't describe what can clearly be seen and understood by most people; (2) however, do amplify and explain what the picture doesn't show. Apart from these, there are no real rules to writing narration, but there are quite a number of hints about the process that may help you along the way.

Writing for the ear. The journalist writes for the eye, but when you are dealing with narration, you are writing for the ear. And there's a world of difference. That generally means your vocabulary has to be simpler and more immediately understandable. For instance, an article in a magazine might read as follows: "They were wed the morning after the raid on the store with the precious stones. The intruders had also sexually violated one of the shopgirls." Film narration would put it like this: "They got married the morning after the jewel robbery. The thieves had also raped one of the shopgirls."

You can't go back. Another essential difference between text and film writing is that in the latter you can't go back. Your writing has to be clear and make its impact immediately. This very much affects the order in which you express things. A news article might say, "Rockefeller, Louis B. Mayer, the Queen of England, Alexander the Great, and Rasputin all loved horses." A film script would put it this way: "Rockefeller loved horses. So did Louis B. Mayer, the Queen of England, Alexander the Great, and Rasputin." In the first version, the meaning of the sentence becomes apparent only at the end. In the film version, we know what we are talking about from the start. Of course, if you wanted the commonality of all these people to be a mystery, you could use the first version. But that doesn't happen very often.

Grammar and slang. Your narration may be grammatical and follow the normal rules of writing, but it doesn't necessarily have to be that way. Your writing does not stand by itself. It is meant to accompany pictures, and the only important thing is the effect of that final combination.

Most of the time your writing will in fact be relatively standard. You will probably avoid anything too archaic or literary and keep to a simple structure. What do we mean by literary or archaic? You could say, "A million dollars sounds like a lot, but compared to the federal deficit it is an infinitesimal amount."

The problem here is that the expressions "federal deficit" and "infinitesimal amount" may be a little too complex for the film, so a simpler version might be, "A million dollars sounds like a lot, but compared to the government's debt, it's peanuts!"

Again it is interesting to look at the language used in the commentary for *The Bigamists*:

When she was 18 Emily married her childhood sweetheart, Paul Rigby. [Then interviews with husbands three and four].

But truly, hold on a minute. Why does Emily keep marrying these guys without getting divorced?

So we have "hold on a minute" and "these guys." Not exactly a great literary style, but a loose colloquial style that works so well in this film.

If we look again at Burke's script on tournaments and knights, we see immediately that he, too, felt absolutely unconstrained about using colloquialisms and slang.

> The only answer was a stronger horse that could take all that punishment. And rearing big horses, as anyone who knows will tell you, *ain't cheap*. . . .
>
> The tournament was a kind of cross between the circus coming to town and a wild free-for-all, where half the time things ended in *absolute shambles*. . . .
>
> You knocked *a guy* off his horse and you took everything. . . .

Standard English and fine grammar it ain't. But it certainly works.

Summary and rhetorical questions. I mentioned that in film, unlike the printed page, you can't stop and go back. But what you can occasionally do—and what makes for greater clarity—is to summarize where you are before moving on to another idea or sequence: "So there were the American soldiers in Stalag Luft Nine. Six hundred of them from all ranks. They had fought the good fight . . . and lost. The question was whether they would simply give up or try to escape. Next morning the German guards found the answer!" The above contains both a summary and a transition to your next moment.

Simple, powerful sentences. Narration seems to work best using short, simple sentences with the main action verb fairly near the beginning. I am not saying that you cannot use more elaborate structures, with multiple ideas and a whole series of dependent clauses, but you have to be much more careful in your writing. Here is what I mean by the simple, strong sentence: "The American troops were young and untried. They came from Texas, from Utah, from Oregon. Few had ever been as far east as Chicago or New York. Now they found themselves five thousand miles from home, ready to invade mainland Europe. It was June fourth. Few knew it, but D-day was only hours away."

Occasionally in my own films I like to use a thought repetition for emphasis in making a point. In *Stalin's Last Purge*, I did this twice.

> In August 1939 the Soviet Union signed a friendship pact with Germany. When German forces invaded Poland a week later Russia watched calmly from a distance.
>
> But the friendship pact was merely illusion, trickery, part of Hitler's power game.

Later in the same film, commenting on a death sentence, I wrote as follows, again using a triple repetition for effect.

For decades the Red Square had provided the background for Stalin's triumphal parades and heroic speeches. And it was here that, according to rumors, the traitor doctors would be publicly executed after a brief trial.

The ax was being whetted. The noose made ready. And the guillotine prepared . . . but the drama would unfold in a very different way.

Directing attention. When you write, you can make the viewer see anything you want. Although there may be a mass of information on the screen, your words will show the viewer what is significant. But your words do more than direct attention. They are also there to give meaning.

We are doing a film about the American South. Suddenly we see a river, trees, a paddle-wheel steamer, houses in the distance, a few horses moving around. What does it mean? Nothing until we add the commentary: "All was quiet, not even a breeze. Few knew or cared that a young man had been lynched on that tree just a day before." Write it that way and all the attention goes to the trees, and the scene takes on an aura of horror. But you could write it another way: "Once there were steamers by the dozen all along the river. They were painted like rainbows and puffed along like Delilah making a grand entrance. Now only one survives, forgotten, desolate, and soon for the breaker's yard." Write it like that and the trees are forgotten while everyone looks at the steamer.

Atmosphere. One of the challenges of narration writing is to add an extra dimension to what can be seen on the screen. We are not talking about adding information or facts, but about enhancing the mood of the film. We are trying to get inside the scene and bring it to life, so that the viewer is fully involved in the emotional experience of the film. As a writer, you want the audience to feel the joy of the child who learns to walk after years on crutches, to understand the sadness of divorce, the isolation of prison, or the excitement of scuba diving.

One way to do this is with careful use of the color words, of adjectives, of words that add texture. The words are there to complement the image, and when everything works in harmony the effect can be tremendous:

In the bitter coldness of the night the jeeps went around collecting their burdens. Husbands said goodbye to wives, sweethearts to lovers.

Faces were pale, lips cold, eyes wet. Few words were said as the last jeeps departed into the clinging mists, carrying the men to the darkness of the waiting planes, loaded bombers, and an unknown dawn.

Below are two examples from *What Harvest for the Reaper*, written by Mort Silverstein. Both show how a judicious use of adjectives can add immensely to the scene. In the first extract, buses are taking black migrant workers north from Arkansas to the work camps of Long Island at the start of the summer.

> Their guide for the 1,800-mile trip will be crew leader Anderson. His charge is thirty dollars. Since none can afford it, they are in debt to Anderson before the trip begins.
>
> The bus marked "special" will take them away from the indifferent towns of Arkansas, past the county seats of Tennessee into Virginia, then over hundreds of miles of sterile highway that bypass great mountains and heartbreaking sunsets, until ultimately they reach Cutchogue, Long Island.
>
> Earlier in the season Cutchogue was a resort, one of the prides of Long Island. The prim town is resplendent with schools, churches, and old homes. It also has a migrant labor camp.

The writing is simple and concise, but very effective. There aren't in fact many adjectives, but the ones used—*indifferent* towns, *sterile* highways, *heartbreaking* sunsets, and prim town—carry a tremendous punch.

At the end of the film, the workers go back to Arkansas, somehow more deeply in debt than when they started the summer. They have been exploited by their bosses and have nothing to show for their months of sweat and grind. This is how Silverstein deals with leaving the work camp for the last time.

> The season which began in the vast darkness of night and soul is now ending the same way.
>
> On the last day this legacy, these odors, these noises, these silences. Three men pack to go home. They have worked for almost six months on the fields of Eden, and are irrevocably mired in debt.
>
> Eight years ago, in a memorable CBS documentary *Harvest of Shame*, the late Edward R. Murrow urged wage, health, and housing reforms for migrant workers. Eight years later, the migrant condition is still the shame of the nation.

Another interesting element of the above extract is the use of words such as *these* and *today*. These words, in conjunction with words such as *here* and *now*, add a sense of urgency and immediacy to the film. They can also tie the pictures to the text when there is really very little connection. Let's assume that we've found some rather indifferent pictures of war. One of the shots shows children wandering around doing nothing. The shot says very little to us until we add in *here* and *these*.

> Here, in the city, there is silence. The bombing has stopped. But few of these children know what tomorrow will bring. Will the fighting return? Will the slogans be repainted? Will hell reawaken in a different guise? No one knows, but today there is calm after the scream, and the city sleeps.

The Particular versus the general. On the whole, particular descriptions work better than generalities. The generalities of narration are soon forgotten, whereas a striking word picture is held in the mind. We are doing a film about banking and have to tell the story of Joseph X. Smith. We don't have much to work with. In fact, all we have on screen are some fairly dull photographs of Joseph as a young man with a cigar and some equally dull photographs of him around age sixty. One version of his life might go as follows:

> He made his fortune with gambling and real estate. Eventually he was worth ten million dollars and opened his first bank. He certainly lived very well and had dozens of women. But the crash of '29 hit him hard. Eventually he lost all his money and lived the last days of his life where he'd started out, around the gambling dens of Kansas City.

Written this way you don't remember much about Joseph Smith. He is a gray character, soon forgotten. But if you particularize the details of his life everything changes:

> He made his first fortune with a ten-dollar bet. He won an oil well that was thought to be dry. It wasn't, and within a year he owned half the town. Later he gambled in Europe with King George V, kept four mistresses who all had to wear the same red velvet dress, had his Rolls-Royce painted green . . . but finished up selling matches outside the gambling dens of Kansas City.

It's a bit exaggerated, but you certainly remember the guy.

The power of words. An old saying has it that pictures don't lie. Well, it's not quite true.

Often, pictures take on meaning only when the narration is added, a point we have been making throughout this chapter. This ability to provide meaning to a scene is a tremendous power, and in many cases you can bend the scene in almost any direction you want.

On screen we see crowds of young people, yachts, a marina, and a regatta in progress. It's a happy season, with everybody smiling and enjoying the atmosphere. Now let's put some words to it.

> They come once a year to celebrate Britain and boating. Soon the yachts will be out, vaunting a pride in old English workmanship.
>
> Today Nelson and Drake would be happy to see that their countrymen still rule the seas.
>
> So, for the moment, and rightfully so, work is left aside as the youngsters cheer on the crews and relax in this festival of fun.

Or we could take a more critical tack:

> They come once a year to celebrate Britain and boating. But while they drink champagne and eat strawberries, the rest of the country is going to ruin.
>
> Yes, it's nice to talk of Drake and Nelson, but wouldn't it be more appropriate to talk of idle shipyards, silent factories, and men out of work? Yes, let these privileged few vent their hollow cheers, because tomorrow comes the silence and the reckoning!

Narration plus interview. Very rarely do you find a film that is all narration. Most films are a blend of narration, sync interviews, and voice-overs. It is therefore worth thinking over carefully how you can best combine all the elements. A good way is to keep the narration very factual and let the voice-overs and sync provide the emotional experience of the film. The episode *Morning* in the Thames Television series *The World at War* provides a good example on this point. Written by John Williams, the film examines the D-day invasion of France by American, British, and Canadian troops. At the point of the extract, the sea invasion is just about to be launched.

> NARRATOR: Never had the channel waters seen such a mighty force. Heading for France were some six and a half thousand vessels of all types, marshaled and escorted by the Allied navies.
>
> Glider fleets were waiting, wearing their D-day markings. The first division would go in by glider and parachute, dropping behind the invasion beaches. Their losses were expected to be as high as seven out of every ten men.
>
> KATE SUMMERSBY (voice-over): They all had their faces blackened because they were going to jump into Nazi-occupied Europe in a very

short time, and you kept thinking, "I wonder how many are going to come back?" Later on, General Eisenhower said, "You know, Kay, it's very hard to look a soldier in the face knowing you might be sending him to his death."

NARRATOR: In the last hours of the fifth of June the airborne troops set out for France.

GEORGE ALEX (voice-over): Butterflies in your stomach, and you're wondering, "What am I doing here? Why did I volunteer? Am I crazy?" And everything's going through your mind, and you're worried and you know it's coming up soon. I was afraid. I was nineteen and I was afraid.

NARRATOR: Many men were afraid that night. They were storming Hitler's Festung Europa—Fortress Europe.

And across the water the Germans waited, not knowing when or where the blow would fall.

PROBLEMS

It's very easy to fall into certain traps while writing narration. Most of the traps or problems are obvious, but every writer falls victim to them sooner or later. Below I have listed a few of the most common pitfalls.

Lists and statistics. Although many individual shots are remembered because of the emotional force of the image, this doesn't work for narration. In fact, one of the most disconcerting things for a writer is to realize that very little of the narration is remembered ten minutes after the film has finished. If the broad details of the message are remembered, that's enough. That said, it becomes obvious why we avoid lists and statistics. They rarely make an impact at the time and are forgotten in five seconds.

Occasionally numbers are necessary, but they have to be used wisely to be effective. When the narrator in the D-day script tells us that "losses were expected to be as high as seven out of ten men," it works because at that point we are eager to know those facts. However, had the writer said, "Losses were expected to be as high as 70 percent," I don't think it would have worked as well because percent is a more abstract term for us, while "seven out of ten men" brings us closer to comprehending the individual deaths.

The task of the writer is to make cool, abstract figures come alive for us in human terms. Brian Winston did this brilliantly while writing the script for *Out of the Ashes*. Brian needed to say that the SS troops, operating in Russia, killed more than a million civilians in just over a year. How could one bring something so monstrously incomprehensible down to earth? This is what he wrote: "Close behind the front lines came the mobile killing squads of the SS. In sixteen months they and other members of the German army shot nearly one and a half million Jews—two human beings a minute for every hour of every day for nearly five hundred days." The last half of the sentence is vital, because only then do we grasp the enormity of the crime.

Wall-to-wall narration. Some filmmakers are reluctant to take up the pen; others simply don't know when to put it down. They overwrite, thus committing one of the cardinal sins of filmmaking. Your narration should be sparse and compact. Say enough to make the point and then shut up. You may think that piling detail on detail will improve the film, but that's rarely the case. More than likely you are just turning off the viewer by the sheer volume of your words. Remember that the picture needs room to breathe and that the viewer needs space and time to digest and reflect on the narration.

Another essential point is that very often narration is redundant, and you are better off letting the pictures make your point. Let us assume we are doing a film about Samuel Clemens. We have pictures of old steamers, river activity, ports, boys on rafts, and generally a rich montage of life on the Mississippi. We could write:

> As he rode up and down the river two characters formed in his mind—one a mischievous rascal called Tom Sawyer, and the other his trusted friend Huckleberry Finn. And, oh, what adventures he would give them and what characters and sights would fill his pages. Tom would get into scrapes, meet villainous tramps, and flee for his life. And Huck would float down the river, seeing all the sights and wonders that Twain himself knew so well.

As I say, we could write it that way—but we wouldn't. Instead, we would stop the narration at the end of the phrase "and what characters and sights would fill his pages." At that point you don't need to say any more because the pictures suggest exactly what Twain is going to write about.

Clichés. Watch out for the cliché, the hackneyed phrase. At one time, all the authors on feature film writing used to enjoy themselves by listing the most popular clichés: "A man's gotta do what a man's gotta do," "Yeah, it's quiet. Too damn quiet!" "There's only one doctor who can help you. And he's in Vienna." We laugh, but we do the same thing in documentary. We see a phrase that is good, and then use it so often that it ceases to have any impact.

A friend of mine used to make children's films about orphanages, resettlement centers, and children's charities. He chucked it when he found that the cliché factor had taken over. He had found one good phrase in his first film: "Do we want children of darkness or children of light, children of despair or children of hope?" When he found himself repeating this phrase in each film he knew it was time to quit.

Writing for different viewers. A problem that arises again and again, particularly when doing documentaries for television, is how to adjust your narration to accommodate a wide spectrum of viewers. For example, if you are doing a film on history, some viewers may know your subject well, while others may know nothing. If you give too much information, you may insult the intelligence of half your viewers, telling them things they know backward and forward. But if you assume that the audience already has a good knowledge of the subject, you may be talking over the heads of the other half of your audience. The answer lies in finding a subtle way of presenting your information so that both sides feel happy.

Let us say we have to do a film about Juan Perón's dictatorship in Argentina. We are talking of events that happened forty years ago, but whose chief characters are much less familiar to us than are Churchill and Hitler. Because we know that half the audience was born after the Vietnam War, we need to establish who's who and what's what. So we could write: "Perón was an army colonel who became a dictator. He led the Fascist Party in his country. He ruled Argentina and gained power in 1945." All the facts are there, though expressed a little bluntly. But by the time you have recited them, half your audience has said, just before turning off the television, "Who do they think we are? Six-year-olds?" You could express facts in a less offensive fashion: "Throughout the forty years since militarism and politics swept Perón into the dictatorship of Argentina, people have wondered when democracy would return to a country governed by generals." In the second version, the facts are given casually and without insulting anyone's intelligence, and everyone is happy.

Difficult terminology. Sometimes you find yourself having to put across difficult concepts with highly involved terminology. This is particularly true of scientific or medical films. The way out of this difficulty is to simplify your language and present the concept visually in a manner that everyone can understand. This may require using graphics or animation, or creating a scenario that demonstrates the concept.

A few years ago I saw a film on Einstein's life and work. Obviously, at some point the film had to discuss Einstein's theory of relativity—not the easiest of concepts to grasp, even for scientists. However, the writer presented the theory in an elegant fashion. He showed an airplane in flight so that we could appreciate that its speed relative to the ground was five hundred miles an hour. He then cut to two men playing catch inside the plane. Given this situation, it was easy to talk about the speed of the ball relative to the plane's motion to the ground. I'm not sure that everyone in the audience understood afterward the significance of $E = mc^2$, but at least they were on the way to understanding.

ONCE THE WRITING IS FINISHED

Scratch track. I mentioned earlier that it's useful to write some tentative narration to help in the first steps of the editing process. You can record this yourself, and the editor can lay your scratch track against the picture. This will give you a sense of how the film is going and will also allow your sponsor or executive producer to react to a more complete film. Once your final narration is complete, it is vital to try it against the film. This time you don't have to bother recording it; instead, you can just read it against the picture. This will give you and the editor a chance to see whether it sounds right and whether your timing is more or less correct.

The narrator. Your narrator can often make or break your film, so get the very best person available within your budget. When the narrator is actually going to appear on camera, you have two additional problems to solve: how to integrate the stand-ups with the rest of the text and how to get a natural performance from the narrator.

The easiest and most efficient solution to the first problem is to write the narrator's text after you have completed the rest of the commentary. You can then see the best way to bring the narrator in and out and also judge how his stand-up text can help move the film along and solve difficult transitional points.

You have various options for solving the second problem. You can write your full text and have the narrator learn it by heart. A few narrators like James Burke can do this, but not many. Second, you can use either "dummy cards," cards placed beside the camera with the full text, or a teleprompter underneath the lens. I don't like either of these methods because the viewer can sense the eyes darting to the cards, and the performance rarely comes over as natural or spontaneous.

I prefer to go over the key points of the text with the narrator and then let him or her simply improvise in front of the camera. It may take two or three tries, but the result usually has more punch than you get with either the cards or the teleprompter. Where your narrator is simply a "voice off," your problems are simpler. Your key concern then becomes to find the best voice to carry the message of your film. Sometimes you have exactly the right person in mind. If you don't, try a few auditions on tape. Have your would-be narrators read a few film passages and then play them back against the picture to see which works best.

Whenever possible, the narrator should see the film through with you in its entirety. After the screening, you can take time out to explain exactly what you are looking for in the film and in the narration reading. Then let the narrator take the text home and read it. When you next meet, he or she will usually have some questions. Do you mind if certain words are changed so that it reads more easily? And do you mind if the narrator rephrases the text slightly because what you have written isn't very clear? This is also the time to discuss once more the style, pace, and mood of the reading—time to specify which passages you want read fast and which slow, which emotionally, and which with humor. Is the narrator clear about what you are aiming for? If so, you can go ahead with the recording.

There are two ways of doing the actual recording. First, the narrator can *record to picture*, with you flashing a little red light every time you want a new section read. The other method is to have the narrator isolated in a recording booth to read the text in one go. I prefer the latter, reckoning that the narrator already has a good sense of the picture and should be allowed to concentrate on the reading with as few distractions as possible.

Generally I try to let the narrator do the reading in one shot without interruption. At that stage, you have indicated what kind of interpretation you want, and if the narrator is any good, he or she should be able to hit it fairly easily. The advantage of letting the narrator improvise is that with any luck, he or she will hit a good rhythm and pace and will be able to work emotionally into the feel of the narration. Obviously, you stop the recording and go back if the reading is wrong, but if you are going to make a comment, be very specific. Tell the narrator you want a passage put more dramatically or more slowly. Indicate specifically which words you want emphasized, and demonstrate what kind of rhythm you want. However, try to avoid too many interruptions in your aim for perfection, because the result may be counterproductive, with the reading deteriorating rather than improving.

In a long recording, watch that the narrator's vocal energy doesn't diminish. If it does, suggest a break. When you're finished, cheek the recording to see if you and the narrator are both satisfied. If not, redo any problematic sections.

The final thing is to record "presence," or "room tone." This is done by recording a minute or so of silence in the narration booth. It may sound funny to record silence, but in fact you are recording atmosphere that will fill in the sound gaps at the head and tail of the narration and occasionally in the middle.

Laying in the narration. However observant you have been during the narration recording, certain faults will show up only when you actually begin laying the track against the picture. You may find that there are problems with emphasis or intonation, that a certain phrase doesn't sound right, or that the balance between the music and narration is wrong. When you spot these points, it's usually easy to call the narrator back to make the changes. You also have to bear in mind that the sponsor or senior producer may require narration changes even at this late stage.

How do these changes affect your budget? I generally tell the narrator that I will want him or her for the main recording, but that I may also call later for minor changes. I then fix a total fee, thus avoiding awkward and costly negotiation at a later stage.

EXAMPLES

Throughout this chapter we have looked at extracts from different scripts to analyze approach, technique, and style. To finish off, we will examine a few scripts at greater length to see how writers develop their ideas.

The first example is from the Canadian film *City of Gold*, which combines personal style, memory, and evocation in a vivid portrait of Dawson City.

Visual	Audio
Children in park	PIERRE BERTON: This was my hometown. And my father's town before me. It's a quiet place. A few stores. A restaurant. Three, maybe four hundred people. Hard workers, most of them.

Old men on porch	On the main street the old men sit on the porch of the hotel in the sunshine, and they talk about the old days . . . the good old days.
Children in park	The park is always full of kids.
Children and town	And after the rain there are always plenty of puddles to sail boats in.
Town views	But I must tell you that this town where I spent my child hood isn't like any other town in the world. This is Dawson City, the center of the Klondike gold rush. History will never see its like again.
Old buildings	Every summer, when the seeds of fireweed drifted across the valley of the Yukon River, we kids used to roam through these decaying buildings. Some of them had been locked and barred for almost half a century.
Old pictures in buildings	You could buy anything in Dawson City, in its heyday, I remember my father telling me . . . anything from oysters to opera glasses. You could buy a dance-hall queen for her weight in gold, and one man did. His name was Chris Johanson, and he lived on Whiskey Hill.
Old steamboat	We played steamboat captain, too. These deserted stern-wheelers were part of a fleet of, oh, 250, that steamed up the Yukon in the stampede days.
Town, old men, atmosphere	Most of the men are gone with the steamboats. Of the tens of

thousands who came here, only a handful found the gold they were seeking. And yet few, I think, regretted the journey to Dawson City, for the great stampede was the high point of their lives.

Chilkoot Pass: stark, ice-covered mountains

The winter of 1897. Beyond mountains two thousand miles north from civilization, the cry was GOLD! And all over the world a million people laid plans to go.
One hundred thousand actually set out.

Miners' faces

Scarcely any of these men were miners. Most were white-collar workers. My father had just graduated from university in civil engineering. All of them had no idea. They were on the way to the Klondike to shovel up gold, and they were going to be rich beyond the dreams of avarice.

City of Gold was written by Pierre Berton in 1956 and still remains a model of scriptwriting excellence. It looks deceptively simple, but it is in fact meticulously well planned.

1. *Introduction*: The first few sentences set the scene and the tone with short, personal, and evocative statements: "There were always plenty of puddles to sail boats in."

2. *Theme*: The theme is then stated quickly and dramatically: "This is Dawson City, center of the Klondike gold rush. History will never see its like again." This last sentence about history begins to move the film along.

3. *Particulars*: Throughout the film, Berton avoids generalities, giving us instead details that heighten the sense of the craziness of Dawson City in the good old days: "You could buy a dance-hall queen for her weight in gold, and one man did." Later, although he

talks about the general types who came, he very quickly gets to the specific case of his father.

4. *Personal memory*: One of the keys to the film is the fluidity with which history and personal memory intermingle. While the father's recollections move the film along, Berton's own memories play their role, too: "We played steamboat captain, too. These deserted stern-wheelers were part of a fleet."

5. *Story progression*: One of the most important moments in the script is when Berton turns from reminiscence and scene setting to actually telling the story of the gold rush. It's all done in one short paragraph. "Most of the men are gone with the steamboats. . . . few regretted the journey to Dawson City, for the great stampede was the high point of their lives. . . . The winter of 1897. Beyond mountains two thousand miles north from civilization, the cry was GOLD!" It's important to note that the transition from present to past is also made pictorially, because at that point the film changes from contemporary footage to animation of the stills from 1897.

James Burke's *Connections* also tackles history, but in a very different, idiosyncratic way. Burke's subject is technological and scientific change, the mere mention of which is pretty off-putting. However, Burke makes science and technology comprehensible to the most ignorant of us in a highly amusing and entertaining way. In *Distant Voices*, the subject is the development of military technology. The film starts with a tease in which you see anonymous hands packing an atomic bomb into a suitcase and carrying it through a crowd. Over this the commentary states: "This is the nightmare of the second half of the twentieth century. A suitcase with an atomic bomb inside it. Once you steal the nuclear material any physics graduate can do the rest."

Burke then slides into the issue of how changes in military technology have caused social and political changes. His first example is the Battle of Hastings in 1066. Here he argues that the Normans won because they used mounted cavalry against the Saxon infantry. However, he adds, the deadly lance of the horseman could only be used because the stirrup had been invented—a small change with overwhelming historical results.

Burke goes on to talk of other changes: the coming of the knights and the rise of the aristocracy. In the extract below, Burke wants to show how the lances of the cavalry were eventually defeated by another technological change: the introduction of the longbow. As usual, Burke's language is casual, full of odd puns and jokes. The language is also directly addressed to the audience, pulling you right into the film.

Visual	Audio
Slow-motion montage of knights on horseback.	By 1250 the big league was a very exclusive club only the very rich could join, thanks in the first place to the stirrup and the way it had led to the fully armored knight on his massive war horse. The aristocrats now made sure the club stayed exclusive: they made knighthood hereditary and took on permanent family names instead of just being "son of somebody." And because the armor covered their faces, they needed identification marks to show in battle so they didn't get clobbered by their own men. These heraldic symbols completed the separation of the aristocrats from the rest. Immensely powerful and immensely rich, the armor-plated upper crust must have felt that they had absolutely got it made.
Burke sync.	By the fourteenth century the knight was a massive, expensive, complex, two-ton war machine, and at full gallop it would annihilate anything coming the other way, except of course, another knight. And then from out of the valleys of South Wales came something that was to take away from the armored knight his four centuries of domination, like that!

Burke in Westminster Abbey, moving around the statue of Henry V.

Let me tell you what happened. Henry, here, had about eight thousand men knocked out by fatigue from marching nonstop seventeen days in the rain. About a mile away across a battlefield of mud were thirty thousand Frenchmen, half of them fully armored aristocrats who'd been up all the previous night, 'cause they'd slept in their saddles because they didn't want to get all their lovely armor dirty. An arrogant, overbearing, effete lot, full of death and glory, and me first.

Pan with Burke as he walks. the morning Henry had some

So when, at about eleven in arrows shot at this mob to get them to do something, any-thing, because they had been standing around arguing the toss about who should lead the French army, oh, since seven in the morning, the French army upped and charged straight at Henry, straight across the sea of mud, straight on to the stakes that the English had put point up in their path, and that was when Henry played his trump card, didn't you?

Burke looks at Henry's sculptured face.

He called up the secret weapon his grandfather had discovered in the mountains of Wales, and when it came into action the slaughter was unimaginable.

Montage of shots of longbow, arrows, and battle in slow motion.

That weapon was the Welsh longbow, and Henry had over one thousand of them. In the hands of a master they were

deadly at one hundred yards—
and in three bloody hours the
French were massacred.

Most of Burke's tricks are obvious, so only two comments need be made. First, Burke often uses a lot of English slang that may be unfamiliar to American ears, so a purist American television station might raise objections to the script on that ground. Second, Burke writes for himself and goes very fast, packing a tremendous amount of information into a few seconds. He just about gets away with it, but I would be wary of emulating his style.

In *The Gates of Time*, I was asked to write a half-hour film on the history of the Old City of Jerusalem. One problem I had was the question of the narrator's stand-ups. As this wasn't a news, verité, or personal history film, I was able to write the core narration before we started shooting. However, as we came to editing, I realized that the film was a bit too loose and could do with a few stand-ups to tie the sequences together. I then went through the film choosing five or six places where I thought a very short stand-up would help. If I wasn't sure that I needed a stand-up, I still wrote one, noting in my mind that I could always discard it if it wasn't necessary or didn't work.

The stand-ups were easy to write, taking only about an hour. The only real problem was to make sure that the entrances into and the exits from the stand-ups were integrated smoothly into the rest of the script.

Visual	Audio
Helicopter shots of Jerusalem.	When he left Palestine in the '20s, the British governor of its capital said, "After Jerusalem there can be no higher promotion!"
	For him, as for millions of others, there was no counterpart to Jerusalem in the history of the West.
	Jerusalem was the center of two faiths and holy to a third. It was the light. The guardian of ideals. The eternal city. The symbol of perfection.
Ground shots: many cars, dense crowds jostling, thrusting.	But as well as the Jerusalem of the mind, there is also the Jeru-

salem of reality. There is the
modern city developed in the
last century, and the ancient
city where over twenty-five
thousand people still live
and work behind medieval
fortress walls.

Sync stand-up.

NARRATOR: And there it is. A
city that has to cope with all the
pressures of the '90s as well as
the gifts and burdens of a
unique history.
And therein lies the dilemma.
How does one preserve and
honor the spirit of the past,
and the legacy of time, and yet
move into the twenty-first
century?
I'm Irv Kaplan, a writer and
broadcaster. In this film I want
you to join me in looking more
closely at the challenges and
dilemmas of this city, and also
some of the solutions. . . .

(*Transitional section omitted*)

Medieval maps of Jerusalem.

NARRATOR (*off camera*):
Following the Crusaders, the
idea of the mystical perfection
of Jerusalem deepened with
the centuries.
Thus the British poet Blake
wrote that his deepest desire
was "to build Jerusalem in
England's green and pleasant
land."

Idealized prints of nineteenth-
century Jerusalem.

Again and again the prints of
nineteenth-century artists show
an idealized image of a Bible
city where Abraham, if alive,
could still walk in peace and
repose.

Archival footage of beggars, cripples, dark streets, foul alleys.	After such romance the reality of nineteenth-century Jerusalem came as a bitter shock.
	Lepers, cripples, and beggars greeted the traveler at every gate.
Crowded, dirty churches, filthy crowds.	Baedeker's guide warned him that rubbish and filth concealed the holy places.
	When Herzl, the pioneer Zionist dreamer, visited in 1898, he wrote, "When I remember thee, O Jerusalem, it will not be with joy. The must deposits of two thousand years lie reeking in your alleys."
British troops enter Jerusalem.	In 1917 British and Australian troops under Allenby captured Jerusalem, ending four hundred years of Turkish rule. For the Allied troops, many of whom were devoted churchgoers, it was a poignant moment.
Narrator sync stand-up	NARRATOR (*stand-up*): After his humble entry on foot through the Jaffa Gate, General Allenby stood close to where I'm standing now. Here he swore to honor Jerusalem and protect its inhabitants. Jerusalem was the *sacred trust*, and its new guardians swore to do all they could for it.

The above film had actually went through a number of drafts till it was finalized and I was happy with it. This often happens. As you work on your film, you will constantly test your ideas against the script and the visuals, and vice versa. This is because filmmaking is not a static but an evolving process. To get your work to yield its maximum potential takes time, effort, and patience. Finally, however, comes the magic moment when it all seems right. Only then can you relax and take it easy.

16

FINISHING THE FILM

THE SOUND MIX

Once you have finished picture editing, you have to prepare and mix your various sound tracks. Here you may be dealing with five or more tracks, the most common ones being the narration and sync tracks, two music tracks, and at least one effects track. Ultimately you are going to mix them down into one master track for 16mm films or two for stereo or video. In film this is done in a dubbing studio; in video most of the preparations are completed in the off-line stage. The *art* of preparing for a mix is the same in film and video, but the actual technique a little more complex for the former. In what follows, the general principles apply to both forms, but most of the practical procedures discussed are geared to film rather than video.

Narration. As director you should be present when the narration is laid in to make sure that the words hit at exactly the right spot. Sometimes you may have to do this by making small changes to the picture. Other times you will have to lengthen the narration by adding pauses (*blank leader*) between words or phrases or by shortening the narration by taking out extraneous words. You have to take care that your editing of the narration doesn't make the text sound awkward or peculiar. For example, you don't want to take out a word and then find that the text finishes on an unnaturally high note or that the sentence ends abruptly. Also look again and again at how much text you actually need. If you have a tendency to overwrite, see if you can lose some nonessential sentences at this point. This will help the film breathe.

Music. Music is usually laid on two tracks so that you can always fade one out, if necessary, as you bring up the other. It's also good practice to leave the picture slightly long until you have finalized the music, as you may want to cut the picture to the beat of the music. If your picture is slightly long, then there's no problem; you can just cut out a few frames. But if the picture is too short, you may be in trouble.

One of the essential things to do, once the music is laid, is check how the music, narration, and sync tracks harmonize with one another. Try to avoid competition. If you have some beautiful music that is more than mood background, make sure it is not laid opposite narration. When this happens, the narration always wins and the music gets lost, because narration is given prominence in the sound mix.

A slightly different problem exists in finding the right balance between music and effects. Many editors put in excellent music and then create very full effects tracks to enhance the film's verisimilitude. That's fine, but make sure the two blend easily. If both are laid down in the same spot, you may sometimes have to choose one or the other, but not both. Either will work alone, but mixed together they may produce a dirty or muddy effect on the sound track that is not pleasing to the ear.

Sound effects. Some of your sound effects will have been recorded in sync, but others will be wild effects recorded on location or effects purchased from a music library or taken from an effects disc. You will probably lay in the first, together with dialogue, as you edit the picture; the latter are laid down when you have finished the music and narration tracks. In other words, the effects track is normally the last track to be laid. Effects bring the film alive, enhancing the sense of realism. Leave them out, and you miss them immediately.

Effects used to be laid down very tediously on 16mm magnetic tape. The standard procedure today, for both film and video, is to send the fine-cut visuals to an effects editor, who will lay down effects and music against the visuals via a computer using a program called Protools. Generally we refer to the process as the audio work station.

Effects are used in two ways: as spot effects and as general or ambient atmosphere. Spot effects are sync effects of doors closing, guns going off, books dropping, feet marching—effects that must absolutely match the picture. General atmosphere effects add to the mood but are not necessarily tied to a spot source. Thus, in films, you often hear birds singing or a dog barking without ever seeing them.

The main question regarding effects is how many you really need. We can put this another way: not everything that you see in a film that makes a noise will require a sound effect. In fact, you may use very few. Your goals are atmosphere and realism, not necessarily authenticity. Laying sound effects is not an automatic process, but one that leaves as much scope for creativity as choosing and laying the music. Thus, the current use of *sound designer* for the person in charge of effects.

You should always record a minute or so of wild sound on every location. When you lay the tracks, this wild sound can be looped either to fill in gaps in the sound or to provide atmosphere.

Dubbing cue sheet. The odds are that you may never even have heard of, let alone used, a dubbing cue sheet. Once considered a necessity, they are now only used in very large productions. In current practice, a good sound work-station system will provide you with all the information needed to mix your film. Nevertheless, you might occasionally have to use the old system, with 16mm magnetic tracks, so I've set out the principles briefly below.

The system works this way. Once you or the editor have laid in all the tracks, you need to make a dubbing cue sheet or mix chart. This is a diagram that shows the entry and exit of each sound on each track, its length, and its relationship to the sounds on the other tracks. The chart will then act as a master guide for the editor and the sound engineer during the mix.

The procedure for making the cue sheet is comparatively simple. The editor puts each track on the editing table, one at a time, and then notes down from the footage counter where each sound enters and exits. This information is entered into a chart, as shown in figure 16.1. A straight line represents a cut; a chevron, a fade-in or a fade-out. Two chevrons side by side, with one inverted, is the sign for a sound dissolve. To make things easier, many editors color code their charts—red for music, blue for narration, and so on.

Studio procedures. The cue sheet for the mix represents your recording master plan, and I like to have two prepared: one for the editor and one for the sound engineer. The editor is normally in charge of the sound mix and tells the sound engineer the desired shadings. However, you as director-producer will have the last word. At the mix, the work print is projected onto a screen beneath which are running footage numbers, which you check against the numbers of the mix chart.

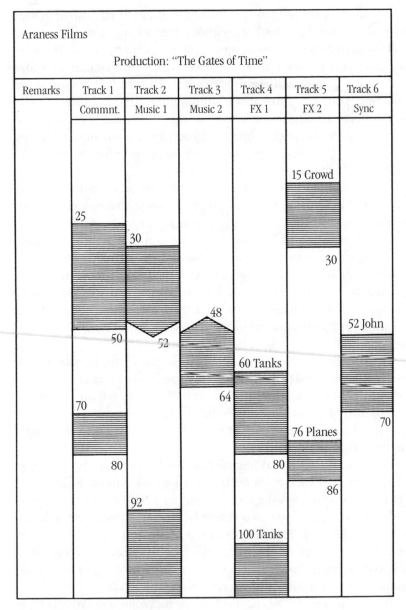

Remarks	Track 1	Track 2	Track 3	Track 4	Track 5	Track 6
	Commnt.	Music 1	Music 2	FX 1	FX 2	Sync

Figure 16.1. Dubbing Cue Sheet

Projection print. In a traditional mix, only a few years ago, a work print of the film was projected in a dubbing theater in which it ran in sync with a number of magnetic replay machines. The capacity for delays and error were extremely high. Today a video print is usually made of the fine-cut film (if one doesn't exist), and the sound is dubbed against the image on a computer.

Mixing the tracks. Your objective is to mix all the tracks onto one balanced master track. You can do this in one go, or you can do it in stages through a series of premixes before tackling the master recording.

If you have a large number of tracks, say seven or eight, it is simply easier to premix a number of them before doing the master. Here, simplicity and ease are the rationale for your actions. But there may be a second reason that is just as important: you may have to make an "M&E" track before the final mix: M&E stands for music and effects, and you always make sure you have this track if you think your film may be translated into a foreign language. If your film is going abroad, say to a French or German television station, they will ask for two tracks, the dialogue track and the M&E track. The station will then translate your English dialogue track to French or German, take the M&E track, and, using both, create a new final mix. The French or the German will then appear to be fully integrated with the music and the effects.

In what order should you do the premixes? There are no rules. Where possible, I like to do a first mix of music and effects (the M&E track), a second mix of sync dialogues, a third mix of the above two, and a fourth and final mix with the narration. If there is time and money for only one premix, then it's customary to do music and effects as a premix, bringing in dialogue and narration for the final mix.

Mixing can be a tremendously tedious process. You must try to pay attention to the way all the elements blend together. Usually you will screen only half a minute or so at a time; using the mix chart as a guide, the editor will tell the engineer how the sound should be matched and recorded for that section. The recording is rarely perfect the first time: the music comes in too loudly or a certain effect isn't heard. The second time you try the same passage, everything works except that the music fade is done badly. So you bounce back and forth until you are all satisfied and can move on to the next section.

When the original quality of sound is not very good, it can often be enhanced, or "sweetened," by the studio equipment. A filter can take some of the hum off your track, or an echo can be laid in to emphasize mood.

What you are looking for the whole time is quality of the sound and harmony between the tracks. When you have finished, you must listen to the playback of the final mix. If something is wrong, now is the time to redo it. In particular, you should check this final mix very carefully against the picture for sync loss caused by the picture's jumping a frame in the projector during recording.

TITLES AND CREDITS

Concurrent with all the preparations for the sound mix are your decisions about titles, credits, and optical effects. The usual practice in film is to mark in opticals, dissolves, and supers during editing. If not, they must be marked in before the film goes to the lab for the negative cut. Title and credits are another story. You may well have left your decisions on these—what they are, where they appear, and how they appear—until the fine cut is completed. But now the time has come for a final decision on these matters.

There are various options for the presentation of titles and credits in film. First, you can present them white or colored on a black or colored neutral back ground, or they can be "supered" (superimposed) over a still or moving picture. The first option is simple, usually effective, and without many technical problems. The second option can look flashier and more dramatic, but it costs more than the simple title cards and can look messy if the lab work isn't of the best quality.

If you have the money and the desire you can also create special graphics, both pictorial and animated, for opening and closing titles. Here, there are no limits except your purse and your taste. When the graphics are done as beautifully and as humorously as in Agnieszka Piotrowska's *The Bigamists*, the result is well worth the cost and the effort.

If you do go for the supers, you have to be careful where you place them. First, the supers should appear on a fairly dark background so that they stand out. It's no use having a white or yellow super over a white sky. Second, you should check that the super doesn't obscure some vital information in the picture. This may mean that your titles or credits are not always dead center, but shifted left or right according to the background.

These days, with computer graphics, you have a tremendous choice available for titles. You may want to go for simple lettering or something very elaborate. The field is wide open to your own personal taste and feelings. For a whimsical film, you might want to try ornately decorated titles. For a medical film, you may want to keep the titles very straightforward.

There is really only one rule: make sure your titles and credits are readable. This means choosing the right size for them in relation to the screen and leaving them on the screen long enough so that they can be read easily. Usually there is no problem with pop-in, pop-out titles or with titles that dissolve into one another. Roller titles or roller credits are another story. Roller credits are often so close together and pass by so quickly that they become completely incomprehensible. Be sure to check the distance between the credits on the roller and the speed of the crawl. Video credits are much simpler to deal with. They can usually be done on your own computer or recorded on a floppy disk at the off-line stage. The disk is then brought in to the on-line studio, where you can play around with style and color as the credits, plus effects, are transferred to the edit in the computer.

MAKING THE PRINT

In film, the final work on the titles and the sound mix should more or less coincide. You can then move on to actually making the print. When you and the editor are satisfied, you can give instructions for the mix to go to the lab, where an optical negative will be made from the magnetic recording. The only thing you should do before that is make sure that you have a duplicate copy of the mix so that if anything goes wrong or if the mix gets lost, you won't have to go through the whole recording session again. At that point you're finished with the sound.

Once you have concluded the work on the titles and the credits, you can leave the film at the lab for the negative cut. This can take anywhere from a few days to weeks or months, depending on the length of the film. When the first answer print is ready, check first that the film is in sync and that the sound quality is good. Second, you need to see that the lab hasn't made any mistakes in the negative cut. This can mean frames or a shot missing, opticals lost, or even, as once happened to me, a shot printed upside down. Finally, you need to check the color quality of the print. Is the color bias right? Are the blues too blue or the greens too pale? Do some scenes have peculiar tones to them? Are some scenes printed too light and others too dark? Does the film have an overall unity to its color?

You'll be asking yourself these and a dozen other questions. Normally the first print will reveal a number of faults, and it is your task to catch them. Once you see what they are, you have to sit down with the lab technicians and see how they can be corrected. The best way to do this is to get your cameraperson to sit in on the color grading and comment on the problems of each scene.

Your film may go through two or three trial prints until you are satisfied you have the best copy possible. The cost of the extra trial prints is usually borne by the lab. All this takes time, but it's worth it because now you have something to show for those months of effort. Now, finally, you have a film you're terribly proud of, and which, even in all modesty, you think might be an outside candidate for a documentary Oscar.

PART FIVE

Special Cases

17

MAKING YOUR FIRST FILM

OK. You've just come to university or film school, you've signed up for Video 101 or Doc Films 117, and you are about to start your first film. You've read a little about the exercise in the course description, and you rather like the idea of yourself as embryo director. In your mind's eye, you see yourself swaggering along with the camera under one arm, the tripod on your shoulder, while all the gray law students secretly envy your choice of career. But along with the excitement there is also some internal trepidation. What on earth am I getting into? What do I know about documentary? Where can I see some examples of short films or film exercises to guide me? This last question is probably the most serious.

Most of us have seen half-hour documentaries or short training films, but they aren't very useful as instructional models. Usually the length, the pacing, the story, and the structure are so different from what you have to do that it is best to just ignore them. The closest thing to the challenge that faces you seems at first to be the five- or ten-minute television news or magazine clip. But that is totally the wrong example for you. Those clips and stories are devoted to television journalism, and they use news techniques. Their approach to filmmaking is very different from yours in terms of both methods and objectives. For example, the films usually tell a breaking news story, are dominated by lengthy interviews and on-screen personalities, and are essentially driven by words rather than pictures. Thus, the editing is often done to a fixed commentary, and all sense of pace or art goes out of the window. So let's forget about them and start from scratch.

The first real documentary challenge at most film schools is usually to produce a seven- or ten-minute film within the space of the ten to fourteen weeks of term. You've probably had a few lessons in camerawork, sound and basic editing, and so as far as technical matters go, you think you are up to scratch. But making a film—well, that's new territory. Where do you begin? By acknowledging that your problem can really be split into two. The first, and hardest, is to find the right subject. The second, and easiest, is to solve all your practical and technical problems.

Before considering concrete ideas, let's think for a moment about what you are really doing. You are producing something akin to a short story or a sonnet. You are producing a short piece of work that is not going to be very long or overcomplex but that nevertheless will leave the viewer with one or two revelations or insights that may fascinate or intrigue him or her. Again, you are going to be the person who opens secret doors. You are going to explain and illuminate situations that have always interested us but that we've never probed. You are going to show us how the flight crew is briefed and prepared before takeoff, how the down-and-outs manage to live from day to day, how clowns practice for their performances, or how an amateur group gets ready for a theater performance.

Ideas, of course, come to you in many ways. You're pulled up by a story in a newspaper. A friend has told you about an interesting character worth filming. You brother has told you about a school down the road that trains comedians. You've heard about a transvestite show and wonder about the background of some of the performers. Now all these subjects have to intrigue *you*. If the idea really holds *your* attention, then you'll find a good way to put it over to other people. In short, the best starting point is to find an idea that is meaningful for you and genuinely intrigues you and is probably about people and their secrets: their secret lives, their secret passions. Of course, if there is no idea that has been brewing for years, you go for one that at least amuses you, fascinates you, and that you'll have fun pursuing. But what is vital is that the idea is focused and practical and has a central idea or theme or curious story that will be easy to tell.

Now you've been mulling over everything talked about above and all sorts of subjects have been revolving in your head. And that's great, and you've probably been asked to discuss them in class. However, before you burst into song and dance in front of your instructor in your effort to show her that you are the Orson Welles or Akira Kurosawa of your generation, you need to ask yourself one thing: is it feasible for me to do my film in the allotted time and under the prevailing conditions? That means, for example, you'll have to dump any films that mean traveling more than five miles from campus. You haven't got the time and the budget. You'll also have to forget that nice idea in which you trace a novelist from first pages to finished book. You haven't got two years to spare. And forget the film about the Secret Service because you are not going to get access. All this means that one of one of your ideas may have been bumped before you even get started. But that's good. It means time hasn't been wasted in chasing an impossible and impractical idea.

Are there parameters and guides for choosing potential stories that can help you focus your ideas before coming to class? Yes. In first exercises it is helpful to go for a subject that is very visual and possibly has plenty of action. If the subject is not visual, how are you going to tell it? You also look for charismatic characters and good storytellers with whom you can go on a journey of discovery. Again, watching the process of creation is always good, whether we are looking at the amateur boatbuilder or the kid who competes in building and flying kites. And you look for people going through change, growth, suffering—whose lives hold you as they reach for the stars or try to pull them selves up from the pit.

As you can see, your starting point is usually people doing interesting things who are willing to disclose their lives and actions to you. But what should you avoid? First, avoid fascinating characters whose stories have no possibility of development. For example, a year ago a student came to me and said she wanted to do a film about a soapbox speaker whom she'd heard on a street corner, and who was there six days a week. The idea was initially intriguing, but research showed that the character had no substance and did nothing of interest besides talk. The second thing to avoid is the waffly subject that sounds good for an essay but is horrendous for a film. Here I am thinking of the student who told me she wanted to do a film about the problems of modern woman in the twenty-first century. Impossible! When I pressed the student, I found there was in fact a small film behind the general subject, which was the story of a seventeen-year-old mother who lived on the streets and wanted to keep her six-month-old baby.

So far we've talked of broad simple principles. However, a few illustrations of some successful films made by the students of myself and friends may help you understand how these principles work, and why.

Underground Musicians is a portrait of street musicians who played and sang in the London subways. This could have been a simple performance film, but it became much more. This was because the director showed us that the musicians had to go through various tests and interviews before they were granted a performance pitch at a particular underground station. It was this unknown information and the scenes of the tests that made the film.

In *Wild Boy*, the opening scenes introduced us to a well-groomed young Chinese man, dressed in evening dress, giving a classical piano concert. The film then cut to the same man at an amusement arcade going crazy as he played music and pinball machines with amazing speed. The catch point of the film was the amazing contrast between the two types of behavior from the one person.

Coffee Shop, made by a Singaporean student of mine, simply contrasted an old-style Chinese coffee shop with a glitzy Starbucks. It was a simple idea, beautifully executed, with the underlying but never-asked question was, What has modernity really brought us?

Marlboro Man was made by a young Stanford woman student and introduced us to the lifestyle of a Marlboro Man, the rangy, handsome cowboy of so many cigarette advertisements. The film showed the Marlboro Man on the range but then revealed that he was gay, had AIDS, and lectured on the dangers of AIDS to schoolchildren. The film's fascination depended on the contrast between the mythical image and reality.

Rehearsal was a classic *in-process* film in which the students followed a theater group from rehearsal to performance. What distinguished the film was that the group met and rehearsed above an English pub, so the pub scenes made a light contrast to the heavier theater scenes.

I was present when all the above films were pitched and remember saying to myself at the time, "Yes, these are going to work." That really wasn't a particularly complex judgment because all the films had the elements we discussed. They were visual, had charismatic people doing interesting things, and revolved around subjects that were of general interest to most people. They did not pose complex shooting situations, and all were shot in just three or four days. Also, very few of them were dependent on interviews.

Now the question of interviews—to use or not to use—always comes up when discussing student exercises. Many of my teaching friends bar their use. I can see why they take that attitude. They are frightened that students will merely reproduce hard news broadcasts and become simple video journalists. They also essentially want the students to think visually rather than rely on words and long explanations.

As is clear from what I wrote on narration, I tend to disagree with this attitude. Interviews and the use of narration are two of the basic tools of film. However, they are complex tools, easily abused—and too often used as crutches when other film ideas have been exhausted. In your first exercises, I would say use interviews if you must, but use them very sparingly.

Once you've found your gripping subject, you also have to consider the few practical and technical issues that confront you when doing your first exercises. Most of these problems are easy to manage or solve.

Crew. Where many first filmmakers go wrong is that they try to do everything themselves. When this happens, you get worried, flustered, overwrought, and touchy. Ideally, you should do your first film with three or four others, each person being responsible for a particular task such as cameraperson, director, and so on.

Research and preproduction. The better your research and preproduction, the better your film. The research will help you make up your mind what, where, and how to film. From there you make up a shooting schedule and make sure you have secured all necessary permissions.

As a first-time director, you are going to feel awkward on your first shoot. People will be looking at you for instructions. And the talent will also be waiting to know what to do. Therefore, the more organized you are, the better. But allow for reshoots. And when things go wrong, as they will, don't worry. Stay cool. You can always come back, and videotape is cheap.

Camera and sound. You've already had a few camera courses, but the odds are you've concentrated on lighting and lenses and focus and all the technical things. And you've probably worked mostly with actors. On location it's going to be different. You are going to have to follow things as they happen, which is another ball game entirely. Here two or three hints that will get you out of most difficulties. Stay away from zooming, stay wide, and fix your frame and hold it. Let things happen in the frame rather than get involved in lots of movement. Finally, give your editor plenty of material to play with. For once, quantity probably matters more than quality.

Talent. From the start you've looked for people who are good on camera. But do they know what they are really getting into? Do they know how much time is involved, and how much you'll be following them around? Will the filming fit into their schedules, and do they really appreciate that they'll be up there on the screen for all to see? Finally, will the talent give you reasonable access to everything you need, and are there restrictions on anything you want to film? If the latter is true, then think twice before getting involved, otherwise you may not be able to get the film you want.

Copyright. Where many students make mistakes is on copyright issues. There is only one rule. If you use photos, music, letters, or archives, make sure you have total permission for use everywhere and anyhow. Don't think that because someone has given you materials for "educational use" that is enough. It is not, and this lack of permission may well limit your piece to a film-school showing when it might have had a festival or broader distribution.

As you can see from the above, most of the things you have to keep in mind are fairly simple. You start off with a good down-to-earth idea; you choose a good crew; you prepare well and you brief your talent—and behold, there's your A grade at the end of the course. And, more important, you hold a great first film in your hand.

18

CINEMA VERITÉ

Cinema verité, or direct cinema, as it is sometimes called in America, is actually a *method* of filmmaking rather than a type of film of the profile or nature variety. *Cinema verité* was the name given to the radical experiments in filmmaking undertaken in the United States, Canada, and France in the early 1960s. Robert Drew, Ricky Leacock, and Don Pennebaker were among those working furiously to perfect a system whereby lighter, shoulder-borne cameras could be used with lightweight, synchronized tape recorders. Their technical break-throughs produced nothing short of a revolution, radically altering structure and approach in documentary.

Some of the practitioners of the new cinema tentatively suggested that cinema verité would do away with the old fiction cinema. Though the approach varied from person to person, the general method of filming necessitated the following:

an evolving story with plenty of incident
no prestructuring
following the story as and when it occurred
a tremendously high ratio of shooting, up to forty or fifty to one
no prompting, directing, or interviewing between the director or
    cameraperson and the subject

>minimal or no commentary
>finding and building the film on the editing table

The results of this approach were tremendously fresh and exciting, certainly as compared with the well-crafted but rather dull, static, and predictable documentaries of the networks. Today it is hard to recall any of the news documentaries of CBS, NBC, or ABC from the 1960s, whereas the cinema verité films of that period are still constantly viewed.

In general, cinema verité films of the 1960s examined personalities, crises, and pop concerts, with some limited political coverage. Starting from that base, filmmakers of the 1970s and 1980s helped extend the range and possibilities of the form, which is still tremendously popular. For various reasons, cinema verité seems to be the most attractive option open to young filmmakers. It is associated with perhaps the greatest films of the 1960s. It also has a veneer of excitement and seems to promise intimacy, truth, and an ability to transcend the crass barriers of old-fashioned documentary—altogether an attractive canvas.

One student described cinema verité to me this way: "It is less manipulative. More human. It gets to the heart of things, and it's more real and direct." I am not entirely convinced. Cinema verité may be all that is claimed above, but I suspect there is another reason for its popularity; it seems to involve less work than do the older documentary forms. You apparently don't have to do any research. You don't have to write boring scripts and boring commentary. You don't have to bother with preplanning; you can just go ahead and shoot. And if you screw things up, never mind; everyone knows the film is made in the cutting room. Indeed, despite its many attractions, cinema verité also has immense problems that are underrated by beginning filmmakers. You must consider them before you race ahead.

SHOOTING DIFFICULTIES

Cost

When you make a cinema verité film, you are entering uncharted regions. Very often you don't know what you will shoot, how much you will have to shoot, and what makes sense to shoot. You just plunge straight in and spend your time waiting to cover the critical moments. But as you don't even know what the critical moments are, the tendency is to shoot and shoot, and that becomes tremendously expensive. Many cinema verité films are shot on a ratio of forty or fifty to one because nothing is preplanned or prestructured. This may mean the purchase and development of fifty hours of film stock. If the film can be shot on videotape, then there are tremendous savings, though editing costs may still be very high. Stock costs are just the beginning. Crew costs then have to be added, and with an indeterminate number of shooting days, these may be tremendously high. Students viewing the marvelous early Drew and Leacock films often forget that these films were financed by Time-Life, which is certainly not one of the poorest corporations in the world.

Postproduction costs can also be astronomical. Not only is editing time likely to be longer than on the structured film, but taking care of the paperwork, transcripts, records, and the like is also likely to be expensive. *A Married Couple*, Allan King's study of a marriage in crisis, was shot on film over a period of eight weeks in 1969. The estimated budget for the ninety-minute film was $130,000. The final cost, due to overruns and the need for extra shooting, was $203,000. Today the cost would be at least $800,000 to $1 million—not very much for a feature, but very high for a documentary.

Finding the Film

Some filmmakers plunge into their films without the least clue of what they will be about. They're just following a hunch. If you film long enough, something interesting will happen. I guess the same rationale supports the argument that if you leave monkeys long enough with a typewriter, they will write *Hamlet*. It seems obvious that one must have a clear concept before embarking on a film, yet many cinema verité filmmakers ignore that at their own peril. You must know what your film is about. It may change direction or emphasis midway, but without that initial clarity you are going to finish up in some very deep waters.

Don Pennebaker took a risk in doing *Don't Look Back*, the story of Bob Dylan's first English tour, but not much of one. Dylan was controversial, colorful, charismatic. Something was bound to happen on the tour, and even if it didn't, the songs would guarantee a reasonably entertaining film. In contrast, the dangers were far greater in Ira Wohl's Academy Award–winning *Best Boy*. Following a brain-damaged adult for a few years could not have been the most promising of subjects. In the end the film succeeds because of the warmth of the subject and his family, the sensitivity of the filmmakers, and the riveting process of change in Philly presented by the film.

I find the basic guide to making cinema verité is to ask yourself, "Do I have charismatic characters involved in interesting and developing situations?" This doesn't cover everything but it is a very good starting point. In the excellent Australian film *Fahimeh's Story*, directed by Faramarz K-Rahber, all those elements were there, and in a sense the filmmakers couldn't go wrong.

In *Fahimeh's Story* we follow the story of an immigrant Iranian woman who marries elderly Australian John. Fahimeh is warm, funny, and dynamic, and her husband John is exactly the opposite, totally dry and dour. So, conflict in character and background can be seen from the beginning. John is Christian and Fahimeh is Muslim. This is also a basis for some problems, though in the end John becomes a Muslim. Fahimeh's children absolutely can't understand why she would marry an old stick like John, so it is also clear that there will be conflict with the kids. And to cap things off Fahimeh's Iranian husband is going to put in an appearance, oblivious to the fact that she's remarried. I mention all this because if you set all these things out on paper you can see easily that the film had a tremendous potential for success.

Michèle Ohayon's very funny 2005 film *Cowboy Del Amour* is another very positive illustration of good characters making good films. The film, mentioned earlier, follows seventy four-year-old retired Texas cowboy Ivan Thompson who, on payment of $3,000, takes American men over the border to meet Mexican women, with a view to marriage. The film is a typical "let's run and see what happens" story. What brings the film to life, and what gave Ohayon confidence in her story, is that Ivan is an amazing character: talkative, quirky, and with wonderful stories. Furthermore, he not only is fascinating to watch as he steers three American men toward their prospective brides but is also very open and expressive on camera. Thus, one of the best scenes in the film is when he talks to the camera and says, "Oh my God. I think she's turning on to me instead of my client. She wants to go to bed with me. What shall I do?"

In *Molly and Mobarak*, Australian filmmaker Tom Zubrycki took more of a risk. When he started shooting, all he knew was that he wanted to follow the trials and tribulations of a young Afghan refugee working in an abattoir in New South Wales. Mobarak was a good choice of a character, attractive and likable, and I assume Zubrycki's first impulse was to follow and document Mobarak's life and problems in his town as he tries to become Australian but also fights to renew his visa. Luck enters the scene when Mobarak meets Molly, a lovely

Australian teenager who teaches him English. Subsequently, Molly and Mobarak seem to be falling in love, with complications being added by the fact that Molly's mother is also quite taken with Mobarak. Here we have strong characters, cultural contrasts, and three crisis threads. Will Mobarak be thrown out of a job? Will he be allowed to stay in Australia? And will Molly and Mobarak stay together or part?

Zubrycki jumped in and was lucky. The problem the filmmaker often faces is that after weighing all the changes and coming to the conclusion that the subject matter is interesting, even fascinating, the film still goes nowhere. Nothing seems to happen. Nothing seems to develop. And in the end, the filmmaker is left with a mass of material without center or focus, and that, truth be told, looks pretty boring.

When the Maysles brothers started filming *Salesman*, the concept probably looked intriguing: follow four Bible salesmen around long enough and something will happen. As it turned out, although the brothers shot some amazing footage, they didn't have a clue what the final story might be about. According to editor Charlotte Zwerin, the real story was found only on the editing table.

> David and I started structuring a story about four salesmen, very much in the order the thing was filmed. Anyway, we started with the four salesmen story, and it took a long time because we started off in the wrong direction. We took about four months trying to make a story about four people, and we didn't have the material. Gradually we realized we were dealing with a story about Paul, and that these other people were minor characters in the story. So the first thing was to concentrate on Paul, and go to the scenes that had a lot to say about him. That automatically eliminated a great deal of the other stuff we had been working on till then. (Alan Rosenthal, *The New Documentary in Action* [Berkeley: University of California Press, 1971])

What to Film

What do you film when you are not sure of the story, you're not sure what is going to happen, and stock is costing you about $175 for every ten minutes of filming? This is one of the greatest dilemmas of cinema verité: when should you start shooting? In action, conflict, or performance films, the answer is relatively easy. You go for the action, the drama, the climax. You shoot the race, getting the beginning, a bit of the middle, and definitely the end. You shoot the soldiers' assault on the hill, including preparations and the moment of takeoff. When you shoot the performance, you make sure you have plenty of backstage material, first entrance, audience reactions, and highlights. But what do you do when your film is about ordinary lives, when there are no clearly defined dramatic points? Do you just hang in and shoot everything? Obviously not. But what are the guides? First, you want to look for the scenes that reveal personality, attitudes, and opinions. This may be by talk or by action. The corollary of this is that you have to be very sensitive to what is happening, listening very carefully and watching.

Often the motivation of when to shoot comes from intuition, from the way someone walks, is dressed, glances at, or observes his or her surrounds. It is the feeling that something interesting may develop if two people talk. As Fred Wiseman once put it, you learn to follow a hunch. Your hunch may not always be right, but it is better to follow it rather than to risk losing a good sequence.

Second, you look for scenes that will develop into something—an argument, a burst of passion, a rejection, a coming together. Even if the scene doesn't develop, are you watching something that is significant in itself to indicate mood or feeling?

Third, you look for patterns over time and try to mark out the most useful time to be around. It might be dinnertime, when all the resentments of the day begin to flare up. It might be late evening, when the kids have gone to bed and the husband and wife are left to face the predicament of their faltering relationship. Anticipation is the key. You have to cultivate the sensitivity to know when things are going to happen or going to break, and you have to be ready.

How to Film

Usually, filming cinema verité implies no retakes. So what do you do if the situation is jumping, but, as usual, you're in a one-camera shoot? You go for the most important sync dialogue and try to anticipate where the next main dialogue is going to come from. Afterward, you try to get the cutaways so the editor will have something to work with, hoping that while doing this, you're not losing too much sync. The essence of cinema verité shooting is not that much different from normal documentary. You try to understand the scene and what's going on, seize the heart of the action, and then go for it.

In the film *Crisis*, Don Pennebaker's task was to shoot a meeting in the White House between President Kennedy and his staff as they discussed the integration of two black children into a southern school. It's interesting to see how he planned to shoot, and then how he changed his strategy because of the evolving situation.

I told the soundman, stay out of the middle of the room. Get the best sound you can but don't get in the middle because I am going to try and get a whole roomful of people. The most extraordinary things were happening in the room. It was the first time we'd ever tried to shoot a roomful of people and it was very hard to do.

The usual rule is you start wide and you end up on whoever is making the scene work, whoever you're interested in, and you come in tight and you watch him—you know, you go in that direction.

In this case I had to reverse all that and keep pulling back, because every time the president would do something or say something, there'd be eight people moving around or changing position, and you realized there was some extraordinary ritual dance going on, which had to do, I guess, with the way power was leaking out of the system. (From P. J. O'Connell's manuscript, "Robert Drew and the Development of Cinema Verité in America.")

THE EDITING PROCESS

In 90 percent of the cases, the cinema verité film is found and made on the editing table. Often the filmmaker senses there is a story but is unsure what it is until the material has been sifted and partially edited. So, the selection of a creative and thoughtful editor becomes even more crucial to the success of the cinema verité film.

In a scripted film, the editing process is fairly straightforward. Since the story line of the film is given, it is usually easy to start at the beginning and, without too much bother, make your way to the end. In a cinema verité film, you often don't even know what the focal point of the film is or what it is about, let alone have the comfort of starting at a beginning and working through to a conclusion.

Where do you begin when you're faced with all these problems? I start by cutting scenes I like and seeing what makes them work and what they reveal to me. At that stage I don't bother with the placement of the scenes within the overall film. When I finish a scene, I write the details about it on a card and pin it to the wall. This work might go on for weeks or months, depending on the film. During this time, a process of clarification is taking place; I am beginning to see connections, lines, meanings. Sometimes this happens in the editing room itself, sometimes when I'm relaxing. It's certainly not a linear process.

Perhaps once a week, alone or with someone else who is seriously involved in the film, I look at the cards on the wall and try to see connections and links. Slowly but inevitably, the thrust of the film emerges.

The complexity of editing a cinema verité film can be seen in comments made by Ellen Hovde, one of the editors and codirectors of the Maysleses' film *Grey Gardens*. The film is a portrait of two unusual women, Edith Bouvier Beale (Big Edie) and her fifty-five-year-old unmarried daughter, also called Edie, and was shot by Al Maysles and recorded by David Maysles. I asked Hovde if the Maysles told her what they were looking for in the film.

> No. Never. They had no idea. Just a sense of two charismatic people, and that there might be a story. . . . When the material came in we just let it wash over us. In general it was very strange. You almost couldn't tell if you had anything until you cut it, because it was so free-flowing. Very repetitive. It didn't have a structure. There were no events. There was nothing around which a conversation was going to wheel. It was all kind of the same in a gross way, and you had to dig into it, try to find motivations, condense the material to bring out psychological tones.
>
> I was always, I guess, looking for relationships. I think we were pushing in film terms towards a novel of sensibility rather than a novel of plot.
>
> I don't think we were clear at all (at least not in the beginning) about the direction we were going in. I think we all knew there was nothing in terms of "action," but what was really going on was not clear.
>
> The main themes that Muffie (my coeditor) and I decided to go with were the questions "Why were the mother and daughter together?" "Was it possible that little Edie was there to take care of her mother, and it was the demanding mother who took care that her daughter couldn't leave?" and "Was the relationship really a symbiotic one?"

GROUND RULES

Cinema verité often makes more strenuous demands on the filmmakers and the film subjects than do typical documentaries. There is usually a much greater demand for intimacy and openness. The filming is frequently done in homes rather than in public places, and the filmmaking itself can take months rather than weeks. In those circumstances, you need to establish a set of ground rules from the start. These help define and smooth the working relationship between you, the filmmaker, and your subjects. The rules will vary with each situation, but certain discussions come up time and time again:

- Time of shooting: Can you shoot at any time and on any occasion, or only at certain defined periods?
- Prelighting: Can you prelight the main shooting areas so that all you have to do is throw a switch (usually the best way), or do you have to set lights each time you shoot?
- Off-limits areas. Can you film anywhere, or are certain places off-limits?
- Recording: Can you record anything, or are certain subjects off-limits?

Obviously, one aims for as broad a permission as possible, hoping that the subject will trust your judgment about when to shoot and when not to.

Roger Graef's *Decisions* is a cinema verité series made in England that deals with big business. The films were shot during discussions over vital decisions made by three huge business corporations, including British Steel. The films were breakthroughs, bringing cinema verité techniques to the corporate world and demystifying the way business works. This kind of filming had never been done before, and Graef's chief task was to gain entry to the corporations, win their confidence, and assure them that the films would be both to their credit and for the public good. The ground rules that Graef laid out between himself and the corporations were as follows:

- The filmmakers would shoot only what had been agreed on by both sides.
- No scoops to newspapers. This was essential because a great deal of confidential information was being disclosed.
- The films would be released only when both sides agreed to it. In other words, the filmmakers weren't setting out to embarrass the subjects.
- In return for the above, the filmmakers asked for total access to one or two subjects they had agreed to film—that is, the right to film at any time and walk in on any conversation.
- The filming would be done without lights and without anything being staged.

When Richard Leiterman shot *A Married Couple* for Allan King, he basically lived in and around Billy and Antoinette Edwards for two months. The three main rules for that film were

1. There would be no communication at all between the film-makers and the subjects;
2. The filmmakers had the right to come at any time, morning or evening, and film anything unless a door was closed; and
3. The subjects were to continue whatever they were doing or whatever they were talking about whenever the filmmakers walked in or started shooting.

I talked some while ago with Leiterman about that shooting, and it is quite clear that what mattered, more than the rules, was the confidence that the Edwards had in Leiterman's judgment of when and when not to shoot. Severe and violent quarrels, including Billy throwing Antoinette out of the house—yes, that was all in. Billy and Antoinette about to make love—that was all right while they were playing around with each other, but off-limits once they reached the bedroom.

Even though you have set ground rules, you still have to proceed with caution and common sense. When John Kennedy was president he gave permission to Robert Drew, Ricky Leacock, and Don Penne-baker to film intimate presidential staff meetings for what ultimately became *Crisis: Behind a Presidential Commitment.* Kennedy had given the filmmakers virtually free access, and yet this is how Leacock de-scribed the filming to critic P. J. O'Connell:

> Pennebaker [the other cameraman] would notice that the President would keep glancing at the camera. And then Penny would stop shoot-ing. Because if he didn't, he knew that within minutes the President was going to say, "Stop." Then you would have the problem of starting again. You have to get a Presidential permission to start again. If he stopped before the President stopped him, then he could decide when to start again. Okay, you're going to miss a whole lot of stuff, but you've got the power to start again.

GENERAL CRITICISMS

Over the years, cinema verité technique has run into a barrage of criticism, and it's useful to be aware of the main negative arguments before you embark on a cinema verité film.

First, cinema verité films are simplistic and nonintellectual. This argument has been used mostly against Fred Wiseman by critics who maintain that his films merely portray the surface of institutions.

Without greater sociological or economic explanations (which he avoids), the films are of limited interest.

I think this discussion can be put another way. Where you are making simple portrait, crisis, personality, or follow-situation films, cinema verité generally works well. Where it doesn't work is in political films or historical films in which we really need to dig deep. Yet not everyone agrees with me.

In 2004 an Israeli film called *Checkpoint* did very well on the U.S. festival circuit. *Checkpoint,* which used no narration, simply looked at half a dozen or so checkpoints on the West Bank where Israeli soldiers checked Arabs civilians. The process was sad and humiliating for both sides. In the end it remained incredibly superficial, as there was not the slightest attempt to explain the background to the situation or the reason for the checks.

Second, casting is everything. The criticism here is that no talent is needed to make a cinema verité film; all you need is a head for casting. Find the right charismatic talent, like the Beatles, Russell Crowe, or a race-car driver, and your film is in the bag.

Third, the portraits are superficial. One of the early claims of verité was that it managed to dig deeper into personalities, that it would penetrate the outward veneer and find the "real" person. This claim is now under severe challenge, as critics argue that, even with verité, the subject is as much on guard as in the old films.

Last, the method is unethical. Here the main argument is that the subjects are unaware of what the film is doing and will do to their lives and their privacy and that the filmmaker is merely exploiting them for his or her own fame and fortune.

Many of these criticisms have to be taken quite seriously. On the whole, though, I think the criticism is overdone. Looking back, it is clear that cinema verité has been handled with compassion and sensitivity by the majority of serious filmmakers, and their works have provided an understanding of people, families, institutions, and social actions that would have been quite impossible with any other method. In short, they have enriched the whole documentary tradition and created an honorable path well worth following.

THE VERITÉ SOAP OPERA

When I wrote the last sentence of the preceding paragraph for the first edition of this book, neither the concept of reality television nor the series *The Real World* and *Sylvania Waters* had yet been born. All are amusing diversions from "the honorable" path. Whether they are worth emulating is another matter, but all three works try to pull verité in new directions.

The Real World hit American television in 1992 as MTV's idea of a documentary entertainment experiment. The music video network rented a New York loft, which it then offered as a home to seven young adults who had never met but who had been selected from hundreds of applicants. A number of video cameras, sometimes singly, sometimes simultaneously, then rolled for three months.

The series is cut in jumpy MTV style and, as *Entertainment* magazine put it, "plays shrewdly to the fantasies of the MTV audience—wouldn't it be a gas to live in a high tech New York loft with a bunch of cool people, to have cameras recording your silliest actions and most personal thoughts, while music from the MTV hit parade plays over everything." Personally, I hated *The Real World* and found it totally unreal and boring. It uses verité techniques to simulate a real-life soap opera, but it leaves you longing for genuine kitsch.

Paul Watson's *Sylvania Waters* (BBC and ABC 1993) is another verité soap. The original shooting took ninety hours of tape, which in turn was reduced to twelve half-hour episodes. In its own way, the series is as compellingly offensive as Watson's 1974 work *The Family*, and just as synthetic.

Sylvania Waters is a suburb of Sydney, Australia, and the series follows—verité style—the life of a comfortably middle-class family. Lucky for the viewers, the family is uncouth and has wonderful problems, like aging, drunkenness, and difficult children.

When the series was shown on the BBC, the reaction of the British was to look down on the family. The series affirmed snobbish anti-Aussie prejudices. As the *Daily Mail* put it, "Britain meets the neighbors from hell."

My problem with both *Sylvania Waters* and *The Real World* is that they lack any authenticity. I am not disturbed by the "shaped" interviews (a breach of verité tradition) or a deliberately crazy shooting style. Both are merely stylistic choices. What troubles me is the filmmakers' inability to probe beneath the surface of things. For verité to work, the filmmaker must be concerned about the subject and must bring some intelligence to the shooting. Merely to switch on the cameras is not enough.

Watching television today, one wonders whether cinema verité has been such a great gift, while series such as *Big Brother* and *Survivor* and cheap docusoaps about taxi drivers, hospitals, Las Vegas, animals, and airports clog the screen. Luckily, in contrast to the soaps, verité is still being used here and there to observe and probe into the deeper places, as seen in *Fahimeh's Story*, *Hoop Dreams*, and *Molly and Mobarak* and in the continuing work of Molly Dineen, Les Blank, Allan and Susan Raymond, Fred Wiseman, and others. So the flag is still there, and it still provides inspiration.

19

DOCUMENTARY DRAMA

When I was a kid growing up in England, I would occasionally visit the British Museum. In the archaeology section, one granite carving fascinated me above all others. This amazing animal had the bearded head of a man, the body of a bull, the wings of an eagle, and the tail of a lion. What I didn't know then, but only realized much later, was that I was looking at the symbolic representation of the fact-fiction film. Like my British Museum sculpture, docudrama is a most peculiar animal.

Fact-fiction, reality-based drama, or docudrama, as I prefer to call it, has become one of the most popular forms of television to emerge in the last twenty years. This hybrid form has embraced single films ranging from *The Flight That Fought Back, Ambush in Waco, Tuskegee Airmen, The Atlanta Child Murders, Into the Void, Strange Justice (the Clarence Thomas–Anita Hill Story)*, and *Pirates of Silicon Valley* to miniseries such as *Sinatra, Blind Ambition*, and *Washington: Behind Closed Doors*. Docudramas have also invaded the feature industry with films such as *Ray, The Aviator, A Beautiful Mind, The Pianist, Hotel Rwanda, Omagh, Hurricane, A Perfect Storm, Schindler's List, Malcolm X, Black Hawk Down*, and *In the Name of the Father*. Because docudrama covers such a broad spectrum of dramatic forms, it helps to see it as divided into two strands, or two totally separate areas.

The biography and entertainment category probably makes up 90 percent of the docudramas we see in the cinema and on television. Films in this category range from *Michael Collins* and *Remember the Titans* to *Erin Brockovich* and from *Dorothy Dandridge* to *O. J. Simpson, Life with Judy Garland* and the Frank Sinatra and Jackson family television series. The category also includes all the current titillating murders of the week.

These films are generally categorized by a desire for the highest audience ratings, an emphasis on entertainment values, and a rather loose regard for the truth. When they are made for U.S. television networks, they tend to fall under the supervision of the drama department rather than news and documentary jurisdiction. (For a fuller explanation of docudrama forms, see Alan Rosenthal, *Writing Docudrama* [Boston: Focal Press, 1994].)

The category of *reconstructive investigations,* though highly honored, is a much smaller category and includes pieces such as *Death of a Princess, Conspiracy, Dead Ahead: The Exxon Valdez Disaster, Tailspin, The Secretary Who Stole £4 Million, Hostages, Who Bombed Birmingham?, And the Band Played On, Dr. Death,* and *Citizen Cohn.*

What we are looking at here is a very serious body of work, much closer to journalism than to conventional drama. Though the works use dramatic forms, characters, and dialogue, the motivating force is that of the restless inquirer and the investigatory reporter. These films want to uncover and reveal for the public good, not just in the name of higher ratings. Their highest goals are to present powerful, enthralling drama that nevertheless also gets as close to the truth as possible. This seems to me the most socially important side of docudrama. It's what gives the genre its moral imperative. It is also the side of docudrama I want to focus on in this chapter.

Sometimes, of course, the two strands overlap, and we get both entertainment biography and investigation. Thus *The Reagans* had both the surface glitz and the gossipy sheen of *The Kennedy Women* while also providing a critical and controversial look at President Ronald Reagan and his wife, Nancy. For its part, HBO's *The Gathering Storm* presented a superb picture of both Winston Churchill's intimate family life and his political battles in the British parliament before World War II.

HISTORY AND CHALLENGES

Documentary drama has a long history, studded with some of the most famous names and films in the documentary pantheon. You could start anywhere, but you would have to include Harry Watt's *North Sea*, Humphrey Jennings's *Fires Were Started*, the work of Willard Van Dyke and Leo Hurwitz, and, more recently, Peter Watkins's *Culloden* and *The War Game*, Ken Loach's *Cathy Come Home*, and Chris Ralling's films for the BBC. This body of work has, however, raised certain theoretical problems. Where is the center of truth in this form, and how believable or suspect is it? These are vital questions, as the basis of documentary is its relationship to truth. In docudrama, however, whole areas seem to be opening up in which fiction is presented as fact, as reality.

In spite of its problems, documentary drama has a tremendous appeal to serious filmmakers. Leslie Woodhead, the creator of some of the most interesting documentaries shown on English television, sees it as a form of last resort: "It's a way of doing things where ordinary documentary cannot cope—a way of telling a story that would be impossible by conventional documentary methods." What is the impossible story? For Woodhead it has ranged from a story about a Soviet dissident imprisoned in a mental hospital to *Strike*, a film about the Russian invasion of Czechoslovakia.

Woodhead's aim has been to re-create history as accurately as possible, and his means—summed up by David Boulton, one of his scriptwriters—are very instructive: "No invented characters. No invented names. No dramatic devices owing more to the writer's (or director's) creative imagination than to the impeccable record of *what actually happened.* For us, the dramatized documentary is an exercise in journalism, not dramatic art."

Woodhead's *A Subject of Struggle* was about an elderly Chinese lady put on trial by the Red Guard at the height of the Cultural Revolution. In 1972, when the film was made, the nature of the revolution was a tremendous puzzle, and no film of any duration had come out of China about it. Woodhead obtained the trial transcript, talked to Sinologists about it, did further research, and then used the transcripts as the basis of a docudrama. In the case of Soviet dissident General Grigorenko, the basis of the film was provided by Grigorenko's detailed diaries, which he had managed to smuggle out of prison.

One of the most famous docudramas of the mid-1960s was *Cathy Come Home*, about the plight of the homeless in England. It was shown three times on the BBC and did a great deal to alleviate the plight of those without shelter or lodging. Scriptwriter Jeremy Sandford came to the subject through the experiences of a close friend who was about to be evicted from lodgings and lose her children. Sandford did extensive background research but put his final script in the form of a drama rather than straight documentary. I was curious about this decision, and when I met Sandford in London, I asked him why he chose drama and actors over straight documentary. Sandford replied:

> Real people are often inarticulate when disaster hits them. There can be flashes of emotion in a live documentary, but these flashes cannot be sustained throughout a film. An actor with an actual script avoids that problem. Also, at this time, cameras were not allowed in the homes for the homeless. Even had I been able to get in and make a television documentary, I wouldn't have been able to do justice to the emotional reality of the people living there. Instead I saw it all in the form of a play—a situation anyone with a social conscience just had to write about.

Sandford has done a number of other docudramas, including *Edna: The Inebriate Woman*, so I pushed him a bit further on justifying the form.

> The justification for it must be, as I have said, that the events portrayed are inaccessible to true documentary treatment, either because they are in the past, or because they lie in some area of secrecy or inarticulacy, such as that to shoot them as straight documentary will destroy the very thing one is trying to show.

Both Sandford and Woodhead provide excellent arguments for the docudrama form. Once the choice is made, the main problems are (1) what form the piece should take to keep it as close as possible to the truth and (2) how to inform the audience about the real nature of what is on the screen.

CHOOSING A SUBJECT

Often a producer will come to a writer with an idea and commission him or her to write a script. But often the idea or the story has to come straight from the writer. The main questions then become

- Where can I find a good story?
- Does it have appeal?
- Can I sell it?

Here, because of space limitations, I just want to deal with the first and major problem, finding a good story.

Your sources are fairly obvious, and it is interesting to look at a few scripts and see where they have come from.

- Books: *And the Band Played On, Good Fellas, Diana: Her True Story, JFK: Reckless Youth*
- Newspaper and magazine articles: *The Killing Fields, Fatal Memories, Andy and Fergie*
- Radio and television: *Chernobyl, Skokie, The Tragedy of Flight 103*

Obviously a great number of sources overlap. While the Chernobyl disaster was happening, it was being covered by every branch of the media and no single branch can claim to be the film source.

What is important, whether your sources are television, radio, newspapers, friends, or books, is consciously searching and looking out for what make a good docudrama. My feeling is that the stories are all around us. I'll give one example.

While writing this book, I caught on television and in the newspapers the story of a small Russian rescue submarine, the *AS-28 Priz*, which was entrapped in cables off Berezovaya Bay and couldn't surface. Eventually Japanese, U.S., and British ships came to the rescue and the seven-man crew was saved just before the air was totally exhausted. What was interesting was that the Russian government had only asked for help after a crew member's wife had revealed the emergency on a local radio station.

Here we obviously have elements for a good docudrama rescue story, but it's a story we've heard many times. What fascinated me as a writer was seeing how the story could be improved by linking it to the story of the *Kursk* disaster. In August 2000, explosions were heard on board the Russian submarine *Kursk*, and it sank 350 feet to the bottom of the Barents Sea. In this case, except for some minor intervention by a Norwegian ship, the Russians refused to ask for help. As a consequence the rescue attempt failed and 118 men died. By combining the stories of these two incidents, and starting off with the story of the *Kursk* submarine, it is easy to see how a docudrama would practically write itself.

PROBLEMS AND SOLUTIONS

The underlying problem of docudrama is that your hands are tied. You can't just invent. You can't neatly sort everything out in the way a fiction writer can because you are dealing with true events and real people. So how do you start?

My own method is to list on a few sheets of paper:

- The factual progression of the story, with all the key dates and times and main characters included
- A few notes on structure and form and possible approaches.
- All the elements that have caught my eye in research: interesting incidents, fascinating characters, main problems, conflicts between people, and so on.

FOCUSING THE STORY

After laying out your lists, you try to focus your story. This means knowing what your story is about and where you are going with it. In most character stories or disaster stories, this is relatively easy, and you should be able to answer your question of story and focus in one or two sentences. For example:

- *Mountains of the Moon*: This is about two men trying to find the sources of the Nile. It focuses on their rivalry in the quest for fame.
- *Diana: Her True Story*: This is about a young girl finding her inner strength as she battles both her husband and accepted social behavior in the British Royal Family.
- *Tsunami*: This film follows the story of three families in Phuket as they become involved in the tsunami disaster.
- *Full Fathom Five*: This film contrasts the bungled attempt to rescue the Russian submarine *Kursk*, with the successful attempt to rescue the smaller submarine *Priz*.
- *The Flight That Fought Back*: This film tells the story of the 9/11 plane passengers who fought back against the al-Qaeda hijackers.

The going gets rough in films dealing with *issues, disasters, and public events*. The story may have captured the headlines, but it can be murder trying to find out what the best story is for the television or feature film. The only way out is to consider a number of possibilities and then focus on the most dramatic, interesting, and entertaining.

Let's look for example at the case of the Lockerbie air disaster. In 1988, a Pan Am jumbo jet was blown up over Lockerbie, Scotland, resulting in the loss of more than two hundred lives. The killers were thought to be Syrians or Libyans. As a result of Libya's refusal to hand over suspects, sanctions were imposed on the country by the United Nations. The relatives of the victims sought millions of dollars in compensation.

Problem: What story would one pursue for television? My writing students came up with various answers:

- The lives of five victims before the tragedy
- The assassins, the plot, and the getaway
- The town of Lockerbie before and after the disaster
- The relatives versus Pan Am

The eventual film made on the bombing by HBO and Granada was called *Why Lockerbie?* Its scriptwriter, Michael Eaton, told me that at first he thought the film would be about the terror groups who made the bomb. As the research continued, he and his executive producer realized there was a second vital story, that of Pan Am and the increasing breakdown of its security measures. The film could then be shaped as two stories that eventually converge in the explosion and conflagration. As Eaton put it:

> It then became a story about two institutions—an international airline corporation and an international terrorist organisation.
>
> And the way I wanted to tell the story was to look at those organisations from the top to the bottom; from the boardroom top to the people who sit by the X-ray machines; from the people who go round the world looking for sponsorship for acts of terror down to the soldiers who carry the bags with the bombs.
>
> So what the film would be was a juxtaposition between the way the two organisations work. And the chill of the story is that in many ways they are not too dissimilar. (Alan Rosenthal, *Writing Docudrama* [Boston: Focal Press, 1994])

CHOOSING THE CHARACTERS

In docudrama, you have to select your characters from real life. In biography films, that's relatively easy, but in other cases your choices can be extremely limited. The most common problem is that you know the story, yet the central characters evade you. Ideally, you want a "hero" who will carry the story in the direction of your choice. Yet very often that ideal character just doesn't exist.

Sometimes you may have to amalgamate characters, as was done with the doctor-hero in *And the Band Played On*. Sometimes you have to give a spread of characters to give enough of the whole story, as in the *The War Game* and the 1992 film *Dead Ahead: The Exxon Valdez Disaster*.

The writer Michael Baker, of *Dead Ahead,* about the Alaska oil disaster, spent an afternoon with me telling me about the difficulty of finding the right characters to carry the story:

> For a long time we were interested in a fisherman we thought would be a focus of tension. There was also a guy called Kelly who almost single handedly launched a kind of wildlife rescue operation . . . So I began to wonder if we could reduce our canvas and look at the film through a Kelly story. Or should we do the captain's story?
>
> And one by one the stories were jettisoned. Kelly's was too environmental. With the captain's story there wasn't a real thread all the way through. He'd been taken off the ship and was then out of the story till the trial. (Alan Rosenthal, *Writing Docudrama* [Boston: Focal Press, 1994])

When the search for the right hero still fails to turn up a plausible central character, he or she may have to be created out of the author's imagination. This was the ploy used by Ernest Kinoy when he wrote *Skokie.* In the film, the central character is a fictitious Holocaust survivor who violently objects to neo-Nazis parading through Skokie. The technique works well and gives us a sympathetic main figure who represents in himself the thousands of objectors to the march. The problem with the use of this device is that it can blur the boundaries between fact and fiction, and it can raise questions of credibility about the rest of the film. When you use it, do so with caution.

THE OUTLINE TREATMENT

We touched briefly on the concept of the treatment in chapter 8. In docudrama you don't have to do a treatment, but this tool can be a great help in fact-based films. The ideal time to write a treatment is after you've settled your questions of focus and character choice.

The treatment is your first attempt to outline the drama. It is normally written as a series of loosely sketched sequences. They can be numbered or not, according to your fancy, and each sequence should indicate a location and the action of the characters. Occasionally, they may contain scraps of dialogue or paraphrase what the characters are talking about. The opening sequences of a treatment I wrote about a British nineteenth-century explorer in Palestine went like this:

1. Lawns of Cambridge University, 1865. Crowds of students. Kings College dominates. Inside the college PALMER thanks audience for making his trip to the Holy Land possible.

2. A desert oasis. Three British officers stretched out in the sun. Officer arrives on a camel and dismounts. He indicates there is no word from PALMER and he may be lost.

3. Luxury house. Dinner is over. Men in evening suits. PALMER points to the map of Sinai, an unknown desert, where the Children of Israel wandered for forty years. "Gentlemen. With my time and your money I intend to bring God to the heathen and make the darkness visible."

4. British headquarters, Jerusalem 1878. Drinks on table. Officers look at Sinai maps. BAGLEY worries that the Turks may have PALMER and the gold will be lost. FRANKLYN suggests he is already dead. BAGLEY, decisively. "There will be hell to pay if the story gets out. Palmer must be found."

As you can see, the treatment is very much written in shorthand form. It's not a literary document. It's not for publication. It's merely a device to help you and the producer see where you are going and what you want to do.

TECHNIQUES AND CAUTIONS

Characters portraying themselves. When you have a strong human or political story, it is worth considering whether the main characters can play themselves. They have been through the situation, lived the events, and can recall the emotions and the dialogue. This method is not easy, but where possible it adds tremendous plausibility to the film, as in the docudrama *Ninety Days*, directed by Jack Gold. *Ninety Days* recounts the experiences of a young, white South African woman sent to prison for political activities under the old ninety-day laws. The film was based on the autobiography of Ruth First, who played herself in the film. After the screening, there was no doubt among the critics that First added a dimension of reality that would have been missing had her part been portrayed by an actor.

Similarly, the National Film Board of Canada made a film in the mid-1980s, *Democracy on Trial*, about a Canadian doctor who, in defiance of the government, ran an abortion clinic out of a deep belief in the rights of women to manage their own bodies. The film shows the running of the clinic, the government prosecutions, and the three or four trials of the doctor until he is pardoned and the abortion laws amended. Here again, the doctor plays himself, adding immensely to the strength of the film.

Kevin MacDonald's Oscar-winning film *Touching the Void* (2004) shows us an interesting variation on the above. In the mid-1980s, two young mountaineers Simon Yates and Joe Simpson, set off to conquer the western face of Siula Grande, a remote peak in Peru. On the descent, Simpson breaks his leg and is gradually let down on a three-hundred-meter rope by Yates. When Simpson goes over a ledge and starts dragging Yates down into the void, Yates makes a decision to cut the rope. Assuming his friend Simpson is dead, Yates continues down. However, Simpson has fallen into a crevice and painfully and incredibly crawls and drags his way back to base.

In *Touching the Void*, MacDonald uses actors, and shooting on location beautifully and dramatically reconstructs the climb, the fall, and the return to camp. However, what gives the film its power is that from time to time we see the real Joe Simpson and Simon Yates talking on camera and telling the viewer directly what happened. Occasionally their voices also float over the pictures. Thus, as the actor playing Yates struggles with the snow, the ice, and the dangers, we hear the real Yates recounting his feelings of pain and desperation. It is as if we are directly inside his head, and the effect is very powerful.

Verification. Most docudramas rely on the audience's belief that what it sees on the screen actually happened or has a very strong basis in fact. This was the main strength of *Cathy Come Home*. At the time *Cathy* was produced, stories about the homeless were regularly making the front pages of most of the English newspapers. Thus, when the drama finally appeared, it resonated with the audience's own knowledge of similar facts and situations.

The film shows its main character, Cathy, at a rundown trailer park. A few months earlier, a radio documentary called *Living on Wheels*, which was recorded on location, had featured exactly the scene Sandford wrote into his film. Sandford then has a fatal fire occur at the trailer park. Again, the incident was based in fact, and many people were already familiar with the appalling number of children's deaths caused by such fires. As Sandford commented:

> Nearly everything in the film was founded on something that actually happened. An incident, like the fight where Cathy strikes one of the staff, was an amalgam of two real incidents. One concerned a principal who threw out one of the inmates of the homes for talking to the press. The other involved the death of a baby and the belief of the inmates that this was due to dysentery. I combined these incidents into a cameo where an inmate writes to a paper about a baby's death. (Alan

Rosenthal, *The New Documentary in Action* [Berkeley: University of California Press, 1971])

Sandford's method was to take a dramatic social situation, research the facts, and then weave a tale based on the facts. A more common method is to take a historical incident or incidents from recent political and general news and reconstruct them, as in *The Trial of Bernhard Goetz, Ambush in Waco,* or *The Atlanta Child Murders.* However, in the latter method, any suspected deviation from authenticity on vital points can shake the believability and effectiveness of the whole film.

This happened in Antony Thomas's *Death of a Princess.* The film showed (via actors) the public execution of a Saudi Arabian princess and her lover for various sexual offenses against Islamic law. This incident was true and had been widely reported in European newspapers. However, the film then went on to show other behavior of the Saudi aristocracy, but many people questioned the basis in truth. Luckily, Thomas was able to answer his critics by being able to verify every accusation he made.

To keep a sense of proportion, it is necessary to distinguish between facts that are crucial to the story and incidental fictions. In *Cathy,* the romantic episodes are incidental fictions, but the trailer fire has to be based on fact; otherwise, the whole film crumbles. In *Death of a Princess,* the scenes in the Saudi household can be taken as general background and unimportant detail. In contrast, the scenes of Arab women picking up lovers in a Mercedes make crucial political and social criticisms. As such they had to be completely true, and Thomas proved that they were.

Accurate dialogue. One of the keys to making effective docudramas is to find the most accurate sources for the dialogues and commentary. Usually these sources will consist of letters, diaries, interviews, and newspaper reports. Sometimes court statements will also provide the basic materials, and this was part of Sandford's working method in *Cathy*:

> It was while I was working on a newspaper series that I came upon the actual case on which the fatal fire in *Cathy is* based. I followed the proceedings in the coroner's court, and then I more or less transferred what occurred to the sound track of *Cathy.* For instance, there is the scene where the girl describes how the caravan [trailer] was filled with smoke and how she escaped with little Gary in her arms. "And what

happened to all the others?" the coroner asks. "They all got burned up," she says. The dialogue is verbatim from the court report.

Accuracy of location and characters. In feature films, the emphasis in location shooting is on cheapness, exoticism, and reasonable working conditions. Accuracy and authenticity are usually the last words mentioned. But authenticity is the key to docudrama, especially as regards period and physical setting. In *Strike*, several hundred still photographs were used to show Poland and Gdansk in the early 1970s. These provided references not only for design, wardrobe, and makeup, but also for casting the actors. In *Ninety Days*, Ruth First worked with the designer so that the feeling of the cell and the South African prison would be as accurate as possible.

Obviously, you are as accurate as your budget can afford. In the 1970s, the BBC made two splendid historical series, *The Search for the Nile* and *The Explorers*. The first told the story of the major African explorers, such as Burton and Speke, while the second recounted the stories of Pizarro, Columbus, Von Humboldt, and the like. Both series were filmed at the locales where their stories took place. The expense was enormous, but the authenticity thus achieved was easily worth it.

The viewer's right to know. It is crucial that you let your audience know whether it is looking at fact, fiction, reenactment, or fiction based on fact. How do we tell the viewer all this? One answer, given by Robert Vas in *The Issue Should Be Avoided* and by Jill Godmilow in *Far from Poland*, is to use sign posting or subtitles that clearly indicate the source of what is happening on screen. Another method is to indicate at the beginning of the film which characters are real and which are fictional, and which ones are portrayed by "real people" and which ones by actors. It is also worthwhile to let the audience know immediately the factual basis for your incidents and your dialogue; this means that the audience understands from the start the nature of your method and techniques. Some people put these explanations at the end of the film; however, I think they are preferable at the beginning so that the audience can put the film into perspective.

Legalities. Questions of libel, slander, and abuse of privacy are likely to arise very frequently in docudrama. Thus, no docudrama script will pass television consideration unless it conforms to network practices in these areas. Each network has its own rules for the genre, and you should familiarize yourself with them before submitting your script. You should also have the script reviewed by your own lawyer, to see that it is not prima facie libelous.

HYBRIDS

In the last five years many filmmakers have started using all sorts of variations on the classic docudrama form. Thus, it has become very popular to insert dramatized sequences into straight documentaries. For example, in the BBC's film on author Arthur Ransome we see the usual paraphernalia of documentary—archives, stills, and talking heads—intercut with long dramatized scenes showing Ransome in Russia, falling in love, and fleeing from the secret police. In another BBC docudrama, on the history of Venice, the Italian narrator guides us around his native city today. For a moment he pauses in an old street and looks through a window. As we follow his gaze we see he is looking at Casanova wooing a young girl. Unfortunately the father comes in and Casanova is forced to make a run for it. And so the film proceeds, half in the present, half in a dramatized past.

Another variation is the reemergence of the type of *Cathy Come Home* and *The War Game* docudrama, in which fictional individual stories are imposed on very heavily researched world or country issues. This approach is particularly seen in *Smallpox* and the three films in the BBC and HBO coproduction series *Dirty Wars*. In the first film in the series, we delve into nuclear terrorism and follow what happens when a radiological dirty bomb explodes in London. In the second film, we look at global AIDS, and in the third we follow the fortunes of a Hutu family involved in the genocidal Rwanda war of 1994. All these films mixed dramatic reconstructions or straight fiction with archives, newsreel, voice-over, and extensive use of CGI technology.

These are just two of the current variations on docudrama. What is clear is that there will probably be more and more permutations of the form and as a writer and director you must stay familiar with all the changes.

EXAMPLES

The inspiration for docudrama can come from anywhere. Often the source is a story in the headlines, as was the case with *The Atlanta Child Murders*. Sometimes a film has its genesis in politics, as in the films of Leslie Woodhead. Sometimes it's biography and sometimes it's history; sometimes it's public and sometimes it's private.

Now most docudramas use the form of a dramatized play; that is, they rely almost totally on actors and eschew familiar documentary elements such as stills and archives. However the fusion of both techniques can produce some interesting results, as seen in the two following examples.

Letters from a Bomber Pilot, by David Hodgson, is one of the best docudramas to come out of England. Presented by Thames Television, it provides an interesting illustration of its source of ideas and is also worth looking at in terms of method.

David Hodgson's mother died in spring 1978. While David's brother and sister were sorting through their mother's belongings, they came across a pile of letters at the bottom of her wardrobe. Dated between 1940 and 1943, the letters were the correspondence between David's older brother Bob and his mother and father and friends. A pilot in the Royal Air Force (RAF), Bob had vanished over Europe in March 1943. The elder brother had just been a shadow of a memory to David Hodgson, who was six at the time of Bob's death. The letters, however, revealed the reality of the missing Bob. Not only that, they also conveyed very vividly the experiences of being a young airman during the early years of the war. Written with humor and honesty, they described the training, the friends, the drinking, the crashes, and falling in love. And, of course, they described Bob's feelings about the military operations.

In addition to its importance to his family, David Hodgson, a documentary filmmaker, felt the story would have significance for the general public. Using the letters as the basis of his script, he started tracing what happened to many of the people mentioned in the letters. The resulting film tells the story of just one of the fifty-five thousand RAF pilots who fell in the war. It is a particular story of one man and one family, but it resonates with anyone involved in the war and serves to tell a younger generation about the immense personal cost of the conflict.

It's a brilliant film, but its method is simple. Narrated by David Hodgson, the film is grounded in a personal point of view. The letters, which form the basis of the script, are sometimes illustrated by library footage and sometimes by acted scenes. Occasionally, an incident or mood suggested by a letter will be fleshed out in a short invented scene. Thus, the talk in a letter of a friend falling in love is followed by a short scene in which two airmen tease a lovesick friend of Bob's named Hughie. What gives the film its poignancy is that a number of the people mentioned in the letters were traced down and interviewed by Hodgson. The friend appears in an on-screen interview that then dissolves into a reconstructed scene with actors. At first, the voice-over of the interview guides the scene, and then the actors' dialogue takes over. These simple techniques work very well, as can be seen below:

Visual	Audio
Stills of Bob as a baby, then various family group shots	NARRATOR: My brother Bob was born the thirteenth of January 1921 in the south London suburb of Norwood. Our mother, Maud, was seventeen when she met a young film cameraman, Jimmy Hodgson, and they were married in 1918. Bob was the second of their children. My sister Joan was two years older.
Bob with model boat; with sister	Bob was a gentle, intelligent Bob child who became enthralled by one of the century's most spectacular developments—flying.
Archival footage of plane taking off; aerobatics; pilot in control tower	He dreamt of becoming a pilot, and his favorite way to spend a Saturday afternoon was watching the planes at Croydon Airport.
Stills of young Bob with model aircraft; mix to still of Bob in the RAF, with other pilots in uniform	In January 1941, eighteen months after the war had started, Bob joined the RAF. He was one of the thousands of young men who wanted to serve in what they all thought was the most exciting and glamorous of the services.
Archival footage of a bomber in training flight	In May he started his training as a bomber pilot.
Title: *Letters from a Bomber Pilot* Various stills of Bob in uniform with friends or family Credit: A film written and directed by his brother, David Hodgson	

Close-up as hand writes letter; up to Bob Hodgson (actor), who reads letter to camera	BOB: 16 Elementary Flying tilt Training School. Near Derby. August 1941. Dear Bill, I start flying Monday. Music: Glenn Miller Story, "In the Mood."
Air-to-air shot of Bob learning to fly small plane, to illustrate Bob's letter	I went up for twenty minutes to get air experience. After about an hour I went up again and was allowed to handle the controls.
Mix medium shot Bob to camera	At first it wasn't so easy, but after a while I began to pick it up.
Air-to-air shots	Samson said that when he saw me, six-feet-four, etc., he thought I'd be as ham-handed as anything. But I seemed quite OK.

The film continues with air-to-air shots, overlaid with extracts from Bob's letters about learning to fly. The commentary then takes over to talk more widely about the policy of the air chiefs and civilian morale at home. This is all illustrated with library footage of bombing raids, destruction, and bodies being buried. Gradually the number of scenes with actors increases.

Visual	**Audio**
Still of Hugh Feast	NARRATOR: Hugh Feast became one of Bob's closest friends. Like Bob, he came from London and was the same age, just twenty. In November 1941 they were posted to RAF Shawbury to learn advanced navigation and night flying. Most RAF stations employed WAAFS (young women serving in the air force) in technical and ground jobs, and not surprisingly, romances blossomed.
Still of Bob, Alf and Hugh Feast	
Archival footage of WAAFS (Women's Auxiliary Air Force)	
Hughie Feast (actor) shuts door and walks to bathroom, watched by his friends.	

Visual	Audio
	Hughie Feast was the first to be bowled over, something his friends treated with schoolboy glee.
Derek Cadman, Alf Kitchen, and Bob Wells	BOB: Now what's Mr. Feast Bob, dolled up for? ALF: He's meeting his WAAF BOB: Again? ALF: He's got it bad, hasn't he. BOB WELLS: This is the third time this week. It's serious stuff, isn't it? ALF: Let's lock his door.
The four split. Bob goes to the bathroom.	
	BOB WELLS: Come on! Let's do it. BOB: (voice-over) Dear Joan.
Close up of hands locking door	
Medium shot of Hughie shaving. Bob peers at him from door. Lads run into dormitory, followed by Bob. Alf at table. Bob goes and lies on bed.	Hughie Feast is going out with a WAAF from the station sick quarters. I believe he is taking her seriously, as when we first chipped him about it he took it with equanimity, but now he loses the wool and gets chipped even more. Tubby's asking Bravington's to send a catalogue of engagement rings to Hughie's home address to give his parents a shock—just innocent fun.
Hughie brushing hair. Wipes face and exits. Hughie leaves bathroom, walks to dormitory door and finds it locked.	Last night Hughie had to meet his WAAF at 6:45. He went into into the bathroom clad only in his trousers and Tubby locked the door of his room, so that he couldn't get the rest of his clothes.
He walks back into the main dormitory, puzzled.	

The scene ends with the friends ribbing Hughie, holding up the room key, and exclaiming, "Oh, this key, the key to your heart. Ah, that one"

As the film proceeds, various people are interviewed about their memories of Bob and how they met him. The interview with Bea Couldrey demonstrates how such interviews are integrated into the film.

Visual	Audio
Still of Bea.	NARRATOR: At the beginning of September Bob came on a forty-eight-hour pass and went to a local dance. There he met a girl called Bea Couldrey.
Medium close-up of interview with Bea.	BEA: My friend Doris and I went went to this dance held by the Home Guard. Not many people attended these dances because the hall wasn't terribly big. I
Pan with dancing couple to see Bea (actress) sitting talking. Bob and his brother and sister enter.	remember sitting on the side and then I saw this very tall man coming through the door . . .

The film alternates between Bea reminiscing over the scene and the actors picking up dialogue showing how Bea and Bob meet and dance together.

In the final scenes, we learn the details of Bob's death were discovered only recently. We also learn that all four of Bob's closest friends in the RAF were killed as well.

Visual	Audio
Still of group of forty-eight young RAF men	NARRATOR: None was more than twenty-two years old. Of the forty-eight men photographed at Bob's initial training
Still as above, showing only ten remaining	wing, it seems likely that less than a quarter survived.

I have emphasized the need for accuracy and detailed research if one wants to raise the level of the film above romanticized biography or fictitious history. To emphasize the point, I have set out below the comments of Leslie Woodhead (producer) and Boleslaw Sulik (scriptwriter) on the sources and treatment of Granada Television's film *Strike*:

Sources

At first sight "Solidarity" might seem to have had a very public birth. Indeed, the extraordinary confrontation in the Gdansk shipyards during late August 1980 looked at times almost like a media event, unique in a Communist country, with the news crews of the world there to watch every development. Our researches have revealed a very different reality.

As the result of contact established during the making of an earlier dramatized documentary we have been able to gain an unusual access to much previously unknown material. . . .

Now after six months of detailed debriefings of dozens of eyewitnesses inside Poland and across Western Europe, and the careful examination of almost one hundred hours of private tape recordings, a quite new version of events in the Lenin shipyard has emerged. By collating all this material, we propose to reconstruct for the first time a precise day-by-day account of what really happened, both in the yards and in Warsaw's dissident community. To focus our research, we have also retained as a consultant one of the key "Solidarity" leaders, the woman around whom the strike began, Anna Walentynowicz.

During the crucial but uneasy first four days of the strike, no journalists or cameras got into the shipyard. We have now managed to obtain private tape recordings of vital incidents during those tense early days, made by the workers themselves at the time. With those recordings and eyewitness reports we have been able to piece together for the first time an accurate account of how the strike began, and how on several occasions fear and confusion nearly caused it to collapse. . . .

The Director and the Designer have visited Poland, gaining access to the Lenin shipyard. As a result, it will be possible to reconstruct in precise detail all the key locations inside the yards. We have also researched and photographed the important dissident locations in Warsaw. As a consequence of this firsthand access, we expect to be able to re-create the most accurate settings in our drama documentary experience.

Treatment

We plan a two-hour dramatized documentary. All characters will be real people represented by actors. All events will follow as closely as possible the sequence established by our research. Sets will recreate as precisely as possible the actual locations: the main gate of the Lenin shipyard, the MKS meeting hall, the presidium, the experts' meeting room, Jacek Kurón's Warsaw flat.

Some use will be made of actuality film events in the shipyard. Wherever possible, dialogue will be an exact translation of the private tape recordings made at the time. Where actual recordings are not available, the dialogue will be compiled from the record of several eyewitnesses. We intend to indicate the different status of these two procedures.

We aim to produce a dramatized documentary which will stand as an historical record of an important event. We believe it will also be compelling drama for a television audience.

The actual start of the film, when it was made, is shown below:

Precredit sequence: Shaky 8mm amateur film. A murky view of a large crowd. A loud, rasping Polish voice is heard. A handful of leaflets is thrown up. The Polish voice fades and the narrator comes in.

NARRATOR: December 16, 1979. The Baltic port of Gdansk in Communist Poland. An illegal demonstration is in progress, filmed by a sympathizer with a home movie camera. On this spot, just nine years before, striking shipyard workers were killed in a clash with police. The speaker at this anniversary protest asks each person in the crowd to return here next year with a stone and some cement to build a memorial. The speaker is an out-of-work electrician called Lech Walesa. But long before the year is over, these people, followed by millions across Poland, will mount an unprecedented challenge to the Soviet order in Eastern Europe, igniting the most serious European crisis since World War II. This film tells how it all began with a strike, which in just seventeen days became a revolution called "Solidarity."

Walesa's distorted voice is heard again and continues as the tense, grainy faces of the crowd swirl past the camera. Suddenly the film flashes orange and runs out. On the blank screen the title stabs out: Strike.

The title fades as factory hooters are heard, followed by muffled sounds of gunfire. Simultaneously, from the blank screen a black-and-white still takes form like a developing photograph.

Still photographs of a rioting crowd in a smoke-filled street. A crowd carrying a dead body on a wooden door. A male Polish voice starts singing and subtitles roll on.

SUBTITLES: Janek Wisniewski fell. They carried him down Swietojan-ska Street. To meet the cops. To meet the tanks. Men of the shipyards, avenge your mate.

The stills sequence continues with images of street fighting and a building on fire, surrounded by a huge crowd. The ballad goes on.

SUBTITLES: Workers of Gdansk. You can go home. Your battle's done. The whole world knows and will say nothing. Janek Wisniewski fell.

The voice fades out and the narrator comes in.

NARRATOR: These photographs were taken in the streets of Gdansk, Gdynia, and Szczecin in December 1970. The terrible scenes were committed to the folk memory, and the photographs have been kept hidden for ten years.

A photograph of a woman bending over a body. The ballad comes back for a final stanza.

A dissident meeting; 8mm film. Several people sit in a drab, anonymous living room. The narrator introduces the group and explains the occasion.

NARRATOR: A home movie record of a meeting in Gdansk, early in 1980. These people are campaigners for the creation of Free Trades Unions in Communist Poland. They are the principal figures of the drama reconstruction which follows.

(Individual introductions follow, starting with Lech Walesa and continuing through Anna Walentynowicz.) Anna Walentynowicz, nearing thirty years of continuous work in the Lenin shipyards as a welder and crane driver. Once a heroine of labor, decorated for her outstanding work record. By August 1980, in lengthy dispute with the shipyard management.

The home movie is now seen to be running on an editing machine, watched by Anna herself.

NARRATOR: Anna Walentynowicz has come to London to help in the preparation of this film. As a central figure in the Polish Free Trades Union movement she has a unique inside experience of what happened. *(Anna cues a tape recorder; her own voice is heard speaking to workers.)* The voice of Anna speaking to Gdansk workers, recorded inside the Lenin shipyard during the strike.

What is interesting in the above is the attempt to show the viewer the authenticity of the sources and all the film methods used. The same approach was taken in another Granada film, *Invasion*, and again the first few minutes are used by the writer to inform the audience about technique and approach.

NARRATOR: On the night of August 20, 1968, the armies of the Soviet Union and their Warsaw Pact allies invaded Communist Czechoslovakia in an attempt to install a new government obedient to Moscow. They had done the same in Hungary a decade earlier. They were to do it again in Afghanistan a decade later. They called it "fraternal assistance."

Title: *Invasion*
Exterior location—day—Austria. The Austrian side of a border checkpoint with Czechoslovakia. In the background all the paraphernalia of a sensitive East-West crossing point: Soldiers, guns, lookout towers, barbed wire. Zdenek Mylnar walks up to the frontier.

NARRATOR (*voice-over*): At the time of the Soviet invasion this man was one of the most powerful politicians in Czechoslovakia. His name is Zdenek Mylnar. Twelve years after the invasion of his country he is an exile in neighboring Austria. He left Czechoslovakia in 1977 after publicly criticizing the Russian-backed regime. Today he is the only man who is free to give an eyewitness account of what happened behind closed doors in Prague and Moscow when the Russians set out to force the Czech leaders to sign away their country's independence. His account, recorded for us under detailed cross-examination and supplemented by independent research in Western Europe and Czechoslovakia, forms the basis of the filmed reconstruction which follows. It is as accurate as our research can make it.

The actor who is to play Mylnar walks across to chat to him.

NARRATOR: All the characters in these events are real people represented by actors. Except where there is a written record, the words spoken are a dramatized recreation of what we believe to be essentially true. The personal recollections of Zdenek Mylnar are spoken by Paul Chapman.

We hear Chapman's voice as he stands with Mylnar.

Voice-over of Chapman: In Czechoslovakia, the spring of 1968 arrived in a genuinely human sense. People shared a feeling that after decades of fear and oppression, their lives had finally changed for the better.

As Mylnar's recollections begin, the music and cheering crowds of May Day 1968 gradually break through.

Mix to library film of singing and dancing in the streets of Prague.

As you can see, the script layout for *Strike* differs slightly from some earlier examples, but as I've said, there are few rules. This was simply the layout style that worked best for Woodhead and Sulik. Hodgson preferred a more conventional layout. It really doesn't matter too much, as long as you and your producer agree as to what works best for both of you.

20

THE HISTORY DOCUMENTARY

In 1990 the outstanding hit of the season for PBS was Ken Burns's seven-part recounting of the American Civil War. In 1992, under the guidance of executive producer Zvi Dor-Ner, WGBH launched its own commemorative series, *Columbus and the Age of Discovery*. And at the beginning of June 1994, one could scarcely turn on a television set without stumbling upon yet another recounting or reinterpretation of the events of D day and the Normandy landings. Later there was a twenty-four-part series on the cold war, and in 1998 the BBC released Laurence Rees's *The Nazis: A Warning from History*. More recently, there have been some stylistically innovative historical documentary series, such as *The Colony* and *The Edwardian House*.

All of these programs illustrate one thing. History has become one of the most basic themes for documentary filmmaking, especially television documentary. One network, the History Channel, is totally devoted to it. The series *The American Experience* has drawn millions of viewers, while the history mystery has become one of the sustaining pillars of the Discovery Channel. And with more than $4.5 million going to produce the Vietnam War series, it has also become big business

And why not? The historical documentary is obviously extremely popular and comes in many forms, including straight essay, docudrama, and personal oral history. It offers tremendous scope and challenge to the filmmaker. Unfortunately, it is also beset with a number of problems, both practical and theoretical. The practical matters include the use of archives, the way programs are framed, and the use of experts, witnesses, and narration. The theoretical problems include interpretation, voice, and political viewpoints. And in the background is an academic voice arguing that filmmakers shouldn't even touch history.

AIMS

When you make a history film you ask yourself two questions: What do you want to do, and for whom? Each of us answers these questions in our own way.

For me, the answer is that I want to put my viewers in touch with historical reality. Using a certain artistry, I want to convey important ideas to people who know little of the subject. I want to encourage the viewers to ask questions after the viewing. I want to tell a good story that will engage both the head and the intelligence, and the heart and the emotions. I want to put the viewers in touch with the past in a way that academics can't. I want to help them keep memories alive. And often I want to recall a forgotten history or an overlooked piece of history that seems to me important.

Again, while the filmmaker is not concerned with the research objectives of the historian, I do believe that he or she can often aid in adjusting historic perspectives. For example, the series *The World at War* slightly shocked British audiences when it implied that the air war, the Battle of Britain, was really won by the efficient use of radar rather than the superiority of British pilots over their German opponents. A recent documentary *The Battle for Berlin* asked a question I had never considered before: why did Stalin sacrifice so many soldiers in his hurry to be the first in Berlin? The answer was that he wanted to be the first to have access to Germany's ongoing nuclear research. This was an interesting observation that few viewers had probably thought about.

FILM HISTORY VERSUS ACADEMIC HISTORY

Many academic historians argue that filmmakers should leave history alone. Their arguments go beyond the individual case to an overall critique of the genre. Real historians, they say, are interested in accuracy; filmmakers, in entertainment. Television producers, they add, are concerned only with gimmicks and show business personalities to introduce the programs. In the end, they conclude, documentaries like Alistair Cooke's *America* or *The British Empire* are myopic garbage put out by blinkered, unlearned journalists, presenting ideological views with which few historians would agree.

Strong stuff! So what can we say?

Of course, there are bad and stupid historical documentaries, just as there are bad books on history, but there are also very good ones as well. And yes, filmmakers do want to entertain (as well as enlighten), but that aim is not incompatible with historical accuracy.

Most documentary producers work with a historical adviser. I admit that advisers are sometimes used simply as window dressing to get the blessing of the National Endowment for the Arts or the National Endowment for the Humanities, but they do have a number of serious functions to perform and can be of inestimable help to the filmmaker. Donald Watt, himself a historian, suggests the following ways that the adviser can contribute to the film:

- The adviser should see that the subject is completely covered within the limits set by the length of the program and the material.
- The view presented of the subject must be objective within the acceptable definition of the term as used and understood by professional historians. It must not be parti pris, anachronistic, ideological, or slanted for the purpose of propaganda.
- The events described, the "facts" outlined, must be accurate, that is, in accordance with the present state of historical knowledge. Hypothesis and inference are all legitimate, but only if they are presented as being exactly that. (Donald Watt, "History on the Public Screen," in *New Challenges for Documentary*, ed. Alan Rosenthal [Berkeley: University of California Press, 1988])

Ideally, the relationship of the filmmaker and the adviser is one of partnership. But in the end, one person has to decide on the nature of the program, and I see that person as the filmmaker. You ignore the historian at your peril.

Part of the disquiet of historians is that they really don't understand the difference between academic and television history. They don't understand what the filmmaker is trying to do and the limits within which we work. Our goals and our framework can, however, can be stated fairly simply:

- We are making television programs, not writing articles for learned journals, but we still want accuracy.
- We are working for a mass audience that can be composed of the aged and the young; the Ph.D. and the person who left school at age fourteen; the expert and the ignorant.
- We have to grab the audience. If the audience doesn't like what we show, it will turn elsewhere. Unlike students, the audience is not necessarily predisposed to what we want to show. We want to entertain, but we also want to inform the audience.
- We cannot reflect; we cannot go back. We are unsure of the audience's knowledge of the subject: some will know everything; others will know nothing. We have to be clear, concise, and probably limited in our scope.
- Our intent is to present a view of history, not *the* definitive view of history.

None of their points are particularly new, since I have covered many of them earlier, but they are worth reiterating because these issues go to the heart of the making of historical documentaries. Clearly, the writer-director who wants to do a decent historical film faces a great many problems. Some of these are discussed later, and where possible I have tried to suggest a solution.

AUDIENCE NEEDS

Historians write primarily for their fellow historians. But what does a film audience want from the filmmaker? My guess is that it primarily wants a powerful emotional experience. This can be vicarious, aesthetic, or the feeling of belonging to a particular group. The question of identity is key. Audiences, I suspect, want to see themselves and their own myths—thus, the popularity of *Who Do You Think You Are?* (genealogy) and *The Colonial House* (how we lived).

On the whole, my feeling is that the popular audience, for whom you are primarily going to be working, rejects extreme experiments in form. Alex Cox's film *Walker*, about William Walker's adventures in Nicaragua in the nineteenth century, with its inventions, flights of fancy, and questioning of history, never found an audience. Jill Godmilow's *Far from Poland* again stayed of minority interest only.

CRITICISM AND PASSION

At the start of this book I made my plea for passion, commitment, and concern in your general filmmaking. I very much believe these objectives also underpin the best of historical documentaries. But passion doesn't mean that anything goes, nor does commitment justify the making of sloppy history. In short, you should still be guided by Donald Watt's suggestions, however deeply involved you are with your subject.

The best of historical films reveal issues in a new way, bring enlightenment, and open new chapters in understanding. I offer three simple examples of what I have in mind. The first is Claude Lanzmann's film *Shoah*, which painfully, unspectacularly, and, in the end, superbly detailed the nature and working of Nazi racial genocide. The second film I have always cherished is *The Agony and the Pity*, by Marcel Ophuls and Andre Harris, which boldly challenged the myth of wartime resistance in Nazi-occupied France. *The Agony* flew against accepted French doctrines, was bitterly opposed when it appeared, but was gradually, finally, accepted as historically correct. And the third film is *Homo Sapiens: 1900*, about the Nazi use of eugenics in murder.

APPROACH

The three paths most commonly chosen for historical documentaries are the broad essay on the subject of choice, the "great man" approach, and the "personal reminiscence" method, all of which overlap to a great extent. The essay form is very common and must be mastered. It can be coldly objective—like the essay on the making of the atom bomb in *The World at War* series—or more subjective and personal, as in *It's a Lovely Day Tomorrow*, John Pett's film on the Burma campaign in the same series. The essay often builds itself around a compact event or episode that offers the writer a clean narrative structure with a well-defined beginning and end.

The *World at War* series, produced by Thames Television in the early 1970s, covered World War II in twenty-six programs. But somebody had to decide how those programs should be allocated. The approach could have been a straightforward chronological recounting of the war. This was not done. Instead, the series was broken up into compact events and partially complete stories. Thus, the Russian campaign emerged from three films about battles, *Barbarossa* (the German attack), *Stalingrad*, and *Red Star* (the siege of Leningrad).

Pacific covers the American invasion of Tarawa and Iwo Jima, while *Morning* deals with D day and the Battle of Normandy.

One of the greatest differences between *The World at War* and previous series, both British and American, is that it never uses officials or experts when the experiences of ordinary people can be used to tell the story. In previous films and series, the revered figure, the expert, or the personality tells the audience what it ought to think. The groundbreaking work of *The World at War* was that it left space for the members of the audience to form their own opinions.

The "great man" approach works the other way. Here, the statement from the beginning (and the attraction) is that history will be seen through the eyes of one of the participants. The film admits its subjectivity and its partisan quality, but it promises entry into the innermost sanctums of the high and the mighty. This approach seems fine to me, since the biases are clear and open. In England, the most famous series made this way centered on the life of Lord Louis Mountbatten, uncle of the queen, a famous war hero and commander, and the last British viceroy of India. In the United States, one could easily imagine a series based on Eisenhower's diaries or Westmoreland's reminiscences of Vietnam.

A variant of the "great man" is the historical biography, which often ranges wider than political history. *Hank Aaron: Chasing the Dream* is a good example of this stream, while Ken Burns's baseball series manages to combine fascinating biography with some perceptive questioning on social and racial matters.

In "personal reminiscence" films, a section of history is told through the stories of a number of people. Often these figures are not particularly famous, but their stories seem sufficiently representative to define an issue or the feeling of a period. Three good examples would be *Nine Days in '26* by Robert Vas; *The Good Fight* by Mary Dore, Sam Sills, and Noel Buckner; and *Seeing Red* by Julie Reichart and Jim Klein. I should add, in fairness, that many academic historians find this approach, or the way it's been used recently, very suspect. I think it has its uses, so long as facts aren't hidden or political events ignored out of partisan considerations.

Nine Days in '26 tells the story of the great general strike in England of 1926, which at one point looked as if it might precipitate a social revolution. It is oral history without pundits, told by those who participated both in making and in breaking the strike. Everyone in the film came to Vas via the same method.

We advertised in various newspapers for people who had something to say about their experience to come forward. We had a tremendous response because this was a crucial event of social history. I certainly didn't go for distortion. I strongly sensed there were different sides to the same truth . . .

We had a tremendous response, and after selecting 25 people after visiting and talking to at least 150 during the research we gradually realized the enormous conflicts, the gulf between the attitudes, the tension, the charge of this whole situation. (Alan Rosenthal, *The Documentary Conscience: A Casebook in Filmmaking* [Berkeley: University of California Press, 1980])

Though, as can be seen above, the range of topics for the history documentary is enormous, there is one area that has grown by astronomic leaps in the last ten years. I am talking, of course, of the historical mystery, the history whodunit. For fun, while writing this chapter, I scanned U.S. broadcast and cable television premiers for one week and came up with the following offerings:

- *The Unexplained: The Deadly Hope Diamond*
- *The Curse of Tutankhamen*
- *The Secrets of the Great Wall of China*
- *Deciphering Nazi Secrets*
- *Pyramid of Death*
- *The Hidden Treasure of the Templars*
- *The Mystery of the Sunken Subs*
- *Bible Mysteries: Sodom and Gomorrah*

I would venture that most of the above were market driven, and arose by someone asking, What sells? and not, What interests me? but maybe I am too cynical. Maybe someone's life passion really was investigating Sodom and Gomorrah and the film was the fruit of years of research. Maybe!

Since these history mysteries can be best sellers, let me tell you quickly how to do them. You open the Bible at random and let your fingers choose a word with your eyes closed. It falls on the high-priest's breastplate. Good for starters. You then add the word *curse*, select an unpronounceable Assyrian name, and have the title of your film—*The Cursed Breastplate of Zophinias III.* You then get yourself a decent researcher and three Ph.D. project advisers. Finally, you must find a presenter who can be either a beautiful twenty-three-year-old maiden who wears see-through shirts in the desert or a gray Sean Connery look-alike with a beard and Indiana Jones hat. And one last thing: although not politically correct, the presenter must smoke a pipe. Use this formula and you can't fail, believe me, and this is probably the most valuable advice in this book!

THE STORY

The story is of prime importance in the historical documentary. This approach may earn academic scorn, but in a visual medium the dynamic story is vital. What we remember from Ken Burns's *Civil War* series are the poignant stories, culled from letters and diaries, and told in the most affecting and moving way. Telling stories is what film does best, whereas it deals with conceptual and abstract thought only with difficulty. This approach obviously affects what one can cover. In seeking only the event, the incident, the intriguing tale, you may distort the broader canvas. The danger is there, and I am the first to admit it.

Robert Kee's series on Irish history for the BBC is a case in point. *Ireland: A Television History* covers eight hundred years of history in twelve programs. If you examine the individual films, you'll see that one is devoted to the great Irish famine of the 1840s, another looks at the story of the patriot Charles Stewart Parnell, while a third covers the Easter rising of 1916. These are all great stories and make superb television, but do they reveal the most important issues and trends in eight hundred years? That is open to debate, and we would have to see what was sacrificed so that these topics might be chosen. But if Kee's dominant motive was to choose historical topics that made for compelling viewing, then he chose well.

What you must do is look for the central theme and then find a concrete way of illustrating it, a finite story that will flesh out the theme. In *Out of the Ashes*, I knew that one of the major points I wanted to make was that innocent civilian populations suffered enormously during the war, and that often this was due to the brutality of the SS and their killer groups. But how to illustrate this? Suddenly, I remembered the story of Oradour, a small village in France. In June 1944, an SS troop entered the village and for no apparent reason massacred more than six hundred people—men, women, and children—in one morning.

During research, I visited Oradour and was appalled at what I found. A cemetery with pictures of twelve members of a family on one grave, seven members of a family on another, all bearing the same date. Oradour was never rebuilt. Instead, its ruins still stand as a grim memory of that obscene day. The Oradour story was intensely moving, and I went back a few months later to film the church, the graveyard, and the silent ruins. In the simplest, most tragic of ways, Oradour summed up an evil and brutality that is still with us today.

RESEARCH

That good research is absolutely vital in the history film goes without saying, and all the methods discussed earlier in chapter 5 apply here. However, in the history film, you have to pay particular attention in acquiring the most up-to-date information, and you also have to try and see that your information is as accurate as it can be.

For years I had wanted to do a film about Stalin's last purges, the savage attacks he made on various Soviet groups and organizations between 1945 and 1953, when he died. I had wanted to do the film in 1988. In the end I made *Stalin's Last Purge* in 2005 and counted myself lucky that I had waited. Why was I lucky? Because it was only in the nineties that Russia opened many of its secret archives of the Soviet years. Access to those archives was essential to my film. Had I made the film earlier much of my film would have been skewed or lacking in detail.

Again, I stress the need to check and double-check the facts and assertions in your film. In making *Stalin's Last Purge*, I wanted to discuss an alleged plot of nine doctors who were accused of wanting to poison Stalin. A key research book I used said the doctors were going to be publicly executed in Moscow's Red Square, and I duly entered this into the script. However, no expert would confirm this, and when I looked at my research book, no source was given for the claim. So reluctantly I took the incident out of the script.

COMMENTARY

The general length of a televised historical documentary is about fifty minutes. This means, roughly, that you can use only about fifteen minutes of commentary, or a quarter of the program's length. In reality you have from about fifteen hundred to two thousand words to play with, which is not a great deal. A tremendous amount of detail has to be left out. You simply will not have time to explore all the ramifications of the Tet offensive, nor will you have time to explore in detail what happened to President Lincoln's family after the assassination. That's why good and effective narration is crucial.

What does narration do best? We have explored this in some detail, but it bears repeating. Narration is excellent for stories and anecdotes and for evoking mood and atmosphere. It is not good at detailed analysis of complex events or abstract thought. This simplification of complex historical and making them understandable for viewer became, in fact, one of the chief challenges in *Stalin's Last Purge*. The idea for Stalin's last purge was conceived through an intricate amalgam of events: the death in a hospital of two major Communist leaders, an accusatory doctor's letter to Stalin, multiple accusations against KGB members, numerous secret meetings of the politburo, signed condemnations, and so on. In the end, I boiled down the narration that explains all this to just a few words:

> Following Ettinger's death in prison a devious plan was forming in Stalin's mind.
>
> He would create an imaginary conspiracy of Jewish doctors intent on murdering Kremlin leaders, then claim the secret police had refused to investigate it. This way both the Jews and the KGB could be purged in one go.

Above all, narration works best when it is related to images. It should point up certain things. It should explain. It should call attention to detail. The narration must not describe the images, but it should make us understand their significance.

VISUALS AND ARCHIVAL MATERIAL

The maker of film histories is doing a visual history. That is what is so confining and so challenging, and what in the end makes the filmmaker's task so different from that of the academic historian. And as a visual history, the materials at hand will be photographs, location shooting, archival material, and witnesses.

The first problem is how to deal with the prephotographic era. The solutions are well known, if not terribly inspiring, and usually consist of using prints, reconstructions, and filming at historical and archaeological sites. Some reconstructions are not bad. Peter Watkins's *Culloden* manages to convey the atmosphere and mood of the last battle between the English and the Scots in the eighteenth century. Others are just awful, like the reconstruction of the siege of Cawnpore in the *British Empire* series.

Another gimmick that has found favor in the last few years is "timeless location" shooting. This artifice demands an as-if jump of

the imagination. We look at today's Bedouins or fishers and are supposed to assume that they exactly reflect life at the time of Jesus or
Mohammed. Sometimes it works, but usually the self-consciousness
of the method is all too obvious and gets in the way of believability.

Archival Problems

The visual photographic record, which begins about 1840, can be problematic as well as beneficial. A few points are worth noting, especially
in regard to archival footage, because it is the basic ingredient of so
many documentary histories.

The first dilemma is that the footage that is visually most interesting
may also be historically irrelevant. Thus, while tank battles of World
War I may be fascinating to watch, they may provide little insight into
the deeper meaning of events. The second difficulty is the misuse and
misquotation of archival film. This happens, for example, when stock
footage of the 1930s is carelessly used to provide background to a film
about the 1920s. The third, and possibly most serious, problem is the
frequent failure of filmmakers to understand the biases and implications of stock footage. One example will suffice. During World War
II the Nazis shot a great deal of footage of their captured populations.
Much of this footage is now used as an objective news record, without
acknowledging that the footage was shot to provide a negative and
degrading picture of those slave populations.

The other side of the coin is that in a visual medium, the very ab-
sence of stock footage may lead to a serious distortion of history, as a
subject or incident simply disappears. Because you don't have archival
footage of the Yugoslav partisan resistance (which, of course, the Nazis
never shot), the subject is never mentioned in the film. In other words,
unless you are careful, the sheer existence of archival material may
dictate the line of your film, whereas it should be subservient to it.

Visual history can often be defective not because events or actions
were physically unfilmable or politically undesirable to film (such
as death camp murders), but because those in a position to do so
thought the events were just not important enough to photograph.
One example was the failure of newsreel operators to record the
famous "Iron Curtain" phrase from Winston Churchill's postwar
speech at Fulton, Missouri.

Archival material can be fascinating, quaint, captivating, magical,
haunting. But it can also be tremendously distancing and unreal. This
is particularly true when you suddenly put black-and-white archival
footage in the middle of a color film. So you must occasionally ask

yourself whether your archival material will work to your advantage, or if there is a better way to do it.

Recently filmmakers have taken to mixing archives with incidental directed scenes. Thus, in a recent British war film we see black-and-white archive of a boat being sunk, and then color footage of men struggling in the water. To the uninitiated it is impossible to distinguish the authentic material from the created material. Whereas one can argue that the latter scene adds atmosphere, I personally am against this practice. Once it becomes impossible to distinguish between the genuine and the false article, all barriers start collapsing. Here I think the answer is to label the reconstruction very clearly for what it is.

Witnesses

The use of witnesses is one of the key methods for enlivening visual history. Sometimes the witnesses merely provide color; sometimes they provide the essential facts of the story. It is interesting that multiple witnesses are often used to re-create the sense of the events. Sometimes the witnesses are complementary, sometimes oppositional. For example, in *Vietnam: A Television History*, witnesses were frequently used to contradict one another or to offer very opposing views. In the episode *America Takes Charge*, a raid on a Vietnamese village is recalled by one of the attacking U.S. soldiers and by one of the Vietnamese villagers. Their accounts of the same event are light-years apart.

Witnesses are sometimes the sole authority for the facts, and therefore the choice of witnesses can be crucial when history is in dispute. One option is to use opposing witnesses, as in the Vietnam series, but most producers seem wary of that method. Yet when this is not done, the results can seem strange at best, and biased at worst. Two series on the history of Palestine serve as good illustrations on this point. Both *The Mandate Years*, made by Thames Television, and *Pillar of Fire*, made by Israel Television, deal with the flight of the Arab population from Haifa after 1945. In *The Mandate Years*, the incident is recalled by a former British army commander who is hostile to Israel and very sympathetic to the Arabs and who claims that the Arabs were forced to leave. In *Pillar of Fire*, an Israeli witness, General Yadin, recalls how the Jews begged the Arabs to stay.

Clearly, visual history is no less contentious than academic history. To cover themselves on controversial issues, U.S. networks now often demand a second corroboration of a statement before they will allow the original to pass.

People's memories are notoriously unreliable, and you must remember that when making historical films. In recalling their childhood, the war, their romances, their successes, and their failures, people will invent and embroider and often not even be aware of it. But as writer and director, you must be aware of this tendency. Often it doesn't matter, but sometimes it matters immensely. Watch also for what I call the "representational voice": the lovable, heartwarming character who smokes his pipe, grins, and tells you what we all felt on that day when the British attacked "on that sad, sad day for Ireland." There's not too much harm in using such characters, but be aware of the game you are playing.

RECENT DEVELOPMENTS

The most recent developments in history documentaries relate to the increasing fondness for using CGIs, and the growth of what I loosely call reality history. There is no doubt CGIs can enhance your film, and provide the vital scene that just doesn't exist among the archives. So in a recent film on the World War II battle for the island of Malta we are treated to a total aerial attack created by CGIs. In its way, the scene is quite spectacular. However, it's totally misleading in that it is unidentified and leads you to suppose it is genuine. Once archive and CGIs are confused all sense of truth goes out of the window, and such confusion seems to me very dangerous.

Regarding reality history, I think we are moving toward a very populist type of film whereby the audience, in films like *The Colony* and *The Edwardian House*, really want to engage with the *presence* and *experience* of history. In these films, what happens is that a modern family is invited to live in an Edwardian house in the dress and conditions of the period, or to pretend they are creating an Australian colony similar to one of two hundred years ago. Here the influence of reality television is very apparent. What is clear is that it is no longer acceptable to ponder history (places, events, people) as significant but absent. Instead, you now have to be there and have the illusion that you are actually experiencing the past.

While these programs are incredibly popular, I personally feel that some of this drive to re-create the past as a vicarious experience is quite mad. The film *Bomber Crew*, for example, has the children of World War II flying a fake mission to see how they cope psychologically with the experience. All this was intercut with real bomber raids of 1945. Another film put volunteers in mock-ups of World

War I trenches and got them to live there for a few days. Again, they were examined to see how they coped psychologically. As they were neither gassed, bombed, nor subject to lethal machine gun fire, I had my doubts as to the worth of the experiment.

What we are really being told here is that history can be a lot of fun if not taken seriously. While all this is fairly enjoyable to a point, and I guess a filmmaker has to learn how to work in this genre, I think we may be in serious danger of dumbing down history. So amuse yourselves, yes, but please go on making history films of worth that actually stimulate serious thought.

THE LOST TREASURES OF JERUSALEM

Since history films are becoming more and more popular, it is becoming vital that the filmmaker knows how to enter the field. If you are lucky, you may be taken on by a television station to work on an ongoing series. The more probable case, however, is that you will have to write your own proposal and pitch it to a commissioning editor or at a film market.

Below I've set out as an example a historical mystery proposal I put forward at a film market in Spain. The tone of the series is obvious. It's intended as a popular (and salable) romp through history with echoes of Indiana Jones and the *Da Vinci Code*. The pitch had a very good response at the market and at the moment of writing I am waiting to see whether the nibbles turn into real bites.

The Lost Treasures of Jerusalem
A three-part television series
    ALAN ROSENTHAL

The year is 70 A.D. Everywhere Roman soldiers are on the rampage. Blood runs in the streets. Bodies hang from the crucifixes outside the city walls. At the pinnacle of Jerusalem's most sacred spot, savage flames ravage the Temple. While fierce fighting rages in its holy courtyards, below its massive colonnades, men secretly carry off its most sacred treasures through dark subterranean tunnels. And for centuries they will lie hidden . . . buried . . . but not forgotten.

For hundreds of years Jerusalem lies abandoned. Its inhabitants have been exiled or enslaved. But now the city is astir. Helena, the mother of the Roman Emperor Constantine, and a dedicated Christian, has come to the Holy Land to look for relics of Jesus. Miraculously she finds the True Cross buried in Jerusalem . . . little knowing that following the discovery men will fight for it, die for it, and then pursue its elusive shadows through the years.

But conquest follows conquest. Soon the devoted followers of the prophet Mohammed sweep in from the south. And as Jerusalem becomes the Muslims' city of dreams, a Golden Dome rises over a sacred rock to commemorate Mohammed's night journey "to the farthest mosque." But here again holiness gives ways to mysteries, and brooding secrets as every one fights for the spot from Saudi warriors and Templar knights, to Jordanian legionnaires and Israeli paratroopers.

The Series

Our three part series is set against this swirling cauldron of Jerusalem.

Jerusalem has seen more blood and conquerors than almost any other city in the world. And via wars and peace it has also assembled riches, treasures, and priceless icons that in turn have inspired love, worship, devotion, lust, envy, and greed.

But intrigue and mystery surround the fate of these treasures. Questions about their destiny, their wanderings, and their location remain unanswered. Our series centers on the hunt for two of these lost eternal treasures and also examines the mysteries and history of one of the most venerated shrines in Islam, a shrine which some say may also contain the secrets of the Holy Grail.

While part of the hunt involves Europe, a major part of our story also takes place underground, beneath the sacred rocks of Jerusalem, a place of tunnels, spirits, legends, and hiding places still largely untouched by the archaeologist's tools.

Thus, we present *The Lost Treasures of Jerusalem* in order to open the hidden doors, the barred vaults and explore the most fascinating of the city's secrets.

The Films

1. *The Search for the Temple Treasures*

One central mystery has fascinated Jews and non-Jews for two thousand years. Are the fabled treasures of the Jewish Second Temple, including the celebrated Golden Candelabra, still in existence? If so, where are they? And who guards them?

The Jewish Second Temple, enlarged and glorified by King Herod, was not just a place of worship, but could be regarded as the Fort Knox of its day. Everyone brought gifts and treasures to the Temple till its vaults were overflowing with jewels and diamonds and sacred objects of gold and silver. Meanwhile, after collecting their taxes the Roman overlords of Judea looked on from the side.

When in 70 A.D. the Jews rose up in rebellion, the Roman general Titus crushed it swiftly and brutally. While thousands of dead lay in the Jerusalem streets, Titus's legions put fire to the Temple and destroyed the sanctuary. But what happened to the treasures?

Were they taken to Rome by Titus? Are they hidden in the Vatican? Did the Vandals transport them to Africa? And why do people say they lie under the Istanbul's Hagia Sophia mosque? And what do the Templars, the legends surrounding the French city of Carcassonne and the secrets of a small mountain village called Rennes-le-Château have to do with the Temple treasures?

But could it be as one Texan archaeologist believes, that the searchers have been following false trails. Could it be that the treasure has been secreted away by the Temple priests and still lies underneath Israel's burning deserts?

In order to find out we will travel back in time to the triumphs of imperial Rome and the destruction of the Second Temple. Then tracing myths and clues, we will journey to North Africa, Constantinople, southern France, and then back to Israel's deserts, all in the quest for the treasures of God.

2. *The Search for the True Cross*

Shrouded in mystery and legend for two thousand years, the Cross of Jesus has been an enigma to men and women around the world. Thus, this most venerated of holy relics, the very wood upon which the holy man was crucified, has been sought after down the corridors of time by noblemen and peasants, kings and paupers.

The story begins in a small church in Arezzo, Italy. Here a fresco by Piero della Francesco tells the story of the origins of the Cross from Adam to Jesus. After the death of Jesus, the Cross disappears till it is found in Jerusalem by Queen Helena. Though it is found with two other crosses, it is identified when it miraculously brings a dead woman to life.

Queen Helena then builds a church to honor the Cross and the place of Christ's crucifixion. But the cross is never secure and over the centuries changes hands many times.

Its moment of destiny comes during the Crusades. Held high by Crusader knights it leads them into battle against Saladin. Captured by the Muslims, it is almost rescued by Richard the Lionheart. But since the middle of the twelfth century, its whereabouts remain unknown. Is it buried beneath some secret courtyard in Syria? Does it lie in some dark Egyptian mosque? Or somewhere in Istanbul? And is that sliver of wood so jealously guarded by the monks of Jerusalem's Church of the Holy Sepulchre really part of the Cross?

Besides the thrill of the search, *The Hunt for the True Cross* will tell the story of how the cross, once the symbol of death and torture, became the most sought out and admired of Holy treasures of Christianity.

To tell the story of the hunt, we travel from the dark vaults of Jerusalem's Church of the Holy Sepulchre to the Horns of Hattin in the Galilee, scene of the Crusaders' last battle under the guidance of the Cross. From there we journey to Egypt and on to Bavaria, Germany, where every Easter people gather from around the world to watch a play about the Passion which reenacts the crucifixion of Jesus.

Interwoven with the journey we also include interviews with archaeologists, theologians, historians, and treasure hunters to tell the story of the True Cross, its history, and its fate. [The third film dealt with the Dome of the Rock, the magnificent golden mosque that dominates the old city of Jerusalem. I've had to omit this part of the proposal because of pressures of space. —A. R.]

21

FAMILY FILMS

> You're wasting our time! I was in the army. Got married. I raised a family, worked hard, had my own business, that's all. That's nothing to make a picture about! It's ridiculous!—Oscar Berliner to Alan Berliner, *Nobody's Business*

> Personal memoirs are always difficult. After all, if there is honest revelation someone always gets hurt.—Lilly Rivlin, commenting on *Gimme a Kiss*

In 1996 an unknown middle-aged schoolteacher called Frank McCourt published his autobiography. The book told of Frank's poverty-stricken childhood in Limerick, in western Ireland. Though many of the related incidents were extremely tragic, McCourt recounted them in an ironic, humor-filled prose that quickly took *Angela's Ashes* to the top of the best-seller list, where it remained for 117 weeks. The message, not a new one, was clear to the publishers. The drama of family relations, if well told and if able to touch some universal chord in the reader, could well find a very broad audience.

Unfortunately, this message has been absorbed to a much lesser extent in film. Today the family feature film in Hollywood has been relegated to the sidelines, allowing the action comic book to handle the main plays. Nevertheless, here and there, the absolutely intriguing family drama creeps through to the main screen in films such as *Ordinary People*, Bergman's *Scenes from a Marriage*, *The Celebration* from Denmark, and Mike Leigh's *Secrets and Lies*.

In contrast to feature films, the drama of family relations—the film that resurrects, analyzes, dissects, and probes family history and interaction—has become one of the main strands of documentary film. But then family film itself is just one example of the growing attention to what one can call the new *personal* film.

This emphasis on the *personal* in documentary is a comparatively recent phenomenon, dating from the seventies onward. It's a revolution due to many causes, not the least being the influence of new film schools, the popularity of cinema verité, the cheapening of film and video equipment, and a deeper social probing by young independent filmmakers. The personal documentary in fact reaches out much wider than family and embraces films on women, the Holocaust, gay and lesbian relationships, problems of minorities, and the AIDS phenomenon. Obviously the categories intermingle and overlap. For the purpose of this book, however, and because of limitations of space, I thought I would merely note down a few observations about the making of family films.

For simplicity's sake, family films can be divided into two groups. First come the family films made by third-party observers. Here I am thinking of films like Allan King's *A Married Couple*, *Fahimeh's Story* by Faramarz K-Rahber, series like Craig Gilbert's *An American Family*, and Bill Jersey's *Six American Families*. Most of these films are done or have been done in cinema verité style, and I discussed their genre problems earlier. The second group of films is what I would call *insider films*. They are revelation documentaries, often concerned with roots and origins, and their creative problems, for a variety of reasons, tend to be more complex than those in films made by outsiders.

The *insider* projects can themselves be seen to split in two—the diary film and the history-cum-analysis film. Examples of the first include Ed Pincus's *Diaries*, Alfred Guzzetti's *Family Portrait Sitting*, and Jonas Mekas's *Reminiscences of a Journey to Lithuania*. What characterizes them is again the use of verité to follow ongoing action and an accumulation of detail over time, which is presented but not usually analyzed, though Guzzetti's film is an exception. In short you go, you shoot, you question, and you edit. And hopefully meaning emerges.

The second and larger group of insider films includes classics like Amalie Rothschild's *Nana, Mom and Me*, Martha Coolidge's *An Old*

Fashioned Woman, Maxi Cohen's *Joe and Maxi*, Ira Wohl's *Best Boy*, Marlon Riggs's *Tongues Untied*, Su Friedrich's *The Ties That Bind*, Michelle Citron's *Daughter Rite*, and Martin Scorsese's *Italian American*. Among the newer films in this group and quite outstanding are Sami Saif's *Family*, Nathaniel Kahn's *My Architect*, Lilly Rivlin's *Gimme a Kiss*, Steve Thomas's *Least Said Soonest Mended*, Alan Berliner's *Nobody's Business*, Deann Borshay Liem's *First Person Plural*, and Jan Krawitz's *In Harm's Way*.

Some of these documentaries, like Nathaniel Kahn's film about his architect father, are portraits. Some are autobiographical confessions. Some are shaped as investigations. What is often common to this group is the need to understand the present through an examination of one's origins. Martha Coolidge wants to know more of her grandmother. Maxi Cohen, Sami Saif, and Lilly Rivlin want to know more about their fathers. Steve Thomas and Deann Borshay Liem want to know more about their mothers. Ira Wohl looks at the problem of a family letting go of its retarded son, while Marlon Riggs examines what it means to grow up black and gay.

Yet all transcend home movies. And this is the biggest task: to make your films ascend and fly, so that they speak not merely to your immediate family and circle but have the ability to touch on the universal and eternal. In short, you are faced with a hell of a challenge.

Now at this point, when you turn and say, "I bought your book, help me," I have to confess I have led you astray. There are no easy solutions. There are no accepted ways of doing things. No pat formulas, no easy prescriptions. But what I can offer are a few hints and a few warnings that, if they don't show you a clear way forward, can at least keep you away from the minefields.

The section that follows addresses the main points to keep in mind.

YOURSELF ON THE BLOCK

Until now you've mostly made films as an outside observer, which is a relatively comfortable position. You've been the third-person essayist and commentator, and you've been able to film and go home to sleep. Now for the first time you are putting *yourself* on the block, and it's not always a comfortable position. You yourself will be up there on the screen, with your own actions liable to be analyzed and criticized not just by strangers, but by your own family, with possible long-lasting effects. Family relations may be strengthened, but they may also be broken. Steve Thomas, for example, found his relations with his mother more than a little strained after publicly showing her coldness to Steve's pregnant sister in *Least Said, Soonest Mended.* So, making family films is very much a walking-on-coals experience. It is not something to be indulged in by the fainthearted.

There is also a slightly schizophrenic quality about the process. As you film you are being split in two. One part of you has to play the participant: the nice girl who adores her grandmother but battles with her mother, or the rebellious son who sees his father as distant and hard with a gentle public reputation at odds with his parental actions. Meanwhile the other part of you has to stand aside and film and wonder how everything will come together. Combining the two roles is not easy, and can be quite painful, so you need to think very hard and long before embarking on the family film.

INDICATE DIRECTION

When you start your film, the odds are you don't know where you are going. You've decided to talk to members of your family about the past, about roots, about a few family secrets. You are intrigued by the problems your grandfather faced on coming to America. You wonder whether the family was happier before Joe died in Vietnam. You are curious about the branch of the family no one ever mentions. So intrigued, but without much direction, you plunge in without much direction. If you are Lilly Rivlin, you just start filming and talking to your aged parents as they lie sick in bed. If you are Sami Saif, you start looking for your father because your girlfriend keeps nagging you into action. If you are Amalie Rothschild, you start shooting your grandmother and only later do you realize the real focus is your mother.

How does all this fit with what I stated earlier, that before you begin you need to establish one defining statement, or one clear underlying concept, that will set you off in the right direction and provide the impetus for the film? "This film is about the search for the atomic bomb." "This video will discuss the role of the university in the twenty-first century." Unfortunately, and for very clear reasons, this rule is rarely observed in family films. In family films we often just do not know where we're going. We work on impulse and feeling. Very often we wander for years uncertain of direction . . . and that's all right. It's all part of the game. You are searching for meaning and it may take years to emerge. *But*—and it's a very big and important *but*—by the time you've finished the film, that meaning and that line must be there.

And it not only must be there but also is usually very important to let the audience see this at the very beginning of the film.

We do this because family films wander all over the place. They often seem to have no clear trajectory and it is easy for the audience to get confused. If you can define a clear line at the beginning, and tell the viewers where you hope to go, then it is much easier for the audience to stay with you and understand your twists, side steps, and convolutions.

In Minda Martin's *Mother's Heritage*, the film opens with an aunt saying, "There were so many emotions at that death. It was a death caused by accident. It created anger. For some reason there seemed to be a lot of, Who's to blame for this? But the real question was not, Who is to blame for the shooting death? but rather, Who is to blame for her life?" This opening has a double advantage. It not only tells us what the film is about—an examination of blame for a life—but also intrigues us by telling us we are going to see events leading up to a shooting, though we don't yet know of whom.

Deann Borshay Liem's *First Person Plural* starts with the words, "I've been several different people in my life. I had three mothers. Three different sets of histories. I've spoken different languages. Had different families. Different birthdays." We hear all this over bleached-out pictures of a pretty Asian woman of about thirty. We are again intrigued, but also know immediately this film is going to be about a search for identity.

For her part, Lilly Rivlin starts *Gimme a Kiss* with a line that hits us all between the eyes. "Who of us knows our parents?" This is then followed by Lilly's brother saying, "What a hell of a life they had"; her sister commenting, "There was no hugging, no kissing"; and Lilly's father saying of the mother, "I always loved her!" Here, with "Who of us knows our parents?" we are presented with a question that all of us have asked at one time or another but have probably never taken any deeper. A second line of inquiry into interparental relations is then opened up by the siblings' comments and the father's declaration that he always loved his wife. The comments of father and children clearly oppose one another, and we know the picture will help show us which view is correct.

DRAMATIC ELEMENTS AND STRUCTURE

The chief fault of films dealing with family relations is that they often wander aimlessly, with little progression, pacing, or conclusion. I've indicated above that you need a good opening to put your film into orbit. But you have to follow up on the promise by delivering the goods. This means a good story, conflict, characters that interest us, scenes that touch us and move us, and a conclusion and closure. Occasionally you strike lucky and can sense many of these things before you begin your film.

In *Fahimeh's Story*, which I referred to earlier, this is exactly what happened to director Faramarz K-Rahber and his line producer Axel Grigor. Before shooting, both men met a vivacious forty-seven-year-old Iranian immigrant to Australia called Fahimeh. Fahimeh had migrated to Australia with her children after an unhappy arranged marriage to a husband whom she could not divorce under Iranian law. Five years later, at the age of fifty-two, she has fallen in love with and married John, a seventy-seven-year-old retired army officer, with his own children. At this point Faramarz enters the scene to be told that the Iranian husband, Hossain, who does not know he has been divorced under Australian law, is coming for a visit. So in fact we have the perfect setup.

First, we have the marriage of two great interesting but absolutely contrasting central characters: Fahimeh, who is warm, funny, emotional, dynamic, and outgoing, and John, who is taciturn, dry, and slow moving. What we obviously want to know is whether time will cement or crack this unlikely association. We then have the children on both sides, who are quite unenthusiastic about the union and even at times extremely angry at the liaison. And finally we have the awaited appearance of the Iranian husband who doesn't even know he's been divorced. It sounds like old recipe instructions. Stir well. Add an egg. Bake for an hour and you'll have a great cake. With the above film ingredients, who can go wrong? In this case not K-Rahber and Grigor, who in the end produced a very fine film.

Again you will probably not be able to define any of these things, story, character, and conflict when you begin your film. Your job is to disinter these elements as you progress and see that they are in place by the time the film is finished.

The most common family film is that structured in the form of a *search*. This could be a search for the meaning of a person's life (which is difficult to bring off) or a search for facts about a life. The second is easier because it is more tangible and often allows *action* as well *recollection* to drive the film.

In Su Friedrich's *The Ties That Bind*, Friedrich explores both her relationship with her German mother and her own ties to the past.

The question that haunts her is whether she has any ties that bind her to the Third Reich. This is the search that must be carried out, whatever the conclusion.

In *Gimme a Kiss*, we learn fairly early that Lilly Rivlin's father was a philanderer. All that is common family knowledge. Rivlin, however, takes the drama further by trying to find out whether it is true that the father had an African American mistress and whether as a consequence of the liaison she has an unknown half brother. This quest adds a terrific drive to the second part of the film.

Deann Borshay Liem's quest in *First Person Plural* is more complex. In her search for identity, she discovers that her true identity has been concealed by fake adoption papers. Further efforts, all documented in the film, then lead her to her true Korean mother. But the final search is to discover whether her allegiance is to her birth mother or to her adopted American parents. This leads to a moving climax in which both families have a very emotional meeting in Korea, talk about their feelings, and help settle Liem's dilemma once and for all.

Sami Saif's film *Family* is based on the classic search for facts. In Saif's case the question is, What happened to my father, and where is he now? Abandoned by his father at a young age, Arab Danish film-maker Saif is urged and assisted his girlfriend, Phie Ambo, to search for answers. Before the filming began, Saif's beloved brother committed suicide and his mother died, leaving Saif grief stricken and more than ever in need of family. As his camera witnesses his search, Saif shows both humor and tremendous emotion during wrenching, gut-searing telephone calls during which neither we nor Sami are sure whether he has found and is indeed talking to his father. Eventually Saif tracks down his family to Yemen, where we witness an extremely moving but also funny reunion with his elder brother.

The quest for self-knowledge, the need for reflection, the searing darts that burn the soul with reverberations of, Who am I? Why am I? What shaped me? may be the hardest search, but a number of filmmakers, like Marlon Riggs, Su Friedrich, and Jan Krawitz, have managed to achieve that.

Jan Krawitz's film *In Harm's Way* opens with a startling image. A building is suddenly blown up, and for thirty seconds, it shatters, crumbles, and slowly disintegrates before our eyes. Over this shot that seems to last for eternity we hear Krawitz's voice defining the pain of her self-discovery:

> For some, there is an event in our lives after which nothing will ever be the same. The ground shifts beneath your feet and you find your-

self adrift on an ice floe . . . gazing at that other part of your life as it
recedes into the distance. You contemplate the wreckage and realise
that the original blueprint is lost forever.

The film then recounts how in 1985 Krawitz was sexually assaulted
and almost strangled to death. It is a hard and tremendously painful
recollection that invites us all to question the pillars of our beliefs and
fundamental assumptions.

FUNCTION AND UNIVERSALITY

Do family films have a function? My personal feeling is that they
very often act as therapy, as a cathartic, purging experience for the
filmmaker. Often they seem to enable the filmmaker to come to grips
with a relationship, as in *Joe and Maxi*, or to settle questions of identity, as in *First Person Plural*. Sometimes they enable the filmmaker
to deal with the loss of a mother, as Minda Martin does in *Mother's
Heritage*, or the tragic loss of children, as Robert Frank does twice in
Life Dances On and *Home Improvements*. But this therapeutic impulse
is not always a necessity. Krawitz's *In Harm's Way*, for example, is
about recounting and revisiting an experience, while *Tongues Untied*
is a reflection on experience. But if the question of *function* is open
to discussion, there is another issue that I would argue is absolutely
closed. Put bluntly it is this: in order to succeed, family films must
have a *universal message*; otherwise they run the risk of remaining
home movies.

So, what do I mean by home movies and why should that be bad?
I would suggest that home movies are generally unstructured and
without a personal voice, are rarely creative, tend to be simplistically
observational rather than analytical, and are of interest to only a very
limited audience. In contrast, the creative family film must provide
some wider social observation. It aims to bring sensitivity, feeling,
understanding, and microscopic investigation to bear onto the complex web of family relations. Occasionally this concentration of gaze
will bring pleasure. Often it will bring pain. But one thing it must do
above all else: it must reveal and illuminate some universal aspect
of human emotions and human actions. It should vibrate for us, the
observers and members of the audience, and bring new meanings
and understandings into our lives. This is easier said than done, but
without these elements, the personal film will remained grounded,
unable to take off, unable to provide inspiration to the wider world
over the horizon.

STYLE

The family film provides ample opportunity for using the widest palette possible. In *Daughter Rite*, Michelle Citron successfully experiments with home movie and documentary footage. Of course there is a catch. The deliberately slowed-down home movies reveal the subtle, nonverbal communications that occur within families, while the documentary footage is fake. The seemingly verité pictures of truth are scripted, acted, and directed. For their part, the authentic documentary images—the home movies—are manipulated to look like experimental film. The question then being posed is clearly, Is there a difference between narrative fiction truth about families and documentary truth?

In the autobiographical section of *Tongues Untied*, Marlon Riggs tries everything from verse to rap, finger-snap jokes, monologues, and group performances. He uses whatever will serve his picture and his aim, and for the most part it works. Possibly the most effective episode is when Marlon talks about his childhood in medium shot to camera, only to have his dialogue broken by close-ups of various lips mouthing the words *nigger, coon, Uncle Tom*, and other intended insults. When Marlon eventually discovers the Castro neighborhood of San Francisco and observes white gay males showing off their leather and their muscles, the whole scene is again enhanced by a very creative sound track that hints at the most intimate of sexual acts.

Unfortunately many of the experiments carried out by Citron and Riggs have become clichés. Overuse has dulled their impact. This is not to say they should not be used, but rather that they should be used with caution, especially with home movies in particular.

The use of home movies and recycled images has become a staple of family films: Mom waving, little kids in beautiful dresses running, big grins, birthday parties, and so on. The problem is that we have seen this so often we stop really seeing what is on the screen. We merely see generic images and often miss their real message. There is also a theoretical danger that Michelle Citron discusses in her book *Home Movies and Other Necessary Fictions*. Citron suggests that most home movies are controlled by the family father and we should be aware of their very controlling viewpoint. I think her concern is overdone but worth noting.

Step printing, and the slowed-down and deliberately blurred images, have also become clichés and should be used with caution. And the warning encompasses archival footage as well. But these are warnings, notes to "handle with care." They are not hands-off directives, because used intelligently, all of these devices can enhance the film. *First Person Plural* uses a tremendous amount of home movie footage. However it is all footage taken by Deann Borshay Liem's father over more than a decade and beautifully documents Liem's growing up and integration into America. The footage provides us with more than passing snapshots. Here a *process* is being illustrated and the key word is *documents*. Similarly Krawitz's use of archival footage in *In Harm's Way* is not generic and randomly atmospheric but consists of newsreels and period instructional films specially selected to illustrate very particular and specific points in her script.

ETHICS

The place of ethics in documentary is discussed at length in chapter 24 of this book, but a short word is due here. When you film your own family, you are entering very dangerous territory. The capacity for harm is immense, and you need to tread very cautiously. You may believe you are working for the public good, or for your own therapeutic purposes, but often you are merely washing dirty laundry in public, even settling age-old family grudges. So be careful.

Questions you have to ask of yourself are, Who benefits, and who is liable to be harmed by your film? Generally your family trusts you. Because of that they allow you access to their thoughts and feelings, which they would probably deny any other filmmaker. Be careful not to abuse that trust. You know more about the possible long-range effects of the film than they do. Be aware of that. Protect them from the harm that they cannot foresee.

Above all, avoid rape with the camera. In his diary project, it seems as if Ed Pincus practically forces his wife to appear in the film against her will. The effect is not pleasant. In *Joe and Maxi*, Maxi Cohen besieges her father, who is really quite angry about being forced into a situation not of his liking. Again the audience is left with a bad taste in its mouth. This abuse is not, however, to be confused with gentle persuasion of someone to appear in your film. When Oscar Berliner tells his son Alan that he is wasting his time filming him, he is really saying, "Persuade me, my life is interesting." There may seem to be only a fine line between the actions of Ed Pincus and Alan Berliner, but in practice the gap is a mile wide.

I would finally add one caution—don't go to the other extreme. Don't be too overprotective. What I mean by this is that in our concern for our loved ones, we can sometimes be too defensive and fail to ask the penetrating and necessary questions. Thus, in Minda Martin's investigation of her mother's life and death, most of the family is interviewed at length except the father. This is a strange omission, as the father would undoubtedly have shed much light on the mother's life. On being questioned on this score, Martin acknowledged the point but told me that she was frankly concerned for her father and didn't want to restir the embers of his loss.

DISCUSSION

To finish off this chapter, I thought it might help you to hear the views of a few filmmakers regarding their approach and thoughts on the family film. What follows is a summary of some of our discussions. First I wrote to Lilly Rivlin and asked her to review a few of the problems of *Gimme a Kiss*.

Gimme a Kiss

Gimme a Kiss looks at the life of Rivlin's father, an attractive man full of energy, who swept his future wife off her feet on a Mediterranean cruise. Subsequently his life was dotted with affairs. Though confessing eternal love for his wife, this was something that the father rarely seems to have demonstrated in practice. As the children say, "There was never any hugging or kissing." While the general life and relations of the parents are analyzed in the early part of the film, the last third is devoted to a hunt by Lilly to find the father's African American mistress and a possible half brother.

While family interviews and stills are used throughout the picture, the spine is provided by Rivlin's filming of her parents. Both are in their late seventies and lie ill and weak in twin beds in a daughter's home. The father is a double amputee after having been stricken with diabetes. The mother has lost her power of speech. Lilly's talks with her father are then dotted throughout the film, as are scenes of the fiftieth wedding anniversary.

> ROSENTHAL: When and how did you start making the film?
> RIVLIN: I started filming and recording in 1985 at my parent's fiftieth anniversary. I even had a professional crew come in and shoot it. Did I know that I would make *Gimme a Kiss* in its present form? Of course not. But somewhere, in the back of my mind, I thought that I would use the material in some way but I didn't know how. However, I have always seen myself as a storyteller of a sort, so somewhere there was the desire to tell a story.

I use the material from the fiftieth wedding throughout the film. My mindset at the anniversary was how can we go through this charade, what a terrible marriage, and the interviews with my parents and siblings bear this out, i.e., the meaning of marriage, and did you ever think of divorce, etc.

ROSENTHAL: **How did you tackle financing?**

RIVLIN: I supported my own habit. For years, I just documented. The scenes of my parents in the last stage of their lives, in adjoining beds in my sister's home: some may wonder, how could she do it, or why? At least once a year, when my sister went on vacation I relieved her from looking after my parents. There was very little else to do, and it is how I am in life. I document things that are intense for me. My parents' marriage has been intense for me. I think I did it because it was so difficult for me to be there, so painful for me to see them in that stage, especially my mother, so that being behind the camera gave me distance.

Finance came slowly. I was rejected by the National Foundation for Jewish culture because the film wasn't Jewish enough. Then a miracle, I got a small grant from HBO which allowed me to put a fifteen-minute preview piece together; then a friend gave a fund-raiser, which really encouraged me, and at the very end, when it was clear that I was well along in the project and would finish in a matter of months, I got a few more grants, more miracles.

ROSENTHAL: **Why did you make the film? What did you hope to gain from it, and what did you think the audience would get out of it?**

RIVLIN: I'm not sure why I made it, I think I needed to tell the story of my parents' marriage, and also show how their marriage affected us, the children. There were so many bizarre aspects to my family life, especially toward the end when I started seeing my parents as characters in a Beckett play. I mean there is my father, the woman-izer, keeping my mother alive [Lilly's father feeds her mother], and she can't express herself in anyway but ironically. In the end, she finally got what she always wanted—his total attention.

I know that my friends and many of those who see the film think it was therapeutic, but I think the therapy happened in the documenting, much before I put the story together in the editing room. My friends tell me that the experience of putting it together was painful, but I think its like women who go through the pain of labor saying afterwards they forgot the pain. I feel the real pain was in the experience of it, of living this story out, but I wanted to do it because I thought it was universal, and that most of us come from dysfunctional families, and the myth of the happy ideal family is only that, a myth. I wanted the audience to be able to identify with this family. It was only when I filmed my sister in 1999, eight years after my parents died, and looked at the material, that I saw how much she suffered. I cried a lot then. I like what Albert Maysles says about my film, "It's a story about love, where it is and where it isn't, and the filmmaker is very skilful in noticing love where it doesn't appear to be."

ROSENTHAL: **What do you think about the ethics of exposing your family and their problems, as well as their love, in public?**

RIVLIN: Yes, that's difficult. I think one reason why it took so long to finish is that my parents had to die before I could deal with the film. It took eight years for me to be able to go back to the material [the filming of the parents in twin beds]. But then it wasn't enough, because as I worked on it with Josh Waletzky, he told me I needed more material in addition to what I had shot. That's when I went out and filmed my sister, brother, aunts, and Rosa, his mistress. And most important, I had to shape it, so even though it is a personal memoir, it is less a traditional documentary then any of my earlier ones. To me it is more like a novel because of its layers and subtexts. Personal memoir is always difficult. After all if there is honest revelation someone always gets hurt.

It's an old question in documentary making, the relationship between the filmmaker and the subjects, so it is especially difficult when in some way I'm telling my own story and that of my siblings and parents.

Initially when I first showed some of my material to HBO, Sheila Nevins warned me that it would look like I was exposing my family's dirty linen, and that this would be frowned upon—that it wouldn't look good. I said I was willing to risk it. I kept thinking that the story I had to tell had revelations similar to those in *Death of a Salesman* and that surely attempting to make art out of one's reality was an acceptable form of expression. Look at all the reality TV on the air. I'm in tune with the Zeitgeist. Why is this happening? Because fiction can't match reality, reality is more horrific then fiction, i.e., the Holocaust, or just read anything about genetic engineering.

ROSENTHAL: **Tell me something about the difficulties of finding audience and distribution.**

RIVLIN: It's terribly difficult. So far I have had a lot of rejections. POV turned it down, but all the people who really love it and appreciate it say, don't worry, it will find its audience. So far, it was shown at the Vancouver Underground Film Festival to an audience of mostly under-30s who would not stop asking questions and talking about their own families. Example of one question: "I came here because I read about your film and I'm a philanderer's daughter. Did you find that as a philanderer's daughter you became a philanderer too?" How's that for direct?

The First Glance Film Festival will show it in March, at the Millennium in the East Village. Makor, the new hip Jewish cultural center on the Upper West Side will show it and it will be shown at the Jerusalem Film Festival. I'm generally getting a positive response, but it's depressing to see how difficult it is to find venues, so I can't get juice up to start the next one, and for an independent that's bad.

ROSENTHAL: **How did your family react to the making of the film?**

RIVLIN: I had no problems with my family as I was making it except for my Aunt Hilda, and you see her reaction in the film. My family was used to me documenting their lives, first as a photographer-interviewer and then with a camera. Now that I've finished it my sister doesn't really want to see it. My brother is ambivalent about it. And the aunts and cousins have yet to see it.

ROSENTHAL: **Were you aware of doing any self-censorship in your filmmaking?**

RIVLIN: As I was getting ready to edit I remember sitting and saying to myself, "Lilly, if this is going to work you have to be a vehicle for the film, you have to be whatever the film requires and you have to be totally honest." I had a fantastic editor, Pola Rosenberg, who receives codirector's credit, and Pola helped me keep this vow to myself. Pola helped me to insert my voice in the film and to keep it from sounding self-serving, which really would have been the kiss of death.

Did I learn anything that I didn't know? After I finished the film and heard some of the reactions I realized that to some people this was a love story. Neither of my siblings, nor I felt that. We were too close, but I can finally understand why a viewer could feel this.

ROSENTHAL: **It seems to me, and I may be wrong, that most of the makers of this kind of film are women. If that is true, why do you think that is so?**

RIVLIN: I think the confessional or journal mode is more a woman's expression than that of a man, except in the case of the sensitive and/or male writer. Women speak about themselves more easily than men do, and I also think that the personal memoir demands reflection and honesty which for a variety of reasons, habit for one, and dissembling in their professional roles for another, is a way of life for men. By way of contrast women speak more from their interior.

When I think of it now, this is a woman's film, and I hope it finds a place out there.

Least Said, Soonest Mended

In 1964 Steve Thomas, then aged fifteen, was living in Bath, England. Unknown to Steve, his twin sister, Val, became pregnant. Quickly she was dispatched to an institution by her parents, where she was hidden away and arrangements made for the subsequent adoption of her baby. Again Steve was kept in the dark. Val then lived for the next twenty-five years (nineteen of them in New Zealand) not knowing where her baby was or whether she was alive or dead. Eventually Val's determination and the curiosity of her daughter, Karen, brought about their reconciliation from opposite sides of the globe in 1992.

Rather than marking the end of the story, this was a new beginning, for this event blew the lid off the tacit family agreement to "let sleeping dogs lie." So in his film we see Thomas, a Melbourne-based filmmaker, questioning his mother about her actions, her silence, and her need to preserve appearances rather than consider the welfare of her daughter. We also see Steve and Val discuss their own feelings in regard to past and present. At the conclusion of the film, we see a meeting between Val; her daughter, Karen; Steve; Karen's adoptive father, Duncan; and Steve's mother. Twenty-five years have passed, but all we hear are banalities as the grandmother locks her emotions away and totally and completely refuses to allow herself to show any regret, or spark of family feeling, toward her granddaughter,

ROSENTHAL: Why did you decide to make the film?

THOMAS: Firstly I wanted to retrace my sister's experience to understand her pain. Secondly, I was fascinated by the very different versions of the same story that each of my relatives carried and wanted to explore these. Thirdly, I wanted to reconcile my family and felt that getting this story out into the open was a necessary first step. I think I probably achieved the first two aims but I was a little naive concerning the last! This is apparent in the final scene when Val plays the piano in the pub. Afterwards Val draws the cover over the piano as mum and Duncan discuss some dead jazz singer. The veil is drawn over her suffering once again, but then, that's life.

ROSENTHAL: Over what period did the filming and interviews of family members occur?

THOMAS: It was researched and written over about six months in 1996. Then it took a long time to get production funding. The filming was eventually done in two blocks in 1999.

I spent a week in New Zealand with Val and her family, recording interviews, etc., early in 1999. A couple of months later I spent three weeks filming in England. I did interviews, etc., with mum, then Karen and Duncan, and finally Val flew over from New Zealand to England for the last week and we revisited the places she was sent to in Bournemouth and London. Finally we brought the whole family together in Bath.

You can see that the chronology of filming isn't quite the chronology used in the film because we cut backwards and forwards quite a lot between New Zealand and England. The chronology (or structure) of the film is the chronology of the events which actually happened, from 1964 to 1999. This is the kind of manipulation of reality which happens in editing a film. The aim is often to stay true to the story one is telling rather than the filming process.

ROSENTHAL: Can you say something about the varying points of view in the film?

THOMAS: The main impetus for the film was for Val to tell her story. The film however, contains multiple points of view, including those of mum and Karen. There's an important distinction here. Although my sympathies lie very much with my sister I did not want to make a film which was judgmental, i.e., about "goodies, and baddies." Life is more complex than that. I wanted everybody to give their own point of view and then leave you, the audience, to make up your own minds about the whole thing.

ROSENTHAL: To what extent do you think the film helped Val to deal with her anger and memories?

THOMAS: I think that making the film helped Val in that it was an open acknowledgment of what had happened to her, which she hadn't been able to speak about for so long. She had been talking about it for some years, to her own family, in a women's group that she attended and to her counselor but this was a more public acknowledgment.

It was hard for Val to revisit those places she was sent to but she says it helped settle things for her and put things to rest. I don't think the anger and the grief she feels will ever be completely cleansed though. For my own part I wanted to give Val the opportunity to tell her story because I've always felt guilty that I wasn't available to her at the time, even though it was not my fault. So the film was my way of trying to make up for that.

As far as mum goes, given her preference to "let sleeping dogs lie," I think her participation was a wonderful gift to the film. She was prepared to talk about the past because she knew it was important to me. Unfortunately, in the short term anyway, the film doesn't seem to have helped her relationship with Val as they are still not able or willing to sit down and talk things through with one another.

ROSENTHAL: **What do you think of the saying, "least said, soonest mended."**

THOMAS: I guess it's pretty clear from the film I am not in favor of that kind of attitude. That approach didn't serve me or my sister to our advantage. There may be times, perhaps with small children, when it is best that they don't know the full story but I think that teenagers are perfectly capable of handling and coping with (given the right support) very difficult issues and tragedies that may happen. Indeed, for our own health and self-esteem we need to be given that opportunity.

The other thing to say is that it's also very hard on the person who has decided to keep information from others. It's a great burden they are heaping on their own shoulders in order to maintain control of events or the people around them.

I grew up feeling that things were kept from me. I could have been of help to my sister, I could have said goodbye to my dad when he died, but I was denied the opportunity to do either. This has caused anger and guilt which I have only become aware of in later life. One result is that I can't abide people keeping secrets! I also empathize with people who are denied their rights or patronized. In short, I have difficulties with "social engineering" however well-intentioned.

So making documentaries is my way of getting things out into the open and sticking up for the underdog. For me, filmmaking is about finding my voice and giving a voice to others. A lot of the films I've made are about the mistakes made by do-gooders and well-intentioned people who feel qualified to say I know what's best for you.

ROSENTHAL: **Are you glad you made the film?**

THOMAS: Sure, although what the film was about shifted for me as I was making it. It started out as an adoption story with the aim of bringing about some sort of resolution for my family. But as the filming went on I realized that it was really a film about the tenacity of family identity and the roles family members play. I realised while filming that I was still playing the role I have always played in my family—that of peacemaker.

I realized that we have never been a family that sits down and has it out with each other, and even though thirty-five years had passed we weren't about to change. Hence mum's basic silence when I asked her what she would say if I said I would have preferred to have known what was happening to Val in 1964. In our family context this rather polite question was tantamount to a revolution.

Such a shift in direction is often what occurs in filmmaking. You set out with a set of beliefs and a hypothesis about what will happen then find that reality refuses to be moulded in the way you intend. So you then revise your hypothesis. Mine changed from, "We have to get things out in to the open and talk things through so that we can resolve the past," to something like, "You can drive a horse to water but you can't make it drink." In this case the horse is my family!

For underneath the narrative of this adoption story (itself an unusual one, as it introduces the audience to the differing perspectives of those involved, for example, the relinquishing mother, the grandmother, the adoptee and the adoptive parent) runs another story—that of family. Through making this film I realized what a tyrant a family, as a unit of relationships, can be. *Every* family has its own rules and ways of communicating, in part to ensure that it *remains* a family. Like separate tribes, each has its own, peculiar modus operandi which tends to be fiercely tenacious. The rules don't change, aren't to be broken and, for better or for worse, we all play by them.

Consequently, although it was something to be grateful for that after thirty years of not mentioning the adoption there was a readiness (if not enthusiasm) among members of my family to talk to *me* about it (as the one long cast in the role of the quiet and sensible one). If I thought they would be ready to talk to *one another*, then I was mistaken. If I was hoping for some family catharsis à la the final scenes of Mike Leigh's *Secrets and Lies*. I was soon to learn that real life is different to fiction!

Thus, this is a highly personal film which gives an account of one adoption story which many women and families will recognize from their own experience, and in the process asks questions (and provides no clear answers!) about the meaning of family and motherhood.

Mother's Heritage

Minda Martin comes from a large lower-class family located in Tucson. There are seven siblings, with Minda the first one to break the bounds and go to a university. Though her father had dreams of being a drummer and her mother aspired to be a singer, none of these aspirations came anywhere near fulfillment. Instead, the family history was one of small-business failures and multiple moves. With time Minda's mother drifted into depression and alcoholism. For a brief time she was hospitalized for a nervous breakdown.

In 1987 Mrs. Martin was accidentally shot and killed by her one of her sons. While cleaning his revolver in the living room the weapon discharged, sending a bullet through the wall, hitting his mother in the next room. At the beginning of the film this specific information is, however, withheld from us. Instead, we are told there has been the death of a woman, but the question asked, and which drives the film is not, Who is to blame for the death? but, Who was to blame for the state of this woman's life? *Mother's Heritage* was Minda Martin's first film and made shortly before entering the California Institute of the Arts.

ROSENTHAL: When and why did you make the film?

MARTIN: I started it soon after I finished my B.A. My grandfather had died, and I moved in to take care of my grandmother, who was alone. This was the first time I had had a chance to talk to her about my mother since my mother's death. In fact it was my first chance to talk to her about anything.

In my documentary class I had seen *Daughter Rite, Nana, Mom and Me*, which both dealt with mothers. I'd also seen Sadie Bennings's videos and Marlon Riggs's films which spoke to me about identity. Gradually the films fired me to think about my mother who had been rather a mysterious figure to me when I was young. So things started to come together. I wanted to learn about my mother and who she was. I wanted to let my mother be known. I wanted to give her a voice.

I started off by interviewing my grandmother, and gradually my perspective changed. I started unraveling mysteries. Previously I had only known my mother through my own perspective. Now I was discovering other facets, and the mosaic seemed a truer portrait. Unfortunately my mother is the only one without a voice . . . her own voice . . . in the film.

ROSENTHAL: Was the process of filmmaking cathartic or therapeutic for yourself or the family? It was such an unnecessary awful death.

MARTIN: Yes, definitely. It was the first time I had tried to come to grips with my mother's death. It was also the first time my family had tried to deal with her death. There had been silence. Denial. Now for the first time questions were being asked that had never been asked before.

ROSENTHAL: **And as you plunged in, where did the money come from?**

MARTIN: It was self-financed. But I was doing it on video and could beg and borrow equipment, so it was no big deal.

ROSENTHAL: **What your family's attitude to your investigation?**

MARTIN: My family was very supportive. But they didn't really under-stand why I was trying to deal with something in the past. Their attitude was, Why do it? Nothing you do can change the present. But I discovered that dialogue *did* change things. It was healing for all of us.

ROSENTHAL: **Did your family have qualms about this whole history being exposed. Not just your mother's death, but the poverty, the alcoholism, the constant moving, and so on?**

MARTIN: I knew I was putting dirty laundry out for the world to see and that my family was being exposed. And it was a traumatic ugly death. But I didn't think anyone was exploited, and I think my family would agree with me on that.

ROSENTHAL: **Were there questions you hesitated to ask?**

MARTIN: My brother Charlie killed my mother. It was an accident, unintended, but it had dire consequences for all of us. And there I was fumbling around. I just didn't know how to ask him, "How do you feel after all this?" Then he said, "Just ask me the question. No one has asked me how I feel." So I said, "The accident was caused because of your gun." And he said "No! The accident was caused because of my fault," and this was the first time he allowed himself to say that.

I know I could have pressed my father more in the film but chose not to. I was angry at my father for not taking care of my mother. He has a tremendous feeling of guilt on the subject. But I have an immense love for him and I didn't want him to see himself any more than he does as a failure.

ROSENTHAL: **As the film evolved how did you work?**

MARTIN: I had quotes, and gradually about halfway through the film I perceived very clearly certain themes I wanted to pursue more deeply. Then I would go back and probe more.

In a narrative film the writer predetermines what will happen. In documentary it's more like life, more open ended. The footage tells you where the film will end. I go as deep and as far as I can. I know I've asked all I could. Sometimes the answers aren't what I wanted. Sometimes the answers lead me to further questions. Sometimes those answers aren't put into the film so that you don't hurt someone.

In Harm's Way

To conclude this chapter, I asked Jan Krawitz, an old friend and superb filmmaker, to let me reprint her synopsis for *In Harm's Way* (working title, *Implosion*). The film is probably more personal memoir and reflection than family film, but it is a very fine illustration of how one gets to grips with the myths and realities of one's life and socialization. It is set out below and seems to me a wonderful model of clear and precise but evocative writing and an excellent example for any aspiring filmmaker.

> All things are contingent, but there is also chaos.—Iris Murdoch

I am applying for a postproduction grant to support *Implosion*, a 25-minute documentary film. The film explores the socialization of children growing up in the late 1950s, and is specifically related to societal threats and behavior. *Implosion* will use my confrontation with anonymous sexual violence as a point of departure for an inquiry into messages about fear and myths of causality and control that have been instilled in women of my generation.

For some of us, there is an event in our lives which irreparably changes the world as we knew it. On July 17, 1985, at the age of 34, I was sexually assaulted and strangled almost to death in Odessa, Texas, while shooting a documentary film about drive-in movie theatres. As a child in the 1950s, I abided by the proffered messages about safety and fear and had a firm belief in causality. I trusted that cars would stop at a red light, that the food I ate would not poison me, and that the men who passed me on the street would not harm me. My socialization left me completely unprepared for the betrayal I felt when confronted with the rage of a violent stranger.

Implosion will explore the disjuncture between a worldview constructed in the 1950s and the reality of adult life in the 1990s. Constructed around a first-person narration that relates both childhood anecdotes and the circumstances of the assault, the film will rely heavily on archival footage which is part of our common cultural experience. My "voice" will provide the through-line for an inquiry into the prevailing attitudes towards safety, fear, and behavior conferred on girls growing up in the fifties. This narration will create a dialogue with the "third-person" authority voice of society—the voice embodied in the "sync sound" of the fifties archival footage comprised of instructional films, newsreels, and stock shots.

The through-line of the film will explore how society (collectively) and parents (individually) attempted to protect children from harm's way with the resulting illusion that we were masters of our own fate. The fifties represented a benign period in history in which nuclear families thrived in the burgeoning suburbs and the global threats of Communism, nuclear war, and polio were presented as controllable. It was against this backdrop that women of my generation developed a "just-world" worldview. We were taught that we could influence what happened to us through our behavior. In instructional films, threats were presented, appropriate behavior was demonstrated, and specific results were guaranteed. A belief system predicated on causality prevailed.

The film is comprised of eclectic archival footage. A primary source is news film (1957–1962) from my hometown Philadelphia television station. With its focus on both local and national issues, it provides insight into the concerns of both families and public figures during those years. The footage is eloquent in its evocation of that era, yet quite specific in its regional relevance to my own experiences. A Philadelphia grade school principal is interviewed about the preparedness of his school to house and feed the students in the aftermath of a nuclear attack. He speaks with confidence about the school's ability to protect the children, but after insistent questioning by the reporter, he reluctantly admits that cafeteria provisions would run out after two days and that the children would ultimately starve to death. The dissonance between "the party line" and reality will be underscored by the intercutting of nuclear test footage in which a typical fifties family (represented by mannequins and a model house built in the desert test range) implodes, with facile scenes from a civil defense film demonstrating that closing the curtains and unplugging the iron before the blast will guarantee our survival.

Another news story depicts Philadelphia policemen descending on public schools armed with pamphlets that tell children not to accept candy from strangers. "Man on the street" archival interviews provide insight into the societal mindset about crime, Communism, morals, and safety. Clips from 1950s instructional films demonstrate how we were taught to avoid risky behavior, take control of our environment, and ultimately, our lives.

My confrontation with sexual violence occurred in a generic motel room in a midsize West Texas town. Motels were a 1950s phenomenon, spawned in the postwar years to accommodate the newly acquired mobility of the American family. A montage sequence combining images from 1950s postcards of motel exteriors (parking lots filled with family station wagons and mothers in shirt-waist dresses) and USIA footage of Americans on the road in 1958 is underscored by a first-person recounting of the circumstances of my assault. The carefree world of the fifties suggested by these images will be undermined by the description of random and anonymous sexual violence occurred there in the eighties.

The film will speak to a wide audience because of its reliance on a body of images and a set of events that are part of our common cultural experience. The viewer will be prompted to reconsider instructional films and news footage from the 1950s with a revisionist sociological and historical perspective.

22

INDUSTRIAL AND
PUBLIC RELATIONS FILMS

Probably more people are employed in making industrial and public relations films than in making documentaries. This has certainly been the case since the 1990s, when small-format video equipment revolutionized the subject. Today, industrial films and videos are in. They are seen as relatively cheap but effective publicity materials, with the word *publicity* being used in its broadest sense. Corporate and public relations filmmaking is a popular and lucrative field, using many staff and independent writers, and it's one worth getting to know.

DOCUMENTARIES AND INDUSTRIALS: THE DIFFERENCE

Many industrial films masquerade as documentaries or docudramas. They slip into the cinemas or onto television under the billing of *Frothy Frolics* or *Young Adventure* or *Head for the Sky*. They purport to be documentaries on the history of wine, nature, or flying, but we realize after two minutes that they are really promos for Napa Valley, Yosemite, or the Air Force. We enjoy them, and there's not too much harm done. They give the illusion of being documentaries because so many of their techniques are the same: location shooting, real people, natural sound, godlike commentary, and so on, but we know they are a horse of a different breed. The main difference, of course, lies in *purpose*. The documentary usually has a strong social drive. It wants to inform you, to draw your attention, to awaken your interest so that some social or political problem can be fully understood and perhaps ameliorated. In contrast, the ultimate purpose of an industrial or public relations film is to do a good sales job. Such films want you to buy something, to support something, or to participate in something. They want a very distinct payoff. You cannot receive an industrial film passively. If you do, it's a failure. The film wants you to receive the message and then jump into action. This can mean anything: changing your bank, joining a health club, supporting a charity, taking up skiing, or going to Bermuda for your vacation.

The action demanded is not always immediate; sometimes the film wants to sow an idea for the future. The Canadian National Film Board's *The Sky* may not send you off to the Rockies immediately, but the image of their beauty and attractions will have been well planted after one screening. The Shell Oil film on historic castles of England doesn't necessarily say, "Come this moment," but the ground will have been prepared.

Sponsors for industrial film can come from anywhere. All you need to be a sponsor is to have a message and the money to put it on film. In practice, the main sponsors are industry, business, universities, museums, tourist associations, government agencies, professional organizations, and charities. Each wants to put out a distinct sales message. These films usually group themselves under seven or eight distinct types:

1. Recruitment and training
2. Promoting a service
3. Attracting tourism
4. Demonstrating a product
5. Building an image
6. Teaching and advising
7. Museum backup films
8. Raising funds

Often the categories will overlap; your film may be promoting a wonderful new medical product or machine and at the same time illustrating the special system or service under which the product is made available to you once a week.

THE CALL TO ACTION

Many industrial films ask you to do something, and the call to action can take many forms. Join the navy. Visit this country. Support this museum. Make yourself into a superwoman this way. Learn automobile repair that way. Your first job is to discuss corporation policy, objectives, and what the management really wants the film to do. After that, your task as a writer is to search out the arguments that will support the film's message, and then find the best way to put them over in the script.

Recruitment. Let's say you have landed a nice fifteen-minute film whose basic message is, "Join the marines." Your first job, after research, is to marshal all the arguments you can to support that action. They might include:

- good pay at a young age
- good sports facilities
- camaraderie
- learning a trade
- seeing the world for free
- serving your country

Your film is then built entertainingly around these points. You might do it by following an eighteen-year-old recruit through his first year, but there are all sorts of ways. The film has to be realistic, and it has to be plausible, and therefore you can often allow some of the problems to come in. Thus, you can say in the recruitment film, "Yes, it's a hard life," and this point might appear in the recruit's letter home. Of course, the inverse message here is that the recruit is proud to be a "real man" and not a "wimp."

Sometimes the recruiting film may be disguised in different wrapping. Some years ago, for instance, British Airways put out a good corporate-image film. You saw a flight crew in training, all the backup service of the company, the concern and attention given to passengers, and the crew visiting different parts of the world. The core of the film, however, was provided by watching a young pilot learning to fly, handling propeller planes, going on to jets, and finally mastering the giant 747. The film was very well done, and if shown in schools, it would probably have induced a rush of recruitment letters to British Airways.

Product or service. In product or service films, your task is, once more, that of a salesperson. With luck, the products or services you are selling can be absolutely fascinating and the task of filmmaking extremely enjoyable. A friend of mine, for instance, was asked to make a film for a worldwide hotel chain. His research took him to Hong Kong, South America, and France, staying all the time at the best hotels. Another friend did a film to boost sales of pure-malt Scotch whiskey. Not only did he get to see and sample the best Highland distilleries, but he had a tremendous vacation in the bargain.

Although I've listed it separately, attracting tourism is really a branch of the selling of product and services. Here you can be selling an area, a region, or even a country. Under the banner of *The Wild Wide World* you are shown the attractions of Rio de Janeiro, the glories of the Arizona desert, and the effervescent thrills of skiing in Aspen. In making these films, which superficially promote themselves as documentaries, you of course never mention that Rio has a lot of crime, that desert scorpions are quite unpleasant, and that prices are sky-high in Aspen.

While doing the research you will be putting questions to the sponsor, whose answers will underpin the script. You want to know what the product does, how it works, why it differs from its rivals, and what its main advantages are.

Corporate image. One of the most profitable areas of industrial filming is the making of corporate-image films. These, too, are sales films, but on a slightly broader basis. Sometimes the image is that of a company, such as American Express or Bank of America; sometimes that of a profession, such as architecture or dentistry. The message of the corporate-image film is not necessarily to buy something or to do something immediately; rather, such films tell us that the company or profession is looking after your best interests.

Sometimes the film is made to sustain an image. The British stock market put out a film in the mid-1990s showing how the stock exchange arose and what fun it was to buy stocks today. This was before the crash of dot-com stocks in 2000. The film itself was screened daily by anyone who came to visit the stock exchange.

In 1992 Union Carbide felt that its image had suffered as a result of the Bhopal disaster in India, when acid gas spewed into the atmosphere from one of its plants. It consequently commissioned a film to show that it was, in fact, a company that was highly attentive to safety and that the gas escape was not its fault.

Teaching and training. Teaching and training films are another category of films that are becoming increasingly popular, particularly in health and sports. One of the most popular videos ever was Jane

Fonda's exercise tape. But that was just the beginning. Now, if you want to repair a car, become a tennis champion, learn yoga, bring up your baby the right way, or fix up your house, there's a tape for it.

Factories, schools, businesses, and hospitals are also big users of the training film or tape, which is an excellent demonstration tool. You can easily take someone through a process and show the right way to do things. You can demonstrate new machines, and you can reach your sales force in different towns and countries.

One of the things that the teaching film does very well is to demonstrate safety techniques, or to provide a warning. Here the minidrama is often used. A few years ago, Film Australia was asked to make a film illustrating the dangers of smoking in hospitals. Their answer was to stage a docudrama of a fire. A patient ignores the safety warnings in a hospital and smokes in bed. Within five film minutes, the whole hospital is ablaze, with eight fire engines in attendance outside and dozens of patients being carried to safety. It was an expensive film to make, but it put across its point.

Museum backup. Another expanding area in recent years has been that of the museum backup film. Here a museum puts up funds ranging from, say, $10,000 to $50,000 to make a film that will greet visitors entering the museum. Usually the film will provide an interesting general background for its exhibits. Following this pattern, the Museum of New York will show a film half dramatized, half based on paintings and still photos, illustrating the history of New York. Similarly the Museum of Jerusalem will employ a film using computer-generated images to show what it was like to visit the Temple at the time of Jesus.

Public service. Public service films lie somewhere between normal documentaries and the sponsored corporate film. Again, they can use any technique, but their usual object is to benefit the public as a whole rather than to publicize a specific factory, business, hospital, or university. Government agencies are one of the main sponsors of public service films, and their subjects vary little from country to country; public health and fighting racism are two of their main concerns. Sometimes the public service film will be sponsored by a private corporation or a special-interest group. Some of the best public service films of recent years have been sponsored by Amnesty International and various church-affiliated human rights organizations.

The public service field is wide open and is often a good entry path for the beginning filmmaker. Earlier I suggested a film to help young children overcome their fear of hospitals. That would be a typical public service film and one that might appeal to a number of sponsors.

RELATIONS WITH SPONSORS

Working with sponsors is an entirely different problem from that of working with television stations. In the latter context, someone usually has some idea of what film and filming is all about. That is not necessarily the case with sponsors.

What are you really up against? Well, first there's the question of knowing your client. Here Ray DiZazzo, a well-known writer on corporate filmmaking, is of the opinion that you'll face everyone from would-be writers, busybodies, and "yessirees" to vacillators, ramblers, and plain-old perfect clients. So be prepared for personality problems. But that's just the beginning.

Even though the sponsor may have suggested the film, he or she may still not be sure it is a good thing. Many sponsors still think film a tremendous waste of money, and even though they have agreed to do something, they may be tremendously lukewarm about the project. That means you will be battling the whole way. Similarly, many sponsors will want to see immediate, concrete results from the film. You must then convince them to be realistic about the short- and long-term effects of the film.

Often the sponsor will tell you that he or she has to feel happy and moved by the film. That's all right, I suppose, but it misses the point: the film is made for the audience, not for the sponsor. Antony Jay, one of the best filmmakers in England, once expressed it to me this way:

> You're not making a film for the company but for the people the company is going to show it to. You're not out to pat the managing director on the back or boost the ego of the chairman. Your job is to capture and hold the attention of people who don't necessarily want to be sold to or preached to, but who merely want an entertaining half hour.

If the audience is moved and happy and does what the sponsor wants it to do, then that's really all that counts.

There are four battles that have been fought with sponsors through the ages but that rarely get immortalized in print. The first battle is for *unorthodoxy.* Try to do something different, try to be a little unusual, try to do a film in a new way, and you may find your sponsor climbing the wall. Your second struggle is the *catalog* controversy. You are doing an industrial or hospital film and your sponsor may ask you to mention every department and piece of equipment in the hospital, or every branch or product of the firm. Resist to your last dying breath. Catalogs have a place in stamp collections, but usually only ruin films. Another major conflict is over *big shots*. Out of the best of intentions, the sponsor may ask you to put in the factory owner, the board of governors, the main contributor, wealthy relatives, and so on. Again, ask yourself whether this naming of names does any good for the film or is simply sucking up to the boss. Last but not least, you may have to wage war over the question of *committees*. All sponsors love committees. But remember one of the wisest sayings of all time: a camel is a horse designed by a committee. Stay clear of committees. Making films under the guidance of committees is the fastest route to disaster that I know.

THE GOLDEN RULES; OR, HOW TO SURVIVE YOUR SPONSOR

But all is not lost. Over the years filmmakers have developed certain golden rules for dealing with sponsors, rules that enable you to survive and make good films.

1. You must find out, right at the beginning, the main message that the sponsor wants to convey. If possible, have the sponsor give you a single sentence that expresses the one central idea that the film should leave with the viewer. If the sponsor can't tell you, then you're in trouble. But if he or she does, then make sure that you focus on that central idea throughout the film.

2. Confirm the elements that are absolutely vital to the film. If the sponsor argues for the catalog or the big shots, try to dissuade them. Apart from that, listen carefully and weigh the sponsor's ideas for their worth.

3. Find one person who is willing to take total responsibility for the film and the script. This saves you going to management and hearing a multitude of different voices, each arguing for something else.

4. Make sure your budgeting is realistic. If you have been given only $7,000 to make a film, make sure that your sponsor doesn't expect the production values of a $70,000 film. You can't pay for a Beetle and expect a Cadillac. This is vital, as many sponsors haven't a clue concerning the true expenses of filming. If they can afford only a modest house, then tell them from the beginning that they cannot expect a mansion.

5. No sponsor is realistic about timing. They all want their films done yesterday. Make sure you give them a completion schedule that is based on actuality and not fantasy.

6. Find out from the sponsor how and where the film is going to be used. Will it play before big audiences or small audiences? Will any informational literature be given out at the time? Will a speaker accompany the film? All these points help you evaluate how you should tackle the film project.

PRODUCTION POINTS

As already mentioned, many public relations and industrial films convey the flavor of documentaries but are far more manipulative. They use many of the same techniques, but they also add one or two of their own.

Identification. The technique of identification occurs again and again in recruitment or training films. The audience is presented with a character with whom they can sympathize and identify: the boy who decides to join the army is like your older brother or the kid next door, or the manager being trained is just like you. Take care that the identification really works.

Audience. If "know your audience" is one of the commandments of documentary, it is even more important in industrial films. You must know for whom you are making the film, as this affects your whole technique, approach, and style.

Real people. You can use actors in industrial films, but I don't like it. I think it is much more convincing to use real people in real situations, slightly guiding their behavior in front of the camera. This approach is also usually more practical. Engineers know how to use tools, surgeons' scalpels, and so on. Put an actor in a complex job and he or she stands out like a sore thumb.

If I am shooting a film in a factory and need certain types, I try to get the manager to let me know who is the most suitable, the most intelligent, and I pick up my "actors" then and there. They are usually terrific and very cooperative. But apart from very simple direction, it is your job to learn from them and not vice versa. For me this means two things. First, I don't ask the actors to do anything they normally wouldn't do. Second, I rarely script casual dialogue. I give the actors the situation and try to find out from them how they would handle it and what they would say. I let them understand the point I want to make, but I leave it to them to put it over in their own way.

Animation and special effects. Animation, graphic or computer, is a marvelous tool for industrial films. Often you have a mass of information that you can't put across by filming in a factory or elsewhere, or a concept that is difficult to illustrate using a physical object. For example, if you want to compare two types of growth over time, animation can be a tremendous boon in making your point simply but effectively.

Again, video special effects, if not overused, can make all the difference to an industrial or public relations film. For example, they are very good at contrasting preparations and results. Let's say you are doing a film on agricultural and flower research. You know you have to show the scenes in the labs, people looking at microscopes and so on, and you know it looks pretty dull. But show that lab scene on one side of the screen, while the other shows a scene shot from a helicopter of dozens of fields of bright flowers, and the film is transformed. This is the simplest of video techniques; there are, of course, dozens of others. The important point is this: if you are doing video, you have at your disposal dozens of effects that would be too costly to do in film, but which can transform the look of your picture.

Humor. Humor is one of the principal tools of the public relations and industrial film, particularly in England. There, the makers of industrial films constantly use John Cleese, who played the befuddled British lawyer in *A Fish Called Wanda*, to write and star in their movies. One common approach is the nitwit who gets into an awkward situation because he or she doesn't have any sense or doesn't know the right way to approach a job. We see Laurel and Hardy try to take a piano into a house through a window; we see somebody ignore advice and build a boat that promptly sinks on its first outing. These wrong methods are then contrasted with the correct procedures.

Voice. In documentary, we are accustomed to a commentator with a neutral voice. But what works for documentary may not be best for the industrial film, where you have many more opportunities to humanize the narrator and add more personal warmth. Once the narrator becomes a character, rather than an anonymous, faceless voice, you have a much greater possibility of reaching out to your audience and talking to them in a direct way. This was a technique that Antony Jay used very effectively in *The Future Came Yesterday*; I have given an example from the script at the end of this chapter.

Approach. The sponsor can tell you the message, but it is up to you to find the most effective and imaginative way to put it over. You probably have a wider variety of techniques available to you than in the standard documentary, including docudrama, but you are still faced with that old question: what approach shall I use?

From Picture to Post was a half-hour public relations film made for the British post office. It didn't have anything specific to sell but wanted the audience to understand that the post office was doing good work. It could have gotten that message across in many ways, perhaps most obviously by touting the speed of mail delivery or automated services. Instead, the film focused on the way stamps are conceived and created. We see four designers faced with different tasks: each has to design a stamp, but on a different subject. One has to do a new design for a portrait of the queen; his method is to make a clay bust and then try different photographs of the final statue. Another has to do a series on bridges, and we follow him looking at bridges in England and Scotland for inspiration. A third has to do a series based on the Bayeux Tapestry, commemorating the Battle of Hastings in 1066, while a fourth has to create a number of designs around what was then the new Concorde supersonic plane. In the last case, all the designs are based on a model.

Each artist uses a different technique, and it is quite fascinating to watch the evolution of the designs. The film is just following the old rules: get a good story, show what we don't usually see, follow process, and you can't go wrong. Eventually we see the final designs and the printing of the stamps. There is nothing complex to the film, but it offers a very entertaining look behind the scenes, and we come away with a greater appreciation of the complexity of making an everyday artifact that we all take for granted.

Tonight We Sing was also a corporate-image film, but one that was also trying to do a selling job. The subject was the Glyndebourne Opera. Going to Glyndebourne is an English tradition. It is a small, beautiful opera house with its own resident company, set among country gardens in southern England. One attends in evening dress, sees half the opera, has a champagne picnic on the beautiful lawns, and then sees the rest of the opera, which is usually a Mozart or Rossini comedy. Although fairly well known in England, Glyndebourne was not familiar to American audiences. Thus, the director of Glyndebourne came up with the idea of a film that would both publicize the opera and sell the idea of "going to Glyndebourne" to potential tourists from the United States.

The filmic concept is simple but effective. At the beginning of the film we meet David, a young American wandering around London. He is on vacation but doesn't quite know what to do. While in a railway station, he sees strange-looking people in evening dress board his train. Once on the train, they drop tantalizing phrases about "seeing the new Duke" and "wondering how the Duchess is." David's curiosity is piqued, and when they leave the train he decides to follow them. And so, out of the blue, he stumbles onto the romantic, fairy-tale world of Glyndebourne, discovering that all the mysterious references are to Mozart's opera *The Marriage of Figaro.*

The film works for all sorts of reasons, but three things stand out. First, David provides the right sort of identification for an American audience. Second, the film is very funny, with the English types portrayed as just this side of eccentric. Third, the film works because Glyndebourne has something well worth telling: it presents great music in a beautiful setting. When you have all these elements, the public relations work becomes simple.

THE FUTURE CAME YESTERDAY: AN EXAMPLE

Antony Jay's *The Future Came Yesterday* was made for International Computers Limited (ICL). Its subject was machine tools and electronic numeric control. To put it mildly, this is not a subject that at first glance makes your heart light up with joy. Instead, you are likely to say, "My God, what on earth does that mean?" The film came to Jay through the enthusiasm of engineering manager Douglas Hughes. Hughes had a lot of ideas about better control systems in ICL's factories but felt that he couldn't talk to the board of directors. They didn't understand his words, and his memos never got read. He felt that the only way to get through was to make the film and demonstrate concretely what he wanted to do. Jay continues the story as follows:

> Eventually we summarized the concept of the film. What we wanted to say was, "We realize that the computer can enormously simplify production control, but first of all we have to reorganize our factory to prepare to use the computer." It was as simple as that.
>
> Here it seemed to me very clear that I had to start *The Future Came Yesterday* with a sequence satirizing an existing factory setup. So I deliberately said nothing in the beginning about new ideas. Instead, I tried to make people agree that the old ones were ludicrous.
>
> When I thought I was familiar with the factory and had grasped the basic ideal I looked through my notes and wrote up a basic commentary that would run about thirty or forty minutes.
>
> Of course, being a film producer and a director, I don't write things down unless I see pictures in my mind, but the concept was very much

that of an illustrated talk. It was the logic of the explanation that had to dominate, not the logic of the pictures. The pictures had to follow.

The discussions for the film, including meetings, planning, and script writing, took four months. The shooting itself was done over the course of two weeks when the factory was totally disrupted. ICL, of course, was not the name given to the company in the film. Instead, Jay invented a mythical company, Universal International, and then had stamps and letterhead made with that name on them.

Below I have set out the first section from the script, called "The Adrian Sequence," which gives a very good indication of the biting and slightly sarcastic style Jay used to start off the film. It's clearly written for a character voice, and it is very much a real person talking to you.

Visual	Audio
Interior design office. Sketch on drawing board with hands doing details. Zoom up to Adrian sketching; he occasionally looks dreamily out of the window.	NARRATOR: Have you met Adrian, our design engineer? Clever chap. University degree. Has lunch in the staff dining room. Doesn't talk to the production people very much. Well, they haven't got much in common. Except that they are going to make what he designs. But that's their problem.
	Look at that job he's drawing now. Every figure and line he puts down is full of implications for the production people. Costs.
Adrian writes ".0005" against a point on the drawing.	Size of machine. Precision of machine. Tooling. Machine loading. Tremendous responsibility? No, bless you. Adrian doesn't worry about little things like that. He's not a computer, and anyway, no one ever tells him.
Pan over to drawing on the floor. Hold, then pan to camshaft acting as paperweight on pile of drawings on nearby table.	Look at his last job. Really beautiful design, that was. first Multiple camshaft. He used that kind of shaft because he knew

	there was a nice bit of bar that size in the lab.
Dissolve to factory interior, second camshaft being machined final stages; pile ready for assembly.	Trouble was, those clots on the floor couldn't repeat it. Had in to go back and design it again. Now it's got the cams and the shaft all in one piece. Real bull-at-a-gate job. Oh yes, it works all right. But there's no satisfaction in that sort of thing.
Interior, design office. Adrian makes quick adjustment sketch. Cut to close up of finished sketch.	Anyway, off this one goes. Five hundred a year, Adrian to designed that for. As it happens, marketing already knows they're only going to want one hundred. But no one has both-ered to tell Adrian. What's it got to do with him?
Dissolve to medium close-up of draftsman's desk with Adrian's sketch being copied by hand.	

The success of Antony Jay's script can be attributed to three things. First, the film uses a wonderful and gently drawn characterization for its main "stars." To this element is added the wit, humor, and person-alized commentary that makes the film informative and entertaining not only to those professionally concerned but also to the average viewer. Finally, the message is kept very simple: we are showing you how a factory can be more logically organized through the use of a computer—if creative and executive personnel can understand one another's problems.

The Future Came Yesterday was made more than twenty years ago but still ranks in my mind as one of the best industrial films I have ever seen.

23

STAYING ALIVE:
THE PRODUCER'S ROLE

It's of no use being the world's greatest filmmaker if, as producer, you can't get your film funded or distributed. In an expensive medium you have to be a businessperson as well as an artist. You have to find a sponsor or you're dead. By sponsor, I mean anyone with money who will support your film. This can be a university department, a television station, an industrial corporation, a government agency, a church, a film distributor, or even friends.

You can interest people by telling them your idea, sending letters, proposals, and so on, but one thing is vital: showing them your previous work. Sponsors want to see your track record. They want to assess what you promise in the future by seeing what you have done in the past. This means you must have some work to show them, which is very hard if you are a student. Film diplomas are fine if you want to teach; otherwise, the more films you can finish or participate in while you are at the university, the better your chances of landing a sponsor.

As a filmmaker you have various possibilities for jobs. The television station and the industrial corporation with its own film unit offer the safest bet. They need films, they have the money to make them, and they can sometimes offer a degree of permanence in the notoriously unstable film world. In reality, though, most of us end up as independent filmmakers and become our own producers. So, how do we raise the money for our films that will change the world?

Abe Osheroff got his $50,000 for *Dreams and Nightmares* through the backing of enthusiastic political supporters. Emile de Antonio picked up the $100, 000 for *Point of Order* while having a drink with a wealthy liberal friend. *Antonia*, by Jill Godmilow and Judy Collins, was backed by the latter's concert earnings.

THE TELEVISION MARKET

One way into filmmaking is to submit your idea to television. Knowing where to turn and to whom to submit your proposal then becomes crucial In the United States this entry route is not easy path, but it can be done, particularly in public television. Occasionally PBS decides to sponsor a documentary series with a marvelous-sounding name like *Great Americans* or *The Living World* or *The Spirit of the Future*. This means that three thousand people apply for grants to make ten films. The odds aren't great, but occasionally a newcomer slips in. Proposals can also be made to independent PBS stations. In theory, each station has a planning department that evaluates proposals. The department is supposed to see whether the proposal fits the station, whether it is unusual or innovative, and whether funds can be raised on the proposal. But little of this touches reality, and I know of hardly anyone who has made a film this way. And there is a further catch. Even if the station accepts your proposal, this may only mean that it will screen the film after *you* have raised all the money. And if the station does raise the money, it will often require an additional 21 percent of the budget as overhead.

The greatest problem for independent filmmakers until recently was that the commercial networks dominated the main television market. Using various arcane arguments, the networks, on the whole, refused to show any documentaries except those made by themselves. That left PBS as the only available national showcase. Cable has now drastically altered the situation. Since the mid-eighties, new cable stations such as the Discovery Channel, Arts and Entertainment (A&E), the History Channel, Turner Broadcasting (TBS), Bravo, and Home Box Office (HBO) have started offering new possibilities both as documentary sponsors and as outlets for finished films.

In Europe things are also improving. First, the European networks, particularly in Germany, are more open to accepting outside suggestions for productions and coproductions. Second, the English broadcast system is opening up to greater participation from independent filmmakers. Channel Four has, of course, been available to the independent since its inception and has either totally or partially funded a great number of documentaries.

FINDING A HOME

For television you could, of course, in the old days, merely write to the station and propose your idea or try to sell it your film. Today it is vital to pinpoint a specific program or a specific department that will really be receptive to the project you are involved in. At PBS, for example, four long-running programs come immediately to mind that are open to independent filmmakers' work but are managed through individual stations.

For starters there is *Nova*, a science series, usually done on film, that places great emphasis on look and stunning visuals. On average the shows are budgeted between $400,000 and $600,000 and can vary from an investigation of in-vitro fertilization to an update on the Dead Sea Scrolls. However, to get a sense of the competition, you must realize that *Nova* only produces twenty shows out of at least six hundred submissions each year.

Nova comes out of WGBH, Boston, which is also the originating station for *Frontline* and *The American Experience*. The main subjects for *Frontline* are politics and world events. This means that one week you may be looking at Iraq, and the next week you may be watching a documentary on the aftereffects of Hurricane Katrina or immigrant youth riots in France. The third series, *The American Experience*, deals with U.S. history, from the American Revolution to the fairly recent past. While the series provided a home for Ric Burns's study of the Donner party, it also found space for Michael Orlov's controversial look at the American reaction to the Holocaust. The fourth series, *Point of View*, is a showcase for highly opinionated documentaries such as Ellen Bruno's *Satya* or Marlon Riggs's *Tongues Untied*. It's worth noting that PBS issues an independent producer's kit that can be obtained by writing to the PBS Development Office.

HBO also claims to have an open submissions policy, but in practice few make it through the front door. Of the three thousand or so pitches and entries per year, HBO only accepts twelve *America Undercover* ideas and two or three miscellaneous projects. Cinema verité is especially favored, and pitches should be limited to three to five pages.

While A&E offers some interesting openings and continues to blossom with *Biography* and *American Justice, America's Castles*, and *Mysteries of the Bible*, the real phenomenon of the last two decades has been the expansion of the Discovery network. Under its banner it now includes Discovery, the Learning Channel, Animal Planet, and the Travel Channel. There are also a Discovery Kids, Discovery Wings, Discovery Health, and Discovery People. The range of the network, which goes in for series as well as individual films, is clearly very broad and makes one feel sometimes that no subject is sacred. For example, while glancing through *TV Guide* for one week I found the following Discovery presentations: *Supernature*, about the supernatural behavior of animals and plants; *The Rise and Fall of the Mafia*; *The Secret World of Toys*; *The Secret World of Speed Demons*; and *Robots Rising*.

The Discovery Channel is very specific about the information it requires from you when making a submission. First, before doing anything, you must sign a release letter for the network, absolving it from any future claim that it stole or copied your ideas. Having signed your life away, you then submit a one- or two-page treatment that besides outlining your idea will include

- The film format
- The production team and the job performed by each person
- Résumé with credits for each member
- Demo tape
- Budget summary, showing how much you expect from the network
- List of coproduction partners
- Production timeline

The necessity of pinpointing your efforts continues when you go overseas and are trying for help from the BBC. Like the U.S. commercial networks, the BBC was closed to the outside for years. Owing to the intervention and pressure of Margaret Thatcher's government, both the BBC and the English commercial stations have now opened their doors to independents. The present rule is that the companies must take at least 25 percent of their output from external sources. Since the BBC produces more than two hundred hours of documentary features per year, there is much time to fill.

The BBC is actually divided into two main sections, BBC One and BBC Two, but both produce documentaries. BBC Three and Four, both new digital stations, also carry documentary. BBC television is based at the BBC TV Center in London.

BBC series have varied over the years, but the main ones at the moment are

- *Reputations*: This, as the name suggests, is the biography strand.
- *Inside Story*, *Panorama*, and *Correspondent* all deal with investigative stories and current affairs.
- *Omnibus* and *Arena*, for their part, deal with music and the arts.
- *Bookends*: Here the subject is literature and literary profiles, such as portraits of Robert Cheever or Elmore Leonard.
- *Everyman*: This focuses on religion and interesting personalities, but in a trendy, nonpreaching style.
- *Horizon*: This, together with *Tomorrow's World*, is the British equivalent of *Nova*.
- *Time Watch* and *Ancient Voices* cover history, the first modern, the second ancient.

For its part the main strands on Channel 4 are

- *Witness* (religion)
- *Secret History* (history)
- *To the Ends of the Earth* (travel and adventure)
- *The Real* (biography)

In order to get your film idea considered, you should send your proposal to the executive producer of each series. Competition is stiff, but it's worth a try. If your idea passes the commissioning editor's scrutiny, it will go before a further selection committee that meets twice a year, usually in April and October. If you get the green light at that stage, you go into production.

Sometimes the BBC is willing to take the initiative in reaching out to independents. In its *Fine Cut* series, the BBC deliberately went out of its way to help various world documentarists realize their most current and passionate projects. The results, according to series supervisor Andre Singer, varied. Four dealt with the horrors of war, while two others centered on the filmmakers themselves. Altogether it was a very worthwhile experiment, ultimately responsible for Robert Gardner's *Forest of Bliss*, Les Blank's *Innocents Abroad*, John T. Davis's *Hobo*, and Peter Adair's *Absolutely Positive*, among others.

In short, the BBC is well worth investigating. What makes things a trifle easier is that the BBC actually issues something called *The Foreign Producer's Guide*. This invaluable pamphlet gives you all the ins and outs of working for the BBC, and the lowdown on current series. It can be obtained by writing to the BBC's Wood Lane, London, office. I would also advise you to look at *Video Age International* that, from time to time, publishes details of television programming, not just in England but around the world.

MARKETING OVERVIEW

It is difficult to assess trends when you are living through them, but looking back, it is clear that the nineties marked a clear revolution in the financing, marketing, and distribution of documentaries. Documentaries became *hot*. Film festivals started paying attention to them. New specialized documentary channels were created. And new terms like "factual programming' and "factual entertainment" started hitting the headlines.

In practice the market is now split into what writer Jan Rofekamp calls the first market and the second market. The first market includes the principal public and private networks in each country. In the United States this means PBS and all the major cable stations I mentioned earlier, plus Court TV. In the United Kingdom we are talking about the BBC, Channel 4, and Channel 5, while in Germany we are referring to ZDF, Spiegel, and ARD. In France the major players are Canal Plus, Arte, FR2, and FR3. The second market includes players like Globo Sat in Brazil, Rai-Sat and CNI in Italy, Bravo and HBO in Latin America, and Canal Plus in northern Europe.

On the surface, all this looks great. In practice, competition among filmmakers for cable slots has created a buyers' market. This has meant that fees in the first market have been considerably reduced. Whereas a few years ago a filmmaker could get a deal for $50,000 of financing, allowing the station four runs in five years for that amount, the current deal is more likely to be $20,000 for two runs in two years. While this means that the rights are available more quickly for the second market, the fees paid for exhibition in this market are considerably lower than in the first. A $2,000 contract for unlimited runs is not likely to make you throw your hat in the air.

Pitching and Film Markets

One recent trend that can be helpful to you in financing and selling your completed program is the expansion of documentary markets. Markets like MIPCOM (in Cannes), NATPE, Leipzig, and MIP-TV have now become essential venues for pitching opportunities, sales, and the exchange of ideas regarding single films and series, financing, and coproduction.

You are probably familiar with the pitch or the fast sell from films like Robert Altman's *The Player*. Here, merely seconds after the film has begun, we are provided with a classic demonstration of the Hollywood pitch when a young eager scriptwriter tries to sell his idea to a bored movie mogul in thirty seconds flat. Well, before you laugh, you need to note that the *pitch* has invaded the documentary scene with some notable success. These days, many documentary markets and festivals—such as Hot Docs in Toronto; IDFA in Amsterdam; Medimed in Sitges, Spain; and Sunnyside in Marseilles—offer you the opportunity to pitch or discuss your film proposal with various commissioning film editors with a view to getting it financed. This is how it usually works.

A film market such as Medimed, in Sitges near Barcelona, sends out an open call for film proposals. The submitted proposals, besides setting out the film idea, also have to include budget, background of the producers, details of funds already raised, and names of any television stations already involved in the project. Later the proposals are vetted by various judges, and from two hundred proposals submitted maybe thirty are selected for the market. That may seem to you like a seven to one chance, but if your proposal is any good, it will probably get through.

At the market itself you then have fifteen minutes to sell your idea before a general audience of, say, sixty people, and a motley collection of twelve or so commissioning editors who may come from the United States, Britain, France, and Germany. Now none of the people present will have read your long proposal, which was merely a means to get you into the market. However, they will have before them a short précis of your film and its budget.

The candidate pitchers normally follow one another at fifteen-minute intervals. This means that you might have eight pitches in the morning, then a lunch break, and another eight pitches in the afternoon. With so many people appearing in so short a time, your job is to make your brief appearance absolutely memorable. In practice, the fifteen minutes at your disposal is split into two sections. First, you have seven minutes to talk about your film and show any visual materials you have prepared. The other eight minutes are then left for questions and reactions by the commissioning editors.

It seems a frightening, off-putting process, but provided you are prepared it really isn't. Also, in order to help novices at this procedure, many markets also provide a training session with an expert to help you get the best out of your presentation pitch. As you have very little time, you have to hit the right bells from the word *go*. You have to explain briefly the length of the film, its story and importance, how much money you are seeking, and for whom the film is intended, Thus, if it is a film of only local interest to Californians, don't expect German television to be interested. What is vital is to explain what special materials you have, as well as any special access to the subject, and why the subject is magical and will captivate audiences everywhere. For a few minutes, you have to become actor and fairground barker. The more confident you are the better it will go, and humor can often help. Recently, in Spain, I pitched the *Lost Temple Treasures* proposal, which I mentioned earlier. Right at the beginning I said "This film is essentially *Indiana Jones* meets *The Da Vinci Code*." And at the end I added, "And if I find the treasures I'm giving up filming to live in luxury in Rio de Janeiro." Low humor, yes, but the jokes reinforced the pitch.

If you are lucky, four or five people in the audience will respond favorably to your pitch. Your job is then to try and meet with them a little bit more at the market, get their names, and follow up by sending the full proposal and pressing your case through e-mail and phone calls. To be realistic, maybe only one or two of the five will turn out to be truly interested. But if they can supply $10,000 or $15,000 toward your film, you are well ahead of the game.

These pitching sessions normally form part of a larger sales market for finished films at an exclusive market or wider film festival. The entry into the market session is similar to the entry for a pitch. You are usually required to send a DVD of your film and its written description to the market officials. These officials will then choose sixty or seventy films for presentation out of maybe five hundred or six hundred entries. The films are then put into the market library and their description entered into a buyers' catalog and guide. Buyers from different stations will then use the guide to select films that interest them and view the DVDs of the same on one of twenty or thirty screens available at the market. If they like your film and are interested in it for their station, the buyers will probably approach you later. In most cases the market organizers will also send you a list of everybody who asked for your film, so that you can follow up from your hometown.

Of course, you yourself are also likely to be very active at these markets. You don't wait around passively, but try to assess who might be interested in your film. You know Discovery likes archeology so you buttonhole the Discovery representative, and tell him to look out for your film. Likewise, you tell the representative from the History Channel that your film *Cursed Concubines* about fatal ladies of Rome is just for her, and she should take a look in the library.

For a novice these markets can be highly instructive and well worth the registration fee. Though these markets are spread out over Europe and the United States, I would say the most useful ones are the Co-financing Forum in Amsterdam (IDFA), the biannual seminar/festival of the International Documentary Association (IDA) in Los Angeles, and the Toronto Documentary Forum.

Advertising and Distribution

While discussing budgets, I advised you to insert an amount for advertising. This is to cover the making of brochures, stills, fliers, and posters that will help get the film out and seen, and any postage and courier expenditures connected with the same. The advertising budget should also cover the making of cassettes and DVDs connected with publicity and any festival fees.

Basically, you need advertising for three purposes: to help you raise money for film production, to send out publicity and background with your film festival entries, and to help sell your finished film.

In order to get financing or to interest a station in backing you, you will of course have written a proposal. However, if you have the money you may decide to splash out on a colorful brochure with picture and photographs. These things are expensive, but they certainly catch the eye more than a few sheets of paper.

Once the film is finished you need to sell it, get your money back, and possibly make a profit. To further these objectives, you need to get information about your film out to stations, festivals, networks, colleges, schools, and journalists. This is done by putting together varied informational packages, which may include a poster, a DVD, biographical information on the makers, reviews, and a good short glossy flier that tells the viewer what the film is about. The flier is important and you should make it as hard hitting and attractive as you can. To help you understand the nature of fliers, I've set out two examples for you at the end of this chapter.

If your film has been made in collaboration with a television station or as a coproduction, then a good deal of the exhibition and distribution work will have been done. However, you are often in the position of facing these problems alone, and then comes the question, Shall I go involved with a distributor or try and do everything myself? My cautious advice is to get a distributor, but be very wary about whom you choose, and check them out thoroughly, because as the old saying goes, "There are thieves, rogues, and distributors."

Every filmmaker I know has a bad story about being ripped off by a distributor. Their letters never receive a reply. Their films seem to vanish into outer space. They never see any bookkeeping records. And worst of all they never receive any money. Given these rather depressing anecdotes, why should you bother with a distributor? Because if you find a good one and an honest one (and they do exist), he or she can get your film into many more places and outlets than you can working alone. That means not they will get your film not only on television but also in home video, educational, and foreign markets.

Now a good distributor comes with at a price, which usually means they take 30 percent to 40 percent of every dollar earned. On top of that they will charge all their expense, which includes making prints, new advertising copy, postage, and so on. But if they can deliver the goods, it's all worth it.

Festivals

Having your film accepted for a festival is always a pleasure. With luck you also get invited to come. There are parties. You meet other filmmakers. There is often good food and wine. And the ego gets positively caressed. All this is to the good. Yet how much success at festivals really affects your career as a filmmaker is another question.

On the positive side, having your film shown at a festival can create a buzz. People talk about it. It may get some good reviews that you can use in publicity. Someone from a television station may see it and like it. A distributor may be interested and want to meet with you. Someone may be struck by your style and ingenuity and decide you are just the director they've been looking for. Festival certificates look good on your wall, and the golden prize statues in your office impress potential sponsors. And being able to say your film was shown at Sundance certainly does no harm on your résumé.

However, there seems to me to be a certain dissonance between what is usually wanted for a festival and the kind of film shown on television. Festivals like films with an innovative style, personal stories, films with political bite, and films that they like to call "on the cutting edge," whatever that means. Generally commentary is frowned upon and regarded as old hat, and anything seen as standard television fare is likely to be thrown in the wastepaper basket. In other words you may have a great festival film but find it is one not suitable for common television. All that means is that the festival acceptance may prove you have skills and artistry, but don't think that is automatically going to help you make a sale.

These days, festivals are sprouting up in every city, town, and hamlet. Scarcely a day goes by without villages like Little Wadlington in the Marsh or Westcliff-by-the-Water announcing they are having a film festival. And why not! One has to live and let live. But on a serious level this means you have to distinguish between the important festivals, that count on your résumé, and those that are just fun. Off the cuff, I would say the five or six most serious general documentary festivals for English-language films are Sundance, Toronto, Amsterdam, Berlin, Sheffield, Hot Springs, Margaret Mead, and New York. These festivals are, however, very competitive and it may be worthwhile to consider whether your film fits into a specialty festival such as one of the numerous lesbian, Jewish, or history film festivals.

These days finding the right festival is very easy. First, you might want to note that the Association of Independent Video and Filmmakers (AIVF) puts out a very useful guide to international film and video festivals. The organization's Web address is www.aivf.org. You can also get long lists of festivals and their specialties by simply looking up film festivals on Google. For festival updates, withoutabox. com is also a useful address for telling you what's happening on the festival circuit.

Documentary Magazines and the Web

The two documentary magazines most concerned with marketing are *RealScreen* (realscreen.com), which comes out of Toronto, and *International Documentary* (documentary.org), which is published in Los Angeles. Both contain the occasionally interesting article but are essentially geared toward selling. With *RealScreen* the emphasis is on what is happening with all the cable shows being done for Discovery and the like. *RealScreen* also publishes an International Factual Broadcast Guide, which contains information on broadcasters around the world. The information is very down-to-earth, and tells you about factual strands, themes, and length of favored programs. The guide also gives you station biographies, the names of commissioning editors, and their contact addresses and e-mail addresses.

Standard features of *International Documentary* include a listing of upcoming film festivals and a monthly guide to cable programming. Its most useful section, however, may be its listing of current funding opportunities telling you what's on offer, where to apply, and the deadlines for grant submissions. It's also worth noting that the magazine's publisher, The International Documentary Association (e-mail: idf@netcom.com) also puts out a useful membership directory and Documentary Survival Guide.

A third magazine I very much like is *DOX* (dox.dk), published in Denmark. *DOX* has been coming out bimonthly since 1993 and has since become essential reading for documentary filmmakers in Europe. However, its European bias shouldn't put off Americans and, in fact, the magazine provides essential information for anyone interested in the European scene. While paying attention to distribution and production possibilities, it also publishes some excellent general documentary articles, probably slightly more academic than those appearing in *RealScreen* or *International Documentary*. It also publishes a useful European Producers Guide somewhat similar to that put out by *RealScreen*.

A few Web sites dealing with documentary have also put in a recent appearance, but the best of them, head and shoulders above the rest, is Docos.com. Although it's based in England, the site's reach is truly global. Put simply, Docos.com is the broadest provider of documentary information I have come across. Its range is truly staggering, and in its free daily news bulletin it covers everything from industry directories to production companies and new books, markets, festivals, and a free showcase for new titles. It is extremely good on coproduction information and advice, and it also runs a unique and remarkable "commissioning engine" that tells producers and distributors who, worldwide, could be interested in producing or financing a given film (www. commissioningengine.com). Finally Docos publishes a fortnightly print newsletter, *DOCtv* (subscription based), which provides a very good analysis of industry trends and is very useful for fast decision making. If I've gone on at length about Docos, it is because I find it less advertisement-cluttered than the magazines and very down-to-earth, and it gives me the information I need speedily and extremely efficiently.

Finally, while discussing Web uses, I would heartily recommend that you look at the *Documentary Cookbook*, distributed by the Center for New Documentary at the University of California, Berkeley. The *Cookbook*—a lovely name—is basically a few pages of very succinct advice on low-budget filmmaking put out by Jon Else and some of the other faculty at Berkeley's Graduate School of Journalism. The question that the booklet asks is this: without compromising journalistic integrity or style, can some films be done for a fifth, a tenth, or even a hundredth of the prevailing cost of films on public television? The answer is yes, and the booklet then goes on to tell you how, and demonstrates the answer by looking at three low-cost films made by Peter Nicks, Lourdes Portillo, and Albert Maysles for less than $100,000. The advice given is very useful, practical, and down-to-earth but is mainly aimed at the journeyman documentary maker who already knows the ropes and is trying to reach a large television audience. Unfortunately, the Web site address of the *Cookbook* is ridiculously long and the simplest way to find the information is just to Google "Berkeley Documentary Cookbook."

GENRES AND FADS

In the very first chapter of this book, I asked you why you wanted to make a particular film. I suggested that often an idea obsessed you. You were pushed toward a certain subject and had no choice. Yet many people work the other way around. They find what sells, and then make a film to fit into that category. We may smile at such an approach, at all the history mysteries, and Bible secrets series, yet realistically we have to be aware of what's going on.

As I write, *Survival, Big Brother,* and *Who Wants to Be a Millionaire?* are all the rage, and *reality programming* the magic words that bring a ray of light to a television programmer's eye. So, do you rush out to film a group of fifteen-year-old boys surviving without McDonalds or Starbucks? Or do you turn your lens perpetually on yet another group of crazies eating, sleeping, fornicating, and pontificating in sealed rooms? I doubt it. By the time this book comes out, those fads will probably have bitten the dust.

But what about docusoaps, or documentary soap operas? Here I am not so sure. This essentially English creation, light years away from Griersonian tradition, has become almost the mainstay of U.K. broadcasting. In the five years between 1999 and 2001, more than sixty-five docusoaps appeared on the major British television channels—no small achievement.

The basic ingredients for the successful docusoap are stunningly simple. First, you take an industry, preferably a service one, or minor business and find a group of people who are slightly charismatic or quirky, and who enjoy being in the limelight. You then follow them for a few months with a crew straight from film school and center in on their disputes, their love affairs, their foibles, and their pranks.

With luck, and high shooting ratios, some interesting stories inevitably emerge.

Starting with driving-school teachers and life at a London airport, British viewers were subsequently given the lives of marriage counselors, trainee journalists, nurses, emergency wards, and investment brokers. A Channel 4 series called *Love in Leeds* followed single women in pursuit of the perfect man.

Not one to miss a trick, the Americans have also embraced the formula, such as with *American High*, which follows the lives of various kids at a high school in Los Angeles. There has also been a series following women in Las Vegas. I sense, however, the formula won't go down quite as well in the United States as in England. It seems to me that American reality drama tends toward action and cop stories rather than daily stories of ordinary human beings. But I may be wrong.

In the end, I think the television enthusiasm for docusoaps is based on financial considerations rather than any philosophic interest in the human condition. Docusoaps offer more returns for fewer bucks. Even allowing for diverse crews and high shooting ratios, docusoaps still come out far cheaper to produce than an hour-long drama or a movie of the week. And as long as the viewing figures aren't that different, docusoaps will continue to get support. They are easy to make, being just an extension of observational documentary, so you might want to consider them. But don't make them with your own money, because by the time you finish your series they may just be out of fashion.

FOUNDATIONS AND CORPORATIONS

So how do you stay alive if you don't want to do another search for sunken submarines, if you don't want to hunt for Nazi war criminals, and if you don't want to do a docusoap on circus performers or ships' stewards? In other words, where do you go for the money if your subject is not sensational, does not make Discovery's heart beat faster, but makes a quiet appeal to the human mind and intelligence and assumes that most people have an IQ higher than fifty? The answer for you is to beat a path to the doors of the foundations and corporations.

Most independent American filmmakers I know who work seriously in documentaries raise their funds through applications to local arts councils and foundations. These foundations have, in fact, become the chief sources of independent film financing in the past few years. Broadly speaking, these agencies are divided into federal, state, and private funding bodies. Generally, government agencies tend to fund research and preproduction, while private organizations are more inclined to give completion monies. Sometimes you will go back to the same source more than once, the first time to cover research and development, the second time for production.

The big hitters among the granting bodies are the Rockefeller, Ford, MacArthur, and Guggenheim foundations; the American Film Institute; the New York Council for the Arts; the National Endowment for the Arts; and the National Endowment for the Humanities. Funding is intensely competitive, and dozens of applicants are turned down for every grant awarded. For example, Barbara Kopple was turned down again and again while trying to fund *Harlan County*, which eventually went on to win an Oscar.

You should note that most state humanities commissions work hand in hand with the National Endowment for the Humanities. Similarly, most state or city arts councils work closely with the National Endowment for the Arts. In addition to all the above, you should be aware of the existence of the Independent Documentary Fund, which is run by the Corporation for Public Broadcasting.

THE FUNDING PROPOSAL

Foundation funding has certain inherent difficulties. Many of these relate to the writing of the proposal, a document that can sometimes reach the length of *War and Peace*. Most foundations require a proposal that clearly states the nature of the film, its objectives and limits, and a well-defined distribution and use program relating to the film itself. Foundations also like to play it safe by requiring the participation of "experts" to provide academic respectability to a project. Such requirements make sense sometimes, but they are obstructions to the filmmaker operating in a field that the scholarly mind has not yet penetrated. What you have to do is acknowledge the basically conservative nature of foundation activities. The art film, the science film, and the educational history film pose few challenges to them. In contrast, the political, investigative, or critical film rarely finds a place in foundation funding without a great deal of trouble.

The peculiar thing is that this setup may favor those who can write good grants over those who are poor grant writers but better filmmakers. This has been acknowledged, so many of the major arts foundations will go out of their way to offer you assistance in writing and framing your grant. Various periodicals can also help you considerably in this grant-writing business, such as the *AFI Education Newsletter, The Independent, Foundation News,* and the journal of the Independent Documentary Association. There are also a number of good books that have come out recently that guide you through the grant-writing maze. Among the best of these are *Shaking the Money Tree* by Morrie Warshawski (Michael Wiese Books), *Money for Film and Video Artists* (American Council of the Arts), and *Get the Money and Shoot* (Documentary Research Inc.).

Most good libraries have a copy of the foundation list put out by the Council of Foundations. This gives you the names and addresses of the major foundations in the United States, together with a list of projects that they support. A few days perusing that list (it is immense) can be worth more than a few dollars in your pocket.

Although we talked about proposal writing in chapter 4, it is worthwhile to look at the subject as it specifically relates to foundation grants.

Unlike the national endowments, many small foundations will simply ask you to send them a short letter describing your project. Later, they may ask for additional details, but in many cases that short letter of about two pages *is the application.* Five things go into it. You need to tell them what you want to do, why there is a need for your project, who you are, the amount of money you are seeking, and why they should support you.

Your letter to business corporations should include

- A list of established corporate sponsors
- The background of the requesting organization
- A request for an appointment

Don't be surprised if your letters to small corporations fail to elicit a reply. That's because you and your project simply don't interest the would-be sponsor, so why should he waste time and money in replying. However, even if you get the slightest nibble, it should be pursued.

It is imperative that your proposal be well organized. If the funding agency has no specific format, then try including these sections in this order:

- Abstract and/or summary
- Rationale for making the film
- Description of the film
- Personnel and grant-overseeing agencies.
- Distribution ideas

- Budget
- Appendixes with letter of support, etc.

All this sounds fine in the abstract, but how does it all work in practice? To show you this process in a little more detail, I asked Nina Rosenblum, a noted New York filmmaker, to allow me to print extracts from some of the grant applications made by her and her company, Daedelus Productions. I think the sections below show the art of grant writing at its best. They are clear, lucid, and appealing; they make very strong arguments; and they brought in the money. The first extract comes from *City of Heartbreak*.

City of Heartbreak, City of Hope: The Photo League's New York Production Grant Proposal

1. Description of Request

We are seeking funds in the amount of $500,000 leading to the completion of a 58-minute color documentary film for public television and nontheatrical distribution on the history of the Photo League, an organization of social documentary photographers which flourished in New York City between 1936 and 1951, and whose collective portrait of urban life in the thirties and forties is comparable in spirit and quality to the rural portrait drawn by the government's Farm Security Administration photographic unit. Should we receive funding, we will begin production on April 1, 1990.

2. Explanation of Subject Matter: Significance to a Broad National Audience; Concepts and Themes to Be Explored

[About a page is taken up describing the Photo League, its history, and its principal members. Then comes possibly the most important part of the proposal: the need and rationale for making the film. —A. R.] We believe that our proposed documentary film about the Photo League will advance public understanding and appreciation of the humanities by exploring a number of provocative themes: artistic responses to social and economic crisis; the impact and manipulation of mass-produced images; the influence of the camera *as an idea* on the writers and journalists, as well as on the photographers of the period. On a deeper level, we believe that the Photo League images are important in themselves because they remind us that even in the worst of times there are moments of joy and triumph, and of sudden grace. . . .

[After about ten pages describing in detail the work of the League and its evaluation by social and art critics, the proposal gets down to the specific structure of the film. —A. R.] It is not the superficial appeal of nostalgia, but rather the palpable appeal of their timeless human content that make the Photo League pictures so compelling and fresh when viewed today. . . .

In particular, our film will highlight the work of five photographers, each in his or her own way typical of one or more aspects of the League at its best: Dan Weiner . . . Marion Palfi . . . Aaron Siskind . . . Walter Rosenblum . . . and Sid Grossman.

Section 3 of the proposal outlines the history of the project, a detailed catalog of the research undertaken before writing the proposal, and the debt owed to various advisers. The later sections describe personnel, production schedule, and budget. Altogether, the proposal runs to thirty-five pages.

The thing that stands out from the proposal is that Rosenblum and her associates have done their homework. They marshal strong arguments explaining why the film should be made and equally convincing arguments about why they can make it in an interesting way.

A few years after *City of Heartbreak*, Rosenblum produced *Liberators* together with William Miles. This was a ninety-minute television special whose subject was the first all-black tank unit to enter combat in World War II. The total production budget was in excess of $800,000 (including promotion and educational outreach), and contributions came from the Corporation for Public Broadcasting, the Donnet Fund, the New York State Council for the Arts, and the National Black Program Consortium. Additional funds came from European coproducers such as Channel 4, U.K., WDR/Germany, and SBSTV/Australia.

Again, the most interesting part of the proposal is contained in the first two pages, which present the rationale and a project description. As in all proposals, these are the vital two pages that have to capture the imagination. They must have punch and must involve, excite, and intrigue the reader. The rest of the proposal merely elaborates on the main topic and assures the grantor you have the right credentials and can pull off the film in the way you describe. These things are important, but it is the first two pages that can make or break your proposal. If you fail to connect with your reader in those first two pages, then your proposal, to all intents and purposes, has gone down the drain. In the proposal for *Liberators*, Rosenblum and Miles manage to intrigue right from the beginning.

Liberators: Fighting on Two Fronts in World War II
Rationale
As we approach the 50th anniversary of America's involvement in World War II, it is time to reexamine the lessons of that conflict, and the legacies we have inherited from an era of both racial confrontation and racial cooperation.

These lessons are particularly germane today. Discrimination and racially motivated acts of violence are on the rise. African-American and Jewish-American relations are in an unfortunate state of disrepair. The civil rights movement has lost its original unity and direction. And the U.S. Armed Forces are once again embroiled in charges of racism and sexism.

The experience of African-American soldiers, whose commitment to fighting for the freedom of their fellow men and women crossed racial lines, illuminates issues of contemporary importance. To this end *Liberators is* dedicated to recording the oral history of the black liberators and reuniting them with the Holocaust survivors.

By telling the little known story of African-American participation in the struggle against fascism, and reexamining the parallel experiences of blacks and Jews during the 1940s, *Liberators* will recover a significant but missing chapter in the collective past of the United States.

Project Description
Liberators opens at the gate of the Buchenwald concentration camp. For the first time in forty-five years, members of General Patton's all-black 761st tank battalion—the "Black Panthers"—have returned to the site of one of their greatest military triumphs. With them is a survivor of the camp itself, returning to Buchenwald and reunited with his liberators for the first time since the end of the Second World War.

As survivor Ben Bender separates from the liberators in order to leave a tribute to his murdered brother, the reminiscences of the veterans reveal a profound resonance with the history of the Jewish survivors.

With the onset of the war, America's racial "dilemma" became a moral embarrassment that had to be faced. The elimination of racism had become one of the avowed aims in the war against Germany. How could America expect to rally its African-American populace while at the same time subjecting them to racial discrimination?

By way of example, in the first hours of America's first battle at Pearl Harbor, Dorrie Miller, a 23-year-old black "messboy" aboard the U.S.S. *Arizona*, took over a fallen crewman's machine gun and brought down four attacking aircraft. He was acclaimed a national hero and awarded the Navy Cross for "distinguished devotion to duty and extreme courage." Yet two years later, when Dorrie Miller was killed in the South Pacific, he was still a "mess boy."

Again, the prose is clear, the rationale for the film very explicit, and the beginning of the project description intriguing. While we see the start of the film very vividly, with the entrance to Buchenwald, we can also see where the film is going, with its fusion of individual stories and the overall picture of racism.

The rationale section also makes one essential point: that the film "illuminates issues of contemporary importance." This needs to be said, otherwise the reader of the proposal may comment: "A fascinating story, but that's all it is . . . a quaint story from the past." The function of the proposal is to convince the reader that the story is relevant now.

The funding proposal for Jon Else's *The Day after Trinity* differs in many respects from the illustrations above. Here, the rationale is largely implicit. In order to understand the present, and present dangers, we must understand the development of the atom bomb, and the story of Oppenheimer, the man who changed the world forever. The key sentence in Else's proposal is: "The film uses Oppenheimer's . . . story as a unifying vehicle in examining several extraordinary events in American history and in juxtaposing these against the present."

The proposal itself does not go so densely into history as Rosenblum's work, but that is because the story of Oppenheimer and Los Alamos is more familiar to us than that of the Photo League. The proposal is also written in a deceptively simple manner, but is in fact extremely powerful. It hits you straight between the eyes with the first sentence: "This is a film about people who build bombs, about the man who brought us into the Atomic Age, and about our rites of passage into that age."

The proposal then unfolds, relating to us the story of a man and events so devastating that we can only wonder why the story was never covered in depth before. Eventually the film was set up through a PBS station in San Jose, and was nominated for an Oscar. One of its cowriters, David Peoples, later wrote the script for Clint Eastwood's *Unforgiven*. Possibly inspired by *Trinity*, English television did a docudrama series on Oppenheimer in the eighties, and Hollywood made its own version of the story under the title *Fat Man and Little Boy*.

The Day after Trinity
Final Funding Proposal
This is a film about people who build bombs, about the man who brought us into the Atomic Age, and about our rites of passage into that age. J. Robert Oppenheimer was a student of poetry, a linguist of seven tongues, searcher for spiritual ideals, and father of the atomic bomb. He lived the life of a gentle and eloquent humanist and, perhaps to his own surprise, became practical architect of the most savage weapon in history. This contradiction lies at the heart of his public and personal drama and is the central theme of *Trinity*.

The film uses Oppenheimer's mysterious and often tragic life story as a unifying vehicle in examining several extraordinary events in American history and in juxtaposing these against the present. It looks in some detail at the spectacular secrets of the Manhattan Project, at Oppenheimer's frenzied war years as director of Los Alamos and technical wizard of Hiroshima. The film then examines his post-war role as "philosopher-king" of American science and his lonely opposition to the Hydrogen Bomb. The final sad chapter describes the secret and terrible 1954 security hearing which brought his career to a sudden end.

These historical elements of the physicist's life are constructed from recently declassified archival sources and woven together with diverse personal narratives from people whose lives today are in some way touched by his work: his friends, his enemies, scientists at Los Alamos, his family, and even a few ordinary people who never heard of him.

It is a rich and evocative story, embodying the most painful ambiguities of 20th Century America, and it has yet to be told on film.

HISTORICAL BACKGROUND

> . . . when you see something that is technically sweet you
> go ahead and do it, and you argue about what to do with it
> only after you have had your technical success.—Oppen-
> heimer, 1951

In the pre-dawn darkness of July 16, 1945, a remote corner of New Mexico was suddenly bathed in a ghastly green light, a light so bright it illuminated half the state and could have been seen from another planet. Detonation of the first atomic bomb at Trinity Site marked what was perhaps the greatest scientific watershed in history, and forever ended mankind's innocence in the face of survival on earth.

Robert Oppenheimer was the guiding force behind that leap into the unknown. Like Fermi, Teller, and the other physicists gathered in the desert that morning, he was a man of conscience and good faith. Brilliant, sophisticated, yet sometimes naive and confused, he was to become our first real scientific hero and the first American scientist to be censured in the name of national security.

His unlikely path to Trinity began in Europe, about twenty years before. There, with men like Max Born and Ernest Rutherford, he experienced firsthand the heady days of the Quantum revolution. He saw the worlds of Newton and Galileo crumble, and helped lay the foundation for a new physical universe no longer conforming to continuous time and space, no longer accessible to the five senses, and utterly foreign to our common experience.

Clearly an immense amount of work was put in by both Nina Rosenblum and Jon Else in the preparation of their proposals. But at stake was funding in the realm of hundreds of thousands of dollars. What their proposals show is that when you apply for serious money you must sometimes become a combination of historian, sociologist, political savant, anthropologist, and theologian. To say merely that your subject is interesting is not sufficient. You have to argue that your film will not only be entertaining—the least of your worries—but that the world will be poorer and less enlightened without it. It's a strange burden. And the wonder is that so many people, like Nina Rosenblum, William Miles, Marlon Riggs, Jon Else, and thousands of other independent filmmakers, survive this rigorous process, get the grants, and in the end produce such great films.

THE FLIER

I mentioned the importance of the flier in drawing attention to your film once it has been completed. Below are a few extracts from fliers that may help you to see how these things are designed and written.

Example 1: Under the Knife

On the cover of the flier we see a color photo of surgeon in close-up. In his hands he holds a scalpel. Across the surgeon's mask we make out the following. "Tom is normal in every way—but one. He has a secret desire, and if others found out about it his life would be ruined. Tom wants to be a eunuch." Then underneath in large letters we see the words, "Under the Knife: A Eunuch's Story."

The cover is dynamic, arresting, and shocking. We want to know more and turn over the reverse side of the flier. Here we read

> Tom lives in a little town in Indiana, population 300. He's an accountant, single, in his fifties. Normal in every way—but one. Tom has a secret desire, and if others found out about it, his life would be ruined. In fact, his wish might be one of the last taboos. Tom wants to be a eunuch.
>
> *Under the Knife* is a one-hour documentary that follows Tom through the process of becoming a eunuch. It is a close and personal look at a forbidden world that few even know exists.

The flier, put out by Alliance Atlantis, then goes on to relate briefly the history of Tom and what happened during an earlier botched operation. It then opens out to tell us about a new doctor who hopefully will do a better job; introduces us to the other eunuch friends of Tom, and tells us a little bit about the history of eunuchs. Finally we are told the picture ends with us following Tom through a new operation that will help him achieve his goal. Then, to wrap up everything, the flier tells us, "In one dramatic hour, *Under the Knife* brings the taboo world of modern day eunuchs to light—shadows and all." It is a very well written flier, short but extremely compelling, and it is worth noting the words and phrases that drag us in: "taboo world," "forbidden world," and "millions who have live as neither man nor woman." So we are back to the old essential lure of documentary. Open secret doors for us, let us into dark worlds, and we will follow gladly.

Example 2: Megalodon

Here the flier's cover picture shows us the red gaping jaws of an enormous shark. Superimposed over the picture are the words "Megalodon, the greatest shark that ever roamed the seas. Do these monsters still survive somewhere in the ocean's depth, waiting to be discovered?" As we absorb the horror of the picture, and memories of the film *Jaws*, we are hit between the eyes by the question, Do they still survive waiting to be discovered? Well let's read the flier and find out.

The information blurb of the flier then goes on this way:

> Was the Megalodon, the greatest shark that ever roamed the seas, an aggressive predator or stealthy assassin? Was this terrifying flesh eater the ancestor of the modern Great White shark? Did the last of its kind die off centuries ago, or do these monsters still survive somewhere in the ocean's depths, waiting to be discovered. In *Megalodon*, with the assistance of traditional and high-tech graphic techniques, leading scientists put their competing theories and reputations on the line.

Again the words are very carefully chosen to whet your appetite. This film is going to be about predators, stealthy assassins, monsters. You read and start to feel a tingling in your spine. Later on the flier becomes a little more prosaic, telling us that in this documentary, "We pit leading researchers against each other, allowing each to make a case for one concept of megalodon." So the film is going to be a bit more than merely seeing sharks swimming around and looking dangerous. But that's fine because we are already hooked.

Example 3: Stalin's Last Purge

Here, in designing the flier for my film, I opted for very bold red lettering with the film's name superimposed over a black-and-white photo of Stalin. Underneath the photo we see the following:

> He saw enemies everywhere and decided to destroy them all in one Great last purge. First the Jews, then his secret service, then his political rivals.
>
> But would he succeed?

The flier itself contained quite a lot of information. Here I gave a lot of thought to the opening paragraphs, which had to arouse the interest of the reader and to the last paragraph which had to ram the story home.

> Shot in Russia, Israel and the USA this one-hour documentary special takes us back to the USSR in the late forties. It is a USSR where Stalin reigns supreme. After the devastating war against the Nazis in which over 20 million citizens have died, Stalin is seen as King, God, Messiah rolled into one.
>
> But the cold war is unfolding, and Stalin's paranoia is increasing. He sees real and imagined enemies everywhere but plans a final to destroy them all. Once more he will let loose the terror. Once more there will be the cry in the night, the knock on the door and the bullet in the neck. . . .
>
> [Final paragraph] Much of the material used in *Stalin's Last Purge* has only recently become available. The opening of the Soviet archives in the 1990s uncovered a treasure trove of secret information about the USSR. These revelations, together with the new interviews and rarely seen archive materials present the viewer with an unforgettable and riveting story about Stalin, and about life and terror in the former Soviet police state.

24

CONCLUSION: PROBLEMS AND CHALLENGES

I hope that this book has given you some insight into filmmaking. I have tried to cover most of the main issues and show you how professionals deal with certain problems. However, some issues don't fall neatly within the previous chapters, and I will therefore deal with those here. They concern the outlook of the filmmaker, the question of perspective, and the challenge of the future.

THE DIRECTOR'S BURDEN

We looked at some of the director's day-to-day problems in chapters 11 and 12, but there are also wider problems that you must confront sooner or later, the most serious of which are ethical. I am presenting this here as a director's problem, but it goes without saying that it is also a matter of serious consideration for the writer.

Ethics

The relationship of ethical considerations to film practice is one of the most important topics in the documentary field. The problem can be simply framed: filmmakers use and expose people's lives. This exploitation is often done for the best of motives; sometimes it's done under the excuse of the public's right to know. Whatever the excuse, though, film occasionally brings unforeseen and dire consequences to the lives of the filmed subjects. So, the basic question is how you, the filmmaker, treat people to avoid such consequences. It's a hard question and one that has existed in documentary filming from *Nanook* through the Grierson years to the present.

Now it has a new dimension added to it because of cinema verité, a technique that allows a closer, more probing view of people's lives, as well as less time for reflection and consideration of one's reactions, than anything that has gone before. Using a lightweight portable camera, a filmmaker can also intrude and interfere in the most aggressive way, as seen in Michael Moore's *Bowling for Columbine* and *Fahrenheit 9/11*.

Many questions lead from the main issue of how far the filmmaker should exploit a subject in the name of the general truth or the general good. Was Claude Lanzmann, for example, justified in filming Nazi war criminals without their knowledge? Does your subject know what is really going on, and what the possible implications and consequences are of being portrayed on the screen? When the subject gave you consent to film, what did you intend and what did he or she intend? When should you shut off the camera and destroy the footage? And should your subject be allowed to view or censor your footage?

There is also the question of economic exploitation. We filmmakers earn a living from our work, building reputations that are convertible into economic advantage. But our subjects generally acquire no financial gain from the enterprise.

Finally there is the matter of fakery. On British television in the late 1990s, this subject suddenly assumed major importance after a number of documentary scandals hit the headlines. In 1996 a film called *The Connection*, made for Carlton TV, about the running of drugs from Colombia to the United Kingdom, was shown to contain a number of invented scenes passed off as real. In 1998 *Rogue Males*, made for Channel 4, was shown to contain similar inventions. Another British film made in the same year, *Daddy's Girl*, which dealt with the relationship of fathers and daughters, had one girl's boyfriend play her father.

One may ask, Where is the damage to the audience since there is so much manipulation in documentary anyway? In physical or financial terms there probably isn't any. However, I think there is an unstated assumption on the part of the audience that says, "We understand editing and camera choice and so on, but given all that we still believe, documentary gives us a higher truth than fiction, and that's why we watch." Fakery attacks that basic assumption, and my advice is stay well clear of it.

Obviously, I think that in the end, most of us can justify what we do. If I couldn't, I wouldn't continue as a filmmaker. But the subject of ethics is tricky, and it is one that you must, as a serious filmmaker, come to grips with sooner or later.

Legal Matters

Whether you work as a producer, director, or writer, you must be aware of certain legal considerations. I am not talking about obvious things such as theft or personal injury while filming, but about libel and slander. These two branches of the law can open up very deep traps that you must avoid if you want to survive. Both these torts deal with an individual's reputation. Broadly speaking, to libel or slander means to defame somebody or to lower his or her reputation in the eyes of the common person. If I call you a slut, a tart, a traitor, a wife beater, an abusive father, or a conniving thief, the odds are that I have either slandered or libeled you. The difference between slander and libel is that the former is a vocal defamation, while the latter is written or filmed.

If you attack someone's professional competence, you can really lay yourself open to trouble. But two points need to be made at this juncture. First, truth is usually a total defense for a charge of libel. Second, in the United States, intent and malice may have some bearing on whether libel has been committed.

Though the applicable laws differ from state to state and from country to country, the penalties in most places for committing libel can be tremendously severe. This means that you must take care, particularly if you do investigatory documentaries.

Normally you are allowed to probe public figures more severely than private individuals, but even then you have to make sure that what you are saying or showing is essentially true and fair. This is something that CBS Television ignored to its own cost in 1982, when it made *The Uncounted Enemy: A Vietnam Deception*. In its film, CBS alleged that in 1967 General Westmoreland had led a military conspiracy to sustain public support for the Vietnam War by deliberately giving the White House a gross underestimate of the size of the enemy forces. Later, two journalists wrote an article alleging that there had been extreme bias in the collection and preparation of the materials for the program. In 1984, Westmoreland brought a libel action against CBS. His case was excellent, but it was eventually withdrawn because of various technical considerations and because of the nuances of malice that had to be proved.

Don't think this warning about libel applies only to subjects like Westmoreland. If you attack your local lawyer or school principal for incompetence, don't think they'll take it lightly. Libel suits are now popular, with big awards to the successful supplicant. So stay clear. Better to use your money for your next film rather than for legal fees and judgments.

Besides libel and slander, one also has to be aware of the right of privacy and the right to the commercial exploitation of one's own life. Whereas the first has been around for some while, the second doctrine argues that your life belongs to you alone, and no one else can benefit from it commercially without your permission. If such a right is upheld, biographical films will become very difficult to do. Both areas of law are, however, in a state of flux, and hardly anyone will venture a committed opinion on the outcome of future cases.

Using Your Wits

As a director, your professional knowledge will take you quite far, but there will be times when your survival and ability to complete the film will also depend on your wit and your scheming. Murphy's law has it that what can go wrong will go wrong. Unfortunately, this law also tends to be true for film. Remember, "Be prepared" is not just the Boy Scout motto; it's also your own. And when things go wrong, that's when you have to call on your humor and common sense.

I am not going to cite all the trials and tribulations of filmmakers over the years, but here are a few of the most common:

- After having agreed to talk, your interviewee balks at the last moment at being filmed.
- You fix an appointment to film somebody, and they forget to turn up.
- One of your crew angers the person you are filming.
- Your sound person gets a toothache in the middle of shooting.
- Your crew doesn't like the long hours, the bad pay, and the fact that they have to share rooms and can't bring their lovers with them.
- The camera breaks down, the wrong film is used, the sound gets out of sync, and you get caught in a revolution.

All these things have happened and will happen again. When they do, that's when you have to call on your wits, common sense, humor, and determination to carry things through.

What we are talking about is making hard, quick decisions in order to get the film done. But you'll also face the situation when the only way to get the film done is to use chutzpah. *Chutzpah* is a Yiddish word, much used in Hollywood, that can be translated as "outrageous cheek." The best example of chutzpah is the lad who killed his father and mother and then asked the judge for mercy because he was an orphan. Chutzpah is guts, boldness, and outrageousness, and it is one of the most essential qualities for a filmmaker. Two short examples will suffice.

In the late 1970s, Emile de Antonio made a film called *Underground*, in which he and Haskell Wexler talked to five members of the Weather Underground, self-confessed urban revolutionaries who had eluded the FBI for years. All the filming was done in secret, but then came the problem of developing the materials. The film was processed through Wexler's commercial company, but the audiotapes, which were very revealing, presented more of a problem. De Antonio explains how he solved it:

> I took the tapes to a sound house and said, "This is a new kind of trans-actional psychoanalysis, and I'll pay you your regular rate if you'll get out of here and let me transfer it myself. You see, I've signed a contract with this shrink, and this stuff is confessions of men and women about their inner sex lives, and the contract states that if anyone else hears it the contract is null and void." So the guy was perfectly happy to take my money and let me transfer. (Alan Rosenthal, *The Documentary Conscience* [Berkeley: University of California Press, 1980])

Another friend of mine, Abe Osheroff, made the film *Dreams and Nightmares*, about his experiences in the Spanish Civil War. Besides looking at the past, Abe also wanted to examine Franco's Spain of the mid-1970s, which was still a fascist state. Among other things, Abe wanted to demonstrate the cooperation of the Nixon government with Franco and decided he could do this by showing U.S. strategic bombers in Spain. However, given the film's argument against current American foreign policy, it was highly doubtful that the Pentagon would release such footage to Osheroff.

Abe's answer was to establish a dummy film company and write a powerful anticommunist script designed for college students. He then sent this script to the Pentagon and told them this anticommunist film needed certain footage. The Pentagon was delighted and sent him all he needed. There was one catch. The letter giving permission for use stated that if the material was used for any other purpose than that set out in the script, the user was liable to a fine or imprisonment. Osheroff's attitude was that if the FBI busted him, it would be fantastic publicity for the film. Nothing happened. So the chutzpah paid off.

THE FUTURE

The question for the future is, Where do we go from here? Old solutions and ideas for documentary writers and directors may not work in tomorrow's world, and the sooner we realize that, the better. How do we face the twenty-first century? What do we want to do, and how are we going to do it? What do we want to say? Should we be putting over the old messages or saying something new? Who will our audience be? Will our films be framed according to past styles or will they be totally innovative? And will we be using the old technology or futuristic equipment we can only dream about now?

Technology and Audience

Taken together, the 1980s, 1990s, and the early years of the new century have been the age of the communications revolution, the age of the videodisc, the VCR, the CD-ROM, and the DVD. With the Avid and other technological wonders, electronic editing in both film and video has taken tremendous strides forward. Cameras have become even more lightweight and miniaturized. Video has become an essential tool in filmmaking. One television cassette takes hours of material, and yet the advent of the videodisc camera may kill tape. High fidelity is the norm. IPods proliferate. The flat television screen and high-definition television have become cheaper and more universal. Cable television spreads, while television satellites orbit the earth, providing filmmakers with international as well as national audiences. Interactive television and digital technology have become the buzzwords.

What it all means is that nothing is sacred: neither the technology nor the classical concept of audience nor the style and manner of film distribution. What we have to do is try to see that the change becomes a blessing and not a curse.

The new computer chip has changed filmmaking in important ways. Because of it, filmmaking has become almost as easy as writing. Filmmakers no longer need to be burdened by massive crews, horrendously heavy lights, and bulky equipment. Instead, one person can go out with a lightweight digital camera and do every single job. But though it's easier today, filmmaking is still a hassle. What I hope to see is a one-pound camera and tape or disc recorder that can go anywhere, do anything, record continuously for four hours, and give images as fine as anything on 35mm or 70mm film. I want to see technology simplified so that the filmmaker's problem becomes *what to say* rather than how to film.

As for distribution, everything is up for grabs. At the moment the market is heavily weighted against the filmmaker, since the main distribution options are television, cable, and commercial distributors. That may change. The spread of satellites will bring a demand for product, and one can only hope that the demand will include documentaries. Perhaps documentaries will be marketed by mail order. Already, electronic systems allow films to be fed privately and cheaply to the viewer-consumer, and documentary has to become part of that system. Individuals can make and market DVDs. Meanwhile, Web distribution promises heaven, though whether the pearly gates are within filmmakers' reach has still to be proved.

The lesson for filmmakers is simple. You must keep up with the new technologies and look for ways to use changing distribution systems to your advantage.

Subject and Style

Subjects change fast. *Nanook* and *Chang* inspired the romance and travelogue films. *Potemkin* and *Triumph of the Will* showed what could be done with political propaganda. Grierson developed the social documentary, and Jennings's poetics boosted war morale. Then even these innovations gave way before new trends. In the 1970s, subject matter ranged from Vietnam and the women's movement to films on the family, interpersonal relationships, and the growing threat of nuclear war. What characterized these films was that many were made outside of television and with a passion that the networks frowned on. Many of them also embodied new techniques and new styles. Until the late 1950s, the accepted form for the documentary was the prewritten script with the visuals conforming to the narration. Cinema verité changed all that, bringing the personal, unscripted film to the editing room. Now, video in its turn is changing the shape and style of films, adding a zip, a flashiness, and an immediacy not seen before.

One of the greatest changes has come through interactive video and DVD. Very often the filmmaker is no longer content to market his or her simple one-hour film. Instead he or she often now also prepares a longer version that contains not only the "master" film but also all the outs, the interviews, and all the research materials and articles. All these "resources" can then be activated and accessed with the flick of a switch. This vision has now become the norm, with all major documentary series now being made available on DVDs.

Of course, change doesn't necessarily mean improvement. The objective is to absorb the lessons of the past and hope that they provide a map to the future.

THE CHALLENGE

In the end, regardless of format or medium, two questions dominate everything: What do you want to say, and how passionate are you about saying it?

If there is a subtext to this chapter, it has to do with commitment: commitment to getting the film done, commitment to a certain set of values, and commitment to share a perspective that implies the world will be a better place for the practice of one's art and craft. Somewhere in there, ethics, craft, and art meet and make magic.

And what does the filmmaker want to do with that magic? Throughout this book, my basic assumption has been that the documentary filmmaker is both an entertainer and a teacher, is interested in the world and wants to change it for the better. And that is true whether he or she works within or beyond the domain of television.

At one time I thought the duty of the concerned filmmaker was to try to bring about social change. Now I am more inclined to see the involved filmmaker as one who bears witness. This "bearing of witness" has two elements. On a modest level, it means the filmmaker is interested in telling us a certain truth—not the only truth or the eternal message, but rather a very personal statement that says, "This film arises out of my background, feelings, and integrity, and on the basis of what I show and how I show it; you can take it or leave it." On a different level of bearing witness, the filmmaker is one who says: "This is our world. See its joys and be happy. But see its sorrow and learn from it, and don't say that no one ever told you what the world was like." This kind of bearing witness is not something that one does logically. It is something that one does compulsively. It is a fire within.

A friend of mine, the very fine filmmaker Robert Vas, once put it to me this way: "I've brought with me a great many things to talk about.

This baggage, this message which nobody asked me to talk about, is absolutely central to me. I can't exist without it. And I must talk about it to audience that never experienced these things directly."

In this book I have tried to tell you a few things about technique. I can't teach you about passion, but I can tell you this: with technique alone you can become a good filmmaker, but you will not become a great one. For that you need passion: passion for the personal message that no one asked you to talk about; passion for the story that must be told and the facts that must not stay hidden.

Appendix
Selected Bibliography
Index

APPENDIX

BUDGET FOR A ONE-HOUR VIDEO DOCUMENTARY, *PEACE PROCESS*

Production Budget for Shooting on BetaSP Video. Project Length: 8 Months

Producer and Staff	Weeks	$ Rate	$ Total
Writer-Producer-Director	28	2,250	63,000
Associate Producer	22	1,000	22,000
Production Assistant	24	750	18,000
Researcher	8	700	5,600
Production Manager/Coordinator	7	1,200	8,400
PR Fringe: 12% of $78,900			9,468
SUBTOTAL			126,468

Preproduction

Travel	Days	Persons	$ Cost	$ Total
Egypt		2	280	560
Jordan		2	150	300
Norway		2	930	1,860
USA(NY–Washington)		2	200	400
Eilat		2	160	320
Taxis and Phones				400
Israel Van and Gas	5		150	750
Per Diems	16	2	50	1,600
Hotels	13	2	150	3,900
Extras				650
SUBTOTAL				10,740

Production Crew and Equipment (with Overtime)	Days	Persons	$ Total
Cameraperson and BetaSP Video	21	1,250	26,250
Equipment Soundperson	21	300	6,300
Accessories:			
Lights, Lenses, Etc.	21	150	3,150
Van Rental and Gas	21	150	3,150
Per Diem Shoot (6 people)	7	50	2,100
Makeup Artist	6	200	1,200
Per Diem	6	50	300
Expendable			500
PR Fringe (USA): 16% of $3,450			552
Helicopter (3 hours)		750	2,250
SUBTOTAL			45,752

Production Air Travel Crew	Days	Persons	$ Cost	$ Total
Norway		5	930	4,650
Egypt		5	280	1,400
Jordan		5	150	750
USA		5	200	1,000
Eilat		6	160	960
Per Diem with Hotel	12	5	200	12,000
Per Diem Eilat with Hotel	2	6	50	600
Extras				2,000
Excess Air Baggage (5 bags/10 flights)				1,500
SUBTOTAL				24,860

Production Israeli Travel	Days	Persons	$ Cost	$ Total
Travel in Israel	7	5	50	1,750
Hotels	2	5	100	1,000
SUBTOTAL				2,750

Travel Costs for Talent	Days	Persons	$ Cost	$ Total
Norway				1,600
Egypt				350
Jordan				150
USA (NY–Washington)				200
Per Diems with Hotels				2,800
SUBTOTAL				5,100
Production Cost Subtotal				78,462

Shooting Stock	Days	Persons	$ Cost	$ Total
BetaSP Tape (70 × ½ hour)			30	2,100
(5 × 1 hour)			60	300
SUBTOTAL				2,400

Archive Material	Days	Persons	$ Cost	$ Total
Rights USA (20 minutes at $3,000 per minute)				60,000
Israel (10 minutes at $1,000 per minute)				10,000
Library/Viewing Days		15	100	1,500
Archive Researcher		15	175	2,625
Copying & Rights to Stills				1,000
Transfer Tapes (15 tapes)			60	900
Transfer Time (20 hours)			60	1,200
PR Fringe: 16% of $2,625				420
SUBTOTAL				77,645

Editing Off-Line	Weeks	$ Cost	$ Total
Editor	18	1,800	32,400
Assistant Editor	10	800	8,000
Avid Rental and Space	18	2,100	37,800
Meals and Supplies		600	600
Transcripts			3,000
Narration, Recording, and Edit			800
Shoot Stills			1,000
Dubs with Time Code			3,000
PR Fringe: 16% of $30,300			4,848
SUBTOTAL			91,448

Editing Online	Days	$ Cost	$ Total
Editing	3	1,750	5,250
Editor	3	500	1,500
Paintbox and Animation (Chyron)			1,500
Sound Editing Effects			3,000
Sound Mix (15 hours)		250	3,750
D 11 Stock for Master			500
Title Sequence			2,000
Music: Original or Cues			3,000
SUBTOTAL			20,500

Office and Administration	Months	$ Cost	$ Total
Rent	7	1,200	8,400
Computer and Printer			2,800
Telephone, Fax, Post	7	300	2,100
Copies, Stationery Supplies			800
Bookkeeper	6	500	3,000
Playback Unit VHS and Monitor			800
Messenger			500
VHS Stock for Dubs			300
Entertainment			600
Shipping			1,200
SUBTOTAL			20,500

Professional	Months	$ Cost	$ Total
Legal			3,000
General Liability			2,500
Production Package			2,500
Errors, Omissions, Liabilities			3,000
SUBTOTAL			11,000

Miscellaneous		$ Cost	$ Total
Research Materials			1,000
Consultants		400	6,000
SUBTOTAL			7,000

Travel and Lodging, Producer and Talent to and in USA	Months	$ Cost	$ Total
Airfare Producer (4 return flights, TA–JFK)		1,200	4,800
Airfare Talent (4 return flights, TA–JFK		2,500	10,000
Lodging Producer (USA)	5	1,500	7,500
SUBTOTAL			22,300
TOTAL			468,463
Contingency 7.5%			35,135
GRAND TOTAL			503,598

Note: Station overhead and publicity not included.

SELECTED BIBLIOGRAPHY

Below I have selected a few books that I think may be useful to you in your work. These books will either help you consider the wider issues of documentary or assist you with very specific aspects of filmmaking. One or two of them, such as the writings of Joris Ivens and Paul Rotha, are simply books that I have long admired and that have very much helped me in my own development.

Barnouw, Erik. *Documentary: A History of the Non-Fiction Film*. London: Oxford University Press, 1993.

Bluehm, William. *Documentary in American Television*. New York: Hastings House, 1965.

Browne, Steven E. *Videotape Editing: A Postproduction Primer*. Boston: Focal Press, 1993.

Burder, John. *The Technique of Editing 16mm Films*. London: Focal Press, 1975.

Cheshire, David. *The Video Manual*. New York: Van Nostrand Reinhold, 1982.

Corner, John. *The Art of Record*. New York: St Martin's Press, 1996

Crittenden, Roger. *The Thames and Hudson Manual of Film Editing*. 2d ed. London: Thames and Hudson, 1995.

Dancyger, Ken. *The Technique of Film and Video Editing*. 2d ed. Boston: Focal Press, 1997.

DiZazzo, Ray. *Corporate Scriptwriting*. Boston: Focal Press, 1992.

Donaldson, Michael C. *Clearance and Copyright: Everything the Independent Filmmaker Needs to Know*. Los Angeles: Silman James Press, 2003.

Gregory, Mollie. *Making Films Your Business*. New York: Schocken, 1979.

Hampe, Barry. *Making Documentary Films and Reality Videos*. New York: Henry Holt, 1997.

Ivens, Joris. *The Camera and I*. New York: International Publishers, 1969.

Jacobs, Lewis, ed. *The Documentary Tradition*, 2d ed. New York: Norton, 1979.

Levin, G. Roy. *Documentary Explorations: Fifteen Interviews with Filmmakers*. Garden City, N.Y.: Doubleday, 1971.

Lovell, Allan, and Jim Hillier. *Studies in Documentary.* New York: Viking, 1972.

Macdonald, Kevin, and Mark Cousins. *Imagining Reality: The Faber Book of Documentary.* London: Faber, 1996

Mamber, Stephen. *Cinema Verité in America.* Cambridge: MIT Press, 1974.

Millerson, Gerald. *Video Camera Techniques.* Boston: Focal Press, 1983.

Nichols, Bill. *Representing Reality.* Bloomington: Indiana University Press, 1991.

Peyton, Patricia, ed. *Reel Changes: A Guide to Social Issue Films.* San Francisco: Film Fund, 1979.

Pincus, Edward, and Steven Ascher. *The Filmmakers Handbook.* New York: Plume, 1984.

Rabiger, Michael. *Directing the Documentary.* 3d ed. Boston: Focal Press, 1998.

Renov, Michael, ed. *Theorizing Documentary.* New York: Routledge, 1993.

Rosenthal, Alan. *The Documentary Conscience: A Casebook in Filmmaking.* Berkeley: University of California Press, 1980.

———. *Jerusalem, Take One: Memoirs of a Jewish Filmmaker.* Carbondale: Southern Illinois University Press, 2000.

———. *Why Docudrama?* Carbondale: Southern Illinois University Press, 1998.

———. *Writing Docudrama: Dramatizing Reality for Film and TV.* Boston: Focal Press, 1994.

Rosenthal, Alan, and John Corner. *New Challenges for Documentary.* Manchester: Manchester University Press, 2005.

Rotha, Paul. *Documentary Diary.* New York: Hill and Wang, 1973.

Silverston, Roger. *The Making of a BBC Documentary.* London: British Film Institute, 1985.

Swain, Dwight. *Film Scriptwriting.* New York: Hastings House, 1981.

Warshawski, Morrie. *Shaking the Money Tree.* Los Angeles: Michael Wiese Books, 1994.

Waugh, Thomas, ed. *Show Us Life: Toward a History and Aesthetics of the Committed Documentary.* Metuchen, N.J.: Scarecrow Press, 1984.

Wiese, Michael. *Film and Video Marketing.* Boston: Focal Press, 1989.

———. *The Independent Film and Videomaker's Guide.* Boston: Focal Press, 1984.

———. *Money for Film and Video Artists.* New York: American Council of the Arts, 1994.

Winston, Brian. *Lies, Damn Lies and Documentaries.* London: BFI, 2000.

INDEX

Note: Italicized page numbers followed by "*ill.*" indicate illustrations that follow page 192.

Alan Rosenthal was born in England, studied law at Oxford, and has made more than sixty films, mainly in the United States, Canada, and Israel. He helped train Israel Television's film staff and has written six other books about documentary and drama, including a book of recollections on Israel, *Jerusalem, Take One: Memoirs of a Jewish Filmmaker.* He has taught at Stanford University and the British, Australian, and Mexican national film schools and is a professor in the Department of Communications at the Hebrew University, Jerusalem. His recent films include *The Brink of Peace,* for WNET New York; *Eichmann: the Secret Memoirs,* for German television; and *Stalin's Last Purge.* Another recent film, *Out of the Ashes,* won a Christopher Award and a Peabody Award for journalism.